ISBN 978-1-5277-9715-4
PIBN 10898998

English
Français
Deutsche
Italiano
Español
Português

www.forgottenbooks.com

Mythology Photography **Fiction**
Fishing Christianity **Art** Cooking
Essays Buddhism Freemasonry
Medicine **Biology** Music **Ancient
Egypt** Evolution Carpentry Physics
Dance Geology **Mathematics** Fitness
Shakespeare **Folklore** Yoga Marketing
Confidence Immortality Biographies
Poetry **Psychology** Witchcraft
Electronics Chemistry History **Law**
Accounting **Philosophy** Anthropology
Alchemy Drama Quantum Mechanics
Atheism Sexual Health **Ancient History**
Entrepreneurship Languages Sport
Paleontology Needlework Islam
Metaphysics Investment Archaeology
Parenting Statistics Criminology
Motivational

*UNDER THE SUPERINTENDENCE OF THE SOCIETY FOR THE
DIFFUSION OF USEFUL KNOWLEDGE.*

· THE

6 2 9 6 4

QUARTERLY

JOURNAL OF EDUCATION.

VOL. IX.

JANUARY—APRIL.

LONDON:

CHARLES KNIGHT, 22, LUDGATE STREET;

SOLD ALSO BY

W. F. WAKEMAN, DUBLIN ; OLIVER AND BOYD, EDINBURGH ; AND JACKSON,
NEW YORK.

1835.

LONDON:
Printed by WILLIAM CLOWES,
Duke Street, Lambeth.

CONTENTS OF NO. XVII.

	Page
Elementary Education in Scotland	1
Public Instruction—Project of a Plan of Moral, Industrious, and Intellectual Education for Females	27
Education of Parish-Poor Children, under the Poor-Law Amendments Act	45
Public Instruction in the State of New York	56
Savings Banks	62
Statistics of Education in England	66
Harrow School	75
Flogging and Fagging at Winchester	84

REVIEWS.

Peacock's Treatise on Algebra	91
Appendix to the Cambridge Edition of Æschylus	110
Müller's Æschylus	118
Elegantiæ Latinæ	122
The Teacher	128
Thiersch's Actual State of Greece	135
Dymock's Bibliotheca Classica	148

Miscellaneous:—Foreign	149
British	176

NOTICE.

The Committee of the Society for the Diffusion of Useful Knowledge are desirous of explaining the degree of superintendence which they think that they ought to exercise with respect to this publication.

It will of course be their duty not to sanction anything inconsistent with the general principles of the Society. Subject, however, to this general superintendence, they feel that the objects of the Society will be better forwarded by placing before the readers of this work the sentiments of able and liberal men, and thus enabling them to form their own conclusions, as well from the difference as from the agreement of the writers, than by proposing to them, as if from authority, any fixed rule of judgment, or one uniform set of opinions. It would also be inconsistent with the respect which the Committee entertain for the persons engaged in the preparation of these papers, were they to require them strictly to submit their own opinions to any rule that should be prescribed to them. If, therefore, the general effect of a paper be favourable to the objects of the Society, the Committee will feel themselves at liberty to direct its publication: the details must be the author's alone, and the opinions expressed on each particular question must be considered as his, and not those of the Committee. As they do not profess to make themselves answerable for the details of each particular essay, they cannot, of course, undertake for the exact conformity of the representations which different authors may make of the same facts; nor, indeed, do they, for the reasons already given, feel that such conformity is requisite.

By Order of the Committee,

THOMAS COATES, *Secretary.*

CONTENTS OF NO. XVIII.

                                                                    Page
National Education in Ireland 193
Report of the Select Committee of the House of Commons on
    the State of Education. 1834   213
On Teaching Singing 243
Grammar Schools—West Riding Proprietary School, Wakefield,
    Yorkshire 254
On writing Latin and Greek Exercises 262
On the Elements of Arithmetic   272
On the Discipline of Public Schools   280

REVIEWS.

Peacock's Treatise on Algebra   293
Woodbridge's American Annals of Education and Instruction . 312
Pott's Etymological Researches   327
Parker's Progressive Exercises in English Composition .   . 338
List of the Universities of Belgium, Holland, Germany, Switzer-
    land, Austria, Russia, Sweden and Norway, and Denmark   343

Miscellaneous:—Foreign   .   .   .   ·.   . 348
    ··   British   369

Index   383

NOTICE.

THE Committee of the Society for the Diffusion of Useful Knowledge are desirous of explaining the degree of superintendence which they think that they ought to exercise with respect to this publication.

It will of course be their duty not to sanction anything inconsistent with the general principles of the Society. Subject, however, to this general superintendence, they feel that the objects of the Society will be better forwarded by placing before the readers of this work the sentiments of able and liberal men, and thus enabling them to form their own conclusions, as well from the difference as from the agreement of the writers, than by proposing to them, as if from authority, any fixed rule of judgment, or one uniform set of opinions. It would also be inconsistent with the respect which the Committee entertain for the persons engaged in the preparation of these papers, were they to require them strictly to submit their own opinions to any rule that should be prescribed to them. If, therefore, the general effect of a paper be favourable to the objects of the Society, the Committee will feel themselves at liberty to direct its publication: the details must be the author's alone, and the opinions expressed on each particular question must be considered as his, and not those of the Committee. As they do not profess to make themselves answerable for the details of each particular essay, they cannot, of course, undertake for the exact conformity of the representations which different authors may make of the same facts; nor, indeed, do they, for the reasons already given, feel that such conformity is requisite.

By Order of the Committee,

THOMAS COATES, *Secretary.*

THE

QUARTERLY

JOURNAL OF EDUCATION.

ELEMENTARY EDUCATION IN SCOTLAND.

IN the first Number of the Journal of Education*, we
pledged ourselves to return to this subject, for the purpose of showing how the emoluments of the parochial schoolmasters may be increased without diminishing their usefulness,
and how several defects at present existing in the Scottish
system of elementary schools may be remedied. During
the last session of parliament, the subject was frequently
brought under the notice of both houses of the legislature,
by petitions from the schoolmasters themselves ; and, as
these petitions have been seconded by a recommendation
to his Majesty's government from the General Assembly
of the Church of Scotland, there can be little doubt that
their prayer will be granted, in one form or another, at no
very distant date. In the meantime, it is of the greatest
importance that the subject should be fully discussed, and
especially that inquiry should be made in what manner the
existing statutes may be most advantageously amended. In
the present article, therefore, we shall first detail the several
provisions of these statutes ; after which we shall point out
the changes and improvements, which have been rendered
necessary by the altered circumstances of the country, and
shall consider the best mode of carrying them into effect.
In the first branch of this inquiry, we shall be led to repeat
some of the statements contained in the former article to
which we have referred ; but for this our readers will require
no apology, as, to serve our present purpose, they must necessarily be a great deal more minute.

When the protestant religion was established in Scotland,
it was proposed by Knox and the other reformers, that the
ecclesiastical revenues should be divided into three portions,

* Vol. i, p. 24.

the first to be applied to the maintenance of the clergy, the second to the erection and endowment of schools and colleges, and the third to the support of the poor. The nobles, however, who had already appropriated the greater part of the church property, declared the proposal to be visionary and impracticable; and it was not till many years afterwards, that a scanty provision for only the first of these purposes was reluctantly drawn from them. But the reformed clergy, even in the midst of their own privations, did not lose sight of the second part of their scheme. In 1567, they procured an act of parliament for the reformation of the universities and colleges, and of all borough and landward (country) schools, and for preventing any one from teaching, either publicly or privately, who had not been examined and found qualified by the superintendents or visitors of the church. Under the authority of this statute, the General Assembly, in 1595, enjoined the presbyteries to visit the grammar schools in all the towns within their bounds, and to " deal with the magistrates for augmentation of their stipends." In 1615, an act of the Scottish Privy Council gave power to the bishops, with the consent of a majority of the heritors, to levy an assessment from the proprietors of land, for the purpose of establishing a school in every parish. This act of Council was confirmed by an act of parliament in 1633 : and, in 1638, the several presbyteries of the Church were recommended by the Assembly to see that these enactments were enforced in their respective districts; that able men were provided for the charge of teaching youth, catechising the common people, and precenting the psalms; and that they were entertained in the most convenient manner, according to the ability of the parish. The subject was again brought forward in the General Assembly, in 1642, when it was appointed, that in terms of former acts " both of kirk and parliament," every parish have a school, for reading, writing, and the " grounds " of religion; that grammar-schools be erected in burghs, presbytery-seats, and other important places; that the ministers and elders, from time to time, visit the schools in their respective parishes, and report to the synods and General Assembly; that it be recommended to his Majesty and Parliament to execute the laws formerly made, and to find out further means for so good a purpose; that Parliament be supplicated to allot a maintenance for youths of the " finest and best spirits " as bursars in the universities; and that a committee be appointed to consider the time and manner of the visitation of schools, and the " best, and most compendious, and most orderly course of teaching grammar." In the year 1649, the Assembly once more recommended to parliament, that whatever had been formerly given, either in burgh or landward parishes, for the maintenance of teachers, readers, and precentors, might not be alienated or taken away.

Notwithstanding the exertions of the church courts, schools were only partially established throughout the country up to the year 1649: the troubles which distracted Scotland during the middle of the seventeenth century, prevented any additional efforts from being made till after the Revolution. In the year 1690, it was declared by act of parliament, that no person should bear office in any university, college, or school, till he had sworn the oath of allegiance, and had subscribed the Confession of Faith: and, to connect the public seminaries still more closely with the presbyterian form of church government, then finally established in Scotland, it was further enacted, in 1693, that all schoolmasters and teachers of youth should be liable to the trial, judgment, and censure of the presbyteries, within whose jurisdiction they were settled, for their sufficiency, qualifications, and deportment in office. But the most important statute of this period was the act of 1696, which appointed, that a school be erected, and a schoolmaster chosen, in every parish; that the heritors or landholders provide a commodious house for a school, and a salary for the schoolmaster, which, exclusive of school fees, shall not be under one hundred marks (5*l.* 11*s.* 1*d.*) nor above two hundred (11*l.* 2*s.* 2*d.*), the said salary to be laid on each heritor according to the valued rent of his land; that the heritors and minister of each parish carry this act into immediate execution; and that, if they fail to do so, the presbytery of the bounds apply to the commissioners of supply for the shire, who, in that case, are invested with full powers to enforce all its provisions. In order to extend the benefits of this act to every part of the country as speedily as possible, the General Assembly, in 1699, instructed all the presbyteries of the national church to use their utmost endeavours to carry it into effect, and also *ordained* the synods to make particular inquiry that this was done. The same instructions were repeated by this venerable court, from year to year, as it saw occasion; especially in 1704, when the Assembly also declared itself willing to concur in any measure for erecting schools, and educating youth, in those parts of the Highlands and Islands, to which the act of 1696 could not be applied; in 1705, when ministers were ordained to take care that none be suffered to neglect the teaching of their children to read; in 1706, when it was recommended to such as have the power of settling schoolmasters, " to prefer men who have passed

B 2

their course at colleges and universities, and have taken their degrees, to others who have not, *cæteris paribus;* and in 1707, when synods and presbyteries were enjoined to send in to the Commission of the Assembly distinct accounts of what parishes had or wanted schools; what were the reasons why they wanted them; what places were in the greatest need of schools; what was the extent of such parishes, and what places in each parish appeared most convenient for the erection of schools. The rebellions of 1715 and 1745, when treasonable correspondence was frequently carried on through means of persons pretending to officiate as private tutors, gave occasion to several additional recommendations by the Assembly, particularly that of 1749, in which presbyteries were required to make watchful inspection of the schools, and of the character and behaviour of the schoolmasters, within their jurisdiction, and to see that all teachers take the oaths to government, and instruct the youth committed to their charge in the just principles of religion and loyalty. When tranquillity was restored, and every part of the country opened to improvement, by the abolition of hereditary juris- dictions, the General Assembly again appointed, in the year 1758, that the presbyteries inquire whether or not a parochial school be established in every parish in their bounds, and, where such schools are wanting, that they make application to the commissioners of supply for having the laws put in execution; and that the procurator and agent of the church be instructed to prosecute such as refuse, at the public charge.

This act of Assembly is remarkable, not only for enjoining the greatest strictness and activity in executing the laws respecting parish schools, but, as being the last on the same subject, which appears in the printed records of the church, for a period of thirty-six years. Hitherto we have seen the clergy exercising a laudable zeal in getting schools established wherever they were needed; but, from this time till near the beginning of the present century, or even till within the last ten years, their efforts as a body seem to have been suspended; and, as there were still many parts of the country without the means of instruction, we are left to infer that the same lethargy, which so long pervaded the dominant party in the Church of Scotland in other departments of their official labours, made them also indifferent to the cause of popular education. In the meantime a lamentable change for the worse came over the schoolmasters themselves. For a con- siderable time after the passing of the act of 1696, their average income was about 19*l.*, a sum which, however

small it may appear in the present day, was sufficient to secure the services of well-qualified teachers, among a people
so frugal in their manner of living as the Scotch then were.
But, towards the close of the last century, owing to various
causes the emoluments of the parochial schoolmasters became
inadequate to maintain them in comfort and independence, and
their office ceased to be an object of ambition. In numerous
instances, they were worse paid than even common labourers;
consequently, when vacancies occurred, the electors were
often compelled to appoint persons who were altogether unfit
for their duties. At the same time, many of those who
were competent in other respects, having lost their self-
esteem, together with the status which they formerly occupied
in society, fell into low habits; and the whole body was fast
sinking into disrepute and inefficiency. To check this growing
evil, as well as to prevent the spread of that unsettled state
of political and religious opinion which was coincident with
the French Revolution, the General Assembly was at length
roused, in the year 1794, to enjoin the presbyteries to make
visitation of all the schools connected with the church, and to
exercise the authority vested in them by law, especially in
enforcing the reading of the Bible, and the learning of the
Shorter Catechism. In 1800 the presbyteries were again recommended to be diligent in exercising those powers, which
the laws of the land had committed to them, respecting the
education of youth; and particularly to call before them all
teachers, whether in parochial or other schools, and take trial
of their sufficiency and qualification in those branches of education which they professed to teach. This recommendation
was repeated in the year 1801. In 1802, the Assembly issued
the following declaration:—" That parochial schoolmasters, by
instilling into youth the principles of religion and morality, and
solid and practical instruction, contribute to the improvement,
order, and success of people of all ranks; and are therefore
well entitled to public encouragement: That from the de-
crease in the value of money, their emoluments have descended below the gains of a day labourer: That it has been
found impossible to procure persons properly qualified to fill
parochial schools : that the whole order is sinking into a state
of depression hurtful to their usefulness: That it is desirable
that some means be devised to hold forth inducements to men
of good principles and talents to undertake the office of pa
rochial schoolmasters : And that such men would prove instrumental in counteracting the operations of those who may
now and afterwards attempt to poison the minds of the rising
generation with principles inimical to religion, order, and the

constitution in church and state: The moderator and procurator for the church are therefore instructed to embrace
every favourable opportunity of expressing the above sentiments, to correspond with the officers of state for Scotland
upon the subject, and to co-operate in the most prudent and
effectual way to forward any plan for the relief of parochial
schoolmasters, and give it all the weight which it can derive
from the countenance of the General Assembly."

In consequence of this declaration by the Church of Scotland, and of the complaints which were sent up from all parts
of the country, parliament, in the course of the next session,
passed the famous act of 1803, which ordains as follows :—
'That, in terms of the act of 1696, a school be established, and
a schoolmaster appointed in every parish, the salary of
the schoolmaster not to be under three hundred marks,
(16*l*. 13*s*. 4*d*.), nor above four hundred (22*l*. 4*s*. 5*d*.) : That
in large parishes, where one parochial school cannot be of any
effectual benefit, it shall be competent for the heritors and
minister to raise a salary of six hundred marks (33*l*. 6*s*. 8*d*.),
and to divide the same among two or more schoolmasters, as
circumstances may require: That in every parish the heritors
shall provide a school-house, and a dwelling-house for the
schoolmaster, together with a piece of ground for a garden,
the dwelling-house to consist of not more than two apartments, and the piece of ground to contain not less than one-
fourth of a Scots acre*; except in parishes where the salary
has been raised to six hundred marks, in which the heritors
shall be exempted from providing school-houses, dwelling-
houses, and gardens: That the foregoing sums shall continue
to be the salaries of parochial schoolmasters till the end
of twenty-five years, when they shall be raised to the average
value of not less than one chalder and a half of oatmeal, and
not more than two chalders ; except in parishes where the
salaries are divided among two or more schoolmasters, in
which case the whole sum so divided shall be raised to the
value of three chalders ; and so *toties quoties* at the end of
every twenty-five years, unless altered by parliament: That
none of the provisions of this act shall apply to parishes,
which consist of a royal burgh, or part of a royal burgh : That
the power of electing schoolmasters continue with the heritors
and minister, a majority of whom shall also determine what
branches of education are most necessary and important for
the parish, and shall from time to time fix the school-fees as
they shall deem expedient: That the presbyteries of the

* A Scotch acre is 1 $\frac{2.6.1.}{1.0.6.9}$ English statute acres.

church shall judge whether candidates for schools possess the necessary qualifications, shall continue to superintend parochial schools, and shall be the sole judges in all charges against schoolmasters, without appeal or review : And that all former statutes with regard to parish schools or schoolmasters be hereby ratified and confirmed, in so far as they are not altered by the express provisions of this act."

The immediate effect of this statute was to prevent the further decline of the parochial schools, and again to make them objects of competition among young men of character and education. Accordingly, as the former generation has passed away, and new appointments have been made, the efficiency of the Scottish schoolmasters has continued to increase. The interest of the established clergy in the education of the people has also begun to revive ; and, of late years, great zeal has been manifested, especially by what is called the popular party in the church, in multiplying the means of religious instruction, by Sunday and other schools. The most extensive, as well as the most successful, scheme for this purpose is that of the General Assembly for promoting education in the Highlands and Islands, which was put into operation in the year 1824*. In the year 1828, as the statute had provided, a small addition was made to the emoluments of the parochial schoolmasters, the *maximum* salary having been increased to 34*l.* 4*s.* 4*d.*, and the *minimum* to 25*l.* 13*s.* 3*d.* The addition was *small* compared with what the schoolmasters hoped to obtain : they had been led by the Lord Advocate of the day and others to expect that the *minimum* salary would be raised to the value of *two* chalders of oatmeal, and the maximum to *three.* In all other respects, the act of 1803 continues in force as it was originally passed, unless where the liberality of the heritors has led them to provide dwelling-houses with more than two apartments, and to erect school-houses in parishes containing more than one school.

Such are the principal enactments, civil and ecclesiastical, for establishing parochial schools in Scotland, and for regulating the appointment, qualifications, and official diligence of the schoolmasters : and that the seminaries of instruction, which have been erected under their authority, have exercised the most beneficial influence on the Scottish people—that they have, in fact, fostered and matured almost all that is excellent and praiseworthy in the national character, admits of no question. But we shall now endeavour to show, that the

* For an account of the General Assembly's Schools, see Journal of Education, vol. ii. p. 227.

system is nevertheless very defective, and that, to keep up its efficiency in the present circumstances of the country, it stands in need of several very essential improvements. We shall also attempt to explain how these improvements may be most speedily and effectually introduced.

The first defect, which we shall point out, is the want of a sufficient number of schools. The law provides that there must be at least one school in every landward parish, and that, if the parish is large, the heritors and minister have it in their power to establish two or more schools, as may be necessary. Accordingly, in the 907 parishes, into which Scotland is divided, there are 1005 parochial schools, attended by between 50,000 and 60,000 children. From the census of 1831 it appears that the population of Scotland is 2,365,807; and if we suppose that, as in Prussia, one-sixth of the population should be at school, instruction ought to be provided for 394,301, that is, for 334,301 more than are in actual attendance at the parochial schools. It is probable, however, that, were the system revised and improved, an additional number of 40,500 might find accommodation in the schools already established by law; and, besides these, there are burgh and other public schools in most of the towns, in which, we shall suppose, there may be taught not fewer than 15,000; society and charity schools, in different parts of the country, furnishing the means of instruction to about 25,000; and the General Assembly's schools in the Highlands and Islands, at which there is an attendance of 6610; making the total number of children for whom education is provided 147,110, and leaving 247,191, for whose instruction no public provision has been made.

But it must not be concluded that the whole of this number is uneducated. In the Lowlands of Scotland, and in some parts of the Highlands, wherever public schools are wanting, or where the parochial schoolmaster is unpopular or inefficient, private schools have been opened, either by subscriptions collected among the people, or as a private speculation by the teachers themselves; and in remote districts, where the children are not sufficiently numerous to support a school, or where they are too widely scattered to meet in one place, it is usual for several families to unite in engaging a teacher, whose services they enjoy by rotation. So desirous are the people of Scotland of having their children instructed in the elements of reading and writing, that, in the country parts, villages, and small towns of the Lowlands, there are upwards of 2000 private schools, and, in the Highlands and Islands, there are 372. We are sure, therefore, that we do not overstate the number, when we suppose that, in the towns and country together, there are as many children in attendance at private as at public schools. But even this calculation leaves upwards of 100,000 destitute of the means of instruction. In the Report of the General Assembly's Committee for 1833, it is stated that 83,397 of these are in the Highlands and Islands; and the remainder is scattered chiefly throughout the large towns.

We believe that the sum of 10,000*l*., which was granted during the last session of parliament to aid in erecting school-houses in Scotland, was intended chiefly for places in which there are no parochial schools; and, if judiciously applied, it will provide school accommodation for a considerable portion of those who are at present growing up in utter ignorance. But it is obvious that, if the design of the original statutes be carried into effect in their amended form, schools for the whole population will not only be erected but endowed; and, consequently, that, in addition to those already established, schools and schoolmasters should be provided for 247,191, or rather perhaps for 200,000, which supposes that the parents of 47,191 are in such circumstances that they either would not or could not avail themselves of an endowment. The necessity of thus increasing the means of public instruction is not removed by the very great number of private schools, as might be imagined. The existence of these in almost every place where they are needed, or where means can be procured for establishing them, is indeed a gratifying proof of the desire of the people to give their children a good education; but the state of many, we should rather say of most, of them furnishes a very strong argument for legislative assistance in making up for the present deficiency in the number of en-dowed schools. This is very clearly shown in a valuable and interesting paper, entitled "Educational Statistics," appended to the Report of the General Assembly's Committee already mentioned, from which we make the following extract :—" If any improvement is to be attempted upon the schools that already exist in the Highlands, the earliest attention is due, unquestionably, to those that have been opened by the teachers on their own adventure. At the stations where these have been placed there is generally an abundant popu-lation, capable of taking the benefits of a regular school, and demanding other instructors than such as they have too commonly found,—a boy, or an aged female, a retired soldier, an innkeeper, or a fisherman. For the most part, the schools of this description are open only in winter, and the teacher of one season is seldom the teacher of the next; and even where a regular school has been attempted, there is a constant apprehension that the teacher will not find sufficient inducement to abide in the place,—his emoluments not exceeding 9*l.* or 10*l.* a year in many parts of the Highlands, nor 3*l.* a year in Shetland. Sometimes, indeed, the teacher's remuneration is not in money, according to his demand, but in produce, according to the liberality of the people; but it may be fairly questioned, whether education does not lose more by the mendicant character thus imposed on the teacher, than it gains by the retention of his services. There is a further evil often attendant upon these schools in this, that by habituating the people to the lowest standard of instruction, they are not without an evil influence in lowering the character of the other schools in their neighbourhood. Such are generally the defects of this class of schools throughout the Highlands, and they will be viewed with the more regret, when it is stated that at every station where they have been placed, there is an evident demand for such regular schools as are given by the educational societies; and that every condition for the interference of these societies would in very many instances be fulfilled. The average number of pupils in attendance at each of the schools now referred to is thirty-six, and the average emoluments of the teachers are 13*l.* a year,— the population being thus at once sufficiently numerous and sufficiently needy to justify and to demand the aid of a charitable institution. In the meantime, however, it will not pass unnoticed, that the very existence of such schools is another proof that the people are most desirous of instruction, and are fully prepared to profit by it." It is proper to remark on this statement, that, though it does not apply with equal force to the Lowlands, it gives a general picture of private schools in every part of Scotland except the towns, in which there are many unendowed seminaries of great respectability and usefulness.

In suggesting how the deficiency in the number of public schools may be supplied, it is necessary that we should revert to two clauses in the act of 1803, namely, the clause which limits the sum to be levied from the heritors, in parishes which require more than one school, to the value of three chalders of oatmeal (51*l.* 6*s.* 6*d.*), and that which prohibits the provisions of the act from being applied to parishes which consist only of a royal burgh, or part of a royal burgh. In these limitations of the principle of the law, and restrictions on its application, will be found the main cause why parochial schools have not been multiplied as the population has increased, and why the lower classes in large towns have been

left in almost utter destitution of the means of instruction.
The first amendment, therefore, in the act of 1803 should be
to withdraw the former of these clauses, and to modify the
latter. By making it imperative on the heritors to build and
endow as many schools in each parish as may be necessary,
without limitation as to the amount of money to be raised for
salaries, education might be provided for nearly as many additional children as are at present in attendance at the parochial schools. In the Highlands alone there are 217 stations,
where schools might be established without interfering with
other schools, either public or private. Connected with the
parliamentary churches, which the General Assembly of 1833
made parish churches, *quoad sacra,* forty schools are required;
and upwards of fifty additional schools should be established
in connexion with the chapels of ease, which were also converted into parish churches, *quoad sacra,* by the Assembly of
1834. For all these stations schools might readily be provided, without any specific provision for the parliamentary
and chapel-of-ease parishes, by merely withdrawing the former
of the clauses in question ; and many of the private schools
referred to by the Assembly's Committee, as well as many of
a similar description in the Lowlands, might be erected into
parochial schools, and filled with respectable and efficient
teachers. The number of children unprovided with the means
of instruction, or left to the chance of being taught in private
schools, would thus be reduced to less than 150,000, which,
it will be observed, is about one-sixth of the population of the
royal burghs, and of the towns which contain more than
7000 inhabitants. A considerable number of these are excluded from the benefit of the laws regarding parochial schools
by the second of the two clauses to which we have alluded ;
but there are obstacles to the withdrawing of that clause from
a new enactment which it would be difficult to surmount.
A modification might be made upon it, however, by which
legislative sanction and public support might be given to
another description of schools, admirably fitted for extending
the parochial system to town as well as rural parishes. We
refer to the Sessional Schools recently established in several
of the parishes in the city of Edinburgh.

In the first number of this Journal will be found an account
of what may be called the parent of these institutions, the
Edinburgh Sessional School ; but it may not be unnecessary
to give here a short history of its origin and progress, and to
repeat the general principles on which it is conducted. The
deplorable scenes of outrage and murder, which occurred in
the streets of Edinburgh on the 1st of January 1812, made

the city clergy anxious to devise some means for diminishing
the mass of crime and misery which was then brought to
light. The scheme first proposed, and carried into execution,
was to establish sabbath schools in all the parishes within the
royalty, to which they gave the name of the Parochial Institutions for Religious Education. It was soon found, however, that the usefulness of these institutions was greatly
limited, in consequence of a very great number of the children, for whose benefit they were intended, being unable to
read. It was therefore proposed that, in connexion with the
sabbath schools, a day school should be established, which
was accordingly opened on the 29th of April, 1813. This
day school took the name of the Edinburgh Sessional School,
from the circumstance of its being superintended by a minister
or an elder from each kirk-session* in the city; the object
of this school is to give instruction to the children of the
poor, in reading, writing, and arithmetic. Five gratis scholars may be recommended by each kirk-session; but the
charge to all the others is sixpence per month. For many
years the average attendance has been about 500; so that the
school-fees, together with occasional donations, and a small
share of the collections made annually at the church doors
for the parochial institutions, have hitherto been sufficient to
meet the ordinary expenses of the school. At first, no particular regulations were laid down for conducting the Sessional School; but, after some years, the system of Dr. Bell
was partially introduced. In the year 1819, circumstances
led Mr. John Wood, Sheriff-Depute of the county of Peebles,
to take an interest in the institution; and that benevolent
individual began by degrees to give so much of his time and
attention to it, that it soon became almost identified with his
name. Under his superintendence, a large and commodious
school-house was erected, and the system of teaching entirely
remodelled. In the latter department of his meritorious labours, Mr. Wood did not adopt the particular views of any
one writer on education, but collected from all what he

---

* For the information of some of our readers, we may explain that a *kirk-
session* is the lowest ecclesiastical court in Scotland, and consists of the clergyman
of each congregation, with a small number of lay elders : it generally meets on
Sunday, after public worship. The next court in point of judicial authority is
the *presbytery*, which consists of all the clergymen within a certain district, with
a lay elder from each congregation : this court meets once a month. All the
presbyteries within given bounds form a still higher court, called a *synod*, which
meets twice in the year. The *General Assembly* is the supreme judicial and
legislative court of the Church of Scotland : it consists of clerical and lay representatives from the several presbyteries, of a lay elder from each royal burgh,
and of a Commissioner to represent his Majesty, and holds its sittings at Edinburgh once a year for about a fortnight.

thought useful, and arranged it into a method of his own. So judicious is this plan of tuition, that it has not only been crowned with complete success in the Sessional School, but has been introduced, either partially or entirely, into many other public and private seminaries, and has, in fact, given a new impulse to the work of elementary instruction throughout Scotland. Its general principles in the teaching of reading are thus stated by Mr. Wood himself, in an account of the Sessional School which he published some years ago : " First, to render more easy and pleasing the acquisition of the mechanical art of reading ; secondly, to turn to advantage the particular instruction contained in every individual passage which is read ; and thirdly, to give the pupil, by means of a minute analysis of each passage, a general command of his own language." Similar principles are acted upon in teaching the other branches, the chief objects of the whole system being to simplify and facilitate as much as possible the labour of acquiring knowledge, to communicate as much general information as the pupils can comprehend, and to train them to habits of mental activity and application.

After the model of this excellent institution, several local schools have been erected in Edinburgh, for the benefit of particular parishes. The first of these was established about ten years ago, in the parish of St. George's, by the late Dr. Andrew Thomson. With his characteristic activity, that distinguished clergyman raised, by subscriptions and collections in his church, about 2000*l.*, with which he purchased the site, and built and fitted up the school-house. Since its erection, the average number of scholars has been nearly 200; the school fees are 3*s.*, 4*s.*, and 5*s.* per quarter, according to the advancement of the pupils ; and the total income of the school is upwards of 160*l.* From this sum, 84*l.* are paid to the master, 30*l.* to an assistant, and 16*l.* to monitors : the incidental expenses seldom exceed 10*l.* The surplus has hitherto been applied to the liquidation of a small debt, which remained from the building of the house ; but, as that debt has now been discharged, it will henceforward go to form a fund for keeping the school-house in repair.

The next local school, according to the date of erection, is the Stockbridge Sessional School, which was established by the West-Kirk Session, from a fund formed by reserving for such purposes one-third of the fees required for the registration of baptisms and the proclamation of banns. The building of the school-house cost nearly 700*l.*; and there is a burden of 15*l.* a year for feu-duty*. The kirk-session gives

---

* Ground-rent, that is, rent paid to the proprietor of the land on which the school-house stands.

an annual salary of 15*l.* to the master, who receives besides
the whole of the school-fees. The average number of scholars
is about 180, and the fees vary from 2*s.* to 4*s.* per quarter.
Many of the children attending this school pay weekly, and
a few are recommended by the kirk-session to be educated
gratis.

Besides these, there are other schools of the same description, and supported in a similar manner, in the southern districts of the West-Kirk parish, in the parish of St. Mary's, in
the New North parish, and in one of the divisions of South
Leith; and more are in contemplation by several of the
ministers and kirk-sessions. We may also mention that
schools upon the same plan have recently been established
in Dublin, by the Rev. James Carlile, of the Scots' Church,
Mary's Abbey, and in Manchester by the clergyman and
session of the Presbyterian congregation.

The object of Dr. Thomson in erecting St. George's Local
School was not only to provide cheap instruction for the
poorer classes in his own parish, but to show the practicability
of extending the parochial system of elementary schools to
large towns : and it is upon the success which has attended
the schools established by him, and by those clergymen who
have followed his example, that we found our suggestion of
amending the present statute, by authorizing the erection of
sessional schools in parishes which consist of a royal burgh,
or of part of a royal burgh, or in which there is a town population of more than 7000. This appears to be the readiest
and most effectual plan for conveying the benefits of education to those children, amounting, as we have seen, to nearly
150,000, to whom no amendment or extension of the act of
1803, which contained either of the limitations already specified, could be made to apply. But the erection of sessional
schools, in anything like the numbers required, could not be
made without an annual grant of public money, similar to
that which was voted by the House of Commons last session
of parliament; for few clergymen have it in their power,
especially in the smaller towns, to raise funds to the amount
collected by Dr. Thomson, or at the command of the West-
Kirk session. There are still fewer, however, perhaps we
should rather say that there are none, who might not at least
rent a school-house, could they obtain a salary for the teacher,
or who might not procure an attendance of children sufficient
to remunerate the teacher, had they the means of building a
school-house. The principle of the grant voted for Scotland,
therefore, as well as of those voted for England and Ireland,
namely, of making schools partly chargeable on the local

residents, might be preserved, though the peculiar circumstances of some parts of Scotland would require some modification in the manner of applying it. The money already granted by parliament has been given merely to assist in erecting school-houses; and in towns like Edinburgh, where the expense of materials and building is very great, and where, as in the case of St. George's school, the number of scholars would be so large that the school-fees would pay the master's salary and defray all incidental expenses, this is all that is necessary. But there are many other places, in which school-houses could be procured at a very trifling expense, and without assistance, while, to make the schools of any essential benefit, it would be necessary to fix the school-fees at so low a rate that they could not support the schoolmaster. The General Assembly's Committee report that they are yearly receiving numerous applications for endowments, accompanied with offers to provide the most ample accommodation. Any public fund, therefore, for the establishment of additional schools, should be applied to the double purpose of erecting school-houses, and of allowing salaries to teachers, as the particular circumstances of each locality might require. Of the sum which might be necessary for this purpose we have no means of forming an estimate, except from the calculations given in the educational statistics formerly quoted. It is there stated that, to complete the education of the Highlands, that is, to furnish instruction to the 83,397, who are still unable to read, would require 384 schools, and the annual sum of 8680*l.* It is also stated that an income of 40*l.* a year, exclusive of the legal accommodations, is enough to secure, in the Highlands, the services of well qualified and able men. In the Lowlands, however, the expense of living is somewhat greater, and we should say that the *minimum* emoluments of a schoolmaster should not there be under 50*l.* with suitable accommodation. Thus, were government to pay, on an average, one-half of the expense of maintaining the schoolmasters, according to the proportion of the above calculations, the instruction of 150,000 children would require 700 schools, with an annual grant of 17,500*l.*; while 1000 schools and 25,000*l.* would be necessary to educate the whole 200,000, for whom there is no accommodation in the schools already established. We know not if either of these sums will ever be allowed by parliament; but we are persuaded that if the latter by itself, or the former, accompanied with the unlimited application of that clause of the Act of 1803, which makes it imperative on the heritors to endow two or more schools in a parish when they are necessary, were placed under the management of the General Assembly's

Committee for increasing the means of education, it would be found adequate for the elementary instruction of the whole population of Scotland.

We proceed to notice another defect in the Scottish system of parochial schools, as it exists at present, namely, that it gives no security that the candidate chosen is the best qualified, or even that he is competent for his situation. The law is, that, within four months after a vacancy takes place, the heritors, possessing land in the parish to the extent of at least one hundred pounds Scots of valued rent, and the minister, shall elect a schoolmaster, who shall be examined by the Presbytery concerning his sufficiency for the office, in respect of morality and religion, and of such branches of literature as by a majority of the heritors and the minister shall be deemed most necessary and important for the parish. The sole right of election thus belongs to the heritors and minister, while the power of induction is vested in the Presbytery. In the examination of candidates, the latter body generally acts upon the recommendation of the Assembly of 1706, by preferring such as have attended college; and, in the majority of instances, there is so much harmony between the Presbytery and the heritors of parishes, that the election by the latter, and the examination by the former, take place upon the same day, and in the same place. But still, from the heritors and minister having the privilege of deciding what branches of education shall be taught in the parish, and in consequence of the Presbytery not having the power of rejecting the object of their choice, unless they can declare him incompetent to teach the branches prescribed, or of immoral character or unsound religious opinions, cases sometimes occur in which, through private influence among the electors, the least qualified, both in attainments and experience, is appointed. It would, therefore, be a very great improvement to the system, were certain qualifications laid down by law, without which no teacher could be elected to a parochial school. In a petition which they presented to the last General Assembly, the schoolmasters prayed that Latin and Greek might be declared indispensable; and the general propriety of this request appears from the fact, that, in the county of Dumfries alone, there were, in the year 1824, not fewer than 500 learning these languages at the parochial schools. This county has indeed been long noted above every other in Scotland, except Edinburgh, for the number of young men whom it supplies to the learned professions: but, though the proportion may be somewhat less in other counties, there are very few parishes in Scotland in which there will not be some who require to be instructed in the ancient classics. It was stated in a former article in this Journal*, that a considerable portion of the students, who attend the Scottish universities, have received no other instruction than what they obtained at the parish schools; and from this circumstance a knowledge of the elements of geometry should be added to the list of qualifications. The improved methods of teaching also require some acquaintance with history, geography, and the outlines of physical science.

Another qualification, not less imperatively called for, is a practical knowledge of the principles and art of teaching. In Scotland, a schoolmaster has no opportunity of making himself acquainted with these, till he has been appointed to his situation, and has acquired them by his own experience : and no system of elementary schools can be considered complete in which there is such an utter want of all provision for the training of teachers. On this subject we shall transcribe the sentiments of two authorities, which ought to have no small weight with those who have the election and superintendence of schoolmasters. " At the same time," we quote from the Report of the General Assembly's Committee for 1834, " it is not forgotten that there is an art of teaching in which every schoolmaster ought to be instructed : and perhaps no greater benefit could arise to éducation than from the general diffusion of such methods as are practised in the sessional and a few other schools in Edinburgh. This, however, can only be accomplished comprehensively by the institution of model schools for the training of teachers to the practice of their calling. These very powerful methods of instruction may be found already, indeed, in a few of the General Assembly's schools, as in those of Arran and Tobermory. In their respective neighbourhoods, the schools of this sort have begot a zeal for instruction, where a zeal for any thing was formerly unknown. They have served, and almost without design, the purposes of a model or training school to many young men who resort to them, seeking to be formed for the charge of lesser schools in other parts of the country,—and declaring, by their voluntary pursuit of these superior modes, the demand which even the common people in these parts appear to have entertained for some considerable improvements in education. By such means the invaluable system now referred to appears to be gradually extending throughout the Highlands. *   *   *   *   For whom, it may be asked, is a model school of the description now proposed to be established ?   It is answered, for the benefit of the entire population.   Incidentally, it may give the higher branches to

* Vol. iv. p. 22.

a few of its immediate pupils, who may either profit essentially by that superior instruction, or who, more probably,
may not profit by it in any considerable degree. The chief
design, however, of such schools will be to teach the ordinary
branches to all with more than ordinary efficiency, and to
prepare a set of teachers capable of instructing in that manner
at their respective stations; and not refusing to carry along
with them, in Christian humility, to the cottages of the poor,
a talent of which it is not one of the least advantages that it
renders the business of teaching so much more agreeable to
the teacher himself."

" It requires but little reflection," says Professor Pillans,
in his Principles of Elementary Teaching, " to arrive at the
conclusion, that the power of *teaching* well is neither a thing
that 'comes by nature,' nor at all commensurate with the
capacity for *learning;* that a great stock of knowledge affords
no proof, scarcely even a presumption, that the possessor has
the faculty of skilfully communicating any part of it to young
minds. To stoop from the pride of superior attainment; to
conceive even the embarrassments that entangle the beginner;
to become identified with the feelings and faculties of children; to anticipate and remove the obstacles in their way to
elementary knowledge; to curb and regulate their little
passions and tempers; and, what is still more difficult, one's
own; to awaken and sustain attention, and know when to
stop short of fatigue and exhaustion; to lead, by short and
easy steps, through a path that to them is a rugged one,
bearing them, as it were, in arms over the worst of the road,
and strewing it with flowers instead of planting it with thorns;
to slacken one's own step, in order to keep pace with the
pupil, instead of expecting or insisting on gigantic strides
from the feebleness of childhood: to do all this is not so entirely a matter of instinct in man, that the power may safely
be left without culture to its natural development. And
with regard to other accomplishments not less necessary,
and yet altogether independent of what a man may know of
Greek and Latin, or mathematics, or any other science of
the seven,—the faculty, I mean, of exciting emulation, encouraging and rewarding industry, inspiring the love of knowledge and of virtue, and so combining and directing the
exertions of all, in one simultaneous movement, that the
whole school shall resemble a piece of fine machinery, all
the parts of which conspire to one general effect—which, in
this case, is the production of the largest amount of useful
acquirement, and virtuous habits; these, I need scarcely say,
are qualifications which it is highly desirable every school-

master should possess, and which there is very little chance
of his ever acquiring without some previous training. Such
a department for this purpose, however, as was, I believe,
attached to the rival establishments of Bell and Lancaster,
and as is now in active operation, in the Model School of the
Society for the education of the poor in Ireland, is by no
means so perfect an institution, as to render it desirable it
should be introduced into Scotland simply and without improvement ; even supposing we had model schools like our
neighbours, on which it might be readily engrafted. It
would, no doubt, be a great benefit to us, who have nothing
of the kind ; but something more, I conceive, is required,
than to bring the future instructor of youth into a school,
where he may see the practical details of teaching going on,
after the most approved method. An opportunity should
also be afforded him of hearing the principles and theory of
the art of teaching laid down and expounded in public lectures, before he sees, or rather while he is employed in
observing, the theory illustrated by example."

According to the Assembly's Committee, then, and to
Professor Pillans, the establishment of model schools, in
which young men would have an opportunity of acquiring
the art of teaching, would be a valuable addition to the Scottish system ; and we agree with Professor Pillans in thinking
that the preparatory training of schoolmasters would be incomplete without an exposition of the principles of the art, and
an account of the various systems of tuition, given in the form
of lectures. Whether attendance on these, and at a model
school, should be made imperative, none being eligible to
parochial schools but such as have been thus trained for their
office, may admit of some dispute ; and an enactment to that
effect could hardly be expected to receive the sanction of
those who at present have the appointment and superintendence of teachers. Nor does it appear to be absolutely
necessary. In a country like Scotland, where there is a
demand for education, and where no schoolmaster, who is
not successful, will be long acceptable, it is the interest of
the teacher himself to be as skilful as possible in his profession. It might be sufficient, therefore, to furnish the
means, and to issue an injunction similar to that which was
laid upon the Presbyteries by the Assembly of 1642, with
regard to grammar schools, namely, that the church courts,
in connexion with the heritors and others interested in education, should endeavour to get model schools and lecture-
ships established in all " burghs, presbytery-seats, and other

important places," and that teachers who had been trained
at these should be preferred to others, *cæteris paribus*.

It will not be supposed that, in suggesting these additions
to the qualifications required of parochial schoolmasters, we
mean to throw any reflection upon those at present in office.
We may state, indeed, without fear of giving offence, that
till very lately the plan of tuition which they pursued was
not the most systematic or the most efficient; but the fault
lay not with them so much as with the system under which
they had been appointed, and which afforded them no opportunity of knowing any other method than that according to
which they themselves had been taught. So far as their
knowledge and experience extend, we believe them to be a
conscientious and laborious body of men ; and, of late years,
they have shown no unwillingness to adopt any improvements which have been suggested to them by those who were
competent and authorized to do so. Of their general character we have already spoken ; and concerning their attainments we have the testimony of both the authorities last
quoted. Professor Pillans states that " a very large proportion of the parochial teachers are men of good education
and very respectable attainments." The General Assembly's
Committee report, " that, from the commencement of this
scheme, they have received applications from not less than
460 candidates for schools; that from that number they made
choice of 293 for examination; that of the candidates examined 139 were found qualified to undertake the charge of
schools of the first or second class; and that, finally, the
most select of those whose qualifications were thus ascertained now form the teachers of this establishment." In
addition to this evidence, we may also state that, in the list
of contributors to the Burgh and Parochial Schoolmasters'
Widows' Fund, there are nearly a hundred probationers, or
young men who, having completed their attendance at college, have been licensed by their respective presbyteries to
preach the gospel, and have thereby been declared competent
to undertake the duties of parish ministers. Our animad-
versions, therefore, are not upon the men, but upon the
system, which, as we are attempting to show, is susceptible
of material improvement.

The small emoluments and accommodation of the schoolmasters have long been complained of as another great defect
in the system of elementary schools in Scotland. It has
been already stated, that, where there is only one school in
a parish, the teacher must have a salary of not more than

34*l.* 4*s.* 4*d.*, and not less than 25*l.* 13*s.* 3*d.*, with a school-house, and a dwelling-house containing not more than two apartments; and that, if the heritors and minister are of opinion that more than one school is necessary, they may increase the salary to 51*l.* 6*s.* 6*d.*, which they may divide among as many schools as they think proper; but that, in the latter case, the heritors are exempted from the burden of providing school-houses and dwelling-houses. It is greatly to the credit of the landholders of Scotland, that for some time back they have not measured their liberality, especially in the building of houses, by the provisions of the statute; and we have much pleasure in making the following extract from the Assembly's Educational Statistics, by which we are led to hope that they would offer no opposition to such an extension of the system as was formerly suggested. "At the same time, it is unquestionable that the Highland heritors have done much for the education of the Highland people, beyond what was required of them by the Parochial School Act. Of them, indeed, it might be expected that above all others they should be alive to the wants of a population that serves them by its industry,—that stands to them so frequently in the relation of immediate dependents,—and that still accords to them, in some instances, an almost feudal attachment and respect. It is found, accordingly, that the Highland heritors have been in general as anxious as became them for the moral and religious education of the people; and that they have not been insensible to the discredit of their estates being laboured by an unlettered population. Their exertions to promote the instruction of the people with whom they are so connected cannot indeed admit of any definite calculation; but it is an easy matter to demonstrate that they must not be estimated as of little importance. There are 315 schools in the Highlands and Islands supported by societies, and each of these schools has been furnished with certain accommodations, very generally contributed by the heritors. It appears, further, that there are 137 schools wholly or partially endowed; and it may be supposed that the endowments have in general proceeded from individuals connected with the Highland districts. There is, besides, a considerable amount yearly subscribed by the Highland heritors to the funds of the several Educational Societies." Notwithstanding the generosity of the landholders, however, which is not exclusively confined to the Highlands, as the school-fees are very low (the usual rates being 2*s.* per quarter for reading, 2*s.* 6*d.* for reading and writing, 3*s.* for reading, writing, and arithmetic, and 5*s.* when the boys learn Latin also), the average income of the parochial schoolmasters throughout Scotland is little more than 50*l.* a year, with very limited accommodation. To show the two extremes of this average, we may explain that, on the one hand, where the parish is partly town and partly landward, and where the schoolmaster derives a considerable revenue, in his capacity of session-clerk, from the registration of baptisms and marriages, and from other perquisites, his emoluments sometimes amount to 150*l.* a year; while, on the other hand, in very large rural parishes, in which it has been judged necessary to divide the legal salary among three or four teachers, their whole income is under 30*l.*, without any accommodation whatever. In the synod of Argyle, there are, in eleven parishes, thirty-eight parochial teachers, whose average emoluments do not exceed 29*l.* In their petitions to parliament, the schoolmasters have generally requested that the *maximum* salary should be increased to the value of three chalders of oatmeal (51*l.* 6*s.* 6*d.*), and the *minimum* to two chalders (34*l.* 4*s.* 4*d.*); and that, where more schools than one are necessary in a parish, the salary of each schoolmaster should not be under the latter sum. They have also requested that the number of apartments in their dwelling-houses should not be limited by statute to two, and that all the schoolmasters in a parish, however many there may be, should be provided with school-houses and dwelling-houses. If the prayer of these petitions should be granted, the average income of schoolmasters with the *maximum* salary would be 70*l.* (including fees), and of those with the *minimum* 50*l.*, exclusive of houses and gardens, which cannot be regarded as too high a remuneration for their invaluable labours. So moderate an increase of their emoluments would render unnecessary any plan for allocating the advance of salary, in proportions corresponding to the merits of teachers, as Professor Pillans suggests; because it would not make them independent of the school-fees, and consequently would not take away from such as are disposed to be careless the only stimulus to exertion, which they are supposed to be capable of feeling. But even if, in some cases, they were exposed to this temptation, we should have little apprehension that many of them would yield to it, or that it would diminish the efficiency either of the body or of individuals. We should confidently hope for the very reverse. The emoluments of a schoolmaster should bear some proportion, not only to his services as an instructor of youth, but to the previous time, study, and expense, which have been spent in preparing him for his office. Till this is the case, teaching will never occupy the rank among liberal professions to which its importance entitles it, nor will well-educated young men be prevailed upon to devote themselves to its labours, except with the view of forwarding their prospects in some other line of life. We are not indeed among the number of those who think, that in order to a teacher's being zealous and conscientious, it is necessary that his ultimate views should not extend beyond his profession; for we have seen that, in Scotland, teachers were never more efficient, and were never more highly respected, than when the office of a parish schoolmaster was considered a stepping-stone to that of a parish minister. But we are nevertheless persuaded that, while every teacher should have a competency, there should be many situations in a complete system of elementary schools, each of which would be an object to a man of talents and learning as a settlement for life. We would therefore have two grades of teachers in point of emolument, such as the preceding scale of salaries would necessarily produce, experience and success in the one of which should form an admitted recommendation to promotion to the other. The hope of obtaining such promotion would furnish an additional motive for exertion to those in the lower class, or with inferior emoluments; while, to prevent relaxation from duty in those of the higher, we should trust to the habits of diligence and application formed in acquiring the necessary qualifications, to the influence of their improved status in society, and to the vigilant superintendence of the church courts.

By the last remark we are brought to the only remaining defect in the Scottish system, on which we purpose to comment, namely the judicial powers of presbyteries. Several former Acts of parliament had entrusted the superintendence of all schools, whether parochial or not, to the church courts; and, by the Act of 1803, the decision of presbyteries in all cases involving the literary qualifications, moral conduct and professional diligence of parish schoolmasters, was made final, there being no appeal or redress, except by an action in the supreme civil court, if a presbytery should exceed the powers vested in it by the statute. At the time the last Act was passed, some law of this kind was absolutely necessary, as, from the many complaints against schoolmasters, the cases before these judicatories were very numerous, and the right of appeal enabled each schoolmaster to remove his case from the local court, by which the circumstances could be most readily investigated, to the Synod or General Assembly, which, in almost every instance, confirmed its decision. In the meantime the delay was most prejudicial to the parish,

in which there was no efficient instruction while these proceedings were in progress. But now, when the character
and conduct of the schoolmasters are so much improved, and
when there is very seldom any occasion of complaint against
them to the church courts, the clause which takes away the
right of appeal should be withdrawn ; and it is greatly to the
honour of the General Assembly, and of many of the presbyteries, that they have unanimously seconded the petitions of
the schoolmasters, and have even presented petitions of their
own to that effect.

But, while schoolmasters should have the privilege of appeal in all cases, in which a regular libel is necessary, and in
which the sentence may amount to suspension or deposition
from office, it would add greatly to the efficiency of the parochial schools, if more frequent inquiry were made into the
manner in which they are conducted with regard to discipline,
regularity of attendance, mode of teaching, and other matters
equally within the cognizance of the church courts,—if presbyteries, in short, were a little more active in their superintendence. At present they do little else than examine the
schools within their respective bounds once a year, and
transmit a report of the number of scholars to the General
Assembly. We are aware that, from their extraordinary
powers, the interference of the clergy is looked upon with
great jealousy by the schoolmasters, and that, from motives
of delicacy, the clergy are very unwilling to interfere unless
in extreme cases. But in so important a matter as the education of youth, the superintendence of its legal guardians
should be something more than nominal. As nothing operates
more powerfully in inciting a careless teacher, and in encouraging an active one, than the examination of his pupils,
the visits of the clergy to the parochial schools should be
more frequent; and the effect would be greatly increased, if
they could persuade other influential persons in the neighbourhood to accompany them, and to take a personal interest in the
labours of the master and the progress of his pupils. The
guardianship with which they are entrusted also implies, that,
as recommended by the Assembly of 1705, the clergy should
suffer no parent to neglect the education of his children ; that
they should pay particular attention to the school-books used,
which, according to the account of Professor Pillans, do not
appear to be the most judicious ; that, like the Assembly
of 1642, they should make inquiry concerning the best
methods of teaching; and that, in a word, they should do
every thing in their power to promote the religious, moral,
and literary instruction of their people. Such active exertions

are not only recognized but enjoined in many of the acts of Assembly formerly enumerated, and are at this moment being made by the Committee, of whose labours we have so often had occasion to make honourable mention. In one of their recent reports they state, that their " appointed task will not find its proper termination, so long as there remains an individual in Scotland unqualified to read, and to peruse the Scriptures for himself." The general diffusion, we should rather say the revival, of the spirit which is breathed in this quotation, is all that is necessary to make the superintendence of schools by the clergy as effective as it once was, and as its powers are ample: and we doubt not but such a state of things would be rapidly hastened by the amendment of the present laws, and by placing in the hands of the General Assembly the means of extending the parochial and sessional system of elementary schools to every part of the country, and to the lower classes in large towns. How far the Church of Scotland is worthy of this confidence from the State, we leave to be judged from the exertions of individual clergymen to establish additional schools in their own parishes *, from the efforts of the church collectively to promote education in India, and especially from the labours of the Committee for increasing the means of instruction in the Highlands and Islands, with another extract from whose Report for 1834, we shall conclude the present article.

" At every period of the Church of Scotland, the parochial clergy have watched with exemplary care over the interests of education throughout the country. It was the custom of the Church to act in this matter almost exclusively by its presbyteries, and by its ministers individually, within their respective bounds. The spirit of the presbyterian form was satisfied by the unobtrusive manner in which one of its most important functions was thus effectively performed; nor is it easy to estimate the services thus rendered by presbyteries and by ministers, in the advancement, protection, and superintendence of education within their bounds. But there are offices in that way which the Church can perform only in its collective capacity ; that is, by its only representative, the General Assembly. By that

* In a country parish known to the writer of this article, there are five day schools, besides the parochial one; three of which—an infant school and two female schools—have been organized by the clergyman, who has also, besides these, established six Sunday schools. One of the clergymen of the city of Edinburgh has the education of 980 young persons under his immediate superintendence. It may be useful to give the details in this latter case, as showing the sort of interest which the Scottish clergy are again beginning to take in the education of youth. They are as follow :—two infant schools, attended by about 100 each ; a senior female school, 90 ; boys' ditto, 60 ; class of religious instruction for children of the better classes, 200 ; young gentlemen's class for religious instruction, 30 ; young ladies' ditto, 80 ; servants' ditto, 120 ; Sunday-school, 200.

organ alone it has influence to win from one portion of the population what may contribute to the Christian instruction of another. If
such aid, therefore, from the general sympathy, be required in any
part of Scotland, it must be considered as the duty of the General
Assembly to seek the means of extending it as far as possible, no less
than it is the duty of every minister to consult and to provide for
the proper education of his own parish. There is, besides, one feature
of the present time that might well suggest to the Church the employment of every instrument it commands, and especially of its
General Assembly, in the care and government of education; and
that is, the extraordinary advances now making in general instruction among the people throughout the country. That instruction is
sometimes almost entirely secular; and in such cases it is satisfactory to observe that it does not appear to have been always considered as sufficient for the whole work of education. On the contrary,
there appears to have been a prevailing expectation that the qualifying
and vital element of religion was still to proceed from the hands of
the Church. It is manifest, indeed, that an instruction merely secular
cannot safely be allowed to proceed alone; and that the greater
progress which it makes, the more it behoves to be accompanied
with an instruction which embraces religion as its most essential
part. In accordance, probably, with some such views, there has
been throughout Scotland, during the last year, a greater promise
than had been given before, of support to the educational measures
of the Assembly. Not a few of the presbyteries have formed themselves into associations in aid both of these measures, and of the
scheme for extending Christianity abroad. The plan may have
some varieties in the different presbyteries; but generally it embraces these essential particulars,—that in every parish within the
presbytery, there shall be for these objects an annual collection, at the
most suitable season of the year; that in such parishes there shall be a
periodical communication, to all who are interested, of intelligence on
the progress of the Assembly's measures; and that the parochial collections shall be thrown together in a common fund, and the distribution of the total amount voted annually by the presbytery. Associations of this kind, if more extended, and if steadily maintained,
will soon enable the Church to effect very signal benefits in education
by means of its General Assembly; and it may be hoped, that when
the Committee are next called on to report, the example may have
been followed by all or by the greater part of the presbyteries
in the Church."

PUBLIC INSTRUCTION.

Project of a Plan of Moral, Industrious, and Intellectual Education for Females.

NORMAL SCHOOLS.

' NOTHING more is wanted than the degree of liberality now advocated, to obtain for Britain at large the invaluable boon of popular education. If dominant sects are listened to, we shall never see the day of its coming ; our people will remain uneducated secularly, uneducated religiously, and continue in their present state of debasement and suffering. It is trusted, it is entreated, that the conscientious of the dominant sects will lay the state of the question to heart. For it has come to this issue : Education to embrace all sects, or no education. Let them not, by holding out, defeat both our object and their own. The government once persuaded that is the alternative (and there can be little doubt that they are so persuaded, and moreover that a large majority of the legislature are so too,) ought not to wait till they succeed in removing prejudices and reconciling clashing interests. On them a tremendous responsibility rests. The state of the country calls for the education of the people with a voice which overwhelms the chill and feeble tone of sectarian opposition. An immense increase of political power has been given to a class, as yet but imperfectly educated. Is it reasonable to expect a wise use of that power without a great enlargement of the means of education ?'

In an age in which there is so decided a tendency towards an amelioration of the existing systems of education, all who have devoted their time and attention to the education of youth are called on to contribute their share of information, in order to assist in solving a question of such vital importance to the happiness of individuals and of society in general. As an introduction to the subject which we shall attempt to discuss, we have selected the above extract from the excellent work of Mr. J. Simpson, a Scotch advocate.

What is the true destination of women ? To be wives and mothers, to watch and preside over domestic duties, to be the ornaments of society, to be competent to give the first instruction to their children, thoroughly to understand the characters of their husbands, and on all occasions to be able to assist them with their advice. But all this necessarily implies a cultivated mind, sound judgment, and great sensibility obedient to the control of reason. Where is the woman who would desire a better lot than to be the wife of the man of her choice, associated with him in one common interest both tending to the same end, educating her children wisely without however quitting her own sphere ; possessing

the affection of her friends, and the esteem and approbation
of society? Where is the woman who would not feel herself
happy, though possessed of a small or even straitened fortune, in passing her life divided between the dearest affections of the mind, and those occupations and pleasures
which delight the understanding and satisfy the heart? Such
a condition is not very difficult to be attained; all agree in
thinking it woman's true position; women themselves generally limit their wishes to it, and ask for nothing more. How
then does it happen that it is the position of so few, and that
the condition of women in society is so often miserable?
It may be attributed, we think, to the general absence of a
good plan of practical moral education, that these evils arise
which the actual state of society aggravates still more.

By education we do not mean merely the lessons given in
childhood; but that progressive instruction acquired during
the course of life, as much by experience as by reflection.
The education of all females is in many respects extremely
deficient; and if this be the cause of their exerting a pernicious influence on morals, so does the positive morality of
society reciprocally exercise a baneful influence over them.
What we here understand by morals, is the totality of opinions,
conduct, and rules of life, and in this sense we may say that
it is in positive morality, and not in positive law, that we must
seek for the radical evil that affects the condition of woman.
Let us begin by examining in what manner, if we mistake
not, the greater part of females in the middle and higher
classes are brought up. The first habits received, are those
of idleness and slothfulness; the instruction imparted is false,
limited, and superficial; the tastes acquired, those of dress
and the world; the ideas imbibed, frivolous, and without any
reflection; and all this being increased by a naturally delicate
organization, they at last forget the substance of everything
to think only of the shadow. The aim of this education is
to furnish women with those external advantages which are
likely to captivate men at first sight, and to obtain for them
the doubtful advantage of a rich establishment which fortune
may perhaps offer them. Few are the chances, however,
that such an expectation will be realized. It is in a great
degree owing to this artificial education of females, that
young men who are fond of study and devoted to scientific
or literary pursuits are deterred from matrimony. Serious
study renders them more reflecting, and consequently more
prudent. A female brought up as we have described, is
simply an object of luxury in a family; and even supposing

a man would wish her to be such, he must first seriously consider whether his fortune is sufficient to meet the expenses of such a wife. Besides, those who have fortunes generally choose a wife who has one equal to their own ; it is therefore easily conceived how very few chances of marriage there are for young women with little or no fortune. A poor man resists his desire to marry through prudence ; the studious man from reason ; and the rich from avarice. In fact, the education of females is not only frivolous, but false and contradictory. They are taught things purely ornamental, and left entirely ignorant of the world and its dangers, life and its realities ; they are cradled in luxury, as if fortune must always smile on them ; their energies stifled as if sorrows would never assail them; their judgment unnerved as if reason would never be useful to them. Instead of moral principles, prejudices and rules of etiquette are inculcated, which are only destroyed by the dearly bought lessons of after experience. With this semblance of education, these habits of indolence and frivolity, this ignorance of the world, these false and confined notions, this soft and vacillating character, young women are suddenly launched into a vicious and corrupt society beset with dangers, where the path is uncertain and every step is dangerous. In the last session of the French Chamber of Deputies M. Delessert spoke thus :—

' The education of females is as worthy of your attention as that of men, and it is necessary that the laws on the education of girls should be revised. I request, therefore, that the Minister of Public Instruction will prepare for the next session a law on this subject.'

To this important motion M. Guizot answered :—

' The system of the girls' schools at the present day is so unconnected and badly understood, that I am compelled to declare myself unprepared with a set of reasonable propositions on the government of female schools ; nor can I yet fix the period when I shall be able to present a memorial on this subject.'

Thus we find the Chamber of Deputies in France recognizing the absolute necessity of a new code of laws on female education. The Minister of Public Instruction, a man fully competent to speak on this subject, admits that the present system in all that concerns female schools is so vague, that he requires much time to arrange his information, and to prepare a new series of resolutions.

The most important of all the institutions of society are those which regard the education of both sexes, because education has the power of determining to a great extent the happiness of individuals, as well as that of society at large.

If we ascend to the origin of all the crimes and evils which disturb society, we shall find it to be the want of a good plan of education; a complete reform in education would bring with it all other reforms which the present state of society requires. As the influence of education on morals, and of morals on education, ought to be simultaneous and reciprocal, one cannot advance at a greater rate than the other; for such a disproportion in progress would only be attended by discord and confusion. We must not then, in our opinion, in a plan of general education, any more than in a plan of social reform, frame theories of ideal perfection, but examine into the actual state of society, and ascertain what may be effected,—in a word, strive to uproot evil by regular progress towards a better order of things. Man has not the power of satisfying at once the whole of his desires : he must limit his designs to what is practicable at the time.

The system of public instruction for the youth of both sexes in France and Belgium, comprises establishments instituted either by the government, or by private persons, religious or lay ; and lastly, free-schools, founded by government or by individuals. This competition of the government with private persons, the laity with the priests, is called *liberty of teaching.* But it necessarily produces confusion in public instruction, and is a great barrier to the organization of it, since, except a few trifling restrictions, every one may teach what, where, and when he will. A complete system of public education is so far from existing in these countries, that no exact statistical account of education can be obtained. The number of schools varies every day, and the mode of instruction pursued in each changes according to the caprice of the director.

This liberty of teaching has these inconveniences: instruction is given without rules, limits, or method ; it becomes in private hands frequently an object of pure speculation ; instructors are induced to embrace it more from the necessity of gaining a maintenance, than from any capacity for such an avocation ; parents, who are themselves usually incapable of appreciating the distinguishing marks of a really good education, find no sure guarantee in any school ; and lastly, it prevents the formation of a plan of general education which would include all the various branches of instruction.

Yet still, in the existing state of society, where all institutions depend on the principle of competition, this liberty of teaching is one of the most valuable privileges, for even its very abuses give rise to improvements.

Can we say what class of society offers sufficient securities to have the monopoly of instruction confided to it? Is it the clergy, the learned laity, the philanthropists, or the government? Neither the government nor any other class of society could at present propose a complete system of public education, which should secure the confidence of all parties in every respect. Competition and liberty of teaching are then indispensable requisites; for the most insupportable of all tyrannies, as a large majority would certainly consider it, would be that which compelled parents to have their children brought up in principles dissimilar to their own. But from this competition itself a *unity of views* ought to arise, the only sure foundation on which to erect a well-organized system. That person or party among all the competitors who can propose the best method, and point out the means likely to insure its success in practice, should be at the head of all education.

Now the government alone possesses sufficient means and power to engage the most enlightened knowledge in accomplishing this object. Government then should be the centre, the focus which, constantly attracting to itself the rich abundance of new discoveries and intellectual improvement, should distribute it through every part of the social body. It will be clearly seen, that we suppose a time when government, through the medium of representatives, will be truly the expression of the people's opinions. For certainly if we impute bad or retrograde intentions to government, and if we deny the efficacy of the representative system in compelling it to keep the path of justice and progressive improvement, there is no reason to expect any good from its interference in education; but on the contrary, we must expect to see the total destruction of all national education when under its direction, and even rejoice at the amount of evil resulting from it. This is an extreme case; but it was the case of France during the Restoration. Years, as they roll by, sweep from the earth whole generations pertinaciously opposed to all improvements; and what are our hopes that the new generations will be more wise? The liberty of the press, and the system of national representation, how imperfect soever, still give some hope that, though government is not as willing and enlightened as we could desire, it will still keep pace with the moral and intellectual improvement of the people. There are countries, Belgium for example, where the liberals complain bitterly that the clergy daily become more active in their attempts to engross all public education. But they have no reason to complain. The field is open alike to all; every competitor may carry there his ambition, or his philanthropy,

The clergy bring both. The liberals, on the contrary, have in this, as in every thing else, the fatal maxims of indifference —' let it be ;' ' let it alone.' The Catholics have gained, and ought to have gained, the ascendency over a party that has neither agreement in views and exertions, nor any perseverance. The principle of competition granted, the arms are equal between all parties; government alone is the strongest of all the competitors, when it will really rouse itself to action; and it will always be the best of all when it wears not the livery of a party. When it does, it is more feeble than any—it is but an instrument.

We should then address the government, in every exposition of a plan of public education. When the government refuses its aid, private attempts may supply, to a certain extent, the want of a more general action : the condition of many may be thus ameliorated, though the mass will remain in their suffering condition ; for society can never be effectually relieved but by institutions capable of including and remedying all its wants. One of the means that belongs exclusively to government, is the command of the public purse.

A plan of public instruction would probably require an increase in the funds already applicable to that purpose ; but there is no increase in the expenditure to which the representatives of the nation would more readily assent, if ever a minister were to submit a plan containing real and vital improvement. The rate-payers themselves would probably as a body be far from complaining, if the cogent reasons for the measure were backed by the authority of the government. The philanthropy of citizens, and how far it might be available when directed to works really beneficial to society, are things yet imperfectly known. In these times men are much accused of selfishness, because they are pent up in a narrow circle from which there is no outlet, and because all institutions tend to make them so : yet there never was a purer spirit of charity, nor a more ardent desire to do good to humanity ; never also did there exist such division in plans and views, never such a variety of systems so vague, so unconnected. In the countries of civilized Europe at the present day, there needs but a determinate end, and the conviction that good must result from it, to induce every one to give out of his abundance, and frequently out of his scanty store. We see every day subscriptions filled that tend in no way to the real public good. What might not be expected from the generosity of the same men, when an object should be presented to them whose aim was the most important of all reforms, one nearly touching the dearest interests of society, as well as those of every individual; and which in the wisdom, the enlightened intelligence, and capacity of the men empowered to carry it into effect, should give the surest guarantee for its accomplishment.

We return to our main subject, the exposition of the improvements which the present system of instruction in girls' schools requires. The most essential of these concern the children of the poor. What is more pitiable than the sight of these miserable little creatures frequently a greater burden to the poverty, than objects of love to their parents, whose intellects are impaired, as well as their bodies, even before they are developed; their after condition is frequently one of certain and inevitable misery. The boys may be fit for labourers or soldiers; but the daughters of the very poor receiving no education at all, are unfit to discharge well the duties of any condition. All this has long been felt; benevolent establishments have been founded for indigent females, infant schools are daily erected; yet all these are but palliatives; they are not sufficient to remedy the evils which affect the condition of this class. General measures are wanting, which without any exception would provide for the future as well as the present. Government ought to act upon that obvious principle of consulting the general interest, which imposes on society the obligation of giving to every member a *moral* and intellectual education,* and more particularly to take all orphans under its protection. Now when parents can neither give their children education, means of subsistence, nor bestow on them the necessary physical cares

---

* In France, the Foundling was erected with this intention. In Denmark, Sweden, and Norway, the children of both sexes receive an education by a master appointed on purpose by the government in every parish. The number of foundlings received, maintained, and educated by the French government—

In 1819	. .	99,346
1820	. .	102,103
1821	. .	106,000
1822	. .	109,000
1823	. .	111,000
1824	. .	116,749
1831	. .	122,981

Expended 8,725,84 francs, or 360,000*l.*

There are besides similar establishments for orphans; now when we examine these with attention, we cannot deny that the children are, in every respect, physical, moral, and intellectual, greatly superior to the neglected children of the poor. Maternal care, clean linen, warmth, food, medical attention, and even social habits, all these advantages form a contrast with the abject misery, filth, and brutality of the greater part of the poor in the towns and villages of France, and in many other countries also. It may be necessary to guard against the possible inference, that we are recommending *Foundling* Hospitals. What we do recommend is, that governments should not allow a large part of the community to grow up in ignorance and brutality, but should check the evil by prompt and efficacious measures.

—not even their daily food—are not these unhappy infants orphans in reality ? Does it not become an imperative duty on society to adopt them as its own children, with the view of so instructing and educating them, as to prevent their giving birth to a race as ignorant and as immoral as the parents from whom they are sprung? It is requisite then that there should be free-schools in all towns and villages, where all children really orphans, or those whose parents have not the means of supporting and educating them, should be admitted.

There might be three different kinds of schools for poor girls. In the first kind, infants from two to six years old should be received; matrons should be appointed, whose office would be to take charge of them, prevent their hurting themselves, amuse them with games suited to their age, allot them easy tasks, accustom them to good habits, and give them true and just answers to every question they might ask. These superintendents ought to be good-tempered, moral, and intelligent persons, fond of children, interested in their little pleasures, and compassionate to their short-lived griefs : for this no great degree of knowledge is required. These schools would be an immense advantage. Most parents of the poorer class really cannot watch over the early years of their children. Forced as they often are to attend to their out-door occupations during the day, they are obliged to abandon them to themselves; or even if their employments be within the house, still they can but give a partial attention to them and must often turn a deaf ear to their complaints and tears.

It would be painful to relate all the evils which arise from the neglected condition in which the working classes are compelled to leave their infants, and to enumerate the accidents, deformities, diseases, which are thus entailed on them through life, or the violent deaths which annually befall so many. What an incalculable benefit would it be to the workman and the artisan, to have large well-aired apartments where they might send their children, either to remain altogether, or only during the day, with the certainty of their being taken care of, and having that attention paid which the parents cannot bestow themselves. If we consider at what a trifling expense so much good might be effected, were it nothing more than a safeguard to the tender years of infancy, it would be a great advantage gained. Infant schools are now very generally established in England, but to make them universal and efficient, the care and protection of government are necessary.* Savings banks, combined with

* See a subsequent article in this Journal on Savings Banks.

infant schools, well conducted, would prove of all means the
most efficient for raising the character of the poorer classes
at present, and securing a future race of industrious and
moral men and women.

Again; these establishments, in which every attention
would be paid to all physical wants, conjointly with the rudiments of moral education given to children in early childhood, would offer such advantages to parents of all classes,
who cannot devote their time to the incessant watching of
their offspring, that undoubtedly they would place them there,
rather than confide them to servants, frequently the first
corrupters of infancy and youth. In education, as in every
other institution, the advantages arising from association are
very great. The more this is encouraged, the more efficient
will education become. Similar to these schools for the
people, there should be schools of a higher order for persons
in the middle class. The care and attention should be the
same in all respects, for there is no essential difference in
early education, how distinct soever the situations of children
may be.

It may, perhaps, be thought that private persons acting on
the principle of competition, would wish to appropriate this
branch of industry to themselves, and erect pay-schools on
their own account, and only leave to government the expense
of the free-schools, or of such for the establishment and
maintenance of which the *aid*, at least, of government is
essential. This is precisely the case where the government
has nothing to fear, whenever it will undertake the task.
The object of a private individual in opening a house of education is always that of profit, or at least to procure a comfortable subsistence. Government, on the contrary, ought
to aim only at public good, and so far from desiring any
profit, it ought to supply deficiencies from the public purse.
But if it has nothing to fear from competition in pecuniary
matters, may it not apprehend rivalry from the merit of instructors? Here, again, the superiority of government shows
itself; for in this case, above all others, it possesses the
means of attracting general confidence by selecting teachers
distinguished by their virtues and talents. It is also the
business of government to form instructresses in normal
schools established for this purpose.

Perhaps it may be objected, that a line of demarcation
between the poor and middle classes is but a sorry basis for
a plan of national education. We answer, that notwithstanding all the prejudices and abuses destroyed, there will
still exist two totally distinct orders of society—those who

possess wealth, and those who have nothing—the working class who labour to subsist, and the affluent, to whom labour is unnecessary. Among women, especially, this is a very great difference: we have the labouring and domestic class, for example, where each individual is obliged to gain her bread by daily work; and the superior class, in which re-munerated labour forms an exception, a grievous necessity, and is submitted to unwillingly. Such is the actual basis on which society is constituted: it is undoubtedly a great misfortune, and it is to be wished, because it would be for the happiness of all, that every member of society should work either manually or intellectually; but still we repeat, society is so organized, and we are obliged to live in it. Education, which is but an apprenticeship to after life, must necessarily be based on positive morality and things as they are. To frame schemes independent of existing institutions, would be to involve ourselves in purely ideal theories, which, though they do infinite honour to the generous philanthro-pists who suggest them, have hitherto remained without any result.

We have stated that there ought to be three different sorts of schools for the daughters of the poor. The first, simply schools for infants that have not attained the age of six years. The second, which we would designate *elementary schools*, should be open to children of the poor from the age of six to twelve. The aim of these schools should be to give them a moral education,—to develope to a certain extent their in-tellectual faculties,—and, lastly, by giving them some trade, occupation, or art, to insure the means of subsistence. Teaching* should be divided into three parts: the first would depend in a great measure on the good conduct, sense, and morality, in the teachers themselves; for instructions imparted in moral conduct are much better when given by example and daily conversations than by lessons and precepts. The second part, instruction properly so called, should be confined to reading, writing, arithmetic, and descriptive geography; a greater amount of knowledge could only prove pernicious to persons who must subsist by their manual labour. The third, which would occupy the greater part of their time, should consist in. work. Under this we rank all occupations of work-women and domestic servants. The schools ought to be an apprenticeship to the different arts of the mantua-maker, milliner, confectioner, laundress, &c. &c. Each pupil should be taught the greater part of these arts, because they

, * See Nos. XI. XII. XIII. of the Journal of Education.

enter into domestic education, but this would not prevent their adopting any one. Now, if we consider what an immense benefit it is when infancy (deprived of its natural guardians) is preserved from the physical evils that menace it, how much greater would the benefit be to poor girls, to have none but pure ideas presented to them, and sound principles inculcated at the same time that they are furnished with habits of industry and means of lucrative employment : and if we feel persuaded that this blessing would extend itself to all the poor female population, beginning from the most indigent, we may naturally conclude that this improvement alone would prepare the way for the complete regeneration of a class the most exposed from poverty to seduction. This education, it is true, would not be conducted beyond the age of twelve, when the body and mind are yet in their infancy; but the first impressions are the most indelibly fixed. There is much to be hoped from the conduct of a child well brought up till that age, and whose future line of life is traced out. If, however, it should deviate from the path of rectitude, it is not its education that must be censured, but that state of society where no step can be made without being exposed to the contagion of bad example. If ever a complete social reform be effected, education will be easy; it will perfect itself in the midst of society; every speech, every action, of others will serve as a lesson. But now, when contact with society destroys the fruits of education, rather than matures them, we must the more carefully watch over the first development of the mind and understanding to prepare the soil for a love of virtue, which alone affords a sufficient warrant for the goodness of after life.*

Moreover, the task of government towards the daughters of the poor is not fulfilled at the expiration of the six years of apprenticeship. The parents who might wish to take

* 'In a well-regulated social order,' says Raspail (p. 230), in his work entitled *Nouveau Système de Chimie Organique,* 'vice and wickedness are anomalies, *sociability* being the ruling propensity. Since civilization has carried the social propensity to so high a point, it is but rational to expect that education should have gradually diminished, and finally entirely worn away, the predominance of a propensity to evil and wickedness; and this, through its operation of *new and good habits,* or by new remedial means exciting the development of a kindred propensity. Those legislators who have written vengeance on the tables of the law, and who, in order (as they pretend) to avenge outraged society, have preferred the cruel and useless infliction of torture to any attempts at ameliorating the condition, or to seeking a cure for him who is ill-educated or diseased, so as to enable him to make ample reparation to the great family for whatever wrong he may have done—those legislators, I say, should be considered as the most wicked among men, were it not that the context of their law evidently proves them to have been the most absurd.'

their children home, should be at liberty to do so, and ought also to have that option during the six years of education. A deep feeling of affection, it is true (excepting perhaps a very few instances,) will always impel them to sacrifice everything for the advantage of their children. Parents would certainly not withdraw their children from the schools, unless they could continue at home the good education thus commenced, and provide the means of subsequently establishing their daughters in some occupation, such as that of mantua-maker and others above-mentioned, or in domestic service. The national education of a part, then, of these poor girls would be completed at the age of twelve, but still a large number would remain of those who are really orphans, or those whose parents, reduced to abject misery, or plunged into vice, could not take their children. These girls, too young to be placed in shops or employed in domestic service, would require a third kind of school. This might be designated a *school of industry,* and should be of a truly industrious nature, containing spacious workshops, where the girls should be employed in all manual labour suitable to the sex. Their time would be divided as in the *elementary schools,* partly between religious exercises, moral instruction, reading, writing, and arithmetic, and part would be allowed for those physical exercises conducive to health. Still the greater portion would be devoted to work, the produce of which would serve to defray the expenses, and form *a fund* ultimately to be given to the pupils. Provided these establishments were well conducted, the expenses would not be considerable, as the girls themselves would do all the work of the house, the cooking, washing, making their own clothes, and keeping the accounts. These industrious institutions would offer a double end of utility. These young girls, having received the national education described, would possess the most desirable testimonials of morality and capacity: the richer classes would feel themselves extremely fortunate in having such places to apply to when they required servants. Generally speaking, servants offer no security for morality; tainted with nearly all the vices of their condition, they are the pest of families, especially the female servants, whom mothers must in some degree admit into the intimacy of their children. The most mischievous consequences often follow in families through the influence and example of immoral servants. We might then rest assured, that the particular care of the education of poor girls intended for service would be an advantage to every class of society. This reform in education would have the immediate effect of reforming morals, for it must be admitted that girls, artless, honest, and thoroughly well brought up, would obtain greater regard from their employers than the present set of servants. Their mistresses more particularly would consider themselves in a manner called on to continue their education, that is to say, to guard them from all immoral contact which might in any way sully their purity or destroy the effect of their early instructions. The servant would become another member of a family, and every inequality, save those of knowledge and refinement, would, in fact, disappear; and this alone would be a great advance in society, at the same time that it secured internal peace to private families. If we have succeeded in explaining ourselves, it will be understood that the girls will quit the schools in rotation from the age of eighteen to twenty-five, for the purpose of being placed in some occupation; those who had passed most time and displayed the greatest ability, to be established on their own account, with that portion from the funds which belonged to them. As these leave the schools of industry, they would be replaced by others from the elementary schools. Thus we might picture the plan of national education complete for the daughters of the poor. From the most tender age they would be instructed in the only kind of knowledge suited to their condition, until they were completely formed in body as well as mind, and furnished also with some art, trade, or acquirement, as the means of subsistence, so that they should not be thrown into the vortex of the world without that well-formed character and that sound practical knowledge, which always command attention, respect, and confidence.

After the schools for the poor, the most important institution is that of *normal schools,** where teachers would be formed for all ranks of society. Without normal schools, there cannot exist a truly national, that is to say, a regular, methodical education, suitable in all respects to the people who receive it. The term national education would be improperly applied to any kind of private establishments, in which each director or proprietor follows his own ideas and plans. This kind of education offers nothing but a mass of vague knowledge, which, having no connecting link with practical conduct or actual life, does not, in fact, deserve the name of education. National education ought to bind and

---

* MM. Levi and Lourmaud have already pointed out a mode of reforming education, by opening in Paris a normal school for the gratuitous instruction of females intended for governesses.

harmonize society by giving it a code of moral, scientific, and practical rules. It ought so to cement the whole social body that it should participate alike in the progress of intelligence and in the improvements of science. It is right, however, to add, that before even a foundation could be laid for such an institution, there is an almost invincible obstacle which presents itself. How can a uniform set of opinions be adopted in a society which acts without fixed principles, without straightforward views,—where the most opposing ideas float about separately, and do not intermingle,—where some are obstinately wedded to old methods, while others inconsiderately embrace every new system?

It is really astonishing how greatly opinions on female education have changed, and how generally the want of more solid information is felt, and yet how very little improvement has been made during the last half-century. The fault is with the old religious and political institutions. We must point out and call into active operation the new elements that have sprung up in society; for many such elements exist, which are nearly unknown even to the society that produces them, but the promulgation of which would meet with no opposition. A superior normal school should be founded, for the purpose of facilitating the progressive improvement of society, through the medium of moral and intellectual education. This institution, however, cannot be surrounded by too many safeguards to prevent it becoming, under the direction of power, or in the hands of innovators, an arbitrary instrument. Parents ought always to have the chief superintendence of their children's education; the principle of competition, with the liberty of teaching, ought therefore to continue, as a matter of right, though we may expect that social improvements, by causing the whole stream of education to flow from the normal schools, will ultimately abolish all schools, the principles and practice of which are not in harmony with the improved state of society.

We conceive the following to be the principal regulations required in the normal schools, the object of which is to form competent teachers for the secondary schools, and generally to furnish the establishments throughout the country with instructresses or well-informed governesses. Such schools would afford women those means, which they have not hitherto possessed, of receiving extended and solid information—of raising themselves to a level with the knowledge of the age—of understanding their own condition—and lastly, of serving an apprenticeship to the important employment of teachers; an employment which, so far from being, as it appears to be thought, within the compass of everybody, requires a particular training, united with some of the rarest qualities and talents. The normal schools founded in the capital (generally the centre of learning) should have a course of instruction which the pupils would follow, in whole or in part, according to their capacities. This course should embrace all the various branches of female education. This instruction should be divided, as with men, into three classes—moral, intellectual, and physical science. The class of morality should comprehend all the instruction that can inform the mind on the general nature of society, and the particular part which women have to fill in it; all lessons, precepts, and learning, which are calculated to produce virtuous propensities and good habits, and inspire them with a love of each other and of humanity; and, lastly, the study of the fine arts, which, at the same time that it unveils the principles of beauty, infuses a love of moral order far better than words can ever do.—The intellectual sciences should comprehend all that can assist in the complete development of the mind, in giving correct views of what really *is*, or rather by leading the mind to observe and judge correctly of all things by itself.

Learning, properly so called, should be entirely subordinate to moral education.

Physical sciences should embrace all the bodily exercises that mature the growth and contribute to health. These exercises assist the moral and intellectual education, for the mind cannot be mistress of its own powers when the body suffers from disease or weakness.—Female professors would be more suitable in these establishments than men; but unhappily the old system of education has hitherto prevented them from attaining the same skill in the arts and sciences. It would then be absolutely necessary at first, in almost every department, to employ men as professors in the normal schools, though the object would be to replace them in course of time by females. This might, in part, be effected almost immediately, for the masters in the female schools ought to be replaced by female teachers from the normal schools as soon as they are qualified. If we find men generally acting as teachers in public and private female education, it is solely because of the difficulty in finding females sufficiently instructed to fill the office. Contiguous to the edifice designed for the public lectures, a house should be appointed to lodge those pupils of the normal school who do not reside in the capital. The rules of this should be as strict as in the school itself; the most scrupulous, even rigid, attention ought to be paid in the admission of pupils*, but still more in the choice of teachers. Equal caution ought to be observed in the admitting out-door students. The normal schools instituted by government, and maintained at its expense, should be pay-schools, except perhaps in a few cases, where government might admit gratis a certain number of pupils, chosen from females who presented themselves as candidates, but whose limited means did not allow them to pass some years of apprenticeship in the normal schools. The other pupils should pay a fixed sum, the produce of which would serve to defray a part, if not the whole, expense of the establishment.

At the same time that the government founds a normal school in the metropolis, it ought also to open establishments for public education throughout the kingdom, in the different counties, districts, or principal towns, according to the wants of the population. These establishments should consist of a house, library, and all other requisites proper for instruction.

Those pupils of the normal schools, pointed out by the teachers themselves as the most distinguished for intelligence, benevolence, and aptness, should be appointed by the government to these schools, there to introduce all the improvements which their experience may suggest in the arts and sciences which they themselves have been taught in the normal school. A certain number of pupils should be admitted gratuitously in these, as in the normal schools; government might also receive an annual interest for the money expended on these institutions; but the remainder of the profits should belong to the teacher. It must be obvious, that the institution of a normal school would greatly improve the condition of that class of females who, unhappily deprived of fortune, and incapacitated for labour by their social position above the lower orders, are yet frequently in a more distressing situation than any of the labouring class, living from day to day in a melancholy and precarious state of existence; indeed, we do not hesitate to affirm that such females are, of

---

* 'The method of instruction, and the general discipline of the school, though very strictly laid down by law (in the grand duchy of Baden), still depend greatly upon the master; and I have had opportunity of ascertaining that the moral condition of a whole parish had been changed by the appointment of a *good* or *bad schoolmaster*, and his continued residence in the place. Were there space, some most striking instances of this fact (in the same grand duchy) might be given, showing the absolute necessity of what have been called *normal schools*, from the immense influence that primary schoolmasters exercise upon the moral condition of the people.— G. T.'—*Education.—Letter III. to Lord Althorp.*

all others, the most to be pitied. Should not society render them some assistance ?—is it not a duty incumbent on it to provide subsistence, or rather the means of obtaining it, for all its members ?—does it not become a more imperious duty, when women are concerned,—ought it not to take them entirely under its protection ? The least it can bestow is an education which may enable them to provide for themselves some art or occupation suitable to the situation in which they were born.

Having claimed for the daughters of the lower orders the only education suited for them in the existing state of society, and which it is the duty of society to give,—namely, one to fit them to become workwomen, artists, servants, &c.—we demand, for the same reason, on behalf of the daughters of the higher orders, an education to qualify them for the only social employment which remains open to them,—that of teaching. Let it be remembered also, that the pupils from the normal schools, who are nominated by government to the direction of other establishments, would not be the only females whose subsistence would be insured ; but that, by a natural consequence, this benefit must extend to all the pupils. The certain result of such an establishment would be, as in the case of mothers and mistresses of shops applying to the industrious schools for workwomen and servants, that the principals of female schools would apply to the normal schools for their teachers and governesses, either for public or private tuition. This class of females would then be saved from the horrors of want; they would have a noble end in view, and the means of obtaining it. What an unbounded influence might not these normal schools thus obtain over private education, through the medium of teachers and servants brought up under their roof and fully trained for their respective duties.

Lastly, let us reflect how this education, so uniform and yet complete, issuing, as it were, from one common source— the normal school—whose pupils had all received the same kind of instruction from properly qualified teachers, would again diffuse this superior intelligence through all ranks of society by their superintendence of private and public education. Let us reflect what an influence education would exercise over the whole community by the exertions of those females who had received the training of the normal schools ; and we can scarcely form an idea, what might be the effects of a national education on morals and opinions, if the government, that is to say, the organ of society at large, became the master and director of it.

Before concluding this article we must answer an objection, which may perhaps be raised, on the score of individual liberty; for in all establishments of this kind, what is most to be feared is that *persons* should be considered as *things*, and compelled to follow certain invariable rules, while the very character of our nature revolts against all restraint. It is then necessary to lay down as a law, that the pupils of the normal school, even those who are gratuitously admitted, shall not be required to take any engagement, nor bind themselves to follow the profession of teaching—not even engage to remain a fixed period in the establishment; so long as they are there, they should follow the rules and submit to the duties imposed, but with perfect liberty to quit the moment they desire.   Even after being appointed to the government schools, they should always have the power of relinquishing their situation, if agreeable to them to do so.   Parents also ought to preserve the right of placing their children either in the government establishments or in private schools.   It cannot be too frequently repeated, that liberty of teaching, so long as it does exist, or rather so long as it preserves the estimation in which it is held at present, renders, in a great degree, a complete national education impracticable; still, under existing circumstances, much may be done by the government showing a model of better schools than any which now exist, and by continually training up a set of teachers who will deserve the confidence of the public. The perfect liberty which every person ought to enjoy of sending his children to private schools of his own choice, would tend to counterbalance any evils that might arise in a system of public instruction under the direction of the government; for no government system could maintain itself in this country, if its schools became less efficient than those managed by private individuals.

The industrious and normal schools would then be for two classes of females, whose education would be determined by their social position.—There remains yet another, much the least numerous and important class in society, that is to say, those whose fortune allows them to consider education as merely a means of moral and intellectual cultivation, so far as it is in harmony with the ideas and wants of existing society.   We must then have a third kind of public establishments, which we would name *intermediate schools*, for those females who seek in education only a methodical development of their faculties, and not the means of subsistence. The object of this third kind of school is nothing more than the improvement of education as it at present exists; but this improvement would be greatly aided by the institution of a normal school, which alone can furnish the means of perfecting a system which shall embrace education in all its parts.

To those women who feel themselves capable, and who have the will to influence public opinion, we address our reflections on a new organization of female education : if government should still refuse to lend its aid towards modifying and perfecting the social body, and education, its foundation and framework, let every member at least concur individually, as much as lies in his power, towards this desirable end.

EDUCATION OF PARISH-POOR CHILDREN, UNDER THE POOR-LAW AMENDMENT ACT.

Important as the results are which we anticipate from the chief provisions of this bold but wise legislative measure (the Poor Law Admendment Act), in checking the headlong course of national degradation, we cannot but attach the highest value to the clause which falls more immediately within the province of the Journal of Education ; namely, that in which the commissioners are empowered to make and issue rules, orders, and regulations for the education of the children in the workhouses. It would perhaps have been difficult to pass through the legislature a distinct and separate bill, giving to three individuals so vast a power of doing good as is contained in these few words. By other portions of the act they have the power of stemming the current of corruption and debasement: by this, of imparting new life to society, by fitting those who in less than twenty years will constitute a large portion of the men and women of the country, to contribute to the national prosperity by pursuing what is really their own interest. Full as the task is of difficulties, we trust, indeed we have every reason to hope, that the commissioners duly appreciate their situation,—that they will meet those difficulties manfully, and, having laid down a well-considered plan of action, will not allow themselves to be swerved either to the right or to the left by any clamour that may be raised against them ; while, at the same time, they pay due attention to any good suggestions that may be offered.

The commissioners, by this act, have a power of enforcing, although not a system of national education which will embrace every individual in the country, at any rate one which will extend to every county, town, and village in it.

They have the power of exhibiting a model of a national elementary school, and if that model be one worthy of imitation, we have little doubt of its being gradually and generally adopted. The object of the commissioners therefore appears to us two-fold :—the immediate one, of educating the children of paupers in such a manner as shall rescue them from their present dangerous position ; and the more distant, but not less important one, of giving an example of a sound practical system of education throughout the country.

The plan to be pursued ought to be founded upon a consideration of the evils to be overcome ; and a knowledge of the more prevalent vices of the parents must point to the mode of dealing with the children. The pauper population consists of the following elements :—In the metropolis and the larger towns, some are persons reduced in circumstances by inevitable calamity, more are persons reduced by imprudence, and the largest proportion are the offspring of vice, confirmed mendicants, thieves, and prostitutes : in the country, there are certainly but few who have ever held a higher rank in society than that of labourer, but then the evil is more widely spread among that class, for in many places it would be difficult to find labourers who have not at some time received parochial relief. The general effect of receiving relief under the old system has been, that those who have once received it appear thenceforth to have their love of independence blunted, and to grow careless of the earnings of labour. The natural springs of prosperity to the individual become dried up, and he knows not himself, and consequently cannot teach his children how to meet manfully the difficulties of life, and to maintain a virtuous and independent position in society. The knowledge of the principles upon which society hangs together become obscured, the real nature of the value of labour and the right of property are forgotten, while the feeling for domestic comforts, the honest pride of independence, and the natural affections, all appear to be buried in one common tomb. To restore a manly tone, and to give a knowledge of their true position in society to that portion of the rising generation committed to their charge, is the duty of the commissioners.

In the workhouses, as at present administered, the method of acting with regard to children is various. We have ourselves lately visited the workhouse of St. Mary-le-bone. This workhouse is in many respects well conducted, and has the character of being upon the best system of any in London

The time both of the adults and the children is properly employed; the children receive instruction in various trades; we saw them at work as tailors, shoemakers, ropemakers, and weavers. But the system is defective in several essential particulars. The separation of the children from the adult paupers was by no means complete, for while at work they were mixed up together. A more fatal mistake than this could not well be made—for if from the good and virtuous, who are advanced in years, youth receive instruction with humility and respect, they are too often liable to corruption from an intercourse with ' hoary vice and grey iniquity.' The literary instruction at this workhouse was of the ordinary description, reading, writing, and arithmetic; which, of themselves, are but feeble agents in fortifying children with principles for their guidance when they go out into the world. The reply of one of the children whom we asked, Why he should not tell a lie? was, having the fear of the cane before his eyes, ' Because he should be punished.' The system of labour adopted, although it may produce the habit of continued application (a matter, we admit, of much importance), cannot give a knowledge of the value of labour, or of the necessity for the right of property. It is true that a few halfpence of their earnings are given to the children weekly, but upon being questioned as to the value of their labour per week, they replied, that it amounted to three-halfpence or two-pence; they appeared to have no idea of their food, lodging, and clothing being given to them in part as a return for their labour—these things they considered as a right, with which their labour was in no way connected.

But in most workhouses there is no system at all; and great corruption arises from bringing the adept in vice into continual close connection with the inexperienced. A workhouse, in most cases, is little less, if at all less injurious to character than a prison. In the London workhouses we have ourselves known instances where female children have been seduced by the agents of disreputable houses; and we understand that the practice is not uncommon. The officers of some parishes, aware of these circumstances, have sent their children out into the country to be kept; but as the persons who receive them do so for their own private interest, and the parishes, in their agreement with them, stipulate for little beyond wholesome food and clothing, it would be almost too much to expect that any sound system should be pursued with reference to the future welfare of these children. Still, however small, this is a step, made by the parishes themselves, to obviate an evil (for the 7 Geo. III. relates only to children under six years of age), and we should feel an inclination rather to improve upon it than to strike out any scheme altogether new. We have lately visited an establishment of the kind at Norwood in Surrey, in which there were five hundred children, kept by a person of the name of Aubin. This establishment, although deficient in many points of importance, possessed sufficient of what was good to assure us of its capability of becoming a powerful engine in benefiting the community. Mr. Aubin appeared to be an intelligent individual, well aware that his only chance of maintaining his establishment was by making it worthy of approbation. We understood that he receives a weekly allowance of 4*s.* 3*d.* for each child; and, to judge from the appearance of the children, the food which we inspected, and the airy lodging-rooms, his mode of treating them must be liberal. Indeed, if we were to find fault on these points, we should say, that the beds were too soft and the bread too white; for we feel assured that a child is not best brought up to contend with the difficulties of life by indulgence and too delicate treatment. A child should have all that is most wholesome and cleanly, but should not be allowed to despise either the hard bed or the brown loaf. Besides, the hard bed is much more wholesome. But Mr. Aubin not only feeds the children well, but also gives them some little instruction in reading and writing, which is valueless certainly for rightly forming the character, but indicates his desire to do what he thinks the best; he also employs them, so as to fix their attention, in sorting bristles of various colours for brushmakers. Having said thus much in favour of the institution at Norwood, we must observe that there appeared to be but little provision made for the bodily exercise of the children, and no system adopted for the purpose of giving them a knowledge of their condition and duties in after life. We have heard, indeed, that at the suggestion of a gentleman who visited the establishment, Mr. Aubin was about to found an infant school, and to apportion a piece of land to the children for gardens; and judging from what we saw, that Mr. Aubin was only desirous of having a good system pointed out in order to adopt it, we consider it to be highly probable that such is the fact.

But supposing the corruption of a workhouse to be entirely put an end to by judicious arrangements, still we are not disposed to allow that all the most serious objections to bringing up children within their walls would be removed. A child should never be degraded—a child should never have to wipe off a stigma from his character which he never can have merited. Some children would be so weighed down by a knowledge of having been brought up in a workhouse, that they would never have a chance of afterwards succeeding in life; while others, more hardy, feeling the world their enemy, would become its enemies in return. The receptacle for those who have been brought to want by either their own imprudence or vice is not a good place for youth to start from in the race of life. It is therefore our conviction, after reflecting on the subject, that the school at which the parish poor children are to be educated ought not to be within the walls of a workhouse. But supposing the commissioners to take the same view of the case with ourselves, will the statute bear them out ?—we are of opinion that it will. The clauses bearing upon this question are as follows :—

' And for executing the powers given to them by this act, the said commissioners shall, and are hereby authorised and required, from time to time, as they shall see occasion, to make and issue all such rules, orders, and regulations, for the management of the poor, for the government of workhouses, and the education of the children therein, and for the management of the parish poor children, under the provisions of an act made and passed in the seventh year of the reign of his late Majesty King George III., entitled an " Act for the better Regulation of Parish Poor Children of the several Parishes therein mentioned, within the Bills of Mortality ; and the Superintending, Inspecting, and Regulating of the Houses wherein such Poor Children are kept and maintained, &c." It shall be lawful for the said commissioners, and they are empowered, from time to time, as they may see fit, &c., with the consent, &c., to order and direct the overseers or guardians of any parish or union, not having a workhouse or *workhouses*, to build a workhouse or *workhouses*, and to purchase or hire land for the purpose of building the same thereon ; or to purchase or hire a workhouse or *workhouses*, or any building or buildings for the purpose of being used or converted into a workhouse or workhouses.'

And where they find a workhouse already in existence, there is a power given not only to alter and enlarge the same, but also ' to build, hire, or purchase any additional workhouse or workhouses.'

Although the first clause quoted gives the commissioners power only over such children as may be in the workhouses, and such as come under the act 7 Geo. III. (this act relates to the sending pauper children under six years of age from London into *the country* to be nursed), the subsequent clauses give them the power of multiplying (with consent of the local

authorities) workhouses as much as they please; for not
only can they build or hire a workhouse where there is not
one already, but they can also build or hire an additional
workhouse or workhouses. And as the act gives them unlimited control in the direction of workhouses, and the
interpretation clause gives a very comprehensive meaning to
the term workhouse*, they may, if they please, allot one
workhouse to grown-up persons, and another to children.
Were they, therefore, to establish a school for the poor
children in each parish or union, such school would, we conceive, come within the comprehension of the statute, and be
a workhouse, although not such a workhouse as would inju-
riously affect the children. Except in localities where there
are workhouses already existing, with sufficient room for the
separate lodging and schooling of the children, the expense
attending such a total separation of the youthful from the
adult paupers would not be much more than boarding them
within the walls of the workhouse itself. If they were boarded
and schooled within the walls of the workhouse, they must
have a school-master and school-mistress : the superintending officer of the union workhouse never could perform the
double duty of attending to the adult establishment and instructing the children. If the establishments were separated,
as we recommend, they might still be sufficiently near to one
another to allow all the economy which the provisioning of a
great number allows.

In this Journal we have constantly enforced the important
truth, that instruction in mere reading and writing is not
education. In no instance was it ever more important to
enforce it than in the present, for such a bare save-trouble
system pursued with regard to the poor children would, we
feel assured, be not merely negative as to good, but probably
foster the very evils which the Poor Law Amendment Act is
intended to destroy.

The main use of education, as it appears to us, is to inculcate sound views as to the objects of life, and to give knowledge and habits that will enable the individual to attain
them. For this purpose he must not only be habituated to
industry, know the value of labour, and respect the rights of
others, but he must be accustomed to derive his happiness

---

* 'The word workhouse shall be construed to mean and include any house
in which the poor of any parish or union shall be lodged and maintained, or
any house or building purchased, erected, hired, or used, at the expense of the
poor-rate, by any parish vestry, guardian or overseer, for the reception, employment, *classification*, or relief of any poor person therein at the expense of
the parish.'—4 and 5 Will. IV, c. 76, sec. 109.

from legitimate sources from the earliest period of his life. All of us love excitement; excitement is indeed life; but to be of real service either to the individual or society, it must proceed from pure and proper sources, and be directed to right objects. The vagrant has been accustomed to the excitement of uncertainty; he has learned to derive a pleasure from the risks of his wandering life, from dishonesty, and from pilfering, and if allowed to come into contact with the more youthful portion of the community, would probably seduce them by his tales of hair-breadth escapes and occasional luxury.

Let us consider how an unexpensive course of education can give, first, a knowledge of the use and necessity of the right of property; secondly, a knowledge of the value of labour; thirdly, a deep tone to the religious and moral sentiments; and fourthly, a due appreciation of what is most valuable in life, considered chiefly with reference to that station in life which the individual is likely to fill.

First, a man born blind cannot possibly form any idea of the nature of colour, and a man who has never possessed, or has not a prospect by exertion of acquiring, any property of his own, cannot readily comprehend the respect that is due to the property of others. We are in the habit of looking at the errors of mankind with an eye of compassion, and are disposed to attribute wrong action in the majority of cases rather to the non-existence of favourable circumstances than to any thing fundamentally depraved in the characters of the individuals. If, therefore, we would have a child learn to respect a right to property in others, we would accustom him to the possession of some from his earliest infancy. His own garden, his own box, his own tools, his own books, are things to be protected and taken care of. If his garden be entered, and his fruit and vegetables destroyed—if his box be broken open, and his tools or books carried off or injured—he will feel more sensibly what an offence want of respect for the property of others is, than if instructed on this head by the best lectures that could be given. The grand object with regard to the majority of mankind is to give them a thorough knowledge of what is right, accompanied by a habit of action in harmony with it.

But property, to have the effect described, must be properly acquired; it must arise from the exchange of labour. If, then, the children have a garden, they must pay a rent for the land; if they have books and tools, they must purchase them. This leads to the second consideration, the inculcation of the value of labour—which there would not be much difficulty in doing if the children were by degrees taught to direct their labour to the acquisition of various articles of necessity, comfort, and utility. If a boy wants a box to put his tools in, for instance, and has not any money to purchase one, he may construct it by his own skill and ingenuity—but the wood and the nails must be purchased—for this purpose he can sell vegetables or fruit from his garden. For this reason we would take care that the children in workhouses had not too many of the conveniences of life given to them gratuitously. Articles almost of necessity should be wanting, until they had tasked their ingenuity and industry to supply the deficiency; much character would thus be developed; the more active and intelligent children would be supplied first. The comforts which they had acquired would excite others to industry until it became a disgrace in the school to be without them. A school conducted on such principles assuredly would fulfil the true end of all education, the development of the natural faculties, and the formation of the character. To train up a child in the way he should go, you must place it in circumstances to desire instruction, and by the exercise of its mental powers you must facilitate its acquirement. This, then, is the first step, and it is to effect this that the friends of education have recently so strongly urged the formation of normal schools for the preparation of teachers. For as a skilful workman depends upon the fitness of his tools, so does successful education depend upon properly educated teachers. In France, the government has established such schools, but it has done more; it has undertaken to provide proper manuals of elementary instruction (the compulsory use of which, however, we could by no means approve); and, among others, one which immediately relates to, and cannot be separated from, this division of our subject, namely, *Les Principes de l'Economie Publique,* a kind of work much wanting in all our elementary schools. Our instruction is too exclusively religious: our duty to man is too little taught, and still less are the principles involved in this second and great commandment developed or explained. On this branch of the subject we cannot but refer our readers to Professor Pillans' evidence before the committee of the House of Commons on Education. Professor Pillans says (question 494)—

' I conceive that the great defect in the system which the church has patronized, particularly hitherto, lies in the extremely limited nature of the information communicated, and the object being almost entirely the making members of the Church of England, and inculcating a blind submission to her, instead of imparting along with religious instruction that general information and intelligence which alone can make a school ultimately valuable to an individual who is to be in the lower walks of life. So narrow and unattractive is the instruction given in the schools which call themselves, by a misnomer, National, that I think it by no means unlikely that a considerable proportion of the pupils, ten years after quitting them, will be found to have lost the power of reading. So *little are their minds* imbued with the love of books or of knowledge by the school business, that they have little temptation, in the ordinary circumstances of a life of labour, to keep up the acquirement. I conceive that by far the most important point to be considered in a national system of education, is the course of instruction that ought to be followed; and that as long as the books perused and the instruction delivered upon them are of an exclusively religious cast, it is vain to expect that school training will contribute materially to form a moral, religious, and intelligent population.'

This is precisely the view that we take of the subject. The object should be to develope the powers of the mind by the instrumentality of elementary education—just as gymnastics are intended to give strength and activity to the powers of the body.

Thirdly. Let us now consider how a deep tone may be given to the moral and religious sentiments. The moral sentiments will, in some leading points, have been effectually cultivated, when a child shall have been led to respect the right to property, and become acquainted with the value of labour. He will then have practically learned justice, industry, and frugality; and we are very much mistaken if the constant necessity that will exist for reciprocal good offices in the management of their little affairs, will not also generate a more accurate knowledge of duty towards their neighbours. Each child will find that simple justice from others towards himself will not be by any means sufficient: he will find it cold, he will want their good will also, and those kind offices of which he who gives takes no account; but he who receives repays in a measure ' pressed down and running over,' and still notwithstanding his payment holds himself. a debtor for ever. The youthful mind will thus be well prepared to receive the seeds of instruction; and every word, as it falls from the mouth of the master, exhorting to justice and truth, good will and brotherly affection, will take firm root in the mind and bring forth fruit. For religion also the mind will be well prepared; there will be a palpable perception of the blessings of the Almighty. There will be already a healthy body, and a contented mind, good will towards man, and an habitual intercourse with nature; and if in addition there be prayers, hymns, and religious instruction, and he who teaches be himself deeply impressed with the importance of what he is saying, it will neither be found that the religious sentiments have been left uncultivated, nor that they are without influence upon conduct.

A right judgment of what is most valuable in life can scarcely fail to be the consequence of a child's mind having been trained in the manner above-mentioned, for he will enter life with some practical experience of character and of things, with habits of industry, and a knowledge of his duty to God and to man ; and he will be fitted to become a better husband, a better parent, and more faithful servant, than if merely instructed in bare reading and writing.

There is, however, one circumstance which we have some difficulty in providing for. The children are the offspring of paupers, and consequently *home* cannot well be appealed to in order to rouse their affections : *home*, that most endearing of all ties, is wanting to them ; the respectability maintained by their parents, cannot be appealed to as a motive for good conduct. This last is a most important circumstance, for even the most profligate men have held the respectability of those from whom they were sprung as something sacred ; when, but for that consideration, they have been ready to outrage every law, divine and human.

Although the parish would be entitled to all profit from the labour of the children as paupers, we consider it essential for the purposes of such an education as would go to the root of the present moral disease, that it should, on the contrary, belong to the children ; and as, by the new law, relief is to be considered as a loan for which the wages of the receivers of it may be attached, and relief given to children under the age of sixteen years is deemed to be given to the parent, the parent will be chargeable for all relief given to the child. It would therefore be desirable that the child should be made acquainted with this circumstance, and be exhorted to exert himself in order to lighten the weight which he must be to his parents. This consideration, when rightly presented, would to many be a powerful stimulus to exertion.

It might, however, be arranged in another manner. All beyond absolute necessaries might be denied to children capable of earning something by their labour, until their industry had enabled them to purchase them. We should, however, for the sake of the kindlier feelings, prefer making the child dependent upon the parent, and exert himself to relieve him of the burthen.

Should, however, a child capable of exertion either refuse to labour, or not appropriate its proceeds to legitimate purposes, he may easily be taught that he who has not earned a dinner shall not eat one, and that even he who misuses his own property will not escape altogether the consequences of his folly. Blows, we feel convinced, from what we have witnessed in the treatment of destitute children by the Children's Friend Society at Hackney-Wick, may be dispensed with. The most obdurate will yield to kindness and to a good discipline, enforced by one whose character commands respect. When punishment is absolutely necessary, a blow is a punishment of the worst kind, for not being directed to the source of the evil, it cannot cure it.

If the system of education here proposed, or any other of a similar nature, were to be pursued, we could wish it to be followed up by instruction very different from what is now given at the national schools. Still, even retaining the literary instruction of the national schools, much of what is sound and valuable would be obtained, and we should not be apprehensive of any very bad consequences from it. As the commissioners would have less prejudice to contend against in introducing some such system as we have here proposed, and retaining with it the literary instruction now generally established, than in making any material change in the method of literary instruction, we should wish them to make one step secure in the first instance, leaving other changes for subsequent consideration.

Among the pauper youth, a considerable number are infants, or very young children, to whom of course the preceding remarks can apply only to a limited extent. Experience, however, has shown that children of a tender age may learn much that will be of service to them in after life. Infant schools have been established for this purpose, and conducted in a satisfactory manner in many parts of the metropolis and other large towns. The commissioners have doubtless taken them into consideration. For parish poor children these schools are peculiarly adapted; for not only would the children themselves derive much advantage from such schools, but much trouble would be saved, as one schoolmistress can keep a number of children happy and employed, who would require twenty nurses to take care of them. We entreat those of our readers who have never visited a well-conducted infant school to lose no time in obtaining so great a gratification—a sight more interesting we have rarely witnessed.

PUBLIC INSTRUCTION IN THE STATE OF NEW YORK.

MM. De Beaumont and De Toqueville, who were commissioned by the French government to examine the penitentiary system in the United States of America, with a view to determine the propriety of adopting the same system in France, have embodied in the report which they have made to the French government on the subject, a considerable amount of information concerning the moral condition of the people in the States which they visited. Among other matters treated of by them, that of public education has not been neglected; and they have given an account of the system of public instruction in the State of New York, which we think it desirable to abridge for the information of our readers.

The legislature has created two special funds, one called the Literature Fund, the other the Common School Fund. The first is appropriated to encourage the higher branches of study; the other to promote elementary instruction.

An administrative board has been formed consisting of twenty-one members or regents, who have in their collective capacity received the name of the University of the State of New York. The governor and lieutenant-governor of the state always form part of the board, and are *ex officio* members of the university: the other nineteen members are all appointed by the legislature. It is the duty of these regents to advise with the state legislature upon the formation and chartering of establishments for promoting the higher branches of study; and the legislature will never act in such cases without the report of the university. Among all the colleges chartered in consequence of their recommendation, the regents annually distribute assistance from the Literature Fund; it is also a part of their duty to inspect the colleges, and to report annually concerning the state and progress of each of them to the legislative body. The regents have also the power of granting medical degrees as well as diplomas in science and belles-lettres.

The second fund, that devoted to the promotion of elementary instruction, is much larger than the Literature Fund. The information which we have derived from the report of MM. De Beaumont and De Toqueville relates almost exclusively to this branch of the subject. At the head of the functionaries to whom the administration of primary instruction in the State of New York is intrusted, is the

'Superintendent of Schools.' It is his duty to distribute annually in the different counties the pecuniary help afforded by the state, and to watch over the execution of the laws enacted for the regulation of public schools. He receives every year a detailed account of the state of instruction in every township of the state, and the result of these accounts he makes the subject of a report to the legislature.

It is obligatory upon each township to establish and support one or more schools, and to provide for this object a sum at least equal to that given by the state: this sum is obtained by means of a kind of property-tax. In every township school commissioners are appointed, who control the proceedings and expenditure of each school within the township. It is their province to select teachers, and to discharge them if they see occasion; but in this case an appeal lies to the Superintendent of Schools.

The money obtained from the two sources above described is far from being sufficient for the end in view; but it acts as an inducement to encourage individual exertion, and at least to ensure public attention to a subject of primary importance. In order to defray the rest of the expenses, each pupil is made to contribute a certain sum. If these payments are at all properly proportioned, the system here described may lay claim to a considerable degree of merit. The state and the inhabitants at large of the townships have an undoubted interest in the plan, and are very properly called upon to contribute towards the success of that undertaking from which they are to benefit through the improving morals of the people; while the pupils themselves have a further and individual advantage, and for this their natural guardians are fairly made to contribute more largely than others whose interest is only general.

In the year 1829, the Common School-Fund amounted to 1,684,628 dollars, out of which the state appropriated to the different townships 100,000 dollars. The payments made by the townships in the same year, amounted to 124,556 dollars; and a further sum of 14,095 dollars was obtained from a separate fund especially applicable to the same purpose. The sum of 238,651 dollars was therefore raised in that year by the joint contribution of the state and the townships; while those who were especially interested in receiving the instruction, paid the additional amount of 821,926 dollars. The total sum, therefore, paid in the State of New York for primary instruction in 1829, amounted to upwards of 1,000,000 dollars, or about 221,000*l.* sterling. The amount paid in that year for the common schools was—

For teachers' salaries   .   663,903 dollars.
For books   .   .   .   247,479
For fuel   .   .   .   92,700

            1,004,082 dollars.

The perpetuity of the Common School-Fund is guaranteed, and its gradual increase provided for by the following clause in the Constitution of the State :—' The proceeds of all lands belonging to this state, except such parts thereof as may be reserved or appropriated to public use, or ceded to the United States, which shall hereafter be sold or disposed of, together with the fund denominated the Common School-Fund, shall be and remain a perpetual fund, the interest of which shall be inviolably appropriated and applied to the support of common schools throughout this state.' This provision of the constitution in relation to the transfer of the proceeds of state lands to the School-Fund, took effect on the 1st January, 1823, at which time the capital of the Common School-Fund amounted to 1,155,827 dollars. In 1833, that fund was increased to 1,735,175 dollars.

Many of the towns have a local fund for the support of schools. These local funds were, in most cases, created by reservations of lots of land for school purposes, in the original formation of the townships. When these lots have acquired value from the increasing population of the township, they have been either sold or let, and the purchase money or rents vested in trustees chosen by the inhabitants. Only the annual revenue is allowed to be applied to the support of common schools ; the capital must be kept entire. From local causes many of these school lots have become very valuable, and in some towns an annual revenue exceeding 500 dollars is derived from them.

In several of the towns a local school-fund exists, which has been derived from a different source. In these towns there was formerly a fund for the support of the poor, but this having been declared by law to be a species of charge which should be borne by the whole county, the town-fund was no longer needed for its original object. An act was passed in 1829, authorizing the inhabitants of any town thus circumstanced to appropriate the poor-fund to other purposes, an authority of which they have generally availed themselves in favour of the Common School-Fund. From all these various sources the whole capital applicable to the purposes of that fund in 1833, amounted to 2,028,000 dollars. The management of the Common School-Fund is confided to the same functionaries who manage the general finances of the state; and the Commissioners of the Land Office have the management and sale of the School-Fund lots, in the same manner as they have of the lands belonging to the other funds of the state. There are 55 organized counties, and 811 townships and wards, in the State of New York. Distributed through these townships there are 9600 organized school districts, of which number 8941 had made reports to the superintendent up to the end of 1831. At that time the reported districts contained 508,878 children between five and sixteen years of age, and of those the large proportion of 494,959 were stated to have attended the schools during at least part of the months appropriated to teaching. In the course of the year 1831, there had been 267 new school districts formed; and the number of districts from which reports were received was greater by 106 than it had been in the preceding year.

The average number of scholars in each school was 55, and the schools were kept open for the reception of pupils during an average period of eight out of the twelve months. The number of scholars given above must be understood to comprehend all who had been on the school lists during the year, and it must not be inferred that each scholar had enjoyed eight months of instruction during that time. The progress of the system of public instruction in the State of New York may be judged from the fact, that in 1816, the number of organized school districts was only 2755, and the children who were taught during that year were returned at 140,106; the number of public schools, as well as of scholars, has consequently increased in fifteen years to the proportion (comparing the numbers at the beginning and end of this period) of seven to two. It is certainly an extraordinary circumstance, and one which shows how highly the advantages of instruction are prized by the inhabitants of New York, that in so considerable a part of the state as was comprised in the returns, thirty-five out of every thirty-six children between the ages of five and sixteen were at some period of the year attending the public schools. If we take into account the many circumstances, which, in a country where the demand for labour is great and labourers are well paid, would induce many to quit their studies before the age of sixteen, we may almost venture to pronounce that every child within the reported districts receives or has received instruction.

There are, besides public schools, other educational establishments, which as they receive no support from the government, are not subject to inspection, and are not included in the reports above alluded to; but these do not appear to be numerous, and it is mentioned that the children of the rich

and of the indigent meet together in the public schools, to
the support of which they contribute according to the means
of their parents.   It is a remark made by the inhabitants of
New York, and the observation might by no means be confined to that state, ' that the poor seize with much more zeal
on the means of instruction offered to them which costs little,
but for which they nevertheless think they pay, than they
evince to avail themselves of the same advantages when
offered as a charity.'   The mingling of all classes of children
in the same schools is encouraged as being in unison with the
republican institutions of the country.   Such a system would
probably meet with little encouragement among people by
whom the artificial distinctions of society are valued ; though
we may observe that this was the case in the former state of
the free schools of England, and still is to a certain extent.

The plan which has been described, and by means of which
the requisite funds are raised, is said to be productive of
various good results.   The public contribution passes from
the hands of the superintendent to the treasurers of 55
counties, by whom it is apportioned to the commissioners of
780 townships and wards, and by these commissioners it is
finally paid to the trustees of 8941 districts.   The trustees
are held accountable to the commissioners for the application
of the money according to the true intent of the legislature ;
and the commissioners on their part must make an annual
report to the superintendent, founded upon the reports of the
trustees.   The machinery thus put in motion engages the
active co-operation of full 38,000 persons, a circumstance in
itself of great value, as tending to ensure a constant and
vigilant attention to the cause of education ; while the regulation which obliges the inhabitants of every township to tax
themselves for the support of the schools, gives an interest
in the subject to each individual.   Accordingly it is found
that the school meetings in every district are very punctually
attended by the tax-payers ; those among them whose property, and consequently whose contributions are the greatest,
are induced to act as trustees, partly in order to secure themselves against the evils that would arise from a corrupt or
careless administration of the funds.   It is mentioned as
another benefit resulting from this mode of contribution, that
the tax-payers who have children are induced to send them
with more punctuality to the schools, and to put themselves
to a further charge by that means, in order to obtain an equivalent for the sum which they are obliged to contribute.
These advantages would be lost, if the supply of the requisite
funds were obtained from the state and the scholars, without
the compulsory aid of the inhabitants of the townships.

The absolute condition on which each township receives its allowance from the state, is, that the inhabitants of each town shall, by a vote at their town-meeting, authorize a tax to be raised among them equal at least in amount to the sum apportioned by the state. Another requirement is, that before the inhabitants of a neighbourhood can participate in the public fund, a school district must be organized, a schoolhouse must be erected, furnished, and supplied with fuel, and that a school must have been collected and taught there by a legally-qualified teacher during at least three months. It is only on a report of all these conditions having been fulfilled on the part of the trustees, that the commissioners of townships are authorized to apportion any part of the Common School-Fund to the district.

The incorporated academies to which allusion has been made as being under the direction of the twenty-one regents, are intended to furnish teachers for the supply of the common schools. These academies are now fifty-five in number, one for each organized county, and for their erection and endowment about 400,000 dollars have been expended from sums contributed by the state and from individual subscriptions. A revenue of 10,000 dollars is annually contributed to these establishments by the state; and in 1827, a sum of 150,000 dollars was transferred from the general funds of the state to the Literature Fund, for the express object of providing education for teachers of common schools, by increasing the apportionments to the academies.

The subject of primary education in the city of New York is treated by the magistrates in a manner suited to its vast importance. A person is employed at a very liberal salary, whose only occupation it is to visit parents in all sections of the city, and to invite and persuade them to send their children to school; and it further appears from the report of the commissioners, that the corporation of New York has passed an ordinance, ' excluding from the participation of public charity all out-door poor, whether emigrants or not, who having children between the ages of five and twelve, neglect or refuse to send them to some one of the public schools.' The public schools in New York have an excellent character, and great efforts have been made of late to increase their number and extend their usefulness.

Our remarks, it will be observed, apply nearly altogether to the fiscal administrative condition of the schools in this state: of their internal working and the value of the education and instruction given, we are not at present able to give any statement.

SAVINGS BANKS.

THE moral improvement of society is undoubtedly the proper end of all efforts for improving the education of the people, and no subject is foreign from the purpose of this Journal which is calculated to contribute to that end. The institution of Savings Banks appears to us admirably qualified to foster an essential class of our social duties, and thus may be said to aid directly the highest purpose of education; while indirectly it works to the same end, by providing the means of obtaining instruction, and probably also by generating the desire for it. It has recently come to our knowledge, by means of a statement to which we shall more particularly refer hereafter, that a large proportion—more than one-fifth—of the deposits in a considerable savings bank in the west of England are made in the names of children. It is probable that similar deposits may have been made in other quarters, and we would gladly hope that the fact is so; for we hold it to be unlikely that parents who are willing thus to abridge themselves of present comforts for the sake of the future comfort of their children, should be unmindful of the greater benefit, in even a worldly point of view, which they would secure to them by means of instruction. A man who exercises the degree of forethought for his offspring which we have here supposed, cannot fail to have observed the comparative unproductiveness of money in the hands of the ignorant; that it is almost sure to be soon squandered in profitless dissipation; while on the other hand, almost every path to worldly advancement is filled by those who have received and profited by sound instruction. We are aware that in thus stating the question we have taken very low ground, and that we might, without stepping beyond the reasonable probabilities of the case, have assumed, that a parent thus anxious for the welfare of his child, would not bound his wishes to such advantages as we have mentioned, but would also attend to the child's moral improvement.

Savings banks may further be said to assist the cause of education by the examples of prudence and self-denial, which they are the means of calling forth in the parents—virtues which, in the case of persons in the poorer classes of life, cannot fail to have a peculiar influence upon the happiness, and consequently upon the character, of their families. What comparison can there be in this respect between the house where everything is managed with order and sobriety, and that in which all that can be taken from the weekly earnings, after satisfying the absolute calls of hunger, is devoted to intemperance and riot? Into this abode, the kindly virtues, so powerful in softening the unavoidable ills of life, can never or but rarely enter; while in their stead will be found those constant strifes and bickerings which alienate the affections and poison every source of enjoyment. It is a common and we believe a wellfounded remark, that the children of persons habitually intemperate seldom resist the contagion of example, that they are almost certain to grow up in the indulgence of the same brutalizing vice which has been so constantly presented to their view and recommended by the practice of those to whom they naturally look for guidance. But it is not necessary that the spirit of improvidence should be carried to this dreadful length, in order to its exercising a very injurious influence upon the dispositions and characters of those children who suffer from its effects. The family of the improvident man must be continually exposed to trials and troubles which would wear the spirits and ruin the temper of the best disposed, and which are but too likely to generate dispositions of recklessness or feelings of morbid misanthropy, under the influence of which it were vain to expect that education should exhibit any of its humanizing and beneficial results.

If we are at all right in the view that has been here taken, we must also be warranted in the opinion that we have expressed, as to the great value of those aids to prudence—savings banks—and justified in recommending every one who has it at heart to better the condition, both moral and physical, of society, to promote their extension by every means within his power.

The paper to which we have already alluded, is a welldrawn-out statement of the accounts of the Devon and Exeter Savings Banks, showing the condition of the depositors under various divisions and subdivisions, the number of each class whose savings are deposited, and the different amounts which individuals in each class have contributed to the funds of the institution. We believe that no similar statement has ever been drawn out by the officers of any other savings bank in the kingdom, although it must be evident that most, if not all of them, possess equal facilities for doing it. The usefulness of such information is so evident, that it must be needless to enlarge upon its value; and we trust that in proportion as the managers of other banks become acquainted with the plans and statements so judiciously formed by the actuary of the Exeter institution, they will be induced to add their part to the stock of our information on the subject. If it were practicable to obtain such statements from every savings bank in England and Ireland, how much light would they throw upon various questions which are now the subject of controversy with regard to the progress and prospects, both physical and moral, of the labouring classes in those parts of the kingdom!

The principal divisions adopted in the statement now under our notice are five:

1. Domestic servants, under three subdivisions.

2. Persons engaged in trade and manufactures, under eight subdivisions.

3. Persons engaged in agriculture, under three subdivisions.

4. Persons belonging to the navy and army, or connected with the revenue offices, under four subdivisions, and

5. Miscellaneous depositors, under three subdivisions.

Besides which, a statement is added of the number of individual depositors of friendly societies, and of charitable institutions and societies, whose funds are placed in the Exeter Savings Bank.

We have already mentioned the large proportion of deposits made in the name and for the benefit of children, and it is gratifying to add that these deposits are made by every one of the five classes above-mentioned. As might be supposed, the proportion is smallest in the first-named class, for the very obvious reason that comparatively few domestic servants are or have been married. Out of 4755 depositors in this class whose savings amount to 152,917*l.*—a large sum to be contributed from wages, which it must be remembered are by no means equal to the rates which are paid in the metropolis—there are still 332 children for whose benefit 3284*l.* of savings have been accumulated. In the next class, that of persons engaged in trade and manufactures, we find 8208 depositors whose savings amount to 224,138*l.*, out of which the large proportion of 50,840*l* has been invested for the benefit of 3568 children. In the third class, that of agriculturists, we find the still larger proportion of 53,933*l.* deposited in the names of 3598 children; the total number of depositors in this class being 6398, and their united savings 159,880*l.* The fourth class we could not expect to find numerous. Many retired officers of the army and navy have it is true taken up their residence in the county of Devon; but persons of that class would probably resort to other means than the savings bank for the disposal of their surplus incomes, and besides, the greater part are probably resident in Plymouth and its neighbourhood, where similar establishments to that at Exeter are opened. Out of 1057 depositors of 40,977*l.* in this class, there is however the large proportion of 423 children, in whose favour 9254*l.* have been lodged.

In the miscellaneous class, which comprises persons of some education, the proportionate number of children is still greater, being 470 out of 831 depositors, and the sum in their names is 12,661*l*. out of 32,654*l*.

On referring to the statistical tables recently compiled under the direction of the Board of Trade, we perceive that the proportionate amount òf savings deposited by the inhabitants of Devonshire is very far beyond that made throughout the kingdom generally. The population of England at the census of 1831, was 13,089,338 ; and the deposits in savings banks in the same part of the United Kingdom on the 20th of November, 1833, was 12,680,512*l*., or a small fraction below twenty shillings for each individual. The population of Devonshire, which amounted to 494,168, have deposited 897,028*l*., or thirty-six shillings and four-pence for each individual : the average amount invested by each actual depositor in the county agrees with the general average of the actual depositors in the whole of England.

This circumstance, so favourable to the labouring classes in the county of Devon, appears to be in a great measure, if not entirely owing to the system adopted by the managers of the Devon and Exeter Savings Bank, for facilitating the deposit of small sums on the part of those who live at a distance from the city of Exeter where the savings bank is kept. For this purpose the managers have obtained the assistance of gentlemen of respectability and influence residing in different parts of the county, and who undertake the receipt of small sums from their poor neighbours, and transmit the same to the managers. At the date of the last report upwards of 130 clergymen and gentlemen were acting in this manner as receivers of deposits and with the happiest effect. By this means many poor and industrious persons have been induced to put aside a part of their earnings, who if they had been without this opportunity of transmitting their little contributions to a distant city, would have been deprived of the opportunity of saving, which is thus offered by bringing the place of safe and profitable deposit, as it were, to their very doors

One of the rules adopted by this well-organized institution provides, that except in cases which in the opinion of the visiting managers appear to be urgent, such as sickness or death in the family, or want of work, no depositor shall receive back the whole or any part of his principal money lodged in his name, except at the expiration of twenty-eight days from the date of a notice to be given to that effect. The length of time which must thus elapse between the forming of the desire to withdraw their money and the day when it can be received, has, doubtless, the effect in many cases of preventing the giving of the notice at all; and in other cases, the time which is allowed for reflection is of the greatest value, as the desire of withdrawing their funds frequently proceeds from a momentary excitement which passes off before the expiration of the notice. Often too, this restraint has the good effect of preserving the poor man's little hoard from the hands of designing persons, who might otherwise prevail on the depositors, by illusive promises of greater advantage, to place it in their hands.

STATISTICS OF EDUCATION IN ENGLAND.

As Education in England forms no part of the general administration, it has hitherto been impossible to make any accurate estimate of the number of children who are receiving instruction in schools of all descriptions. The reports of various societies, such as the National School Society, and the British School Society and others, enable us to form a pretty exact estimate of the operations of such societies; and the number of children who are under the direction of these societies, is a large part of all those who receive instruction. Still there are numerous schools belonging to religious sects, of which either no reports are published, or, at least, none that are comprehensive and satisfactory; nor is it an easy matter in some cases to procure such reports. As to the number of private schools, by which we mean all those that are solely under the management of an individual or individuals, not responsible to any person or body of persons, no information at all can be obtained.

With a view of endeavouring to ascertain the Statistics of Education in England, the late government requested returns to be made to certain questions from each town, chapelry, and extra-parochial place in England and Wales. As some of our readers may not have seen the form of the paper issued on this occasion, we give it at full length.

' HOUSE OF COMMONS.

' *Veneris*, 24° die *Maii* 1833.

' Ordered, That an humble Address be presented to his Majesty, that he will be graciously pleased to give directions, that there be laid before this House,—

" A return of the number of schools in each town, parish, chapelry, or extra-parochial place; which return, after stating
the amount of the population of the said town or place according to the last census, shall specify;—1. Whether the
said schools are infant, daily, or Sunday schools;—2.
Whether they are confined, either nominally or virtually, to
the use of children of the established church, or of any other
religious denomination;—Whether they are endowed or unendowed;—4. By what funds they are supported, if unendowed, whether by payments from the scholars, or otherwise;
5. The numbers and sexes of the scholars in each school;—
6. The age at which the children generally enter, and at
which they generally quit school;—7. The salaries and other
emoluments allowed to the masters or mistresses in each
school;—and shall also distinguish—8. Those schools which
have been established or revived since 1818;—and, 9.
Those schools to which a lending library is attached."

' In pursuance of which Address of the House of Commons, his
Majesty having given directions to his Secretary of State for the
Home Department, to use his best endeavour to obtain satisfactory
answers to the above questions, Lord Viscount Melbourne hereby
requests the overseers or overseer of the poor of every parish or place
in England and Wales to answer the said questions (in so far as
they are applicable to each parish or place) in the manner pointed
out on the following page of this sheet;—or in case there should
be no school whatever in the parish or place, to return this sheet
forthwith, with an answer to that effect, signed by such overseers or
overseer;—but if there be any school or schools, the particulars of
which are known to them or him, to insert answers to the questions applicable to such schools;—or if there be schools, the particulars of which are unknown to them or him, to send a printed copy
of the Address (herewith enclosed) to each schoolmaster or schoolmistress in turn, requesting written information from them severally;
—and, in any case, the overseers or overseer will return such
answers, or their own answer or answers (as the case may be), with
this sheet;—on the outside of which a proper direction is printed for
duly returning it to the Home Office.

' MELBOURNE.

' *Home Office, Whitehall,* 1833.

' **** *The Schoolmaster or Schoolmistress to whom this order is delivered by the overseer will be so good as to answer the following
printed questions, in so far as they are applicable to his or her school.*

' *Infant Schools—*
   Specifying
     The number of infants in each school? _____
     And of what sex? _____
     At what age do they usually enter, and at what
     age do they usually quit school? _____

' *Daily Schools—*
   · Specifying
        The number of scholars in each school ?_____

    And of what sex ? _____

    At what age do they usually enter, and at what
    age do they usually quit school?_____

Sunday Schools—
   Specifying
        The number of scholars in each school ?_____

    And of what sex ? _____

    At what age do they usually enter, and at what
    age do they usually quit school?_____

' *Endowed and other Schools—*
    Whether an endowed school or schools ?_____

    If not endowed, by what funds supported ; that is,
    whether by payments from the scholars, or other-
    wise ? _____

    If by salaries, or other allowed emoluments, be
    pleased to specify particulars ? _____

' *Religion—*
        Is any school confined (nominally or virtually) to the
        established church ? _____

    Or to any other denomination or religious persua-
    sion ? _____

' If any of the above schools established since the year
1818, be pleased to specify the date when they severally
· commenced ? _____

Is any lending library of books attached to any of these
schools ? _____

    Be pleased to insert any observations which occur to
    you relative to the above questions, or any of them.

    Signed this_____ day of _____ 1833.

                                   Schoolmaster at _____
_____ Schoolmistress at _____

' (*For Schoolmasters or Schoolmistresses.*)'

This is the circular which the overseer has had to deliver to
the schoolmaster or schoolmistress. The circular addressed
to the overseer, in which the answers were to be entered, is
the same, with the following additional head :—

' What the total number of schools of every kind ; including
herein (with the above Infant, Daily, and Sunday schools)
Boarding schools, and any other description of schools not
above-mentioned? With similar particulars as to number, sex,
and age of scholars.'

The design of the government was good; but two things were necessary to render this measure efficient. The government should have been able to compel the overseers to make careful returns, and to give them sufficient power for procuring the necessary information, which in some cases will have been withheld; the second necessary thing was a well-digested formula or table of inquiries. Both these essentials were wanting, and of course the returns must be both defective and inaccurate. We believe that in many cases the overseers have taken great pains; and we know that in other cases they have taken very little. Still we do not deny that the returns will be of some use, though it is easy to see how great the amount of error may be owing to the two defects just pointed out. If education formed a part of the civil administration, there would of course be no difficulty in obtaining complete returns of all the schools under the direction of the government: and as to the schools of all kinds not under the direction of government, a tolerably accurate return might be insured, from the circumstance of there being in every parish some responsible persons connected with the government schools, who might be empowered to obtain the necessary statistical information, as to such schools as are directed by societies or belong to individuals. If any system of national education existed, the legislature would know what was doing in their own schools, and they might infer what was probably doing in others; and thus they might from time to time, frame such a series or table of questions, as would certainly bring in a mass of valuable information. The table of questions given above, shows pretty clearly that the framers of it were not well acquainted with the subject of inquiry. We propose to make a few remarks on this table.

Infant Schools.—The religious sect under whose direction each school is, should have been mentioned under this head. Of course it will appear under the head of *Religion*, if the returns are complete; but this will only tend to introduce confusion.

Daily Schools.—As we have a head of *Endowed and other Schools* which comes after, it is impossible to say what are meant by *Daily Schools.* Endowed schools, as a *general* rule, are daily schools only, as far as the endowment goes, and many in the north of England are strictly, in practice, *only* daily schools: but many are boarding-schools also, at the same time, under present circumstances.

Sunday-Schools.—A great number of children who attend Sunday-schools also attend day-schools; and the returns ought, therefore, to show how many children who go to the

Sunday-schools also attend the day-schools. The religious sect under whose direction the Sunday-schools are, should have been stated under this head.

Endowed and other Schools.—The head of endowed-schools is one that is tolerably distinct, but still there is room for error here also. The endowments of some schools, which were small, have been merged (we suspect illegally in some cases) in national schools. What *other schools* are we cannot conjecture. The intention was probably, that this head should contain all except those not included in the first three heads and under *endowed schools;* but as the first three heads do not comprehend determined classes of schools, it follows that the classes included under *other schools* are undetermined also.

Religion.—This head, as it stands, appears to us to be useless. It was also injudicious to insert the words 'nominally or virtually.' Those who know what country parishes are, will easily conceive that the word *virtually* will sometimes puzzle the overseer.

It must be quite clear to every person who reflects on the subject, that the form in which a table of questions for circulation is drawn up, has not necessarily anything in common with the form in which the whole results will ultimately be arranged. The object of the table questions is to get the greatest amount of information, and to ensure its accuracy: the object of the table in which the collected information is ultimately registered, is to put the whole in that form in which it will be most useful to the public. It may happen that with these two different objects in view, the form of the questions and the form of the results will be altogether different.

In the table of questions simplicity is everything. The answers should be as much as possible in figures, and no remarks or observations, such as are asked for in this printed paper, ought to be called for. Under present circumstances we are inclined to think that the head of Religion should have formed the basis of the whole division of the table of inquiries ; and not because it appears to be of any great importance to ascertain the exact proportions in which each sect contributes to the extension of education, but because this division, as we shall show, points out the easiest mode of getting precise answers. It perhaps might have been advisable first to have made a division of schools into public and private, though it is probable that some error would have come in here also ; and certainly some schools that were placed under the head of *Private* would appear again under some of the minor divisions, such as *Night*-schools, &c. Still the division into public and private is intelligible, and a few words would explain clearly what was meant by a private school. It should be stated under private-schools whether they are day or boarding schools, or both ; for boys or girls, or for both.

The subdivision of the public-schools would be the following :—

The National-School Society has now spread itself over nearly all England and Wales ; their schools are the schools of the Established Church, and they are so numerous that they would form a distinct head of inquiry. The division of them into day and Sunday schools would be easily ascertained under this head. We consider it to be no objection to this and the following division, that many children, not of the church of England, are in the National schools, and that the British schools comprehend children of all persuasions. The object of inquiry should be to ascertain *how many* children are educated in the country, and *how* they are educated. The form of questions which will bring in the best answers on these two heads, is the best form of inquiry.

The British-School Society, though less in numbers, also forms a separate class, and would make a distinct head of inquiry. Both the societies, it is well known, publish reports, but this is no reason for not making the inquiry about them in another shape. The schools of both these societies are of course included in the government returns made in compliance with the printed form, but we propose the present division because it is more simple.

The *other* schools should be asked for under the heads or subdivisions of the several religious sects ; all the sects have schools strictly their own (though they may admit, as they often do, all who are willing to come), and they are the only parties who can say what description of schools they are, and who can give the other particulars of inquiry touching them. It is no objection to this mode of subdivision that the number of heads in the printed formula would be increased. The whole number of sects is not very great, and even if it happened that some which consist of a few congregations only were omitted, the error would be nothing compared with the errors that must necessarily exist in the returns according to the late formula. It may also be observed that as the answers ought to be given entirely in figures, a tabular form more comprehensive and compact than the one issued by the government would easily be devised.

The head of Endowed Schools is a necessary one, but we are aware that there are causes of error in this head which will not be easily obviated.

Some classes of schools would require distinct heads independent of religious distinctions: they are, adult-schools, schools for the deaf and dumb, schools for the blind, night schools, mechanics' schools and institutes, schools of industry, and a few other classes of schools.

It will appear from an inspection of the government questions, that the recent inquiries refer only to one of the two things which such an inquiry should ascertain. If the returns were perfectly correct, they would show very little indeed beyond the number of schools and the number of children taught; but they will contain hardly any information on the more important head of inquiry—how the children are taught. We hardly blame the framers of the questions for omitting all inquiries on this head. In the present state of education in this country, it seems almost hopeless to expect that any set of inquiries, however well framed, would produce satisfactory returns as to the kind of education given.* Even were the books used in each school included in the returns, this would give very little real information as to the actual state of instruction: this information can be got in no other way than by long and personal acquaintance with schools of various kinds. We believe that the general character of the education in this country may be known better by active individual inquiries than by any answers to government questions, so long as education is not a branch of the civil administration. We know pretty well the kind of education given in our grammar schools, in our ordinary boarding-schools, in the National schools, &c.; and if more precise information were wanted, we believe it could only be got by sending out some active commissioners with full powers for making inquiry into all kinds of schools, taking such large portions or districts for examination as would enable us to form tolerably safe conclusions as to the state of education in the districts not examined.

The following statement about the schools of Bolton, in Lancashire, has been drawn up with care by a friend in that place. It is not complete because no individual possesses the means of making such a statement complete; nor is it proposed as a model in its arrangement, but it shows what the materials are in a large town, with respect to which a table of inquiries should be framed :—

'Out of a population of nearly forty-two thousand, about one-fourth are receiving instruction in day and Sunday schools. The returns recently made to government, aided by further inquiries, give the following particulars of the state of education in this manufacturing town :—

* See Mr. Rickman's judicious answer (15), in the evidence before the Select Committee on Education, p. 3: also the rest of his answers.

	Boys.	Girls.	Total.
Paid day-schools . .	1741	1342	3083
Charity day-schools .	458	287	745
Total number in day-schools . .			3828
Sunday-schools . .	3432	4306	7738
Paid night-schools .	311	115	426

' From this statement it would appear, at first sight, that 11,992 are enjoying some of the advantages of education. It is not, however, strictly so; because a considerable number of the children in the infant and lower schools, are also sent to Sunday schools. The proportion of such would have been a proper subject of inquiry in the late returns, as the information cannot be expected through any other channel.

' The *acquirements* made in these schools are pretty accurately ascertained. Out of the number of scholars in the day-schools, about one-fifth, or seven hundred, receive a good common education, including grammar, geography, arithmetic, history, &c.; and a small proportion of these, some knowledge of Latin. At the free grammar school, the classics are taught, in addition to the usual branches of education; but out of 120 boys who are educated there, it is not believed that many make much progress in the classical authors, unless with a view to obtaining an exhibition at the university, which forms part of the endowment.* At the two other endowed day-schools, the course of instruction is on a lower scale, being intended for the children of working people. In the higher class of paid schools very little attention is given to what are called 'accomplishments,' as will be obvious from the fact that no teacher of any of the modern languages, drawing, or dancing, finds sufficient encouragement to reside in the town. The remaining four-fifths who attend the day-schools learn little more than the elementary arts of reading and writing, and some few, perhaps, arithmetic. In the Sunday-schools nothing is taught but reading and writing, with religious instruction. The night-schools and the Mechanics' Institution come in aid of these schools, and enable those who have no other opportunity to get some knowledge of arithmetic. A good library is attached to the Mechanics' Institute, which is resorted to by some of the reading operatives; and libraries are established in connexion with many of the Sunday-schools and dissenting places of worship. There are also two other libraries in the town, one a public one, upon a liberal basis, containing about 1500 volumes; and another of a more select sort, instituted about the time of the French revolution, and still retaining in its designation, as well as in its management, the spirit of that intolerant period. It bears the name of ' The Church and King Library.' Besides these, Bolton has no institutions for the advancement of education.

' The number of day-schools is about eighty; of which forty-four are for children between the ages of three and nine; fifteen for girls

* This school, according to the Report of the Charity Commission, has an income of 485*l*. 10*s*. 6*d*.—See *Journal of Education*, No. 16, p. 353.

only, from five upwards; seven for boys only, of the same age ; and the rest for pupils of both sexes, between the ages of four and twelve.   The average period of attendance in the day-schools is six years and a fraction.

'Below are some of the data from which the above results are obtained :—

	Boys.	Girls.	Total.
In paid day-schools—			
Superior education . . .	311	386	697
Common ditto . . .	1430	956	2386
In charity day-schools—			
Superior education . . .	120	0	120
Common ditto . . .	175	120	295
Infant schools . . .	163	167	330
	2199	1629	3828
In Sunday-schools—			
Parish school . . .	430	720	1150
St. George's school . . .	310	490	800
All Saints	75	125	200
Methodist—old and new connexion	1464	1744	3208
Primitive and Independent Me-			
thodists	370	340	710
Independent schools . .	430	570	1000
New Jerusalem . . .	69	39	108
Catholic school . . .	110	120	230
Unitarian	174	158	332
	3432	4306	7738
In night schools—			
Mechanics' Institute * . .	185	0	135
Cæteri	176	115	291
	311	115	426

'If these returns are in the main correct, there must be several thousands of children without instruction.   Taking the population at 42,000 and the number of families at 8000, the average must be nearly two in a family of an age to require education.   This would give about 14,000 who should be at school, more by 2000 than the number given in the returns ; and if from that number we deduct 1000, who attend both day and Sunday schools and are thus reckoned twice, there will be 3000 who receive no instruction at all, not even the limited instruction of the Sunday schools.   Can this be the actual state of the case?'

* A night-school forms part of the plan.

HARROW SCHOOL.*

In the Fifth Number of this Journal an account was given of the present system of instruction at this school. The publication referred to in the note, seems to be one of that class which originate in the desire of the residents near an Endowed Grammar School, to give publicity to the statutes and will of the founder, with a view of reforming abuses, or what by some people are considered to be abuses. Such publications are especially useful, when they concern schools which were either excepted from the act appointing the charity commission, as Harrow school was, or belong to districts not yet examined by the commissioners. The main design of such a publication as this, is, we presume, to show that the governors do not strictly observe the statutes and rules of the founder. Our object is not to insist upon the propriety of compelling governors and trustees of endowed schools to observe regulations, many of which at the present day are either useless or positively mischievous; but to show the necessity of giving to all our endowed schools an enlarged code of rules suitable to the present time. The governors of Harrow school would not certainly consult the interests of that establishment, if they followed in all things the undoubted meaning of John Lyon's statutes. But, on the other hand, if governors of endowed schools can modify the statutes according to their pleasure, or even according to their best judgment and most honest intentions, what security is there that they, or some who follow them in their innovations, may not entirely pervert the property not only from its destination, but from all useful purposes? The only security is to frame a new set of rules for all endowed schools in England, and to make the trustees and governors immediately and periodically responsible to some central authority, without the tedious form of appeals to Courts of justice or the Crown as visitor.

As the nature of John Lyon's foundation is of a mixed kind, we will briefly state what it is. The Free School of Harrow was intended for the instruction of the children of Harrow parish, but the master, with the consent of the governors, can take other children for his profit. Part of the lands of John Lyon were intended for the building and support of the Free School, according to the rules by him laid down; and for the preaching ' thirty good learned and godly sermons yearly

* Orders, Statutes, and Rules, to be observed and kept by the Governors of the Free Grammar School at Harrow-on-the-Hill, in the County of Middlesex. Founded by John Lyon in the year of our Lord, 1590. Published by Order of Vestry under the direction of George Padmore. London. March, 1833.

for ever, in the parish of Harrow-upon-the-Hill.' Twenty pounds also, are to be annually distributed among sixty of the poorest householders of Harrow parish; and twenty pounds yearly for 'fowre poore scollers' at the universities; two at Gonville and Caius college, Cambridge, and two at such colleges in Oxford as the governors shall think best. These exhibitions, in consequence of the improved value of the estates, have been raised to twenty pounds per annum each, according to a statement made in the introduction to the vestry's publication; but this appears to be an error, as we shall afterwards show.

The rents and profits of certain estates at Kilbourn and in the parish of St. Marylebone, said now to be worth 4000*l*.* per annum, (see *Introduction*) are appropriated by the will of John Lyon to the repairing of the roads from Edgeware and Harrow to London, and for the maintenance of certain other roads specified. The other estates also are said to have increased much in value. 'The disbursements are made by the governors in paying the masters' salaries and the exhibitions, educating poor children, relieving decayed housekeepers and widows, and by the payment of a certain sum annually to the National School, repairing the roads, &c. &c.'—*Introduction.*

The discretionary powers of the governors under John Lyon's 'Orders, Statutes, and Rules,' are pretty ample, as we may observe from the following clause :—

' I doe, in the name of God, straightly charge the keepers and governors who now be or any time hereafter shall be, as they will answere before God and the Lord Jesus Christ, to be carefull and faithful in the just and true disposition, execution and performance of all and singular the things herein menconed belonging to their charge, and to see and provide that the whole profitts of the said lands, the yearely rents, all ffines and other comodities whatsoever thereof in any wise arriseing or comeing, be wholly imployed and bestowed to and for the uses intents and purposes herein menconed and declared, in the best and most beneficiall wise that may be to their skill and knowledge; and if any overplus be, the same to be safely kept in stock towards necessary charges, and parte thereof to be given and bestowed for the help and releife of poor marriages and other such good and charitable purposes within the said parish of Harrow, at the discrecon of the said keepers and governors.'

The governors have thus the power in the present improved value of the estates, of doing either much good or harm ' at their discrecon.' We hope they have not done much for the 'helpe and releife of poor marriages.' The whole value of the estates does not appear to be known to others than the go-

* Some say that this is an exaggerated estimate, which is not unlikely.

vernors. ' Mr. Padmore (p. 40) applied at the office of Mr. Decimus Burton, the agent of the governors, to learn the amount of the present rental of the estates, without being able to obtain the information required.' There is no reason, as far as we can see, from the ' Orders, Statutes, and Rules,' why Mr. Padmore should receive the information, or any other inhabitant of Harrow, on making a similar application. John Lyon intrusted his estates absolutely to the six governors and their successors, with directions, ' in case of their being divided in opinion, to apply to the right honourable and most reverend father in God, the Archbishop of Canterbury for the time being, with humblest request to his Grace to expounde, order, and determine such doubt, or variance.' The parishioners of Harrow have no power of interfering in any way with the governors, all of whom, however, ought to be ' honest and substantiall inhabitants within the said parish of Harrow.' The vacancies in the body of governors are filled up by the survivors. It appears that this part of John Lyon's will, as to the governors being inhabitants of Harrow, is not observed, though it is a positive rule of the founder;* and as there appears to be no court which has jurisdiction with respect to the election or amotion of members of corporations, the governors may elect whom they please to the vacancies in their body.

By the ' Orders, &c.' of the founder, the ' schoole-master,' (head-master) must not be ' under the degree of Master of Arte,' and the usher, now called the under-master, not ' under the degree of Bachelor of Arte,' at the time of election. Nothing is said as to their being in orders, though it is clear that the founder contemplated the possibility of the head-master being a clergyman, as he declares that if either the school-master or the vicar of Harrow shall be considered competent to preach ' the thirty good, learned, and godly sermons,' and if the schoolmaster can preach the sermons without any hindrance to the teaching, the governors may choose him or the vicar before any other, and give to the person so chosen, ' the ten pounds for his paines therein.' As the vicar, we presume, can prevent any person from preaching in his own church, without his permission, we suppose that he preaches the sermons himself; or probably they are not preached at all. The governors can, if they please, under the clause above quoted, increase this payment to above ten pounds.

Though John Lyon had a wife Johan, he ordered and ruled that the head-master and usher shall be ' always single men unmarried:' if they marry, they are to be turned out. This

* ' Those governors of the school who are resident in the parish, are in the habit of sending their boys to the school upon the foundation.'—*Journal of Education,* vol. i. p. 4. See also further as to the decree in the Rolls.—Lord Aberdeen is at present the only governor not resident in the parish.

rule is not observed now, though it is as imperative as it can be. Nobody would wish to see such absurd regulations enforced, which would manifestly be to the detriment of the school, but the existence of such imperative rules, and the violation of them at the same time, are decisive reasons in favour of a complete reformation of the orders of John Lyon.

The salary of the head-master was fixed by the founder at forty marks per annum, ' for his stipends and wages for teaching, ordering, and governing of the schollers of the saide schoole,' with five marks additional for wood and coals. The salary of the usher was twenty marks, with an allowance of five more for wood and coals. We do not know whether or not these salaries have been raised with the increased value of the property. Such an increase of salary is within the power of the governors, and, as it seems, would be a very proper use of their discretion.*

The boys who are to enjoy the allowances at the universities are to be chosen out of the Free Grammar School (if there be competent scholars in the school); they are to be chosen by the governors, ' of the most apt and most poore sorte that be meete, the poore kinsfolke of me the said John Lyon (if any such be), and such as are borne within the said parish of Harrow, being apt to learn, poore, and meete, to go to the university, to be preferred before others.' The following statement, from the account of Harrow School in the Journal of Education, will show the present condition of these scholarships.

' Almost every boy in the sixth form, and many of the fifth form, offer themselves as candidates for those scholarships. The course of study, therefore, preparatory to their examination, may be considered as a necessary part of the education of every boy of average abilities who rises into the fifth form. The governors' four scholarships of fifty guineas a year each, to be held for four years, have been recently founded by the governors of the school. The boy who gains one of them must go either to Oxford or Cambridge; but he may enter at any college of either university.'

These scholarships, though here said to have been recently founded, appear to be John Lyon's scholarships, erroneously stated in the publication of the Vestry to be now 20*l.* a year each; for there are no scholarships mentioned as belonging to the school, except these and the two Sayer's scholarships, founded recently by the late John Sayer, of Park Crescent, Portland Place, London.

These scholarships are certainly not disposed of according to the terms of John Lyon's orders; but we do not for this

* See the decision in the Rolls' Court (hereafter mentioned) as to the sums laid out on the Master's house.

reason infer that they are not well disposed of: we merely observe the discrepancy between the orders of John Lyon and the present practice. The Letters Patent of the 14th of Elizabeth, granting John Lyon a license to establish his school, and constituting the keepers and governors of the school a corporation, particularly mention that two of the scholarships are for Cambridge and two for Oxford. These Letters do indeed empower the governors to make statutes and rules touching the school, with the advice and consent of the Bishop of London for the time being; but so that these statutes be not contrary to the statutes and ordinances of John Lyon, made and to be made.

The regulations of John Lyon, as to the admission of children into the school, are unintelligible, as they are printed in the Vestry's publication. It appears that his main design, in all his bequests, was to benefit the parish of Harrow, and, among other things, to establish in it a free grammar school for the children of Harrow parish; but he also intended that children from other parishes should be admissible, for the profit of the head master. The clause is as follows : ' And a meete and competent number of schollers, as well of poore, to be taught freely for the stipends aforesaid (viz., the forty marks and the twenty marks), as of others to be received for the further profitt and comoditie of the said schoolemaster, shall be sett downe and appointed by the discrecon of the said keepers and governors, from time to time.' Another and a subsequent clause is,—' The governors of the said Free Gram mar Schoole, or the more parte of them, for the time being, shall have the authority, with the consent of the said schoole-master for the time being, to admitt children into the said Free Grammar Schoole.' The last regulation appears to render the master's consent necessary for the admission of *all* scholars, though we believe that the founder could not have meant this.

In 1831, the total number of boys in the school at mid-summer was 214, of whom only 15 were upon John Lyon's foundation : at present, we are informed that the number is probably about 260, with about 15 or 18 on the foundation. Those boys on the foundation are exempt from a charge of ten guineas a year which all the rest of the boys pay to the head and under master, under the name of schooling, and likewise from the payment of one guinea per annum for school charges. In all other respects they are on the same footing with the rest of the boys ; and the invidious distinctions, which exist in such schools as Eton, are said (Journal of Education) not to exist here between the boys on the foundation and those who are not. This, however, is to be

attributed to the very different nature of the foundations of
Eton and Harrow. It would appear that Harrow School
must have lost nearly altogether its character as a free school
for the parish. The necessity which is imposed on each boy
of having a private tutor would of itself be a formidable objection to the poor, if, as we understand the statement in
the Journal of Education, and as we are also informed by
the best authorities, each boy, including those on the
foundation, is compelled to have a private tutor to whom he
pays 20*l*. This is the sum mentioned as paid for a private
tutor by those who lodge in the head master's house, and
the same sum is paid by the boys who lodge in other houses.
In the Journal of Education, it is said, that it is the 'invariable
practice that each boy should have a private tutor;' and in
fact no boy can get on without one. This appears to us a
complete departure from the intention of John Lyon, in the
case of boys on the foundation.

The 'Orders, Statutes, and Rules,' as printed in this publication, are prefixed in it to a decree of Lord Chancellor Elles-
mere, made in the 9th of James I., on a Bill of complaint exhibited by the then Attorney-General against the governors.* It
seems that the Rules are not very accurately or completely
given. It is stated in the Introduction, that John Lyon ' adds a
singular clause, that the master shall not receive any girls into
the school.' This clause does not appear in the Orders, &c.,
printed in the publication of the Vestry ; and there is other internal evidence that the Rules of John Lyon are not complete in
this publication. (See the Introduction.) The original Rules,
we conjecture, are in the chest in which ' shall be kept all the
deeds, evidences, and writeings that shall appertaine to the
lands and tenements of the corporation of the said governors,
or in any wise concerning the corporacon.'

· The following summary of the proceedings in the Rolls'
court as to this school is from Vesey's Reports, vol. xvii.
(Case of Harrow-School, the Attorney-General *v.* the Earl of
Clarendon, Rolls, 1810, August 17th.) This information
stated, among other things, that five of the six governors did
not reside in the parish ; that they were not duly appointed ;
that few or none of the children of the inhabitants of the parish
or town of Harrow, have been educated there. It complains
that the children of Harrow parish cannot be sent safely or
properly to the school, on account of the number of foreigners

* We have compared the printed rules with the original in the Harleian
Collection, 2211, British Museum. In this MS. the rules are not immediately
prefixed to the decree, as in the Vestry's publication, which, however, appears
to be a correct transcript.

(pupils from other places), who are chiefly the sons of the nobility and gentry of the kingdom, and who constantly scoff at and ill-treat the other boys. The information further states, that the children of Harrow town or parish, if sent to the school, are apt to imbibe the extravagant and expensive ideas, as well as the pernicious habits of the young men of fortune admitted into the school. The information prayed an account of the revenues, the removal of the governors not duly appointed, and the appointment of others; with a reference to the master to approve a plan for the better regulation of the school, &c. The defendants in their answer admitted that for many years past persons had been chosen governors who were not inhabitants; but that they were fit persons, and no injury had arisen from it. That all the governors, not actually resident in the parish, can travel to Harrow for the purposes of the school in two hours. They admit that few children of Harrow parish come to the school, but that they have never been refused to be admitted, and have even been encouraged to come. They say that the school is a school for classical learning; that, however wise the intentions of the founder might have been, the school is not now adapted generally for persons of low condition, but better suited to those of a higher class. Such prevailing opinion, it is stated, is the chief reason why a greater number of poor children of the inhabitants have not attended the school; and some parents have alleged as a reason for not sending their children, that they lived too far from the school, and could not bear the expense of boarding their children in the town; and others have objected to the expense of purchasing classical books.

As to the ill-treatment of the parish children by the others, it is said by the defendants, that instances may have occurred, as may have been the case with other boys in so large an establishment; but that the masters have invariably repressed such conduct by every possible means. They admit that the expenses of foreigners are necessarily considerable, though always checked by regulations and the vigilance of the masters; but the children of inhabitants who choose to attend the school are put to no expense whatever, except purchasing necessary books; unless they choose to attend other masters, who form no part of the founder's plan. That, as to imbibing the habits and manners of others, or expensive and extravagant ideas, there is no danger of the kind but what necessarily arises from boys of different fortunes and situations in life being brought together. That more children do not come from Harrow parish, because few of the inhabitants are desirous that their children should be educated in classical learning: the defendants conceiving that this was intended as a school for teaching grammatically the learned languages; and not for the instruction of the children of Harrow in general learning.

The Master of the Rolls decided that the court had no jurisdiction with regard either to the election or amotion of corporators of any description; that where, for want of an heir of the founder, the crown becomes the visitor, it is by petition to the Great Seal that the removal of a governor from the corporate character which he *de facto* holds is to be sought. Mr. Williams, one of the governors, to whom a part of the school estate was let, was ordered to deliver the premises up, and to pay rent to the full value, if it should appear that the rent he had paid fell short of that full value ; and the relators were declared entitled to have inquiries directed, to ascertain whether the estates are properly and advantageously managed, with a view to prospective regulation, if any should appear necessary. It was further decided that the purposes to which, after providing for the sustentation of the school, the surplus income is to be applied, are partly specified by the founder's rules, and partly left to the discretion of the governors. But, as it appears that the application of the income is not in all respects agreeable to the directions of the founder, it was decided, that it is fit that it should for the future be fixed and ascertained by a scheme; having a due regard, on the one hand, to the founder's directions, and, on the other, to the alteration of circumstances that may have taken place since his time, and which may be such as to render a literal adherence to his rules adverse to their general object and spirit.

The complaint as to the alleged conspiracy against the parish boys was declared not to be satisfactorily made out ; and the reason given for there being so few parish scholars appeared to be that few of the parishioners wish to give their children a classical education. Any restriction as to the number of foreign scholars could not be consented to by the court, except such restriction as the founder himself prescribed. The school clearly was not intended solely for Harrow parish : it was for the gratuitous instruction of such as chose to receive the kind of education there offered, and for other scholars not of the parish who might choose to resort there.

The complaint as to the expenditure on the Master's house, which was one of the grievances alleged by the relators, was decided to be unfounded.

It was also said that the course of education and internal discipline might be altered by the governors, and that they are expressly authorized to alter the rules of the founder. But, it is added, that if there should be any substantial deviation from the principle and purpose of the institution, the visitatorial authority may with propriety be called on to interpose.

This decision appears, with one exception, to be a fair one, as far as the imperfect copy of J. Lyon's statutes enables us to judge. The governors are *not* expressly authorized to alter the rules of the founder. Elizabeth's letters-patent expressly declare that the Governors' rules are not to be contrary to the ordinances and statutes of J. Lyon, a clause which undoubtedly limits their powers in certain directions positively and completely. The school, it is true, appears to be a grammar school; and, therefore, if the inhabitants of Harrow want other instruction, and not instruction in grammar only, they must seek it elsewhere, or pay an extra charge for it here. It may be observed, however, that as the governors have changed the rules in many instances, and in some certainly for the benefit of the school, they might have taken the same liberty, had their views of education been otherwise than very narrow, as to the kind and amount of learning to be taught in this school. John Lyon's rules as to this being a pure grammar school are not more strict than John Lyon's rules as to the masters not being allowed to marry. The Master of the Rolls decided that rules should be made partly with regard to the alteration of circumstances since J. Lyon's time; which is a very reasonable decision. In conformity with these altered circumstances, the masters are allowed to have wives; and as the masters have had *their* liberty enlarged, it would not be unreasonable to enlarge the course of instruction which John Lyon (it is said) limited, or intended to limit, to grammar, *i. e.*, the Latin and Greek languages. The decision clearly recognises this power in the governors. But changes made in the rules of founders are made only so far as may suit the particular views of governors and trustees: they do not make them on any general or broad principle. We should certainly not be advocates for any change which would prevent the resort of foreigners to the school; but for the benefit both of foreigners and natives, we think that other things besides Latin and Greek should be a part of the regular school course, and should be given gratuitously to those on the foundation. And this leads us to the last remark that we have to make. The Master of the Rolls says, ' That the school was for the gratuitous instruction of such as choose to receive the kind of education there offered.' Nothing is said by the relators as to the 20*l.* for a private tutor, which we may therefore, perhaps, safely infer is a regulation made since that date, and clearly against the decision of the Master of the Rolls.

FLOGGING AND FAGGING AT WINCHESTER.

PERSONAL violence as a mean for correcting errors in judgment, defects in moral character, and the ebullition of passion,
although it has now been for some time condemned by the
good sense of the reflecting portion of mankind, is still
not only retained, but is almost the only regulating power
made use of in the public schools of this country. Whether
inflicted by the formal and indecent castigations of the master,
or by the authorised violence of the præfect,* or the more lawless passion of the stronger, it is the indiscriminate application
of what, as a remedy, is ineffectual, as a punishment inconsi-
derate, and as an exercise of power, cruel. A blow may inti-
midate, but it never can convince. Does it necessarily follow
that, because you are angry, you are so with reason ? It is
the business of education to form a manly and upright character, and yet, most inconsistently, an appeal is made not to
the fear of doing wrong, but to personal fear. And many a
father and master, who would scorn the character of a coward,
endeavours, throughout the whole course of childhood and
youth, to influence those under his charge by working on their
timidity. When Galileo was imprisoned until he denied his
theory of the earth moving round the sun, and the conviction
of his understanding arising from reasoning founded upon observed facts was attempted to be overturned by an appeal to
the infirmity of the body, he replied—' I will deny it, but my
denial cannot alter the fact.' If a boy errs from wrong judgment, we cannot understand how flogging will be the means of
correcting it. Such a proceeding is more likely to generate an
idea of the injustice of the master, particularly if it be accompanied by violent passion. If a boy errs wilfully, the object
should be to make him feel ashamed of his conduct ; but if
you inflict an ignominious punishment, the shame will be of
the punishment and not of the fault ; and consequently, if he
can contrive to commit the fault secretly so as to escape the
punishment, he will not feel himself disgraced by what he has
done. But supposing the same personal ignominious punishment to be equally inflicted for offences morally wrong, and those
which, in their own nature, are indifferent, but still are offences,
as being infractions of the regulations of the master, it will
follow either that those things, which in their own nature are
indifferent, will be considered as bad as those which are morally
wrong.; or that those which are morally wrong will be considered as venial as those which, in their own nature, are indifferent ; and as the offence is no disgrace, so neither will the
punishment be considered as such. In either case a most

* Præfect is the designation of the head boys or monitors of Winchester school.

melancholy confusion of ideas is the consequence, which we think we are able, without much difficulty, to trace in the character of many individuals. We cannot refrain from extracting an eloquent passage from Montaigne, in which he forcibly touches, in his quaint language, upon this subject.

' Ostez moy la violence et la force: il n'est rien, à mon advis, qui abastardisse et estourdisse si fort une nature bien née. Si vous avez envie qu'il craigne la honte et le chastiement, ne l'y endurcissez pas : endurcissez le à la sueur et au froid, au vent, au soleil, et aux hazards qu'il luy fault mespriser : ostez luy toute mollesse et delicatesse au vestir et coucher, au manger et au boire ; accoustumez le à tout : que ce ne soit pas un beau garson et damaret, mais un garson vert et vigoreux. Enfant, homme, vieil, j'ay tousiours creu et jugé de mesme. Mais, entre aultres choses, cette police de la plus part de nos collèges m'a tousjours despleu : on eust failly à l'adventure moins dommageablement s'inclinant vers l'indulgence. C'est une vraye geaule de jeunesse captive : on la rend desbauchee, l'en punissant avant qu' elle le soit. Arrivez y sur le poinct de leur office, vous n'oyez que cris, et d'enfants suppliciez, et de maistres enyvrez en leur cholère. Quelle manière, pour esveiller l'appetit envers leur leçon, à ces tendres ames et craintifves, de les y guider d'une trongne effroyable les mains armées de fouets ! Inique et pernicieuse forme ! joinct, ce que Quintilien en a très bien remarqué, que cette impérieuse auctorité tire des suittes perilleuses, et nommement à notre façon de chastiement. Il n'y a rien tel que d'alleicher l'appetit et l'affection : aultrement on ne fait que des asnes chargez de livres ; on leur donne à coups de fouet en garde leur pochette pleine de science ; la quelle pour bien faire, il ne fault pas seulement loger chez soy, il la fault espouser.'

And Socrates in Plato's Republic, book 7th, says—the lessons that are made to enter by force into a child's mind do not take up a lodging there.

Quinctilian powerfully reprobates the system :—

' Cædi vero discentes, quanquam et receptum sit, et Chrysippus non improbet, minime velim, primum quia deforme atque servile est, et certè, quod convenit, si ætatem mutes, injuria: deinde, quod si cui tam est mens illiberalis, ut objurgatione non corrigatur, is etiam ad plagas, ut pessima quæque mancipia, durabitur: postremo, quod ne opus erit quidem hac castigatione, si assiduus studiorum exactor adstiterit. Nunc fere negligentia pædagogorum sic emendari videtur ut pueri non facere, quæ recta sunt, cogantur ; sed cum non fecerint, puniantur. Denique cum parvulum verberibus coegeris, quid juveni facias, cui nec adhiberi potest hic metus, et majora dicenda sunt ?'

Quinctilian, while he reprobates the system of flogging children, never for an instant imagines it possible that stripes could be deemed a suitable punishment for youths of a more advanced age; but we have seen in one of our public schools (at Winchester) youths, and even bearded young men, com-

pelled to submit to the indignity of a flogging.   One great vice
inherent in such a system is, as the author just quoted suggests, the deficiency which must exist of a principle of conduct when the fear of punishment has been removed.   And so
we find it; young men let loose from school, particularly
those whose parents have neglected to exert their influence,
plunge into every description of extravagance; they know
no rule of action—they are ignorant of the reasons for moral
conduct—they have no foundation to rest upon—and until
they have been severely disciplined by the world, are extremely dangerous members of society.   What sufferings to the
unfortunate individuals themselves might be spared, by a more
humanizing and a more rational system of education.

Upon entering a public school there is no circumstance
which so immediately and so entirely occupies the attention and
thoughts of a boy, as the singular relation in which he finds himself placed with regard to his schoolfellows.   There is a custom
existing in all, or nearly all large public schools, sanctioned.
by length of time and invariable usage, by which the boys are
divided among themselves, independent entirely of the will and
authority of the master, into three distinct classes,—the
higher—the middling—and the lower.   The higher class, in
addition to each individual member of the class having a boy
allotted to him as a sort of personal servant, have the privilege of ordering and commanding to the lower, whatever
their will and caprice may dictate, and of enforcing those
commands by the united power of their whole body—
which being composed of the oldest boys in the school is of
course irresistible;—2. the middling class, although they cannot give a command except to some boy allotted to each of
them as a servant, are themselves exempted from servitude;—
3. the lower class are the slaves and drudges of the school,
performing the most menial offices, subjected to the most wan-
ton caprice, and often to the most cruel personal ill usage:
their condition is like that of women in uncivilized communities, tyrannized over because incapable of resistance, and whose
oppression is only bounded by the caprice of their husbands.

We will give a few particulars respecting the public school
we ourselves are best acquainted with—Winchester.   On
a cold winter's morning the unfortunate juniors have to rise
an hour before their masters to boil water for them to
wash in; they have to watch out of doors, without hats,
in order to notify the exact moment the schoolmaster goes
into chapel, in order that their lazy masters may be neither a moment too early nor too late.   If, after chapel, it
is the pleasure of a senior to enjoy a game of fives, half-

a-dozen unfortunate juniors are sent for, and although they
have not the pleasure of playing, they have to watch and run
after such balls as the senior has been too clumsy to strike
accurately, or has wantonly struck in another direction for the
express purpose of giving them trouble. Should any of them
be not sufficiently attentive or active in performing this duty,
it will be his fate either to be placed under the wall to be
struck by the ball, or to receive some blows from the bat upon
the hand, or from the clenched fist upon the head. During
school hours there is a greater, although not even then an entire,
equality, but the moment they are over, it is at an end. Instead
of going to breakfast, after several hours' fasting, the unfortunate juniors have either to prepare and serve their masters'
breakfast, or to toast bread for any of the privileged class who
may choose to order them. We remember having often seen
some twenty unfortunate juniors round the fire on a morning
with toasting forks of their own making, some under the legs
of the others, some poking their bread through some little
crevice in the mass of bodies, and others unable to get in at
all,—the strongest of course obtaining and maintaining the
best places,—while a brute of a fellow, with a long whip, has
lashed those whose strength or skill has not enabled them to
procure a place. As soon as this operation is finished,—for
which, if done ill, they are rewarded with blows of the clenched
fist upon the head,—it might be imagined that they would be
allowed to eat their breakfast in peace;—no such thing: they
are then obliged to stand at the top of the hall, there to be
ready to minister to the wants, whims, and caprices of any of
the seniors who may please to call them, and if they can contrive, while there, without knife or table, to find time to swallow
down their bread and butter and cold milk, they are lucky
fellows;—if they are sent on errands, this is often out of
the question. School hours, again, give the juniors not much
relief, as they are expected to have learned their lessons during
play hours, and we have just seen how they have been occupied. School hours at an end, the gates are opened, and
there is liberty for the boys to go out and enjoy themselves.
It might be thought that now, at least, the juniors would be
permitted to do so; no such thing. One of the senior boys
sends them to watch out at cricket, that is, to run after the ball
when others have struck it, without participating in the pleasure
of playing, receiving blows on the head, as usual, for any want
of attention or skill; or to play at foot-ball, that is, to be
pushed about, and to have their shins kicked at the pleasure of
the seniors. Well do we remember the dread that such orders
used to inspire, and boys would hide themselves, expose them-

selves to be flogged, or otherwise punished by the master, or even pretend illness in order to escape this odious tyranny. Although dinner is a more peaceful meal, supper is a repetition of break- fast; and bed-time, so far from being a time of rest, is often that in which tyranny is exercised to the greatest extent. Tossing in the blanket, tying toes, bolstering, &c., although matters which, when boys are of the same size and age, may be laughed at as puerile amusements, become subjects of more serious consideration when exercised by the older upon the younger, who are utterly unable to defend themselves, and who would be most soundly thrashed if they presumed to return one joke by another. (See Note at end of the Number.)

To the fagging system we think is mainly attributable the want of independence, both politically and in private life, which has characterized too many of our countrymen,—a servility without an object,—an unmeaning, unaccountable subserviency to the will and caprice of others. That in Turkey men should abase themselves in the presence of those in power, we are able to understand ; there is a bowstring in question. We can understand, too, the cringing of servility, degrading and disgraceful as it is, when a place or a pension can be obtained by the practice of it; but we cannot understand that habitual self-humiliation which is practised every day in society, where men without character or talent are receiving the homage of whole circles because they are in possession of hereditary title or wealth, neither of which the admiring crowd have any chance of participating in. The man who is habituated to be a slave is well schooled to be a tyrant, for he who has forgotten his own rights is not likely to bear in mind those of other people. The abject slave and the insolent tyrant are inva- riably united in the same person. The eunuchs of the East are a notable instance of this.

In Turkey, says a modern traveller, ' from the top to the bottom of the ladder is a gradation of servitude. The Grand Vizier kisses the Sultan's foot ; he bows to Mohammed. The Pasha kisses the Grand Vizier's foot : the Bey the Pasha's : the Aga the Bey's ;' and while the one party debases himself, the other ignominiously spurns the crawling reptile, which he is ready himself to become at a moment's notice to his own superiors. But a sensitive regard for individual independence invariably characterizes those who extend a benevolent disposition to all the world, and who would be grieved even inadvertently to wound the feelings of another. The humbling of the growing spirit of youth, which is the great ruling principle of our public schools, is every way objectionable. We cer- tainly should be careful to correct its abuse or excess, but we think that a boy cannot be too early characterized by a spirit of independence, a term which we use in the proper and good sense, and beg our readers so to understand it.

From the moment that the mind is capable of distinguishing between right and wrong, we would teach a child to judge of his own actions by this sole criterion, and never by the unexplained approval or disapproval of others. Let him use his own reason, and be assured of the rectitude of his purpose, and act boldly. Errors in judgment we would never punish; we would correct them by pointing them out. There is generally a delicate sensibility in youth of the nobler stamp of character, which renders them easy to be corrected in this manner when blows will either damp the spirit or render it sullen or incorrigible. The regular practice of calmly and kindly pointing out the errors which a child must necessarily fall into, will be more likely to check arrogance or over-weening conceit than any rough treatment. A blow is not a reason; and if no weightier argument is adduced, a boy with a tolerable capability of endurance is likely to consider his logic as accurate as that of the person who gave the blows: and although the fear of punishment may induce him to keep the opinion to himself, he still retains it to bring out when he can do so without the fear of personal injury. Mr. Bulwer, in his work entitled 'England and the English,' says with much justice,—

' The only moral principle at a public school is that which the boys themselves tacitly inculcate and acknowledge; it is impossible to turn a large number of human beings loose upon each other, but what one of the first consequences will be the formation of a public opinion, and public opinion instantly creates a silent, but omnipotent code of laws. Thus among boys there is always a vague sense of honour and justice, which is the only morality that belongs to schools. It is this vague and conventional sense to which the master trusts, and with which he seldom interferes. But how vague it is, how confused, how erring! What cruelty, tyranny, duplicity are compatible with it? It is no disgrace to insult the weak and to lie to the strong; to torment the fag and to deceive the master. These principles grow up with the boy; insensibly they form the matured man Look abroad in the world, what is the most common character? that which is at once arrogant and servile. It is this early initiation into the vices of men, which with some parents is an inducement to send their sons to a public school. How often you hear the careful father say, "Tom goes to Eton to learn the world." One word on this argument: your boy does not accomplish your object; he learns the vices of the world, it is true, but not the caution which should accompany them. Who so thoughtless as the young man escaped from a public school? Who so easily duped? Who so fair a prey to the trading sharper and the sharping tradesman? Who run up such bills with tailors and horse-dealers? Who so notoriously the greenhorn and the bubble? Is this his boasted knowledge of the world? You may have made your boy vicious, but you will find that that is not making him wise.'

This is all true with the exception of lying, with regard to which our experience of Winchester enables us to say that it was condemned in that school at least. In fact, it was the only vice which appeared to meet with condemnation from the public opinion of the boys; for the most blasphemous swearing, the most disgusting and indecent language, and outrageous tyranny, were of daily and hourly occurrence. In addition to the evils we have mentioned as consequent upon the fagging system as permitted at a public school, the health is frequently seriously and permanently injured; and timid characters are often so completely destroyed, as never afterwards to be able to oppose ordinary courage to the difficulties of life. By the supporters of the system it will be urged, that boys ought not to be brought up too delicately; that the knocking about and roughing of a public school is but a foretaste of the world they are about to enter, and well fits them to conduct themselves in it with spirit and propriety. We too would wish to habituate children to endurance; we would have them patient of suffering, of heat, of cold, and of fatigue; we would not have them faint at labour; we would wish to rouse the spirit, but not to dull the affections; we would not bring them up either as tyrants or slaves, to console themselves when slaves with the idea of one day being masters. To inflict an injury should be to them pain, and we would not have them submit to one in silence.

Force is in all cases brutal, for it is the mere effort of the animal uncontrolled by that moral understanding, which is the characteristic of a man as distinguished from a beast. Force therefore should not be the ruling power in a school, either in the community which the boys form among themselves, or in the government which the master exercises over the boys. We would have a boy comprehend why his action was wrong; we would therefore rather point out his error than flog him for it. As a master, we should prefer being known to the boys as a friend who had no interest but their own, and who was more ready to assist them in correcting faults in their character than to punish them—instead of being considered as a person of superior strength, whose will was in direct opposition to their happiness, and whose only object was to find out faults for the purpose of inflicting bodily pain. We would use our *influence* to induce the elder boys to let their intercourse with those younger than themselves, be characterized rather by kindness and good will than by ill usage and hard blows. With regard to the fagging system, we would use our *authority*, and abolish at once this odious and demoralizing usage.

REVIEWS.

A TREATISE ON ALGEBRA.

A Treatise on Algebra. By George Peacock, M.A., F.R.S., &c., &c., Fellow and Tutor of Trinity College, Cambridge. Cambridge, Deighton, 1830.

In some previous articles we have suggested methods of teaching the first principles of arithmetic and geometry to beginners. At the time, we neglected the higher science of algebra: partly on account of the very great extent and importance of the subject, for those who are to become mathematicians; and partly because it is extremely difficult to draw the line which separates the elements from the higher parts. For reasons which will appear in the course of this article, though the transcendental part of every one of the mathematical sciences aids in giving clear views of the first principles, in none is this so much the case as in algebra.

A description of the work before us in a small space would not be an easy task. We shall take the opportunity of presenting some general views of the subject, and then proceed to inquire in what relation they stand to the subject-matter of this article. That we shall be always intelligible to every reader we cannot promise; but, to the best of our knowledge and belief, such considerations should be understood (we do not say *admitted*, but *understood*) by every one who pretends to teach algebra as a preparation for the higher mathematics.

The general notion entertained of the mathematical sciences, namely, that there is perfect security and evidence from the very commencement, contains a sort of *petitio principii*. It is true only of a beginner who has already mathematical powers and habits: that is, of one who has gained what it is usually presumed can only be gained from the studies of which the assertion is made. Dip a mathematician in Lethe as to the *results* he has learned, but let the powers of his understanding remain in all the strength derived from the manner in which he came by these results; let him then recommence his mathematical course, and he will no doubt be able to propose objections, and understand the answers. He will establish every point as it ought to be established to the most critical eye of reason; and principles which are now deferred, not because they require foundation, but because the power of abstraction is not yet sufficiently strong in the mind of the learner, would be, in the case supposed, the most proper and easy ground-work. With the ordinary beginner the case is of course different. The same want of grasp which would prevent him from understanding the answer, also makes it impossible that he should originate the objection ; and if he is satisfied during every part of his algebraical career, it is either because care is taken that the difficulties are kept out of his way for a season, or because he is satisfied with anything that his instructor may say. Here then are two methods which comprise much the greater part of all teaching on this subject : the first consisting in the rejection, either temporary or permanent, of all the difficulties which arise from the confined views of the student ; the second, that of meeting them by authority. Among the latter, we include all such explanations as the student cannot understand; which if he receives at all, it must be because he has them on the word of those whom he believes to be wiser than himself.

Against both methods we have decided objections. With regard to the temporary postponement, it seems to us that the matter is not mended, because the difficulties for the most part are of such a nature that habits derived from other parts of the science are not those which are required to surmount them. To learn how to use a term or a symbol in a limited sense, though a most necessary preliminary, is not all that is required for preparing the mind to grasp the extension of its meaning, and to get accustomed to pause upon it wherever it occurs, to make sure that what is only true of the limited sense is not fallaciously asserted of the more general. We will take an instance from common life, which will place the nature of the difficulty before all our readers, whether mathematicians or not. We learn the use of the word ' to see' when we are very young. When we become older, we know that our primitive meaning of this term applies to perception by means of the action of light on the eyes, and at all ages we rest convinced that we cannot see in the dark. But in time we learn another use of the word, by the same habit which taught us the first; any conclusion which the reason can draw, even from the other senses, is represented as an act of sight. We may easily *see* that Rossini's style differs from that of Handel : there is no one who does not *see* the guilt of murder. But none (except a felonious punster) would advocate the abolition of all responsibility between sunset and sunrise, because he could not then clearly see the difference between right and wrong.

However odd the preceding illustration may appear, it is much to the point, because the extension of terms is one of the greatest difficulties of algebra. All jests are only very obvious fallacies, and may always be made to furnish illustrations of those which are less apparent. Its application is as follows : suppose it were proposed not to let children hear the extended* use of any term until they arrive at an age to understand the process employed; that is, the phrase ' to see' would always have its primitive and physical sense, so that it never could be used, except as connected with the idea of a perception which is impossible in the dark. No doubt such an education would close up several sources of misconception ; but it would also deprive the mind of several most important modes of invention. Would this, we must ask, be a good preparation for the common use of language ? We believe most people would answer in the negative, and we affirm that extension, if not learnt in childhood, would never be learnt at all. We see by daily experience, that invention of new words (if indeed it ever take place, in the strictest sense) is the act of *men ;* while *children* never invent words, but invariably extend those which they already have. Indeed, in common life, it would be difficult to show more than a single English word† which has *really* been invented in modern times.

While on this part of the subject, we really wish that the idea could be entertained without ridicule, of forming a dictionary of euphonious monosyllables and dissyllables, which have no meaning, for the supply of new terms when wanted. We doubt if ever a word could be thence brought into *common* use ; but had such a process been legitimate, we should not have had in *science* to labour through such words as numerator, denominator, multiplicand, &c., which are in constant use, and with unenviable correctness‡ have never been abbreviated.

The great difference between mathematical and common extension is in the apparently immense steps which are made by the former. We say apparently, because so convenient is the usage found, that the extensions have almost universally been made as matter of practice, before the principle was correctly understood.

Leaving the temporary postponement of such difficulties, as tending rather to increase than diminish the labour of mind to which it is thus admitted we must ultimately come, we proceed

---

* We have used this word here in preference to *metaphorical,* because we do not believe the latter word really expresses the way in which we actually come by the manifold use of terms.

† The word *cabal* (if the historical story be true) comes most near to the title of new-invented.

‡ One of the benefits of the diffusion of knowledge will, we hope, be the clipping of scientific terms by the great master of language—the common people.

to consider the question of the entire abandonment of them. It may be asked why we do not substitute new words in place of the extension of old ones? To this the answer is twofold. In the first place, by so doing, we of our own accord relinquish analogies which have been the most efficient guides to discovery. We require the substitution of a new word at the very point at which our previous investigation has almost removed the difficulty of extension. For, to the habits of a mathematician, as we have observed, the extension is no difficulty; and the process of reasoning and comparison by which the necessity for a new term appears is, *pro tanto*, the formation of the habit, for want of which the new word is proposed instead of the extension. The extension is always found to come very naturally at the end of a particular process: this process cannot be avoided, merely by proposing that its result shall be differently expressed. And all that we have said of new words and of words altogether, equally applies to symbols, which are the *words* of algebra.

The second argument, which is practically the stronger of the two, is the fact, that unless the student learns words as they are used, no matter whether properly or improperly, he cannot read that which has been written. Let us suppose a tutor and pupil to set out with a clear view of their mutual contract. The tutor has notions of his own, which he considers reasonable, in opposition to universal practice. The pupil, it may be supposed, wishes ultimately to read, let us say, the works of Laplace. If the tutor, knowing such to be the view of the other party, choose to persist in his own system, it is clearly his duty to make the other party aware of what he is about to do, and to give him his choice between Laplace and himself. And the pupil will do wisely to prefer the former; for since, take which course he may, he is obliged by his ignorance to act upon the authority of others, even in the system on which he shall learn a science of pure reason, he will do better to choose the greater authority. And he may depend upon it, in nine cases out of ten at least, that those who have most reputation* *among the learned* are the best guides to those who have not knowledge to judge for themselves.

This brings us to the subject of meeting the difficulties by authority in all its various shapes. Whatever we may think of this sanction as a guide to the road, we would reject it altogether as to the details of the voyage. The little bit of knowledge (be it ever so little) which is gained day by day should be a real and satisfactory addition to the working faculties of

* We must not be supposed to mean the popular estimate of scientific character. The Newton of the world at large, is not the Newton of philosophers.

the mind. . But even here we must put a limit to the student's rights. If he ever wishes to become a mathematician, he must not reject absolutely any proposition because he does not understand it. To make his own powers the test of what is to be learned or not learned, at the outset, would be equi- valent to supposing he has all (as to thinking power) that he wants to acquire or can acquire. How then can he reason cor- rectly (which is indispensable) while he is supposed to be without the power of rejecting what he thinks wrong? To take a case; suppose that the demonstration proposed is as follows : ' A is B, B is C, C is D; therefore A is D.' Suppose that he sees the two latter propositions with sufficient clearness, but that he is either dubious about ' A is B,' or even entirely of the contrary opinion. He must not receive this proposition on the evidence of his tutor, or of the treatise he reads, neither of which are worth anything, except where they produce conviction. Neither must he stop his course on this account. But, seeing that he has completed the proof of the proposition ' A is D,' except only that he does not receive ' A is B,' he is entitled to con- clude that ' if A is B, A is D.' He may then proceed with the subsequent propositions, remembering always that such as depend upon ' A is D,' or in any way follow from it, are hypo- thetical, and not demonstrated until the fundamental pro- position, ' A is B,' shall have been established. His reasoning will then be perfectly correct : for he must remember that reasoning is not the affirmation or negation of propositions, but the right deduction of them from one another; and that though the *certainty of mathematical conclusions* depends upon that of the fundamental propositions, the *correctness of mathematical reasoning* has nothing whatever to do with that circumstance. And the very process of retaining an hypothe- tical conclusion, and deducing its consequences, keeping in mind that the latter partake of the uncertainty of the former, is, for the purposes of every other branch of learning, as well as of common life, one of the most useful that can be devised, and one of the most neglected. There is a manner in which children (*sub rosâ*, we have done it ourselves) amuse them- selves with dominos, by placing them upright behind one another, in such a way that when the first falls, it knocks down all the others. This is what the older children must play at. They are reasoning correctly, provided they place propositions before their mind in such a way, that if any one fall, all its successors fall after it; and this is the plan which the deepest proficient must follow, as well as the be- ginner. For he must be a bold man who is not prepared to think it possible, even in mathematics, that he may to-morrow refuse to admit that, which to-day he considers unquestionable.

There are two *succedanea* which we have not alluded to, because the first is almost without advocates, and the second without defenders. The former is the rejection of what we may call symbolical algebra, on account of its difficulties; the second, its adoption without the difficulties of extension being properly placed before the student. The first confine themselves to general arithmetic, and entirely shut themselves out of algebra as a science of investigation of methods ; the second deface arithmetic itself by retaining arithmetical terms, without making it appear that they do not use them in their arithmetical meaning. We cannot agree either to relinquish the richest vein of mathematical science that ever was opened, at the bidding of the first; or to give up existing treaties with Cocker, at the pleasure of the second. We will, therefore, give each a question, and leave them : from the first we should be glad to know a purely numerical method of finding divisors of the second degree of $x^2 + 1$, and also a clear explanation how it happens that the—in their language—absurd expression $\log (-1) \div \sqrt{-1}$ will never arise, except when the rational process would yield $3\cdot14159$. To the second we propose the following as a question of pure arithmetic : supposing a pupil aged fourteen years to receive quantities less than nothing (arithmetically speaking) on the word of a tutor, how much greater than infinity must be the credulity of a newly-born infant ?

There are abundant attempts to simplify the mathematical sciences, and make them very easy. Of the elementary works which issue from the press, a large proportion professes to teach algebra and geometry almost without the trouble of thought. We will not call this *charlatanerie*, because we know that the original fruit of a man's own mind always appears so clear in comparison with what he has read, that it needs not even self-love to make him suppose it will be equally clear to others ; and it is as difficult to fix the extent to which simplification may be carried, as to define the boundaries of human power. Therefore, we are always pleased to see a new annunciation of a geometry or algebra with all the difficulties removed, because, though sometimes only a trap, it is as frequently the index of something like a new and original work, which, being in no respect harder than its predecessors, may add a mite to the materials for future constructions. We have seen within a century, that the works which at the beginning of that period were too difficult for most teachers, are now the elementary treatises of students. In another century, it may be that all those obstacles of which we now treat shall equally have ceased to exist. But of this we may be certain, so boundless is the subject, that however much may be made 'clear to the meanest capacity,' a field of difficulties will always remain to exercise those who will think upon them. The mathematician will never sit down at the limits of his science, to weep that there are no more worlds to conquer; and therefore those general principles which we now find it useful to apply to what we call the elements of algebra would immediately find their proper employment, even though every child in the kingdom were to become in one moment intuitively cognizant of all that is already known. Therefore, though morally certain that algebra is, at this moment, in spite of all that has been written, a very difficult science, we are disposed, instead of abandoning the causes of embarrassment, to put them fairly before the student, and to try what time and thought will do for him: convinced that by such an experiment only can we expect to find out what is the best way of proceeding.

Let us consider for a moment what is the end proposed in teaching algebra. Certain habits of mind are to be acquired, certain methods of calculation are to be demonstrated to be true, and made easy by practice. To obtain this end, books are written (we speak of school-treatises) in which from beginning to end there are no difficulties except what arise from mere complication of processes. That which has few letters is always easy; that which has many is always hard. How are we to explain this circumstance, consistently with what we have said of the real difficulties of algebra? In this manner:—so much of the incomprehensible as is necessary to the partial view there taken, is laid down in rules; and, what is the grand secret, the examples furnished to the student are so contrived, that they shall exhibit just what the rule is good for, and no more. The learner is much in the position of a boy set to tend tame cattle, which are used to a limited range, and to herd together within it: but this is not the way to acquire skill and strength to use the weapons which shall bring down the wild bull or the tiger; and we imagine our algebraical student would be in no condition to deal with a newly-caught example out of the mass which might be proposed. In speaking therefore of the greater part of our elementary treatises, we consider them as good for the instances they give, and no more; we have never seen independent power obtained by means of them. That which the student afterwards acquires he has to labour for afresh; he struggles with an algebraical principle while he is already deep in the Differential Calculus, and gets his first

ideas of a common process of numbers out of his treatise on
mechanics. All the sciences are taxed, each in its due proportion, to furnish elements of algebra; and the reason is that
the books on that science are mostly filled with useless rules,
in order that every name known to arithmetic may have its
counterpart in algebra, and that the second science may seem
a *literal* translation of the first.

This account may be considered exaggerated as applied to
many foreign treatises, and to some of those which have been
published of late years in this country. But we do not speak
of that small fraction of the whole which is called university
education, but of the algebra taught in the multitude of private
schools. There the proposed habits of mind are not formed,
because there is more of rule than of reasoning; the intended
facilities of calculation are not given, because, to save trouble,
a few rules are substituted for wide and difficult principles,
such rules being incapable of application beyond their own
letter, and almost sure to fail the student in the very first
instance in which he ventures beyond the little collection of
examples which is arranged for his use.

In the same manner as the learner is left to acquire what is
really useful in algebra from the subsequent sciences, as he
best may, so the works on this subject seem intended to teach
him what he ought to have known before, namely, arithmetic.* How to learn the former science without a thorough
knowledge of the latter is a secret we have not yet discovered,
though it has been attempted in thousands of instances every
year. Though the former is founded upon the latter, (at present entirely†,) or, in Mr. Peacock's phrase, which is preferable, *suggested* by it, yet the former is expressly constituted
and defined to include a large class of relations, which it cannot
be the object of the latter to consider. Arithmetic numbers
and counts, according to any rule that may be laid down;
algebra points out what the rule must be, whether any rule
can be devised or not, and if not, how it happens that the particular case in question admits of no rule, and what modifications it must undergo before the establishment of a rule
becomes possible. By arithmetic we add or subtract; by
algebra we find out whether to add or subtract. The latter is

* We speak here as much of facility of computation as of knowledge of principles. Few students who begin algebra have even the necessary practice in the
management of fractions to prevent very simple applications from being laborious.

† Formerly it was not so, but partly on arithmetic, partly on geometry. We
still retain the vestiges of this in algebraical language; but the connexion, according to Vieta, was so close as to place such expressions as $a^2 + a^3$ among the
number of impossibilities.

therefore a science of investigation, without any rules except those under which we may please to lay ourselves for the sake of attaining any desirable object. The hypotheses, the meaning of the symbols, however laid down, are in our own power : subject only to the great rule of all search after truth, that nothing is to be asserted as a conclusion, more than is actually contained in the premises.

But in drawing the distinction just alluded to, it must be remembered that every species of arithmetical *investigation* is a part of algebra ; and in reference to the distinction, we use the term arithmetic in the most common sense, as implying no more than computation by rules. But when we say that students do not previously learn arithmetic, we use the word in its wider sense, as implying the species of investigation which they might learn while employed upon numbers.

The first glimpse of the manner in which algebra breaks beyond the province of arithmetic may be, according to the widest notion a learner can form of it, very easily given. The latter is a part of the general science of quantity. Its province is number, and number only. In geometry, it enters in the form of proportion ; and the Fifth Book of Euclid, which is a purely numerical speculation, is the foundation of its application to that science, the investigations being conducted by what we must call an algebraical method.

But in considering the relations which may exist between one line and another, we find the twofold notion of length and direction. The first can be estimated arithmetically ; but not the second, unless we introduce the arithmetical science of quantities of an entirely different nature, namely, of angles. If therefore we ask for a symbol which will represent a line both in direction and magnitude, it is plain that we require something which is not in the province of arithmetic directly applied to linear quantity.

Let us turn to another magnitude,* which we are of necessity in the habit of estimating, and which we call *time.* We have here, by well-known methods, the power of numbering or counting ; but the relations implied in the words *before* and *after* are as much beyond the reach of arithmetic, as those of north or south in geometry. There is no arithmetical symbol which at once expresses a number of days, and also whether that number is to be reckoned forwards or backwards from a given epoch.

Here arises a point of comparison which, at an advanced

* The mathematical definition of magnitude is, anything to which the terms greater or less may be applied, and such that two things of the kind may be compared by a common unit,

H 2

stage of his progress, must strike the inquirer. When we speak of north and south, we have also an idea of an infinite number of directions which are neither north nor south ; but, according to our notions of this relation, they lie between the two. But when we consider time, we find that we have no complex idea connected with duration, which appears neither to express before nor after, but something between the two. We know *before, at,* and *after,* but no other modes; and this we say is evident enough from the ' nature of the case,' which words must always be interpreted to mean that we wish to have something to say about what is above our faculties. But whether, if we had higher faculties, such relations would open upon us, or whether no such thing would happen, is not essential to our present question. The bearing of the comparison upon our present object is simply this : that when we have acquired an algebra sufficient for the purposes of geometry, that is when we have symbols and operations which will consistently express and combine all the conceivable varieties of length and direction, we shall have gained notions too general to be applied to our ideas of duration. We can imagine a fixed point to represent a particular epoch : points on the left to represent anterior epochs, and on the right, posterior epochs, on the scale, as we should express it, of an inch to a year, or any other. But in the right line chosen will lie all the analogies which we can conceive to exist between duration and a right line. If therefore we were to apply a perfect geometrical algebra to the consideration of a question connected with time, we might conceive a problem which, though geometrically considered, should be possible, yet, *mutatis mutandis,* should have no intelligible counterpart.

We may take other objects of calculation in which a boundary, instead of appearing we know not how, or ' by the nature of the case,' to speak learnedly, merely exists by the common habitudes of life. A sum of money is either to be received, paid, or retained, and we do not usually consider any other possible circumstances. Here the analogy of geometry is true to the same extent as in the former case. It should seem then that a system of representing and combining relations of magnitude which is fully equal to the wants of geometry, may be considered as sufficiently extensive for those of every other subject in which calculation is involved ; but that arithmetic, which treats of absolute magnitude only, cannot be sufficient, because it has no means of representing relations which are as necessary to the specification of the conditions of a problem as the knowledge of the absolute magnitudes which it treats of.

A mode of viewing the subject so general and abstract as the

preceding would, we may be sure, not be the one which was first adopted. It is the characteristic of all the sciences, indeed of all branches of human knowledge, that the combined machinery of a thousand years may be made apparent in all its details, in a shorter time than was found to be necessary for the perfection of one of its parts. A shipwright's apprentice does not begin his career by burning a tree into the form of a canoe; his first step is not regulated by his powers of invention, but by those of perception, and any tool, however skilfully imagined, is put into his hands, provided he is able to understand why it is constructed. So we imagine must it be in teaching algebra; it certainly is so in teaching geometry. Analysis is considered out of the question for some time; there is no acquired power of investigation. Is there more in readiness for the study of algebra? We suspect not, but at the same time we think the writers of most elementary treatises must have been of a different opinion. Because algebra is considered an analytical art, it seems to have been imagined that learners must be analysts from the very beginning. And the attempt has been to make them analysts by rule; and to make them masters of every case that may arise, by telling them the result to which some of their predecessors have come in a few cases, without insisting on any one of the principles by which these results were obtained.

The present system might be abandoned, were it only upon the principle that algebra for the sake of its results is of little use, except to those who intend to cultivate mathematics to a considerable extent. This we think can hardly be disputed; how many of those who learn a certain portion of school algebra, say to quadratic equations inclusive, ever find occasion to apply anything they have learnt in the common business of life? If they have gained, which we hope has been the case with many, some quickness of calculation and extended range of perception in questions of number, it is no more than they might as easily have acquired upon a different system, which gave the same quantity of thought and reading. A walk for exercise, without any other object, may be taken in one direction as well as in another. But to look at our treatises, we should suppose that a certain number of specific operations were necessary to some daily application of the science; and that, at whatever sacrifice, these were to be first secured. This is not the case: take some of the rules on which great stress is laid; say, what is called division, involution, evolution, and the *numerical* solution of equations of the third and fourth degrees. We presume that many a person who has toiled at these operations has pleased himself by the reflection that at least he was doing something which deep mathematicians

were always doing, however little wish he might have to use
them in such a capacity. But we say that these rules are of
very infrequent occurrence ; that several of them arise out of
an attempt to create analogies between arithmetic and algebra,
which are forced and inconvenient ; that the mathematician
always proceeds to the same end in a different way, which
gives him a clearer view of the nature of the result which he
wants ; and that, take the whole *Mécanique Céleste* from one
end to the other, the three first-mentioned operations would
hardly occur once,* and might certainly be easily avoided.
The numerical solution of equations occurs in a few instances ;
while many simple principles, not mentioned in our books, are
to be applied in almost every page of the work mentioned.
And under this defect, the advantage of works written by men
so well versed in the actual state of analysis as Mr. Peacock†
appears conspicuously ; because, independently of any other
merits, they show what is actually taking place in the world
of science, and are not merely new editions of works which
have previously appeared on the matters of which they treat.

We have yet, before we enter properly on our task as re-
viewers, to consider how algebra might be taught to a mathematician who has forgotten the subject, but retains the
powers of mind he derived from it ; or, which is the same
thing, to a student who possesses a high capacity for generalization. But by this word hangs a tale. We cannot proceed without explaining what is the mathematical meaning of
the term. We are, of course, as true Baconians, suspicious
of general propositions ; we have heard many objections to
algebra altogether, as a science of alarming generality ; and it
is a sort of proverb that *In generalibus latet error.* This is
the only proverb that we like ; for it destroys all the rest, and
ends by committing suicide. What is such an apophthegm but
a very general proposition, so unlimited in the ideas which it
conveys, that it may, on some occasion, become a weapon on
any side, and gain force against some one position by the
authority which it derives from having been used in a thousand
different senses by a thousand different people ? Few very
specific propositions ever became proverbs ; which are garments
of conversation always ordered without measuring, because

* It is difficult to give the student an idea of the extent to which some processes, fundamental in appearance, are practically useless. The process of
finding the sides of a spherical triangle by means of the angles occupies as prominent a place in most treatises of trigonometry as any other case. Delambre,
who had perhaps more experience in this subject than all the men of his time
put together, says it never came before him but once, and then he could as
well have done without it.

† See the Report of that gentleman to the *British Association* on the present
state of analysis, published in the second volume of their Transactions.

we know that if they do not fit, they will stretch. As against algebra, the preceding saying of the wise has been terribly distended from its original dimensions; if there be any meaning in it, it is this: that general conclusions drawn from particular premises are likely to be false, sometimes at least. That is, we may not assume that what is true of A, B, C, and D, is therefore true of the whole alphabet; or induction, however numerous the facts on which it is based, is liable to fail as a guide to perfect truth. But there is another process to which the name of generalization is given, perhaps improperly, and out of which the generality of algebra springs. It does not arise from drawing conclusions wider than the premises will logically admit, but from arbitrary conventions by which terms in common use are made to signify less than their vulgar meaning implies, the algebraical meaning being always a part, and not the whole, of the common meaning. On this point much depends; when an algebraical term is converted (by express hypothesis for the time being) into the arithmetical term which corresponds to it, it is by super-addition to the algebraical meaning, the latter, as far as it goes, being already the arithmetical meaning. To the mathematician we have supposed we present the algebraical meaning; to the common student we present at first the whole arithmetical meaning; and, when the necessity arises, we show him the convenience of restricting the sense he has hitherto used, of throwing away part of what was necessarily considered as implied in the word, retaining only those propositions which are true of the restricted meaning, and of course rejecting those which are true only of the fullest meaning of the word. It therefore follows that certain formulæ may be chosen, not as consequences of any meaning given to the symbols, but as the definitions of the symbols themselves. For instance, we know that if $+$ and $-$ have their arithmetical meaning,

$$a + b - b = a.$$

But we cannot say that this equation implies the whole of the arithmetical meaning; for it only constitutes such a relation between $+$ and $-$ as would equally exist if the former signified subtraction and the latter addition; or, if the former signified the raising of a power, and the latter the extraction of a root, $+$ might stand for *to the right,* provided $-$ stood for *to the left.* Indeed the preceding equation merely expresses that $-$ is an operation of a contrary effect to that denoted by $+$.

Now what we insist upon is this, that there is no magic virtue in $+$ and $-$ by which the first must mean addition and the second subtraction. In giving our own signification to these arbitrary symbols, we are at liberty either to let them remain, subject only to the preceding equation, free to signify any two inverse operations, or to restrict them by further definition, so that each shall signify one only of two sets of inverse operations, and the other the other. Or we may further confine + to mean either addition or subtraction, provided that — means the other. Whichever we may choose, there is only one question for the student. Are the consequences asserted of the definition such as are logically deducible from it, and no others? Of the convenience or inconvenience he is no judge; it could never be supposed in geometry, that the tyro should form an opinion upon the propriety or impropriety of the definition of a straight line, provided he see clearly what is meant. And in algebra we should say the same thing of the student, even were his power of abstraction as great as we have supposed it must be, before this first and most abstract mode of viewing the question is presented to him.

It is but a small class of readers who would readily enter upon the development of the preceding views; they will find principles of this description in the work before us fully carried out. In justice, however, to Mr. Peacock, we state that all that is said in this article contains only our own opinion, except where the contrary is specially mentioned.

We will now suppose ourselves proceeding with a person moderately skilled in the processes of algebra, habituated to the most usual applications of it to geometry and mechanics, but who has never paid much attention to the real import of the symbols which he uses, and perhaps has never thought at all upon the subject. Many such we know are engaged in teaching, who if pressed to explain the meaning of any really algebraical symbol, say the isolated negative quantity, would not be able to do it to their own satisfaction. In most cases we have found the magic word 'conventional' applied to the purpose, and there the matter ended. Our object in writing this article was to give the ideas of such persons a good bewildering shake, to the end that they might see, though our limits do not allow us to place the whole before them, that there is more in the subject than is 'dreamed of in their philosophy.' We should call the attention of such a one first to the well-known fact, that the truth of his theorems depends entirely on the meaning which the fundamental symbols receive; and that if +, —, a, b, &c. had been used in other significations, there would have been no reason to expect that the same combinations of them which now express truths would have formed the theorems of the new science. This would be easily granted; but we should then ask, whether it might not be possible so to vary the meaning of the signs, as to make an entirely different algebra, which should nevertheless present exactly the same theorems in form as the old one, the forms having different meanings. For instance, when a and b are numbers, when $\times$ means multiplication, $+$ addition, and $-$ subtraction, we know that

$$(a + b) \times (a - b) = a \times a - b \times b.$$

But are these the only significations which can be attached to $+$, $-$, $\times$, a and b, that the above may be true? Certainly not; a very material alteration may be made in one only, and the theorem will remain true. Let $\times$, instead of meaning that the preceding and following numbers are to be multiplied together, mean that their sines are to be multiplied together, all other things remaining the same; the above equation will still remain true, and will become the well-known trigonometrical formula

$$\sin (a + b) \sin (a - b) = \sin{}^2a - \sin{}^2b.$$

A formula might remain true under an alteration still more at variance with common notions; that is, when the ordinary meaning of a sign is changed in some parts of a formula, and not in others. For instance, take the evident equation

$$(a + b) + (2a + 2b) = 3a + 3b;$$

let the sign $+$ retain its ordinary meaning, only where it is placed between the two sets of brackets; but in every other case let it imply, not the *sum* of the preceding and following quantities, but the diagonal of the rectangle constructed upon two lines represented by those numbers, with any arbitrary linear unit. The preceding theorem will still remain true.

Instances such as the above only exemplify changes of meaning which do not alter the truth of particular theorems: the question we ask is, can any change of meaning be proposed, affecting some or all of the symbols of algebra, but not affecting the truth of any one theorem or method? This may seem something like asking, whether two different languages might have all their words in common, but with different meanings, in such manner that by writing a treatise on astronomy in the first language, we write, *totidem verbis*, a treatise on music in the second. There is a reason why we should feel pretty confident of the negative on the second point, and another why we cannot be so sure of the same as to the first. The words of a language contain a vast number of independent conventions ;* here the latter term is properly used. Etymology apart, and considering words merely in the way in which children come by them, there is no process deducible from the

* The 'primitive convention' of language, like that of government, is a convenient hypothesis, but a dubious fact. Both are meant to preserve popular rights, against the assumption of divine attributes ; which are equally invaded by those who make truths of all their phrases, and laws of all their wishes.

sense which we affix to the sound *astronomy* which is any
guide as to what it is right or wrong, or even convenient or
inconvenient, to signify by the term *music.* But in algebra,
conventions which are really of the nature of affixing meanings
to arbitrary sounds or symbols, are few; while semi-con-
ventions strongly dictated by convenience, but not imperatively
deduced by logic, are numerous. The equation $a^\circ = 1$ is not
pure convention, neither is it strictly inferred: it is at our
pleasure to make a° stand for the logarithm of a; that is, there
is nothing against such a supposition in the elements of algebra, and we might with care conduct all future operations
conformably to such a definition. But it is highly convenient
to let a° stand for I, because these are methods derived from
the first principles, which will be continually leading us to
write a° in the place of 1; and in fact, we shall never be led
to a° by any operations of algebra, except where a different
and intelligible process would have substituted 1. Therefore
we say, *let* $a^\circ = 1$; but the word is a great deal more like
' I think we must *let* $a^\circ = 1$,' than ' We are perfectly free to
choose a meaning for a°, and therefore *let* it be 1.'

The smallness of the number of independent conventions
which exist in algebra may therefore render it highly probable that an equally small number of other independent conventions might create another science, differing in the truths
it expresses, but not in the manner of expressing them. In
like manner one sentence consisting of a few words might,
by conventional alterations of signification, readily be made
to give any other meaning. But the best mode of showing
that the question can be answered is to answer it; which
perhaps our readers may think we should have done at first,
but which we deferred because we thought the preceding considerations would give those who have not yet seen this view
of the subject, the necessary insight into our meaning. The
answer is as follows:—*

Let $a\ b\ c$, &c. indicate, not numbers, but lines, all in one
plane. Let each symbol be significant not only of the length
of its line, but of its direction; that is. let two lines of the
same length, but in different directions, be different things, requiring different symbols. Let $a + b$ mean the diagonal of
the parallelogram described on the lines a and b; or if they do
not meet in one point, of the parallelogram described upon
parallels to them which do meet in one point. Let $a - b$

* The reader may see a full account of the rise and progress of this system in
Mr. Peacock's report cited in the note to page 90, and a detailed demonstration
of the consequences asserted in the subject of this review, as well as in Mr.
Warren's Theory ' *Of the Square Roots of Negative Quantities,*' Cambridge,
1828.

mean the inverse of the preceding; that is, a being a diagonal of which b is one side, let $a - b$ be the other side. Let an arbitrary axis be chosen; and let $a\,b$ imply a line containing as many units as the product of the units in a and b, but inclined to the arbitrary axis at an angle which is the sum of the angles made by a and b with the same. Or in general, let four lines be called proportional, when, in addition to the relation between their lengths required by the arithmetical meaning of that word, they satisfy the following condition: that the first makes the same angle with the second which the third does with the fourth; and let $a\,b$ mean a fourth proportional to 1 (measured on the arbitrary axis) a and b. These hypotheses being made, it will follow that every theorem which expresses any relation of ordinary algebra will now express a geometrical truth; and it will be found that every formula which is true in the one algebra will be true in the other. For example, the formula

$$(a + b) \times (a - b) = a \times a - b \times b,$$

which in common algebra expresses that the sum of two numbers multiplied by their difference is equal to the difference of their squares, will now be a compendious representation of the following geometrical theorem:—

Let there be two straight lines (a and b) passing through a given point in an axis, on which an arbitrary line 1 is measured, and making angles α and β with that axis. Through that point draw lines as follows: (I) the diagonal of the parallelogram made by a and b; (2), a line parallel and equal to the other diagonal; (3), a fourth proportional to the unit (1), and (2), inclined to the axis at an angle equal to the sum of the angles of the diagonals; (4) a third proportional to the unit and a, inclined at twice the angle α; (5) a third proportional to the unit and b, inclined at twice the angle β; (6) the remaining side of a parallelogram of which (4) is the diagonal and (5) one side   Then shall the lines (3) and (6) coincide in magnitude and direction.

Now a little consideration will make it appear, 1st, that so long as all the lines are measured in one direction, there is no difference between this and the common algebra; 2nd, that there are no impossible quantities in the new algebra, or at least that none of the forms which are impossible in the old algebra are impossible in the new. For $a - b$ when b is greater than a, is possible, since the diagonal of a parallelogram may be less than one of the sides. Again, $b\,\sqrt{-1}$ must denote a line equal in length to b, and making with the axis an angle greater by a right angle than that which b makes with the axis.

One of the principal hypotheses in the preceding, namely, that each symbol carries with it its own direction as well as length, need never be made after its consequences are once established. For a line whose length is a, and which is inclined to the axis at an angle θ, is legitimately expressed by

$$a \, (\cos \theta + \sqrt{-1} \, \sin \theta)$$

containing explicit symbols of direction.

We now proceed to the use which may be made of this new supposition by a person unhabituated to take that general view of the subject which modern algebra has for a long time required.

The theory of the simple negative quantity has long been established on grounds which we have always considered clear and satisfactory, though not easy to a beginner. The theory of the square roots of negative quantities, up to the promulgation of the system which has been briefly stated in the preceding pages, was never considered by us as standing on the same species of evidence. Demonstration there undoubtedly was, of an order superior to what is found in any kind of knowledge except mathematics and mathematical physics; but it seemed to be of a kind more approximating to that of the latter than of the former. We are convinced few could say that experience was not a direct part of the ground on which their confidence in this branch of pure mathematics was built. To the nature of the foundation we did not object; for we never felt disposed to assert, that we would have all the relations of quantity deducible on our own terms, or that we would not have them at all. We could admit either Aristotle or Bacon as having pointed out one way to truth; but we should have taken leave to have dissented from either, if either had asserted his to be the only way, requesting him to add ' as far as he knew.' At the same time, we presume that it would always have been desirable to have the strongest kind of evidence ; just as it is to be wished that the celebrated axiom on parallels in geometry could be dispensed with, though geometry itself is not to be rejected until that can be done.

The question about impossible quantities will, we conceive, be set at rest by the system of algebra above-mentioned. Though it appears to rest upon geometrical considerations, yet that is mere matter of illustration, not of necessity. Let the symbols of the new algebra differ from those of the old only by accentuation, or some similar difference : it being understood that the distinction is to represent the difference of meaning. Our definitions will then be expressed by such equations as the following :—

Extended Algebra.		Old.

$a +' b$ means $\sqrt{a^2 + b^2 + 2\,a\,b\,\cos\,(\alpha - \beta)}$

$a \times' b$,, $a \times b \begin{cases} \text{To be used in such equations as the} \\ \text{last, with the angle } \alpha + \beta. \end{cases}$

and so on : in which, though the term angle is employed, it may be as the representation of the angle of *analytical* trigonometry, the definitions of which are not necessarily based on geometry. We have then the following argument :—

1. Since the results of the new algebra are always true, and have a direct arithmetical, or, if we please geometrical, meaning, as well in the case where common algebra is impossible, as in any other :

2. Since among the results of the new algebra are to be found all the results of the old, and since the ' new algebra reduces itself to common algebra (as far as the meaning of symbols is concerned) in all cases in which the disappearance of the angles, or (see preceding page) the elimination of the symbol $(-1)^{\frac{1}{2}}$ takes place :

3. It follows that all those results which have been deduced by what in common algebra are called impossible quantities, may be deduced by the same steps from the new algebra, in such a manner that every step between the hypothesis and the result may be capable of an arithmetical exhibition of the meaning of both sides of every equation, which, though complicated, shall be always intelligible.

This will explain how it has happened that no error has ever arisen from the use of the square roots of negative quantities, that is, from the application of the principles of numbers to things which were not number, or any (then) conceivable modes of quantity. It is as if a race of calculators had no conception of fractional parts, but only of whole numbers. They would call fractions impossible,* and would be surprised to find that operations conducted with these inconceivable quantities were true and intelligible, whenever they happened to give whole results. In time would come to be understood the extension by which fractions are formed from whole numbers, after which the name of impossible would be dropped. So, in the present case, the methods and results of an extension have been matured, before the extension itself has been formally made. And as the consequences of this extension are developed and methodized, it may not be unreasonable to sup-

---

* It is curious enough that some older arithmeticians (among the rest, the illustrious Cocker) call fractions *negative* numbers, and seem not to be very clear about admitting them at all. Vieta objected to subtraction altogether, and always, where he could, avoided what he called the '*vitium negativnis,*' meaning any subtraction, even of the less from the greater.

pose that the impossible part* of the new algebra will appear, and in time dictate the manner in which it is to be interpreted.

The length to which these remarks have run renders it necessary for us to reserve the remainder of this article to the next number. We have yet to consider in what degree it is practicable or desirable to make any part of the preceding enter into the method of teaching beginners. But we are convinced that no one will see the true meaning of algebra, who does not master the difficulties of the preceding considerations.

de Morgan.

APPENDIX TO THE CAMBRIDGE EDITION OF ÆSCHYLUS.

Appendix ad Editionem Æschyli Cantabrigiensem novissimam. Confecit Jacobus Scholefield, A.M., Græc. Lit. Prof. Reg. Cantabrigiæ e prelo Pittiano. MDCCCXXXIII.

THE 'last Cambridge edition' of Æschylus, referred to in the title which we have prefixed to this article, was published in 1830, and was a second edition of a work which is entitled 'Æschylus. Recensuit Jacobus Scholefield, A.M., Coll. Ss. Trin. nuper Socius et Græcarum Lit. Prof. Reg. Cantab. MDCCCXXVIII.' Now if a person of tolerable scholarship, but unacquainted with the University of Cambridge, were told that the Greek professor in that university (the successor of Porson) lectures on Greek 'to crowded audiences;'† that Æschylus has been the subject of two courses of his lectures; that he is a university examiner; that a passage from Æschylus, and generally one on which the professor has remarked, forms a part of his examination; the person in question would naturally presume that these publications of Professor Scholefield may be taken as a fair specimen of the kind of scholarship which now prevails at Cambridge. If the supposed person were then to examine this edition of Æschylus under this impression, he would naturally conclude that, in a knowledge of the Greek language, the University of Cambridge is much behind its continental contemporaries. This, however, would not be a true conclusion; for many Cambridge scholars—we might be permitted to instance the translators of Niebuhr, and the authors of several of the articles in the Philological Museum— are not only well acquainted with the present state of ancient learning, but also fully competent to improve it by their own exertions.

---

* Has it not done so already? In several cases where the exponent of an exponent has been not purely numerical, circumstances inexplicable by common rules have been observed.

† Journal of Education, No. IV. p. 245.

The faults which we complain of in the edition of Æschylus and the Appendix are not trifling; they are of such a nature as to show that a professor of the Greek language is unacquainted with the great progress which philology has made in the last thirty years, or so strangely prejudiced as to make no use of the works of his fellow-labourers. His notes savour so little of the scholarship of 1833 that we could have believed, while reading them, that we had fallen on some posthumous commentary of Tobias Damm, or a series of extracts from Dr. Butler's voluminous annotations. The University of Cambridge seems to be destined for a long time to feel the effects of her refusal to allow Porson to edit Æschylus in his own way, inasmuch as every attempt made by Cambridge men to correct or explain this poet has been a signal failure. Butler, Blomfield, and Burges, by their mode of editing the whole or part of his plays, have, as far as in them lay, rendered the study of the finest specimen of the Greek drama unprofitable ; and now, after all that has been done for Æschylus since the publication of the last of Blomfield's plays, Professor Scholefield comes into the field with a new edition, as the satyrical drama to the tragic trilogy of editions in which the son of Euphorion has been so unmercifully handled. Before we proceed to justify this general censure, and to show how difficult and how unprofitable it would be to study Æschylus in Mr. Scholefield's edition, we will make a few observations on the way in which this author might be edited so as to make the study of his plays both profitable and easy.

In the first place, then, we should have a good and cheap impression of the text and fragments by themselves,—such a one, for instance, as the Oxford reprint of Dindorf's edition, though the text of this is not altogether such as we could wish. A copious and complete commentary (either in good English or intelligible Latin) would also be necessary to explain all the peculiarities of construction, and to take advantage of the opportunities furnished by the poet's $\dot{\rho}\acute{\eta}\mu\alpha\theta$' $\acute{\iota}\pi\pi o\beta\acute{\alpha}\mu o\nu\alpha$ of illustrating the etymology of the Greek language ; such a commentary should also fully and correctly discuss the allusions, which so frequently occur, to the history, mythology, and plastic art of the author's age and country. Of the manner in which all this might be well done an elaborate specimen has been given by C. O. Müller in his edition of the Eumenides ; and the true method of correcting the text of this poet, and this is a point which our commentary should not overlook, has been beautifully explained and exemplified by H. L. Ahrens, in what Müller calls his *inhaltreiche Abhandlung,* 'de causis quibusdam Æschyli nondum satis emendati.' If Æschylus were thus edited and explained, his works might be made the medium of much useful information, and would at the same time cease to be a sealed book to the many in this country who pretend to have had the advantage of a classical education.

Mr. Scholefield has a very different view of the mode of editing Æschylus. In the first place he has published a dear edition of Æschylus : the Oxford Dindorf, a beautifully printed volume, is published at less than half the price of the 'last Cambridge edition.' Mr. Scholefield's edition is incomplete as concerns the fragments; bad as concerns the text; deficient in every kind of collateral information ; and accompanied with foot-notes, written in very odd Latin, and of which it is not too much to say that nearly all of them are either trivial or incorrect ; that they either contain nothing which is not already known to any well-taught schoolboy, or something to which a scholar will decidedly object. It often happens that critics and authors differ in opinion, and this is the case here, for we observe that the Professor says in his preface—that he has edited Æschylus, so that he may now be studied *optimo cum fructu.*

We do not doubt that any person moderately acquainted with the Greek of Æschylus will assent to the opinion which we have formed with respect to Professor Scholefield's edition. A few selections from his notes will, however, not be amiss, by way of proving what has been said. We will first make some remarks on the notes which are found in the first and repeated in the second edition, and then turn to the pamphlet named at the head of this article:—

Suppl. 339. αἰδοῦ σὺ πρύμναν πόλεος ὧδ' ἐστεμμένην. ' πρύμναν πόλεος, i. q., πάγον.' Professor Scholefield has overlooked the allusion to the custom of crowning the sterns of vessels with garlands, and seems to suppose that the height of the stern is the thing principally referred to.

485. ' αἰδοῖον εὖ ῥέοντα πρόξενον λαβεῖν. Vix potest esse *benigne loquentem,* ab Homerico ῥέω dico.' We should be glad to know in what part of Homer Mr. Scholefield has found ῥέω, *dico?* Wellauer's explanation is perhaps right, or at least intelligible, provided the text is right,—' de oratione regis benigne fluente dictum fere existimaverim.' Or ῥέοντα may be used in a sense like εὐροῇ. Pers. 593. ed. Well.

896. ποίοισιν εἰπὼν προξένοις ἐγχωρίοις ; ' πρόξενοι, i. q., προστάται, &c. Ar. Pac. 684 ; infra 940. Hæc fere Butl.' Professor Scholefield and Dr. Butler, therefore, suppose that the proxeni were the same as the prostatæ, or protectors of the resident aliens,—and this, too, in the face of the passages quoted by Mr. Scholefield. It is surprising that he did not

perceive that the relationship between the king and the public messenger of another state was different from that subsisting between him and the suppliants whom he had received into his protection.

Pers. 219. ' Retinui vulg. δράμνμα utpote ab ἔδραμον formatum.' The reason given for retaining δράμνμα is a proof that the elements of Greek etymology have not formed part of the Professor's studies.

Prom. 21, 2. ' Luc. xi. 64. ἀνεῴχθη τὸ στόμα καὶ ἡ γλῶσσα. Mox in 23—5. cf. locum pulcherrimum Deuteron. xxviii. 67.' We copy this note as a specimen of the numerous references to the sacred writings which the editor often makes. In this instance, at least, the references are perfectly useless.

Sept. 62. ' Vide Pors. Med. 523. Sed potuit Æschylus Ionicam formam retinere, etiamsi Euripides Atticam mallet. In Pers. 411. omnes in νηΐ consentiunt.' From this we infer that the editor supposes νηΐ to be an Ionic, and not an Attic form. Perhaps this notion originated in the following note to Blomfield's edition on Pers. 414—' Formæ Atticæ erant ναῦς ναΐ. Ionicæ νηὸς, νηΐ.' The Attic forms were ναῦς, νηΐ, as we hope all good schoolboys know.

We refer to the note on Agam. 993, for a specimen of the mode of translating Greek into Latin,—πλέον φέρειν is rendered by ' opem ferre.'

Choëph. 222. σκέψαι τομῇ προσθεῖσα βόστρυχον τριχός. ' τομῇ sc. τομαίᾳ τριχί. cf. 161.' τομὴ does not signify ' hair cut off,' but 'the place from which it was cut,' as will be proved by ἐπειδὴ πρῶτα τομὴν ἐν ὄρεσσι λέλοιπεν, Il. A., and Thucyd. ii. 76, ἀπὸ τῆς τομῆς, and by the obvious meaning of the context of this passage of Æschylus.

955. ' Casus autem felici jactu utentes retrocedent (*e contrario cadent*) iis (*Oresti et Electræ*) qui domum e mutatâ fortunâ obtinebunt omnia et videre et audire sperantibus.' This translation shows that Mr. Scholefield has neglected the meaning of the word μέτοικος, and that he has not seen that, according to his reading, which is perhaps a true one, the construction must be ἱεμένοις πεσοῦνται, ' shall fall out to the wish of,' similar to the phrases ἀσμένοις ἐλθεῖν, βουλομένῳ εἶναι, &c.

1000. νῦν αὐτὸν αἰνῶ νῦν ἀποιμώζω παρών. ' Nunc eum (Ægisthum) laudo *quoniam ultus sum*, nunc defleo mortem ejus praesens *et ab exilio reversus.*' Although we are unable to pronounce with certainty on the meaning of this line, we are quite sure that Mr. Scholefield's ' laudo quoniam ultus sum ' is not the meaning. Some lines may have been omitted by the transcribers; if the present reading αὐτὸν be correct, the pronoun refers to φόνου, and not to Αἰγίσθου; and αἰνῶ retains its proper meaning. See Buttm. Lexil. ii. 112.

Eumen. 668. ' τὸ δεινὸν, reverentiam.' Professor Scholefield
has very unnecessarily gone out of his way to make a mistake.
The next line shows that the words do not mean an *effect*
but a *cause* of terror—was Furcht erreget, as Müller has it.

931. νικᾷ δ' ἀγαθῶν ἔρις ἡμετέρα διὰ παντός.   ' Certamen uter
plus beneficiat.' This is certainly not the meaning ; the translation is inconsistent with the context, and cannot be forced
from the Greek.   The construction ἀγαθῶν ἔρις ἡμετέρα is the
same as καὶ τὸν ἐμὸν μελέας πόσιν Ἕκτορα. Eurip. Androm. 107.

The Appendix is characterized by the same errors and tri-
vialities as the edition itself.   In v. 425 of the Supplices, Mr.
Scholefield classes τύμπανον, ἀμπλάκημα, πίμπλημι, πεισίμ-
βροτος, ὄμβριμος, together, as if the μ was inserted in all these
words on the same etymological principle.   The word ἀμπύκων
gives occasion to this remark ; it is also added, that, in the list
of words given above, μ may be inserted or omitted.   But this
is not the case : its insertion is, in some of the words, necessary ; in others, such as πίμπλημι, it is omitted in particular
forms, such as the compound ἐμπίπλημι, where the reason for
omitting it is precisely the same as the reason for inserting it
in πίμπλημι—euphony, and nothing else.   This μ, however, it
is added, cannot be omitted in ἄμπυξ, ' siquidem ἀμπ. est ἀμφὶ.'
It appears, then, that υξ is a termination—a conclusion to
which, we think, few scholars will come.   We do not think
that ἄμπυξ is of the stock ἀμπέχω : vowels are not treated in
this unceremonious way.   We have the form ἀμπυκάζω, in
which the element πυκ is manifest, and this element exists in
ἄμπυξ with ἀνὰ prefixed.

In the Persæ, 205, there is nothing similar in the constructions βωμὸν προσιστάναι, πάγον προσίζειν, and κίνδυνον ἐκστῆναι.
In the two former, the accusative relation is to be accounted
for from the motion implied ; in the last from the entire
change of signification—ἐκστῆναι, with an accus., signifies ' to
avoid,' with a notion of fear implied—cf. Soph. Aj. 82, φρο-
νοῦντα γάρ νιν οὐκ ἂν ἐξέστην ὄκνῳ.

Pers. 152.   We have often had occasion to remark that
every language has an arrangement of words peculiar to itself,
which arrangement is one of those characters of a language
that is an essential and not an accessory.   It is the outward
form and representation of the order and connexion of thought.
Now in the two following lines,

ἀλλ' ἥδε—θεῶν ἴσον ὀφθαλμοῖς
φάος—ὁρμᾶται μήτηρ βασιλέως,

one would suppose there could be no difficulty ; we have placed
the two dashes to show where a reader who comprehends
the meaning would make a pause.   Yet Mr. Scholefield gives

the following note in his Appendix—'constructio certe est, ut videt Schutz. ἥδε ὁρμᾶται φάος ἴσον ὀφθαλμοῖς θεῶν.' Such notes are worse than trifling: they are mischievous, as they tend to prevent a student from ever learning the language.

Pers. 825. '*forsan* melius Schutz. e Schol. interpretatione legit κεχρημένον, *sapientiæ inopem.*' On this passage Blomfield remarks—'forsan tamen rectius scriberetur κεχρησμένον.' A proper study of the language would remove such doubts, and prevent editors from confounding forms connected respectively with χρά-ω and χρη-ίζω, or χρῄζω.

Prom. 241. ἀλλ' ἀϊστώσας γένος τὸ πᾶν ἔχρῃζεν ἄλλο φιτῦσαι νέον. 'Omnino dele punctum post πᾶν, cum ordo verborum est, ἔχρῃζεν ἀϊστώσας γένος τὸ πᾶν φιτῦσαι ἄλλο.' In place of cum .. est, we venture to suggest the emendation, 'cum .. sit.' Nothing can be more injurious to a student of Greek than this imaginary 'ordo verborum.' The right order of the words is that which Æschylus has given; any other would take from the force of the passage.

We do not exactly know what Professor Scholefield means in his next note (on v. 351) by his reference to the Greek text and English version of St. Paul's Epistle to the Gal. iii. 4; nor are we aware of any difficulty in the very common union of εἰ and καὶ which should render a reference to an Hellenistic writer necessary.

Sept. c. Thebas, 213. 'Restat in hoc loco difficultas, quam neminem moratam esse miror. Quænam enim syntaxis est τῆς εὐπραξίας σωτῆρος? Quod supplet Scholiastes, τῆς ante σωτῆρος certe desideratur. De generis enallage nemo dubitabit; sed propter constructionem subest corruptelæ suspicio.' Fortunately Æschylus has not put a τῆς before σωτῆρος: in that case there might have been a difficulty. Those who will read the words in the order in which they stand cannot mistake the meaning.

700. ita—utqui—studemus, we believe to be a solœcism. See Plautus, Curcul. ii. 1, 2. Quando Æsculapii *ita* sentio sententiam *utqui* me nihili *faciat* nec salvum *velit*.

Agam. 477. We do not transcribe this facetious note, lest some reader should complete the Professor's scale of comparison: Blomfieldii nota—pene ridicula; Wellaueri nota—magis ridicula; Scholefieldii nota—plane ridicula.

530. πόθεν τὸ δύσφρον τοῦτ' ἐπῆν στύγος στρατῷ; 'locus obscurus, &c. &c.' If any of Professor Scholefield's readers agree with him in thinking this an *obscure* line they have to thank him for making it so. It is quite clear that στρατῷ is governed by ἐπῆν, and that στύγος, like its synonym στὺξ (Choëph. 532), does not mean 'malevolentia,' but 'any cause

of abhorrence or fear,' and so construed the meaning of the line is obvious. We agree with him that στρατῷ is not *populus*, as Wellauer says ; but who will translate the line as Mr. Scholefield does ?—*Unde tibi supervenit hæc adeo ingrata erga exercitum malevolentia ?*

566. ' νικώμενος οὐκ ἀναίνομαι, *non invitus vincor;* quasi plena constructio esset, νικώμενος οὐκ ἀναίνομαι νικᾶσθαι. Sic in locis apud Blomf. Gloss. Sic etiam in Suppl. 58. ἀκούων δοξάσει (ἀκούειν).' Here we have the construction of a verb with a participle explained by the addition of an infinitive of the very same verb which is participially expressed ; and that, too, in the case of a verb, the peculiar signification of which in this construction has been explained by two scholars, with whose notes most Greek students are well acquainted.—(See Elmsley and Hermann on Eurip. Bacchæ, 251, [248].)

595. ' Sed apud Soph. Aj. 651, simile proverbium occurrit. βαφῆ σίδηρος ὥς.' There is no similarity between the *proverbs*, as Mr. Scholefield calls them.

1422. ' Constructio esse videtur παρυψώνημα χλιδῆς εὐνῆς τῆς ἐμῆς. *Opsonium clandestinum voluptatis lecti mei*, vel ut *Schulz, lecto meo cumulum voluptatis addidit.'* This is a successful attempt to pervert the meaning of a plain passage, by inverting the natural order of the words. According to the Professor, we have the following absurd sentence— ' Here she lies, and her death has brought me a secret enjoyment of the pleasure of my bed.' As if the death of Agamemnon and Cassandra would not have the effect of inducing Clytemnæstra and Ægisthus to throw off the restraint under which they might have previously carried on their intercourse, rather than make their cohabitation clandestine. The meaning of the passage clearly is—' I have slain Agamemnon in revenge for my child's murder'—(ἀγὼν νείκης παλαιᾶς, 1351,) but his paramour has also perished, and her death has brought me an additional, a subordinate, an accessary gratification of my pride, namely, ' one touching my bed,' that is to say, ' I have not only avenged my child, but I have also, by the murder of this concubine, indulged my jealous spirit.' Χλιδή we take in the same signification as in Od. ix. 888 ; the word never signifies ' voluptas.'

Choëph. 736. In regard to the old nurse's talk, which Mr. Scholefield has been pleased ' exscribere in lectoris gratiam,' we really do not see anything to object to in Mr. Dindorf's punctuation, which we suppose is included in the Professor's sweeping censure.

804. Professor Scholefield's translation of this passage proves how necessary it is that an editor of Æschylus should

be well informed as to the usages of the Greeks. In the first place, he translates οὐριοστάτην ' intensam,' by which, we suppose, he means (in reference to the first part of the compound) ' going with full sail,' ' full,' ' earnest ;' but this rendering gives no force to the second part of this synthetic adjective. In parathetic combinations both parts of the compound retain their full force, but the latter or verbal part of the synthetic compound is generally the most forcible. We do not think, therefore, that Professor Scholefield has been able to appreciate the remarks which Blomfield makes in his Glossary, though we are quite sure that this word is to be explained (as Dr. Blomfield seems to have understood it), by the application of ἵστημι and its derivatives, (as στάσις μελῶν, Aristoph. Ran. ; στάσιμον μέλος, Aristot. Poet. ; παραστάτης, Aristot. Polit. iii. 4.) to the formation of choruses. In the next place the Professor has suffered Dr. Blomfield to mislead him, as to the meaning of χρεκτόν: χρέκειν means ' to beat' in general, and its application to the beating of the lyre is only a secondary signification. We must remark also, that the flute and not the lyre was the instrument used by mourners. (See e. g. Iph. T. 146.) The passage to which he refers (21) χοὰν . . . κτύπῳ shows that the beating of the breasts is alluded to ; and that ·such is the case is clear, from another passage of this play, so beautifully and certainly emended by Ahrens, and by him restored to the chorus (444) ; for μεθίεναι χρεκτὸν γοητῶν νόμον is nothing more nor less than κόπτειν κομμὸν νόμοις ἰηλεμιστρίας.

Eumen. 497. ' Aldina lectio ἀναστρέφων non improbabilis est, eo sensu unde v. 23. δαιμόνων ἀναστροφή.' But in this sense the Greeks said ἀναστρέφειν πόδα, Eurip. Hippol. 1176, or ἀναστρέφεσθαι, Od. xiii. 316.

Our views of what an edition of Æschylus ought to be differ altogether from what Professor Scholefield has produced, and it is therefore needless to carry our remarks farther, as they would all be to the same general effect.

It is our object rather to direct attention to the imperfect and inaccurate mode of studying a Greek author, implied by the publication and republication of such an edition, than to point out particular errors ; though of these there is, in our opinion, a plentiful supply, considering the meagre and limited nature of the Editor's remarks. It is much to be regretted that such a book should have got, as it appears to have, a firm footing in the university of Cambridge. The better class of tutors, we are aware, will not fail to point out its errors and defects, but there are unfortunately many among them who must be content to take what is offered.

(118)

MÜLLER'S ÆSCHYLUS.

1. *Æschylos Eumeniden Griechisch und Deutsch mit erlauternden Abhandlungen von* K. O. Müller, Göttingen, 1833.
2. *Anhang zu demselben.* Göttingen, 1834.

THIS is the work which we have mentioned in the preceding article. A general commendation of Müller's contribution to the already long list of German works illustrative of the Greek Drama would have been sufficient to introduce his book to the English student without a separate notice, had he not been already reviewed by two of his countrymen in a spirit and upon principles of which we cannot approve. Müller concluded his preface with a protest against Professor Hermann's setting him right before the public with a dictatorial sentence, like a judge who has been asked for his opinion, ' before,' adds Müller, ' he has even in the least convinced us that he really possesses a clear conception of the connexion of thought and of the plan of one tragedy of Æschylus, or in general of any one specimen of ancient poetry; and yet it is to the attainment of such conception that, in our opinion, the efforts of philology at the present day ought principally to be directed.' Now it seems that this protest, and the remarks which precede it, have been considered as a sort of challenge by the Leipzig School of Philologers, and two champions have accepted the challenge of the Göttingen professor, the redoubted Hermann himself, and a former pupil of his, Mr. Fritsche. Their strictures have been answered at some length by Müller in an Appendix to his book, and we think satisfactorily. Indeed, the specific errors in this translation and the accompanying essays are so few, that Müller's two antagonists have, in their eagerness to find fault, objected to translations which are manifestly right, and have proposed emendations which, by their own tacit admission, are untranslateable. It is not, however, on the particular blunders of Messrs. Hermann and Fritsche that we would insist; Professor Müller is perfectly able to defend himself against his veteran opponent, and has wit enough to enable him to turn into ridicule the petulant presumption of his younger antagonist. We would rather direct the attention of the English philologer to the two assumptions virtually made by Hermann and his pupil; namely, that verbal criticism is determinable by and dependent upon the mind of an individual critic (in the present instance of Mr. Hermann); and, consequently, that it is not an art: secondly, that grammatical considerations alone are to determine the necessity for an emendation and the eligibility

of an emendation proposed ; and, therefore, that a comprehension of the connexion of thought in the whole work, and
a knowledge of the subjects treated of in the work which
may be derived from other works are not necessary for that
purpose.   Proceeding on these suppositions, Hermann has
made a series of attacks on those editors of Greek books, who,
like Müller, have ventured to act as if they thought it possible
for a scholar to emend a passage differently from Mr. Hermann,
and yet be correct in his emendation ; who have been bold
enough to assert that it is more difficult to correct a detached
fragment in Athenæus than a passage in an entire play ; and
parodoxical enough to assume that philology and archaiology
are in some measure connected, and not altogether independent
of one another.

As we imagine, from the sort of scholarship which has generally thriven in England, that our countrymen would rather
be inclined to favour the Leipzig party, we feel it due to our
conviction of the superiority of Böckh's method of editing
Greek authors, to make a few remarks on the worthlessness of
verbal criticism, pursued merely for its own sake, and carried on by a process of guessing, the certainty of which depends on the sagacity of the individual critic.   The uncertainty of emendations thus introduced into the text of ancient
writers is shown by the number of Hermann's criticisms
which have been already eschewed by their author; and the
barrenness of all speculations on the true reading of a given
text, speculations directed neither by nor towards a knowledge
of the subjects of the particular work, must be sufficiently
evident to all persons who will take the trouble of comparing
Burney's Tentamen (where the choruses of Æschylus are
altered to what was supposed, in the then state of Greek syntax, to be grammatically *possible,* in order to meet the exigencies of an hypothetical system of metres) with the arrangements of two or three of the same choruses in Ahrens' essay,
where emendations are introduced for reasons suggested by the
connexion of thought, and the general scheme of the poem.
But, although the results of the two methods of criticising are
so apparently conclusive in favour of the archaiologers, this is
not the only argument which can be advanced against the position of Hermann and his school ; their method may be also
shown to be theoretically defective.   For a method which proposes to do by guesswork that which may be done by system,
which proposes to render independent of art that which naturally falls under it, and which would reduce to the standard of
individual capacities that of which a common standard already
exists, must surely be liable to the charge always brought

against bad methods, namely, of not attaining the object proposed in the best, the shortest, and most certain manner. And
this is the fault of Hermann's school; the result has been an
almost universal failure of the disciples of that school where-
ever they have attempted comprehensive criticism. Indeed,
Hermann's own success in many points must be ascribed to
his having deviated in practice from the method of criticising
which he now wishes to vindicate and maintain. The first to
adopt the style of criticism which is so offensive to Messrs.
Hermann and Fritsche was the late Dr. Schleiermacher; who
showed, after an accurate perception of the connexion of
thought in Plato's works, that he was enabled not only to
arrange them as to their philosophical correlation, but also to
correct with some certainty the words of his author in many
corrupt passages. He was followed confessedly by Böckh in
his edition of Pindar, (see Dissen. apud Böckh, Præf. vol. iii.)
and Welcker, Ahrens, and Müller have subsequently applied
the same principle to the elucidation and correction of Aristo-
phanes and Æschylus. Of the labours of the last-named of
these scholars, we shall now give a short account, in order that
the English reader may be able to form a notion of the advantage of attending both to the subject and language of an author,
in preference to confining his attention to the words only.

The book, the title of which we have prefixed to this article,
is a new edition of the Eumenides of Æschylus, with a German translation and essays, containing much collateral information respecting the subjects treated of in the play and connected
with it. Of the text, we need only say that it is the most
satisfactory recension of a play of Æschylus which we have
ever seen. Müller has not, indeed, collated any new MSS.,
but the comprehensive view which he has taken of the poem,
and of its external relations, has enabled him to introduce
nearly one hundred and fifty corrections more or less important, into the text of Wellauer—(a considerable number of
which, however, he has borrowed, with due acknowledgments,
from his guessing predecessors); the effect of these alterations
is such, that the once nearly inaccessible Eumenides may be
now read without much difficulty. Not, however, that we
entirely agree to all Müller's emendations: for instance, no
doubt it would have been better to borrow in l. 204, ἦρχεσεν
from Wellauer, than to adopt, as Müller has done, Bothe's
ἀρχίσει; and he now prefers to his former reading πένεσθαι
(211) after Hermann, the reading τίνεσθαι proposed by Messrs.
Hermann and Fritsche, a reading which we consider to be
certain. Again, in v. 169, we would substitute for ἔστιν οὗ,
which is assumed from Hermann, ἔκ γ' ἐμοῦ, as nearer to the

unmeaning ἐκείνου of the MSS. We also do not like the
ἐκχολοῦσ’ in 823. But these objections are of little importance. Of the translation as a poem, it would not become us
to speak; that is a question for the author's countrymen to
decide. As an interpretation of the Greek it is very good, and
we have no doubt that it would convey to the unlearned reader,
the same ideas that the original calls forth in the mind of the
scholar.*

To examine fully and fairly the two explanatory dissertations
which follow the play would require a volume, so replete are
they with new views or old remarks in a new form. We must
be contented, therefore, with a brief description of their contents. The former of these two dissertations is an essay on
the representation of the play; in this, among other subjects,
the long disputed question of the number of the chorus is decided by internal evidence in favour of the number fifteen:
and the choral songs are arranged according to a method, as
new as it is convincing, which the author was led to by his
clear view of the scope of the whole play. In the other dissertation, the political circumstances under which the Eumenides was composed are first discussed, and in this part of
the essay we find some inferences as to the aristocratic feelings
of Æschylus, founded on passages from his writings which we
do not consider sufficient or satisfactory. We do not discover
anything in the account given in the Persæ of the landing on
Psyttaleia which should prove that the poet was ‘a warm par-
tizan of Aristeides;’ nor can we infer from the observation of
the messenger, (Pers. 341) ἀνδρῶν γὰρ ὄντων ἕρκος ἐστὶν ἀσφαλές,
that Æschylus disapproved of Themistocles’ plan of fortifying
Athens and the Peiræus, or that he was generally ‘an opponent’ of that statesman (see Müller, pp. 119, 120). Our
author next proceeds to discuss the Greek notions of the duty
of avenging the murder of one's relations, the pollution incurred
by the murderer, the mode of washing out the stain of blood,
and other points connected with the criminal law of Athens.
And in this part of the essay, which is somewhat lengthy, although there is little which is absolutely new, there is much
that deserves the attention of the student of Greek antiquities,
on account of the methodical arrangement of the authorities
and of the application of the discussion to the full explanation
of the latter part of the play. In the third part of the second
essay, which treats of the Eumenides in a religious point of
view, we have principally to remark the new light thrown upon

---

* There are, however, a few mistranslations. For instance, we would substitute for Müller's translation of l. 931, the following—doch überwältigt
Zeus. . . . und der Wackeren Streit, der unsre, für immer gesiegt hat.

the Œdipus Coloneus of Sophocles, by the exhibition of the hero of the piece as a person devoted to the Demeter Erinnys (Müller, p. 169, *seqq.*), and the most ingenious and convincing development of the idea of Zeus-soter, as the predominating notion in the whole trilogy (p. 186, *seqq.*). The fourth section is taken up with an application to the Oresteia of certain æsthetical principles, which have been long admitted and adopted on the continent : and this we consider, though perhaps the least original, at all events the most instructive part of the essay to him who, following Hermann's mode of reading a Greek play for the words only, has never arrived at a full conception of the beautiful unity of an Æschylean tragedy as a work of art, and of the mutual dependence and harmony of its apparently unconnected parts.

In concluding this brief account of what Müller has done for Æschylus, we hope our readers will not be satisfied with our concise description of his work, but will study it themselves. We are sure, they will unite with us in thinking that it will be a new and not undesirable event in the history of British philology when a work shall appear from one of our professors, exhibiting as much taste, learning, and good sense as the Göttingen edition of the Eumenides.

ELEGANTIÆ LATINÆ.

Elegantiæ Latinæ ; or Rules and Exercises illustrative of Elegant Latin Style, &c.

To be able to write Latin prose with accuracy is an acquirement, which, even at the present day, will not be undervalued by any good scholar. Indeed the advantages derived from the labour necessary for this attainment appear to be one of the best parts of our Latin studies. The occasions for turning this acquisition to any practical use may be rare, yet in endeavouring to imitate the style of the best Latin authors, we gradually acquire a more correct knowledge of the precise signification of the words, and a delicate perception of the idiom of the language, as well as of what is harmonious and proper in the structure of its sentences. We are, consequently, better enabled to read, understand, and enjoy the Roman writers. The truth of these remarks will not perhaps be questioned; and if they are correct, they show how necessary it is that every learner who is desirous of something more than a mere smattering of Latin should devote a considerable portion of his time to composition in that language.

Now let us consider what assistance towards the formation

of a pure Latin style can be derived from such works as the Elegantiæ Latinæ. A correct and appropriate mode of expressing our ideas in Latin can never, we venture to affirm, be acquired by the study of mere rules and their exemplification ; the assistance which such rules give is hardly worth mentioning compared with that which may be obtained from a well-conducted practice of translation and retranslation. In order to be able to write Latin, or any other foreign language, the memory must be well stored with words; there must be a readiness and facility in using them ; a clear conception of their peculiar and distinctive meanings ; judgment must be exercised in selecting one in preference to another ; and they must be arranged in an idiomatic and harmonious order. Now how is it possible that all this can be effected by rules, or how can any exemplification of rules be sufficiently extensive, or of such a nature, as to furnish the student with all these requisites ? But the method of double translation, especially when under the direction of an able teacher, is nearly sufficient of itself for all the purposes which we have mentioned. By means of such translations a large store of words is laid up, their significations are distinguished, the propriety and harmony of connexion and arrangement are observed, and the ear itself is gradually trained to the rhythm of the language.

In turning English exercises into Latin, as an exemplification of some rule, the student may perhaps, so far as the rule directs him, write correctly ; but how is he to perform that part of the example for which no direction has been given ? We cannot suppose that he is already prepared for this ; because this supposes that he can write Latin, and· if so, exercises are unnecessary. Nor is this all ; for as there are in every English sentence, proposed as an example, subordinate parts, for which no rule is given, and as these must be generally more numerous than those to which the rule itself applies, the consequence is that such parts will often be translated incorrectly, and more time will be employed upon this incorrect writing than upon that which is intended to exemplify the rule. Under such a system it is not likely that the student will ever acquire a pure Latin style. We will explain what has been said by a particular instance. The first rule in the Elegantiæ Latinæ is, that the word *vir* is used when the praise or excellence of any one is mentioned ; and this is the example :—

· ' A man of the greatest virtue and honour has been cruelly put to death by a man of the most abandoned character.'

There can be little doubt that the student would here use the word *vir* for a man of *the greatest virtue and honour ;* and

homo when translating a *man of the most abandoned character ;* but what is he to do when he comes to the other parts of
the sentence—how is he to know what Latin answers to the
English, and what should be the arrangement of the words?
If he cannot manage all this, most of what is written will be
miserably incorrect and barbarous; and if he can, such exercises will be of little or no use.

There is also an objection to the manner in which the examples of the Elegantiæ Latinæ have been selected. The language of Cicero is that which is usually taken as the standard,
and it is to the imitation of this author's lucid arrangement and
flowing periods that writers of modern Latin are generally ad-
vised to apply themselves. But many of these exercises are
taken from other authors; and in some cases even from poets:
this appears to be injudicious, because such exercises cannot
enable the student to acquire that style by which his future
progress in the language will be estimated; nor will he, by the
promiscuous use or imitation of various styles, become thoroughly acquainted with the distinctive peculiarities of any
one. Perhaps even the common idiomatic expressions of the
language will not be impressed upon his mind in such strong
and marked characters, as if he were thoroughly master of
one good author. The language of some particular author
should first be fixed upon as a model for the young scholar's
imitation ; and as Cicero is not only the most copious Latin
writer, but as his works offer so much variety in the subject
matter, they seem best adapted for the purpose.

Notwithstanding these objections, the Elegantiæ Latinæ
contain many good remarks; and it is probable that these
Rules and Exercises may be used with advantage, in connexion
with the constant practice of translation and retranslation.
But it would be a pity that any person should spend his time
and labour upon these Exercises, in any other way than that
which we have just suggested, with the fallacious expectation
of thus acquiring a pure Latin style.

We concur pretty nearly in the remarks of Mr. Kenrick
prefixed to his ' Introduction to Greek Prose Composition,
Part II.   Syntax.' *

' It is an inconvenience which attends all teaching of languages
by short examples, that the connexion is necessarily destroyed; and
as no other language has such a perfect and beautiful continuity by
means of its particles as the Greek, none suffer so much by the destruction of the original integrity of a period. The best remedy for
this unavoidable inconvenience is to intermix double translations
of longer passages with the use of the Exercise Book. Double

* London: John Murray, Albemarle-Street. 1834.

translation alone does not fix the attention with sufficient distinctness on the rules of construction; the Exercise Book alone may teach the rules of construction thoroughly, but will never give the genuine colour of antiquity to the style.'

Mr. Kenrick, in these Exercises, has frequently given a little assistance to the learner in foot-notes, independent of the general precept or rule placed at the head of each series of exercises. These foot-notes have apparently been added with the view of obviating the difficulty already stated, with respect to the Elegantiæ Latinæ, by aiding the student, as far as it is practicable or desirable, in rendering that part of the example which does not come under the rule. This seems a good plan; but even with this aid, some pupils will be much embarrassed with those parts of the sentence to which the rule does not apply.

We exhort those who are using the Elegantiæ Latinæ *alone,* to adopt some more efficient system, and to save themselves or their pupils the bitter disappointment of labouring hard for an object which, in this way at least, we do not believe to be attainable. Of all those who have spent many years on the study of Latin, and even on the practice of Latin composition, how few are there who can write a page of Latin with tolerable ease and accuracy; and still fewer are those who have derived from this discipline the advantages which would attend it, if followed up on a good system. To attempt to write a foreign language, when we make the attempt on sound and rational principles, is a sure mode of getting a better insight into the language, even if our actual proficiency in writing it should never be very great. But under a judicious system of teaching Latin, such as once prevailed in this country, before dictionaries were known and rules invented, we believe that the power of reading a good Latin author, and of writing tolerably good Latin, will always go together.

THE TEACHER.

The Teacher; or Moral Influences employed in the Instruc- *tion of the Young. Intended chiefly to assist Young* *Teachers in organizing and conducting their Schools.* By Jacob Abbott, Principal of Mount Vernon School. Revised by the Rev. Charles Mayo, LL.D., late Fellow of St. John's College, Oxford. London. Seeley and Sons.

In the Preface with which Dr. Mayo has introduced this little volume to the English reader, we find the following passage:

' Whenever improved principles of popular education are advocated, this difficulty is invariably started,—" Where shall we find persons competent to execute these views?" Men must be trained, they must be taught to teach, educated to educate. We have had enough of books adapted to disguise the ignorance of the teacher and perpetuate that of the pupil; we must now form *men;* we must bring the living mind in contact with mind, the living heart in contact with the heart.'

Judging from the evidence afforded by Mr. Abbott's book, we should say, that in his case the want here expressed has been satisfactorily supplied; that he *has* thus trained himself to be a skilful teacher; and that he has not only acquired the art of conducting the education of children upon sound and rational principles, but has also succeeded, to a considerable degree, in explaining his views and recommending his plans to the adoption or imitation of other teachers.

The business of teaching is entered upon by different persons with very different feelings: some few are led to adopt this profession from a real love for it, but by far the larger number of instructors regard the labour as an odious drudgery.

In a great majority of cases, those who are forced by circumstances to pursue a course of active industry have had the particular branch which each has adopted, determined by accident rather than by any predilection for the employment. It may, and doubtless often does happen, that the profession embraced is even disagreeable to the individual; and where this feeling is not overcome, it will be useless to expect any great success. In every case the indulgence of such feelings of dissatisfaction is unwise; but with those who, through the chances of life, have been led to undertake the duty of teaching, it is worse, and may be pronounced even criminal, since it unfits them for the performance of a duty, on the conscientious discharge of which depends the formation of the characters of numbers who, in their turn, will influence the welfare of society.

It is the principal object of Mr. Abbott, to show how the labour of teaching may be converted into a pleasing and exciting occupation. This end he accomplished in his own case, by calling into exercise his ingenuity for devising plans by which his scholars might be converted into instruments for assisting in their own instruction. He provided for himself a continual fund of amusement by contriving means for acting through the instrumentality of others, and of thus accomplishing a great effect by slight efforts of his own; the source of the pleasure thus attained is described as follows :—

' Looking at an object to be accomplished, or an evil to be remedied, then studying its nature and extent, and devising and executing some means for effecting the purpose desired, is, in all cases, a source of pleasure ; especially when, by the process, we bring to view or to operation new powers, or powers heretofore hidden, whether they are our own powers or those of objects upon which we act. Experimenting has a sort of magical fascination for all. Some do not like the trouble of making preparation, but all are eager to see the results. Contrive a new machine, and everybody will be interested to witness or to hear of its operation ; develope any heretofore unknown properties of matter, or secure some new useful effect from laws which men have not hitherto employed for their purposes, and the interest of all around you will be excited to observe your results ; and, especially, you will yourself take a deep and permanent pleasure in guiding and controlling the power you have thus obtained.

' This is peculiarly the case with experiments upon mind, or experiments for producing effects through the medium of voluntary acts of the human mind, so that the contriver must take into consideration the laws of mind in forming his plans. To illustrate this by rather a childish case : I once knew a boy who was employed by his father to remove all the loose small stones which, from the peculiar nature of the ground, had accumulated in the road before the house. He was to take them up and throw them over into the pasture across the way. He soon got tired of picking them up one by one, and sat down upon the bank to try to devise some better means of accomplishing his work ; he at length conceived and adopted the following plan. He set up in the pasture a narrow board for a target, or, as boys would call it, a mark, and then collecting all the boys in the neighbourhood, he proposed to them an amusement, which boys are always ready for, firing at a mark. I need not say that the stores of ammunition in the street were soon exhausted, the boys working for their leader when they supposed they were only finding amusement for themselves.

' Here now is experimenting upon the mind : the production of useful effect with rapidity and ease, by the intervention of proper instrumentality ; the conversion, by means of a little knowledge of human nature, of that which would have otherwise been dull and fatiguing labour, into a most animating sport, giving pleasure to twenty instead of tedious labour to one. Now the contrivance and execution of such plans is a source of positive pleasure ; it is always pleasant to bring the properties and powers of matter into requisition to promote our designs, but there is a far higher pleasure in controlling, and guiding, and moulding to our purpose the movements of mind.'

The principle which Mr. Abbott has here familiarly exemplified must always, in a greater or less degree, be called into action for the governing of communities, and there can be no good reason why that which is found so efficacious, or, more properly speaking, so necessary, in carrying forward the operations of government, should not be also efficacious in the management of that little world,—a school. The element to be acted on is the same in both cases, with this difference only, that the minds of children are more easily acted upon through the greater degree of deference and respect which they entertain towards a judicious teacher, than is usually felt by masses of grown up men for those by whom they are restrained and directed.

A great number of plans are described in this volume by which the ends of interesting the teacher, and at the same time of securing the co-operation of the scholars, are said to have been attained. These plans may all of them have been judicious in their conception and successful in their application, under the circumstances in which they were applied. We do not, however, think they would be equally successful in cases where the previous social discipline of the children in their parents' houses may have been different from that pursued towards those who were the subjects of Mr. Abbott's plans. This, however, is of small importance. If the principle for which Mr. Abbott contends be correct, it is comparatively of little moment that the plans by which that principle has been developed in one case are not strictly applicable to all other cases. The object of the author appears to be anything rather than that of prescribing unvarying rules for circumstances which must be varying; his object is explained to be principally the imparting of interest to the business of teaching, and it would in fact be defeated by the adoption of any unvarying system, since no man can be supposed to take so great an interest in following out the plans of others, as in testing the efficacy of methods which are the produce of his own invention.

The object of teachers must be the same in all cases—that of giving knowledge and forming the pupil's character. It is in the means of pursuing that object that the invention of instructors must be tasked; and the point to be steadily kept in view—that of interesting both teachers and pupils in their mutual labours—will perhaps be best attained not only by each instructor adopting his own plans, but also by producing as constant a variety in the mode of executing those plans as is consistent with the steady pursuit of the object to be attained. This position has been well exemplified by Mr. Abbott, in the following passage :—

' Intellectual effort, in new and constantly varied modes, is in itself a pleasure, and this pleasure the teacher may deepen and increase very easily by a little dexterous management; designed to awaken curiosity and concentrate attention. It ought, however, to be constantly borne in mind, that this variety should be confined to the modes of pursuing an object which is permanent and constant, and steadily pursued. For instance, if a little class are to be taught simple addition, after the process is once explained, which may be done perhaps in two or three lessons, they will need many days of patient practice to render it familiar, to impress it firmly in their recollection, and to enable them to work with rapidity. Now this object must be steadily pursued. It would be very unwise for the teacher to say to himself, my class are tired of addition, I must carry them on to subtraction, or give them some other study. It would be equally unwise to keep them many days performing example after example, in monotonous succession, each lesson a mere repetition of the last. He must steadily pursue his object of familiarising them fully with this elementary process, but he may give variety and spirit to the work by changing occasionally the modes. One week he may dictate examples to them, and let them come together to compare their results, one of the class being appointed to keep a list of all who are correct, each day. At another time, each one may write an example, which he may read aloud to all the others, to be performed and brought in at the next time. Again, he may let them work on paper, with pen and ink, that he may see how few mistakes they make, as mistakes in ink cannot be easily removed. He may excite interest by devising ingenious examples, such as finding out how much all the numbers from one to fifty will make when added together, or the amount of the ages of the whole classes, or any such example, the result of which they might feel a little interest in learning. Thus the object is steadily pursued, though the means of pursuing it are constantly changing. We have the advantage of regular progress in the acquisition of knowledge truly valuable, while this progress is made with all the spirit and interest which variety can give.

'The necessity of making such efforts as this, however, to keep up the interest of the class in their work, and to make it pleasant to them, will depend altogether upon circumstances, or rather it will vary much with circumstances. A class of pupils, somewhat advanced in their studies, and understanding and feeling the value of knowledge, will need very little of such effort as this, while young and giddy children, who have been accustomed to dislike books and school, and everything connected with them, will need more. It ought, however, in all cases to be made a means, not an end;—the means to lead on a pupil to an interest in progress in 'knowledge itself, which is, after all, the great motive which ought to be brought to operate in the school-room as soon and as extensively as possible.'

It is not intended by the limitation in the last paragraph to recommend that means of giving interest to the studies of older pupils should be neglected; and that, as regards them, reliance should be placed altogether upon the desire of extending their amount of knowledge. On the contrary, it is expressly recommended, that as frequently as possible the connexion between their studies and the practical business of life should be taught and exemplified, by seizing upon the occurrences which are passing in the world, and showing in what manner the studies in which they are engaged can be rendered subservient to the better understanding of those occurrences, and towards assisting the pupils in the regulation of their conduct when they shall be called upon to take a part in the active business of life. The example, which is given in the volume before us, of the manner in which this may be accomplished, is not, in our opinion, one which it would be advantageous to imitate. Questions connected with party politics (such questions are included in Mr. Abbott's scheme) call for the exercise of a greater share of judgment, as well as of knowledge, than can well be expected from a youth who is pursuing his studies at school; and there is great danger lest, without intending it, the teacher may imbue his scholars with his own particular views. An intelligent tutor will always be able to extract from the events which are passing around him means for exercising the minds of his pupils, without having recourse to this class of subjects. One of the highest motives which it should be the business of every instructor of youth to awaken in the minds of his pupil, is the desire of being a useful member of society, and nothing will tend more forcibly to implant and strengthen this desire than the consciousness of possessing the means of usefulness.

Another advantage resulting from this course will be, that the judgment of the pupils will be cultivated : they will be so trained as to form their own opinions upon various subjects, as they present themselves, and thus be fitted to take their station in the world, where they may have no guide to consult, or where their judgment, if not well cultivated, may be in danger of yielding to the false opinions with which they come in contact.

In following up the plans which have here been mentioned for exciting and interesting pupils, it is by no means the object to convert the business of instruction into a pastime. In fact, one of the great ends of education would be missed if children were thus, as it were, cheated into the acquirement of knowledge, for they would not be trained to that habit of steady application, nor accustomed to that struggle with difficulties, which is essential to the formation of a firm and good character, and so absolutely necessary to success in real life. Mr. Abbott seems to be fully impressed with this truth when he says :—

' Even if the work you are assigning to a class is easy, do not tell them so, unless you wish to destroy all their spirit and interest in doing it; and if you wish to excite their spirit and interest, make your work difficult, and let them see that you know it is so—not so difficult as to tax their powers too heavily, but enough so to require a vigorous and persevering effort. Let them distinclty understand, too, that you know it is difficult—that you mean to make it so,— but that they have your sympathy and encouragement in the efforts which it calls them to make.

' Another way to excite interest, and that of the right kind in school, is not to *remove* difficulties, but to teach the pupils how to *surmount* them. A text-book so contrived as to make study mere play, and to dispense with thought and effort, is the worst text-book that can be made, and the surest to be in the end a dull one. The great source of literary enjoyment, which is the successful exercise of intellectual power, is by such a mode of presenting a subject cut off. Secure, therefore, severe study. Let the pupils see that you are aiming to secure it, and that the pleasure which you expect they will receive is, that of firmly and patiently encountering and overcoming difficulty ; of penetrating, by steady and persevering effort, into regions from which the idle and inefficient are debarred, and that it is your province to lead them forward, not to carry them.'

The description which is given of the system pursued during four years in Mount Vernon school is exceedingly interesting. The statement is too long for insertion here, and it would be difficult to make any extracts that would give a fair view of the plans and principles which are laid down for the guidance of the scholars. The whole chapter may be studied with advantage by every one engaged in superintending the education of youth.

One of the most interesting portions of the volume is the chapter on moral discipline, a branch of education little considered by many teachers, but one which is of far greater moment than the whole catalogue of studies which ordinarily fill up the measure of school learning. The system described and recommended by Mr. Abbott is similar to that already explained, as applied to other branches of education : the pupils are themselves to be made active instruments in forming their own moral characters. Where means can be found for interesting them in the examination of their own motives and principles of action, there can be no question but that, in securing those aids, more will be accomplished than would be likely to result from the best lectures or advice of a tutor, unaccompanied by the co-operation of the pupil. The circumstances in which we ourselves have taken a part as actors will always make a deeper and more lasting impression, than those in which we have been merely spectators. We cannot better illustrate this position than by quoting from Mr. Abbott's volume one of the scenes which he has inserted in order to explain his system.

K 2

' The subject for the moral exercise to-day is *Prejudice.* Each boy may take one of the papers which have been distributed, and write upon them anything relating to the subject. As many as have thought of anything to write may raise their hands.

' One or two only of the older scholars gave the signal.

' I will mention the kinds of communication you can make, and perhaps what I say will suggest something to you. As fast as you think of anything you may raise your hands, and as soon as I see a sufficient number up, I will give directions to begin. You can describe any case in which you have been prejudiced yourselves, either against persons or things.

' Here a number of the hands went up.

, ' You can mention any facts relating to antipathies of any kind or any cases, where you know other persons to be prejudiced. You can ask any questions in regard to the subject, questions about the nature of prejudice, or the causes for it, or the remedy of it.

' As he said this many hands were successively raised, and at last directions were given for them to begin to write. Five minutes were allowed, and at the end of that time the papers were collected and read. The following specimens, transcribed verbatim from the originals, with the remarks made, as nearly as they could be remembered immediately after the exercise, will give an idea of the ordinary operation of this plan.

' " I am very much prejudiced against spiders, and every insect in the known world, with scarcely an exception. There is a horrid sensation created by their ugly forms, that makes me wish them all to Jericho. The butterfly's wings are pretty, but he is dreadful ugly. There is no affectation in this, for my pride will not .permit me to show this prejudice to any great degree, when I can help it. I do not fear the little wretches, but I do hate them."

' This is not expressed very well. The phrases " to Jericho," and " dreadful ugly," are vulgar, and in very bad taste. Such a dislike, too, is more commonly called an antipathy than a prejudice, though, perhaps, it comes under the general head of prejudices.

' " How may we overcome prejudice? I think that when we are prejudiced against a person, it is the hardest thing in the world to overcome it." '

' A prejudice is usually founded in some unpleasant association connected with the subject of it. To connect some pleasant association with it is therefore the best way to overcome the prejudice against it.

' For example, to take the case of the antipathy to the spider alluded to in the last article. The reason why that young lady dislikes spiders is undoubtedly because some unpleasant idea is associated with the thought of those insects, perhaps, for example, the idea of their crawling upon her, which is certainly not a very pleasant one to any body. Now the way to correct such a prejudice is to try to connect some pleasant thoughts with the sight of the animal.

' I once found a spider in an empty apartment, hanging in its web in the wall, with a large ball of eggs which it had suspended by its side. My companion and myself cautiously brought up a tumbler under the web, and pressed it suddenly against the wall so as to inclose both spider and eggs within it. We then contrived to run in a pair of shears so as to cut off the web, and let both the animal and its treasure fall down into the tumbler. We put a book over the top and walked off with our prize to a table, to see what it would do. At first it tried to climb up the side of the tumbler, but its feet slipped from the smooth glass. We then inclined the glass so as to favour its climbing and to enable it to reach the book at the top. As soon as it touched the book it was safe. It could cling to the book easily, and we now placed the tumbler again upright to watch its motions.

' It attached a thread to the book, and let itself down by it to the bottom of the tumbler, and walked round and round the ball of eggs apparently in great trouble. Presently it ascended by its thread and then came down again. It attached a new thread to the ball, and then went up, drawing the ball with it. It hung the ball at a proper distance from the book, and bound it firmly in its place by threads running from it in every direction to the parts of the book which were near, and then the animal took its place quietly by its side.

' Now, I do not say that if anybody had a strong antipathy to a spider, seeing one perform such a work as this would entirely remove it, but it would certainly soften it; it would *tend* to remove it. It would connect an interesting and pleasant association with the object. So if she should watch a spider in the fields making his web. You have all seen those beautiful regular webs in the morning dew, (" Yes, sir; yes, sir!") composed of concentric circles, and radii diverging in every direction? (" Yes, sir!") Well, watch the spider when making one of these, or observe his artful ingenuity and vigilance when he is lying in wait for a fly. By thus connecting pleasant ideas with the sight of the animal you will destroy the unpleasant association which constitutes the prejudice. In the same manner, if I wished to create an antipathy to a spider in a child, it would be very easily done. I would tie her hands behind her, and put three or four upon her to crawl over her face.

'Thus you must destroy prejudices in all cases, by connecting pleasant thoughts and associations with the objects of them.

' "I am often prejudiced against new scholars without knowing why."

' We sometimes hear a person talk in this way, " I do not like such or such a person at all."

' " Why ? "

' " Oh, I don't know ; I do not like her at all. I can't bear her."

' " But why not? What is your objection to her ? "

' " Oh, I don't know ; I have not any particular reason, but I never did like her."

' Now, whenever you hear any person talk so, you may be sure that her opinion on any subject is worth nothing at all. She forms opinions in one case without grounds, and it depends merely upon accident whether she does not in other cases.

' " Why is it that so many of our countrymen *are*, or seem to be, prejudiced against the unfortunate children of Africa? Almost every large white boy who meets a small black boy insults him in some way or other."

' " It is so hard to overcome prejudices that we ought to be careful how we form them."

' " When I see a new scholar enter this school, and she does not happen to suit me exactly in her ways and manners, I very often get prejudiced against her, though sometimes I find her a valuable friend after I get acquainted with her."

' There is an inquiry I should like very much to make, though I suppose it would not be quite right to make it. I should like to ask all those who have some particular friend in school, and who can recollect the impression which the individual made upon them when they first saw her, to rise, and then I should like to inquire in how many cases the first impression was favourable, and in how many unfavourable.

' " Yes, sir; yes, sir."

' Do you mean you would like to have the inquiry made?

' " Yes, sir."

' All, then, who have intimate friends, and can recollect the impression they first made upon them, may rise.

' (About thirty rose, more than two-thirds of which voted that the first impression made by the persons who had since become their particular friends was unfavourable.)

' This shows how much dependence you can justly place on first impressions.

' " Is it not right to allow prejudice to have influence over our minds as far as this? If anything comes to our knowledge with which wrong *seems* to be connected, and one in whom we have always felt confidence is engaged in it, is it not right to allow our prejudice in favour of this individual to have so much influence over us as to cause us to believe that all is really right, though every circumstance which has come to our knowledge is against such a conclusion? I felt this influence not many weeks since in a very great degree."

' No, it would not be prejudice in such a case. That is, a prejudice would not be a sufficient ground to justify withholding blame. Well-grounded confidence in such a person ought to have such an effect, but not prejudice.

' The above may be considered as a fair specimen of the ordinary operation of such an exercise. It is taken as an illustration, not by selection from the large number of similar exercises which I have witnessed, but simply because it was an exercise occurring at a time when a description was to be written. Besides the articles above quoted, there were thirty or forty others which were read and commented on. The above will, however, be sufficient to give the reader a clear idea of the exercise, and to show what is the nature of the moral effect it is calculated to produce.'

Mr. Abbott's work is altogether one of the most interesting

and practically useful which we have lately seen. Though we do not agree in all respects with the author, we can safely recommend his book to all classes of teachers who are anxious to discharge their duty faithfully. They will find much well worth adopting in the general management of schools; and where they may not feel inclined to follow the author, it is probable that their inventive faculties may be roused to devise something better suited to the circumstances in which they are placed. Mr. Abbott is not one who dogmatizes in matters of education; he gives us the benefit of his experience and thought, and then leaves us to help ourselves. Teachers are already under great obligations to Dr. Mayo for what he has contributed to the improvement of education; and for the re-publication of the present work he is justly entitled to their gratitude.

ACTUAL STATE OF GREECE.

De l'État Actuel de la Grèce, et des Moyens d'arriver à sa Restauration. Par F. Thiersch. 2 vols. Leipzig. F. A. Brockhaus. 1833.

THOUGH many of the facts contained in these volumes are now matter of notoriety, and many of the speculations have lost their interest by the actual course of events, this work is still, in many respects, worth the attention of those who have studied the past history and formed conjectures on the future prospects of regenerated Greece.

It has been often said that Thiersch was sent to Greece on an official mission by the King of Bavaria, and the author has accordingly thought it necessary (vol. i. pp. 307-326) to explain the motives for his journey. By the Protocol of London, Greece was to be independent, and to have a king chosen from some royal family of Europe, not excluded by the terms of the Protocol. Professor Thiersch, who is well known as a scholar, and one who had paid great attention to the affairs of Greece during the late struggle, immediately set about thinking of a proper person for the kingly office, and accordingly made a proposition on the subject to the King of Bavaria, whose subject he is. From his own statement it appears that the king gave no answer to his letter of Sept. 10, 1829, in which he proposed that Prince Otho, the king's son, should be the future King of Greece: but though the king gave no direct answer, he was too considerate to allow the Professor to be damped by apparent indifference; he thanked the writer through his secretary, M. de Kreuzer. Thiersch next ad-

dressed himself to M. Eynard, then at Paris, who had long taken
an active interest in the affairs of Greece, and proposed to him
also Prince Otho as the most suitable person in Europe for
the newly-created kingly office.   He also took advantage of a
favourable opportunity which offered, to write on the same
subject to the Emperor of Russia, inclosing a copy of the
letter to M. Eynard, and assuring his Imperial Majesty that
the King of Bavaria was entirely unacquainted with its contents.   M. Eynard, adopting the idea of the German Professor,
used all his influence to procure the election of a prince who
was a minor; and among the princes in this predicament none
could come into competition with a son of the house of Bavaria.
France accordingly proposed one of the sons of the Bavarian
King, and Russia would have consented, but the English
members of the conference objected to a prince who was a
minor, and finally Leopold of Saxe-Coburg was chosen, in
compliance with their wishes.

On the resignation of Leopold (March 21, 1830), the throne
was again open to competition, but the negociations were inter-
rupted by the events of July of that year, which drove Charles
X. into exile.   Both Charles X. and his ministry were favourable to the Greek cause, and it was the proposition of
Polignac himself that the island of Eubœa should form a part
of the new kingdom.   The conference of London was recom-
menced under the administration of Lord Grey, and the choice
of a king again became a matter for deliberation.   In September, 1830, Thiersch learned at Berlin that the new French
government was favourable to the claims of Prince Otho, and
that there would be no opposition on the part of England;
but at this time a new difficulty presented itself.   John Capodistria, the President of Greece, it was now generally known
cherished a strong desire to retain the dignity with which he
had been only provisionally invested, and to be the founder of
a new dynasty in Greece.   Professor Thiersch had acquainted
the President with the measures which were adopted by him
and his friends to secure the election of Prince Otho, but receiving only evasive replies from the Count, and having daily
more reason to suspect his sincerity, the Professor determined
to pay him a visit, and readily obtained the king's permission
for that purpose.   On the eve of his departure, the Professor
applied to the king through a third person, in order to learn
his majesty's views as to the chief object of the journey.   His
majesty's answer was in accordance with what he had said from
the commencement,—that he did not wish to impose his son
on the Greeks in any way whatever, and that the most satisfactory thing to him would be that the nation itself should

ask for Prince Otho, if he was to be their sovereign. The king also gave Thiersch a letter of recommendation to the President.

. On his arrival at Nauplia, the Professor had several interviews with the President, in which the old politician, according to our author's account, embarrassed by the difficult position of affairs, and having to deal with one who was fully on his guard, could get nothing from him that might compromise, in the slightest degree, the interests of his royal master, and his own future reputation as one of the pacificators of Greece. Two days after his last interview with the President, Thiersch set out to visit the interior of the Peloponnesus, and on arriving at Nemea he heard the intelligence of Capodistria's assassination (Oct. 8, 1831). The confusion that followed the President's death was in some degree abated by the arrival of the news, in the following year, that the conference of London had offered the crown of Greece (February, 1832) to Prince Otho. The Professor received the intelligence of this long-desired consummation of his labours and his wishes, on his arrival in the island of Syra (March, 1832) from a visit to the coasts and islands of Asia Minor.

From this statement it is not difficult to infer the precise nature of the mission to which we owe the account of the ' actual state of Greece.'

A large part of the first volume is taken up with the history of the Greek government from the death of Capodistria to the dissolution of the mixed government, which was soon after followed (Jan. 30, 1833) by the landing of King Otho at Nauplia.

It would perhaps be difficult to give any considerable degree of interest to the history of Capodistria's administration, and to the series of intrigues and petty movements with which this unhappy country was distracted during the latter part of the President's life, and still more after his assassination. Nor do we think that Professor Thiersch has treated the subject in a way to render it at all attractive. His narrative is often confused, indistinct, and sometimes unintelligible; nor do we think it possible to draw from it, were it worth the labour, a fair estimate of the blame attaching respectively to the different parties, and to the agents of the foreign powers. The writer himself was largely mixed up with affairs at one period. (p. 80, &c.) Though not professedly holding any public appointment, circumstances made him in some degree a public character, and accordingly he does not fail to inform us of the active part which he took in several transactions.

The character of Capodistria has been differently repre-

sented by his friends and enemies. As the short-lived admi-
nistrator of a country to which the recollections of three
thousand years are attached, and one which is now called into
a new and doubtful existence, he claims a notice which otherwise would not be his due.   Like many of those who play a
prominent part on the theatre of the world, he was a weak and
ill-educated man, raised by circumstances to power, to which
he clung with an obstinacy of purpose proportionate to his
consciousness that he was nothing when detached from the
accidents to which he owed his importance.   The judgment
of Thiersch on this renowned diplomatist is neither harsh, nor,
on the whole, so unfavourable as we might have expected ; but
the defects of his character and his unfitness to govern the
Greeks are points made sufficiently clear.   He could not write
the language of the people whom he was sent to govern ; nor
had he the slightest sympathy with the heroic character-of
those men who had endured nine years of war and privation,
and who had placed the name of Mesolónghi in the annals of
their history by the side of Marathon and Platæa.   The President's settled purpose from the commencement was to establish his own power in Greece and to transmit it to his family.
To carry these views into effect, he stopped at no act, however
illegal.   He began by dissolving the legislative body (τὸ
βουλευτικὸν), and putting two of the members in prison who
protested against this abuse of power ; and all his subsequent
acts were of a piece with this arbitrary proceeding.   To par-
ticularize the pitiable intrigues and the various acts of oppression by which he roused against him a whole nation who, on
his arrival, had received him with open arms, is not necessary
here.   His public acts, mean, cruel, and contemptible as they
were, may perhaps find their apologists and defenders; but
the guilt of instigating a son to murder* his father (p. 15) is
a blot on the Corfiote which justifies all the suspicions of his
bitterest enemies.

The President had no taste for learning or the arts : he was
a stranger to the ancient recollections of the country which he
had come to govern, and declared, after visiting the Acropolis
of Athens, ' that it was a heap of rubbish, and that nobody
but those whose heads were turned could attach any importance
to such stuff.' Yet after all the author describes him as a man
' who had not naturally a bad heart, but had been corrupted
by vicious intercourse with others, and hardened by experience.

* Thiersch asserts this on the authority of the son himself. Though the
President, as we are told by the author, could not *write* Greek, he could, it
seems, speak at least as much as this—Θέλει εἶναι ἡ εὐτυχία σου, ἐὰν σκοτώσῃς τὸν
πατέρα σου—which is as much as to say—' If you will only get rid of your
father, your fortune is made.'

Besides he was governed by the strongest of passions, that of power, and blinded by excessive vanity. His conversation was animated and varied. He was never at a loss what to say, and indeed took all the conversation to himself: full of the idea of his own superiority, he only listened to his own voice, without troubling himself about the opinions of others. His wish was to be loved, and hence he could relish even hypocritical marks of attachment and respect. He was temperate and industrious ; his table, his furniture, and his mode of life, everything showed him to be a man of simple habits, and averse to splendour.'

The arrest and imprisonment of Peter Mauromichali* were the immediate cause of the President's assassination, who fell by the hands of Constantine and George Mauromichali, as he was entering the church of St. Spiridion (Oct. 8, 1831.) In the republican days of Greece, such an act would have been considered as the just punishment of a cruel tyrant, and the assassin might have had his statue placed by those of Harmodius and Aristogeiton. Constantine was immediately killed, but George Mauromichali, after escaping for a short time, was tried by a court-martial, and shot.

The most interesting part of Professor Thiersch's work is the second part, ' On the Situation of Greece and the Means to be adopted to restore it to Tranquillity.' As to his general speculations on the foreign policy, the commerce, finance, and innumerable other subjects, touching the present and prospective state of Greece, we are of opinion that, with some occasional exceptions, there is a great deal of vague talk without any definite meaning ; and on various points we think the learned Professor out of the sphere of his studies, and not always correct. But an educated and reflecting man, to whom the ancient history and language of this interesting country have been so long familiar, could not fail to make numerous valuable observations ; and, accordingly, some of the chapters in the book are not only of the highest interest to the general reader, but still more so to those whose early associations have been connected with the language and monuments of ancient Greece.

The population of Greece (Part ii. § 3.) is of a very mixed kind, viewed with reference to their occupations and the various degrees of education. There is a nomadic or pastoral class, a class of cultivators of the soil, and a body of enterprising merchants and able seamen : in the interior, there are captains who cannot read or write ; and men of extensive and solid acquirements, united with a great aptitude for business.

---

* See the events as they are told in an anonymous work, entitled ' Sketches in Greece and Turkey. London, 1833.'

' From the heroic times to the French revolution, every generation has left here its impress and its manners. The middle ages, and those near our own times, still exist by the side of Hellenic antiquity and Byzantine institutions ; for here conquerors have succeeded one another without altering the basis of society, and no change, at once moral and political, has acted with sufficient power to re-cast the perishing memorials of past ages, and make them harmonize with new wants and new laws.'

, There is a pretty marked distinction among the inhabitants of the three great divisions of Greece—Rumelia or Greece north of the Isthmus, the Peloponnesus, and the Islands. The inhabitants of Rumelia have retained a chivalrous and warlike spirit, with a simplicity of manners and mode of life, which strongly remind us of the pictures of the heroic age, and of that social state which the historian of the Peloponnesian* war has described as existing in a large part of northern Greece at a time when Athens had attained a high degree of civilization. The Peloponnesus, with the exception of the Mainiotes, was completely under the Turkish yoke before the late revolution. Some few families of Klephthes maintained themselves in the mountains and enjoyed a kind of independence.

, ' The islands (p. 219), by their connexion and their commerce with Europe, are nearer a state of civilization. In most of them the houses, furniture, dress, food, and lodging are in the Frank fashion ; and it is like being transported into a different age, when you leave Helicon or Parnassus—where you have seen, in a wretched cabin, the husband, wife, and children sleeping on the ground, on one side of the fire-place, with the asses and oxen on the other—and arrive at Tenos or Náxos, where the houses are furnished in the Venetian fashion, and where all the conveniences and comforts of life are found. And though the mode of living may be considered as somewhat old-fashioned, it is framed altogether after the social usages of western Europe.'

, The soil of Rumelia is, in general, cultivated by Bulgarians, Albanians, and Vlachians (Βλάχοι), under which last term the three are generally comprehended. In eastern Greece, Parnassus with its impregnable natural bulwarks, is the only place where the Hellenic race has maintained itself, and speaks the Greek language with some purity ; in the mountainous parts of western Greece, there are also some remnants of Hellenic stock. The Vlachians are a robust, industrious, and honest race, but possessed of neither the regular features nor lively character of the Greeks. Mingled among them are the captains and their

* Thucyd, I. 5, 6.

soldiers, called pallicari (young people), who are trained to the
sole profession of arms, and often extort from the unresisting
peasant the hard-earned fruits of his labours. Besides the
peasants and soldiers, there is an active and intelligent body
of proprietors, merchants, and artisans in the towns, and
among them some of Greek stock. Mesolónghi, though neglected by the government of the President, had recovered some
of its trade ; and Calaxidi, at the entrance of the Gulf of Sa-
lona, is now a thriving place.

. The population of the Peloponnesus consists nearly of the
same races as that of Rumelia; but the Peloponnesians are
more ignorant and less honest than the Rumeliots. The
Albanians occupy Argolis and a part of the ancient Triphylia.
Among the rest of the inhabitants, who all speak Greek, there
are considerable social differences : the cultivators of the plains
are not the proprietors, all their lands belonging to the state,
or to the rich families. These cultivators are less industrious
than the little proprietors in the mountainous districts, whose
houses and lands are in a much better condition. The population of the towns is of a mixed character, as in Rumelia, but
there are among them many wealthy Greek families, who, under
the Turkish government, had an active share in the administration, which they exercised for their own profit and to the disadvantage of the rest of the community. Were this class now to
gain a political ascendency, and a kind of territorial title to
nobility, they would keep the country in a state of servitude
more unfavourable to industry than the dominion of the Turks.
The military chiefs of the Peloponnesus owed their existence
to the war of independence ; and their soldiers were merely
peasants who came from the plough and have returned to it*.
Scattered through the country, and collected in the towns, is a
class of small dealers and artisans, who bear the character of
being industrious, frugal, and honest. The Mainiotes form a
separate class of the population : they are generally called
Mainiotes from the name of one of their districts, but their
true name, which they have never lost, is Spartans. They
occupy the lofty and sterile mountains between the gulfs of
Laconice and Messenia, the representatives of a race driven
from the sunny valley of the Eurotas to the bleak and inhos-
pitable tracts which they still occupy, though the plains which
are spread out below them are no longer held by a conqueror,
and the fertile lands lie uncultivated for want of labourers.

In the islands there is a similar mixture of Albanians and
Greeks. The Albanians of Hydra and Spezzia have long been
known as active traders and excellent mariners : the Hydriotes

* Compare Thucydides I. 141. αὐτουργοί τι γάρ εἰσι Πελοποννήσιοι, &c.

made great sacrifices for the cause of independence in the late
war; the Spezziotes, more prudent and calculating, increased
their wealth and their merchant navy. The island of Syra,
which has long been the centre of an active commerce, now
contains the remnant of the population of Psara and Chios.
The Psariotes are an active and handsome race, and skilful
seamen: the Chiots, following the habits of their ancestors,
are fond of staying at home and attending to their shops and
mercantile speculations ; they amass wealth, but they employ it
in founding establishments of public utility, and in the education of their children. In Tenos, the peasants, who are also the
proprietors, cultivate the vine and the fig even amidst the most
barren rocks: in Syra, Santorin (Thera), and at Naxos,
they are the tenants of a miserable race of nobility, whose
origin is traced to the time of the Crusades, and who still retain the Latin creed of their ancestors. Besides these various
elements belonging to the kingdom of Greece as at present
constituted, Thiersch enumerates various bodies of Suliotes, of
people from the heights of Olympus, Candiotes, many Greek
families from Asia Minor, Phanariotes, and others, who have
emigrated or been driven by circumstances within the limits
of the new kingdom. And we must not omit, says the author
(p. 230),—' a crowd of physicians, literary and scientific men,
and young politicians, who have come from Paris, frequently
with democratic opinions, and with a smattering of the knowledge which is there preached in the streets—all of whom
contribute to increase that great variety of character, manners,
and opinions, which marks the motley population of Greece.'
    The northern limits of Greece are a line drawn from the
Gulf of Arta to that of Volo, but the exact course of the line
has not yet been definitively fixed, or, at least, as far as we
can learn, is not yet made public. The ancient Acarnania on
the west, and the valley of the Sperchius on the east, are both
within the limits of the new kingdom. The statistical information of the author is partly founded on the documents in
the Statistical Office established by the President at Nauplia ;
but as this information was both inexact and incomplete, the
author corrected and enlarged it by actual inquiry on the spot,
and by the assistance which he derived from the bishops and
démogérontes. The modern provincial divisions of Greece
are called Eparchies: of these the eastern part of northern
Greece contains eleven, with as many chief towns, and 585
villages. The calculations as to population are founded upon
a conjectural estimate of houses or families, which gives about
130,200 for the population of this part of Greece. The western
part of northern Greece, comprehending a part of the country

of the Locri Ozolæ, Ætolia and Acarnania, is divided into eleven eparchies, with a conjectured population of 76,000, making the total of Northern Greece about 206,000.

The Peloponnesus, in extent, differs little from Northern Greece, but it is more populous, better cultivated, and altogether the most important part of the new kingdom. It contains thirty-five eparchies, with a population of 429,250, according to the author's estimate: this includes the Spartan population of Maina, as well as the Spartans in other parts of south and south-eastern Peloponnesus.

The large island of Eubœa, and thirty-two inhabited islands in the Ægean, form the insular portion of Greece, with a conjectured population of 176,185. The total population of the whole kingdom will, according to these estimates, be only 811,435, on a surface calculated by the author at 1100 (German) square miles, or 23,595 (English) square miles. This is more than one-third and less than one-half of the area of England and Wales, which have a population of 13,897,187; but the population is not double that of the agricultural county of Kent, which has an area of about 1500 square miles. Before the war, it is supposed (p. 272) that Peloponnesus and Northern Greece contained a population twice as large as that now estimated for the whole kingdom: some eparchies have lost more than half their population. The islands in general have suffered less, with the exception of Eubœa and Hydra.

Greece is a mountainous country, containing few extensive plains, but numerous small and often fertile valleys. The mountains, such as Parnassus and most of those in Attica and Megaris, are chiefly composed of calcareous rock, which, however, varies much in its quality. Slates occur in the ridge of Œta, in Helicon, and several of the mountain masses of Messenia and Arcadia. The calcareous formation characterizes most of the islands; but as we advance to the east granite prevails in the grey and barren rocks of Myconos and of Delos. The mineral wealth of Greece is little known, and with the exception of the mines of Laurium in Attica and a few of the islands, the mining branches of industry do not seem to have been prosecuted either with ardour or success by the ancient inhabitants of this country. Thiersch (p. 274) says that the gold, silver, copper, and lead, found in Attica, at Chelcis, and in the islands of Siphnos and Seriphos, are far from being exhausted: iron abounds in Scyros, at Tænarum, and in Eubœa. Abundance of coal also has been discovered in Eubœa, and other beds of the same useful mineral are expected to be opened in Elis. The forests of Greece have been in a great measure destroyed: still there is a considerable quantity of wood in Eubœa, on Parnassus, Helicon, in the Megaris, and especially in Arcadia and the heights of Taÿgetus. The pine is one of the most common trees, but the author adds that, towards Thessaly, there are still noble forests of oak; and, as we learn from other authorities, the timber of the Peloponnesus often occurs of majestic size and of many varieties. Great damage is occasioned by the shepherds setting fire to the brushwood and even to the forests themselves, in order that the ashes after the heavy rains may fertilize the ground and produce fresh pasture for their cattle. The author, on his route from Elatea to Thermopylæ, passed through a forest of majestic oaks, of which he counted more than two hundred blackened and injured by the flames. In many parts the pine trees are tapped in order to procure the resin, and then left standing to die and wither away. The demand for wood also for ship-building, and the absence of all proper control over the felling of the timber, has contributed to the present state of devastation.

The physical character of Greece is yet but imperfectly known, and the few and hasty glances that the traveller or the antiquarian explorer has cast upon it, serve more to excite than to satisfy curiosity. Within the narrow limits of the continental part of the new kingdom, nature has presented perhaps more varieties of surface, soil, and climate, than are crowded together anywhere else within the same limits. And to no spot on the face of the earth is such a series of recollections attached—from the dim and indistinct forms of the mythical ages, through the long historical period of a nation's existence, which, though humbled, debased, and mingled with foreign blood, still lives and speaks the language of ancient Greece.

The numerous sites of antiquity which still remain to be explored promise a rich harvest of discoveries, which cannot fail to throw light on the domestic usages, the social life, and the whole history of the nation. But perhaps few subjects present more curious matter for inquiry, and are at the same time so closely connected with the present interests of Greece, as the remains of those great works which were undertaken for the draining of the country and the securing it against inundations. The narrow valleys and plains of Greece sometimes contain small lakes, or are so formed as to be liable to be converted into marshes and swamps by the closing of the cuts by which they were once kept dry. In this way (II. p. 16) some of the richest levels in Arcadia and Bœotia have been rendered almost useless; for the waters, rising to a great height in the winter time, do not subside in the summer soon enough to allow the land to be profitably cultivated. The fertile lands about the Lake Copais in Bœotia, the most extensive plain in all Greece, are so deluged by the rising waters of the lake in the winter-time, that the cultivation of the country round its banks is annually decreasing. 'The old men of Livadia say, that within the last fifty years the marshes have approached nearer the town by more than a league. Out of twenty conduits or outlets which once existed there is only one in tolerable condition, and if unfortunately this should be choked up like the rest, the inundation would reach, on one side, to the base of Parnassus, and on the other to eastern Bœotia, where it would seek an outlet in the valley of the Asopus. We should then see the times of Deucalion restored, and one might sail from Helicon to Parnassus over entire provinces buried in the water, with their towns, villages, and fields*. That which may happen to the plains of Bœotia and Phocis, has already occurred in the valley of Phonia (in Arcadia). The smaller of the two subterranean outlets from the lake was choked up twenty years ago, and the larger ten years after. Since this time, the waters, having no outlet, have gone on rising: the whole valley of Phonia is already covered with water ; twelve villages situated on the slopes of the mountains have been swallowed up, and others to the north are threatened with the same fate.'

The basin of the Lake Copais is one of the most interesting parts of Greece. The late survey of Captain Copeland shows, that from the outlet of the Bœotian Asopus to the commencement of the low flats which fringe the Gulf of Zeitun, a mountain-barrier lines the Bœotian and Locrian shore of the Euripus, and allows no outlet for any stream from the interior of the province. *Ktypa,* near the narrowest part of the Euripus, is 3401 feet high; a mountain near the ruins of Larymna is 1855 feet ; and a mountain near C. Stalamata, north of Larymna, 1146. From this last a range of mountains runs westward into the interior, of which Talanta is one, forming the northern boundary of the basin of the Copais and Cephisus, and separating it from the basin of the Sperchius and the Gulf of Zeitun. There can be little doubt that the level of the Lake Copais is considerably higher than that of the Euripus ; the author indeed asserts, without stating any authority, that the lake is more than a thousand feet above the sea ; but this may safely be denied, or at least doubted, till it is proved. The lake is separated from the sea by the range of Mount

---

* See Pausanias, IX. 24, as to the tradition of the Bœotian Athens and Eleusis being destroyed by the rising of the Lake Copais ; and the curious description of the plain of Bœotia in Strabo. (P. 406, Casaub.)

Ptoon, which is about four or five miles across.   Between the
eastern end of the lake and the coast the subterranean channels
still exist, with the shafts or wells communicating with them,
which unfortunately are now choked up.   (ii. p. 23.)   Professor Thiersch explains how this ancient work is to be restored,
for the mode and means of doing which we refer to his book;
such projects involve many more difficulties than he̋ takes into
his account.

This great work for draining the Copais is one of the most
ancient memorials of Greek civilization, coeval with the wealth
and political importance of the Bœotian Orchomenus.   The
destruction of this ancient city probably caused the conduits
to be neglected, the consequence of which was that the waters
of the lake recovered a part of the territory which the industry
of the ancient inhabitants had won from it.   ' In the time of
Alexander, the great Crates of Chalcis began to restore the
subterranean communications, and he succeeded so far, in
spite of the troubles in Bœotia, which prevented the completion of the work, that the sites of the ancient Orchomenus, of
Athens, and Eleusis were discovered on the banks of the
Triton.   Since this time the passages have been again choked,
and, as we have remarked, only one is now open.   If we may
trust the examinations made on the spot by the chief persons
of Livadia, there are the traces of twenty conduits.   Several of
them communicate with the surface by wells or shafts, from
which it would appear that these works are constructed similarly to the aqueduct of Polycrates * at Samos, of which I discovered the course; and that of Tenos, which has been lately
discovered and restored.   We observe the same construction
in the conduit (*emissarius*) of the Lake of Alba Longa, cut in
the midst of the Latin mountains, and still remaining, after the
ravages of the barbarous ages; the same kind of conduit also
drained the Lake Fucinus (Celano), which they are cleaning
out at the present time.'

It should be observed that Strabo (p. 405) makes the river
Cephisus discharge itself into the sea near Larymna of
Bœotia; but he does not probably mean to say that this was
an original and natural outlet of the river.   In another passage
(p. 406), he says, that ' a chasm opening close upon the lake
and near Copæ, made an underground passage for the water
thirty stadia in length, which received the river.   The Cephisus
emerged at Larymna of Locris, where there is a lake of the
same name, and then entered the sea.'   A small stream is
marked in Capt. Copeland's chart as entering the sea near the

---

* See the curious description of this great work, Herod. iii. 60.

ruins of Larymna, which, if it is not a mere mountain-torrent, must be the outlet of the Cephisus. Whether the ancient drainage of the Cephisus was altogether a work of art, or whether, in this singular country of earthquakes and subterraneous water-courses, advantage was taken of some great operation of nature, is a question that may perhaps be decided by future inquiries on the spot.

The reader may compare with the general observations and sometimes rather loose remarks of Professor Thiersch, those of Colonel Leake ('Travels in the Morea,' iii. cap. 26) on the Pheneatice and the *Zerethra* of the Peloponnesus. The account of the attempt made by the Turks, in 1776, to clean out the great canal of the Stymphalia is exceedingly curious. (Thiersch, p. 19, &c.)

Our limits do not allow us to enter upon the consideration of the various topics of administration, commerce, finance, education, and numerous other subjects which the learned author has discussed. To do justice to such varied matter would require dissertations as long as those in the work itself, many of which are, in our opinion, more amusing than convincing. That any man should be able to form a sound judgment on the almost endless topics which enter into the work of Professor Thiersch could hardly be expected; and though we think few persons, with the limited time allowed for observation, could have collected more facts than the author, we are inclined to think that a more lucid arrangement of them might have been made, and sounder conclusions drawn, by many men of much smaller acquirements. Judging from some slight errors as to facts, which are observable here and there, we do not feel such confidence in the accuracy of all the author's statements, as to consider this sketch of the present state of Greece perfectly unexceptionable authority. The work has evidently been drawn up in a hurry in order to prevent the ground being occupied by others; and to this we may perhaps attribute the author's innumerable crude, disjointed, and often impracticable plans, through the darkness of which certain glimmerings of good sense now and then appear.

To give his opinions a wider circulation, the author has written in French, a language of which he has shown himself not quite a master. In a postscript to his preface he regrets 'que les sept premières feuilles soient si gravement défigurées par des fautes d'impression, contre la langue et le sens même ; il n'était pas possible d'y remédier sans amener de nouveaux retards.' We regret that we are obliged to add that the errors, both typographical and others, are not confined to the first seven sheets. We have never yet seen a book

from a man of Professor Thiersch's ability and learning so ill
written, and so overrun with typographical errors.   Even the
classical names, which are of frequent occurrence, are barba-
rized in almost every possible form, owing either to his own
carelessness or that of the correctors of the press*.

DYMOCK'S BIBLIOTHECA CLASSICA.

THE reader will perceive in the advertisement leaves of this
Journal, some remarks in reply to the review of ' Dymock's
Bibliotheca Classica.' (Journal, No. XII, p. 298, &c.) This
advertisement would have appeared in the last Number, but
for a mistake which it is unnecessary to explain here.

On all occasions, when an author feels dissatisfied with any
review in this Journal, we invite him to give his reply in the
advertisement sheets of the same Journal, in preference to any
other periodical, or even, if he likes it, in addition to his reply
in any other review.   In this way, the readers of the Journal,
having the evidence on both sides before them, may judge for
themselves.   We do not think it necessary to institute a fresh
examination of the ' Bibliotheca Classica,' though we are not
unwilling to do so, and even to enter more at length into the
subject matter of it : we shall be content if the review and
the remarks upon it are compared.   Whatever errors of any
kind the authors of the ' Bibliotheca' may detect in the review,
will be so much fairly deducted from the censure passed on
their book, and so much blame on the editor for allowing even
the minutest error of a contributor to pass unnoticed.

With reference to the last paragraph in the remarks on the
review, it is necessary to observe, that, independent of the
numerous errors in the ' Bibliotheca,' there are two specific
charges made against the plan of the work : the first is, that
the ' Bibliotheca' contains a very large amount of useless matter; the second is, that it omits an equally large, or larger,
amount of matter useful and necessary.   And to this last
charge, it is no answer to say that the work is intended merely
for a school-book; for if the charge is true, it is not suitable
for a school-book, though intended to be a school-book : and
further, the authors themselves have fixed the standard by
which their work may be fairly tested, by telling us, as they do
in the preface, that the ' Bibliotheca Classica' is designed to
render separate treatises on geography and antiquities quite
unnecessary.

* Since writing this article we have learned that the Commissioners are now
employed in retracting the ground for the purpose of completing the formal and
official Map which is to constitute the line of separation between Greece and
Turkey; and their labours are expected to be very shortly brought to a close.

MISCELLANEOUS.

FOREIGN.

FRANCE.

The Royal Printing Press at Paris.—THIS establishment is in possession of fifty-six distinct sets of Eastern characters, comprising all the known styles of writing of the Asiatics, whether ancient or modern; it is also possessed of sixteen sets of characters peculiar to those nations in Europe who do not make use of the Latin character which we ourselves employ. With regard to the latter, the Royal Press has at its command forty-six complete sets, in all their various forms and sizes. The whole of these types weigh 375,000 kilogrammes (7387 cwt.) at the least; and as the characters required for an octavo page weigh about 3 kilogr. (above 6 lb.), the establishment has, in its own stock, the means of composing 7822 octavo sheets, which would form nearly 260 volumes, or about 125,000 pages. The number of presses which it has in use would enable it to work off 278,000 sheets, or nearly 580 reams of paper per diem, which is equivalent to 9266 octavo volumes, supposing them to consist of thirty sheets each. This prodigious command of means places it in a situation to keep 5000 forms of type set up, which are called for by the public departments, and in this way to economise both labour and expense very essentially. The consumption of paper for public purposes which actually takes place in it, year by year, amounts to between 80,000 and 100,000 reams, or between 261 and 326 reams per working day, which are distributed among the several public departments and boards. The number of workmen commonly employed amounts to about 350.

Teachers in Elementary Schools.—The master of every such school (and one at least is to be established in each district) is nominated by the Minister of Public Instruction, and receives, besides a salary of 200 francs (8*l.*) or upwards, certain fees for pupils, as fixed by the district authorities, which the collector of taxes levies upon the parents. Every individual, too, who has passed his examination as teacher, and can produce a certificate of good conduct from the mayor of the district, is at liberty to open a school. All towns, possessed of a population of more than 6000 souls, are required to establish an elementary school of a superior class, and to pay the master a salary of 16*l.* (400 francs) at the least, besides which he is entitled to a fixed fee for each pupil. And every department is required to erect a normal school for the education and formation of teachers.

Law Students.—The French schools of law were re-organized under the decree of the 15th March, 1804, which laid down certain regulations prescribing the subjects to be taught, the courses to be pursued, the nature of the examinations to be passed, the degrees to be given, &c. The decree requires that all pupils desirous of obtaining a certificate of competency as attorneys (*avoués*) should follow a full year's course of study, and submit to an examination; if desirous of a diploma of licentiate, which is necessary in order to obtain admission into the class of barristers (*avocats*), they must have previously passed through a three years' course of study, and four examinations, as well as have held a public disputation; and lastly, if desirous of obtaining the more elevated rank of a doctor, they must have pursued a four years' course of study, passed six examinations, and held two public disputations. A later law, that of the 10th of May, 1806, converted the schools of law into faculties of law, and declared them an integral member of the imperial university of France. There are at present nine courses of law delivered in the faculty of law at Paris, the ninth being the new course on constitutional law; the others treat, 1st. Of the civil code; 2d. Justinian's Institutes, or the elements of Roman law; 3d. Civil proceedings and criminal legislation; 4th. The Pandects; 5th. The Commercial code; 6th. Administrative (practice of) law; 7th. The history of law; and 8th. The law of nations. Nine professors and eight adjunct-professors (*professeurs suppléans*) are attached to this faculty; they are chosen by open competition (*concours*); and the pupils and students are in number between 2000 and 2500. The diplomas annually granted are as follows:—Diploma of competency about 140; to bachelors, from 980 to 1000; to licentiates about 650; and to doctors about 25 or 30. One half of them are granted by the school of law in Paris; the remainder by the schools of Aix, Caen, Dijon, Grenoble, Poitiers, Rennes, Strasburg, and Toulouse; the last-named university grants about one-third of those emanating from these provincial establishments. The amount of fees received by all the schools of law in France is about 31,250*l.* (781,400 francs) per annum.

BELGIUM.

Free University.—In opposition to the exclusively Roman Catholic University, which has been opened at Mechlin, subscriptions are raising in the Netherlands with a view to found a university in Brussels, the benefits of which are to be open to parties of every religious persuasion. The first meeting of the Provisional Council took place in the Museum at Brussels, on the 8th of August, and appointed Mr. H. de Brouckère their president. It was determined at this meeting to circulate twelve hundred lists for subscriptions (scrips for shares), and to divide the council into sections for the purpose of forwarding the object in contemplation with as little delay as possible. A plan for the general details of management is to be drawn up by Messieurs H. de Brouckère, Delvaux de Salve, Dumortier, Laisné, and Baron, the last of whom has been chosen secretary. The discussion and settlement of the arrangements con- ¬cted with the different faculties have, been distributed as follows : ˙·e faculties of ' law' and ' political science,' Messieurs H. de ːre, Blargnies, Barbanson, and Verhaegen ; for ' medicine,' ɪnd Guillery ; for the ' sciences,' De Puydt, Dumortier, and ; and for the ' belles lettres and classics,' Vautier and Baron. ɔintments of professors are to be made until the whole ar- ːnts are completed.

---

rsity of Mechlin.—A Belgian paper announces that the ː Ram, a professor in the Ecclesiastical Seminary in Mechlin, ɪ installed as rector of the New Catholic University in that nd empowered to nominate all the professors. This indi- ɪ editor of the ' Nouveau Conservateur Belge.'

HOLLAND.

ns' Correspondence.—M. Uylenbrock, Professor of Physics ronomy in the University of Leyden, has recently published ɪrto volumes, containing Huyghens' Correspondence with ː, L'Hôpital, Vaumesle Duilliers, and Hubert Huyghens. jority of the letters are in French ; and the remainder in The originals are preserved in the Public Library at Leyden.

GERMANY.

ADT.—Great improvements have been made of late years in establishments for the education of youth. Independently ligh School and the Technical Seminary, there are no less hteen public and eleven private schools in this small state. ɲber of pupils in the whole of these establishments is 2978.

ɛN.—The number of students resident in the past winter (1833-4) was 362, of whom 50 were not natives of Elec- ɪse ; the remainder consisted of 136 from the province of Iesse, 102 from that of Starkenburg, and 74 from that of Hesse. The population of these provinces is, for the ɪ,000 souls ; for the second, 257,000 ; and for the last, it follows that the proportions of students from each are, Hesse, 1 in every 2000 souls ; in Starkenburg, 1 in every ɪd in Rhenish Hesse, 1 in every 2567 : the average for the ːctorate is 1 in every 2304.

ɪ.—*Grammar Schools.*—The whole number of these in- stitutions in the kingdom of Saxony is fourteen ; and at the close of 1833, they had 81 head teachers, 66 assistant teachers, and 1847 pupils, which gives an average of nearly 10 teachers and 132 pupils to each school. We subjoin a few particulars of the principal schools :—

	Classes.	Teachers.	Pupils.	Departures. In all.	For some University.
Kreisschule (school of the circle or department) at Dresden . . .	5	15	350	79	35
Gymnasium at Bautzen			108	70	13
Do. Zittau			93	13	6
Lyceum at Annaberg .	3	6	76	15	5
Gymnasium at Freyberg	4		150	17	11
Lyceum at Zwickau .	4	6	50	23	6
Do. Schneeberg			109	49	16
Gymnasium at Plauen	3	8	151	30	11
St. Thomas' School at Leipzig . .	6	11	168	18	18
St. Nicholas do. do.			214	18	18

Students' Dress.—This part of academical discipline appears in past times to have been an object of no small concern to the ruling powers. In 1618, for instance, the Elector Augustus required the students in his dominions ' to make use of *respectable* clothing' (*erbarer kleidung*), and prohibited them from ' wearing hacked, slashed, or parti-coloured garments;' but he is much more particular in the directions which he gives to their teachers, whom he thus admonishes:—' The youths are not to be apparelled like country boors (*landsknechte*), but in a decent, respectable way; and they are not to wear slashed garments, but such as are worn by pious (*frommen*) and respectable persons. And they (the teachers) are not to allow any among them to appear in slashed and puffed-out breeches, hats dangling with feathers, large broad sleeves like sacks, or the like.' From another of the orders issued by the same prince it may be inferred, that custom and perhaps necessity had given even the youngest of his subjects a right to wear arms about their persons; for he says, ' none of them shall be permitted to carry daggers, and if they bring arms (*wehren*) to school with them, the teacher must require the same to be delivered up to him, and hold them in safe keeping until the youth leaves the school.'

The Book Trade.—The Saxon ministry have recently communicated to the Committee of German Booksellers at Leipzig, a proposal laid before the late Congress of Envoys at Vienna and actively discussed in it, for placing the book trade of Germany upon a broader and securer basis. The proposal assigns the Diet of the Confederation as the court of appeal for any matriculated member of the Corporation of United Booksellers, in whose case the laws of such body shall have been infringed, and no redress given him by his own government. No printer, proprietor of a circulating library, author, antiquary, bookbinder, or hawker, is to expose stocks of books for sale, or become a publisher. Piracy or the unauthorized reprint of books published in Germany is to be abolished. Copyright and protection against piracy are to be secured by the deposit of two copies of every work previous to its publication. Any member guilty of pirating a work so deposited is to lose his matriculation in the corporation for life, to be expelled from it, and to forfeit his privileges as a regular dealer : the pirated edition to be confiscated, and the offender to be liable to an action for damages. Five years are to be allowed for the sale of such works as shall have been pirated previous to the establishment of the corporation ; but such works not to be allowed to circulate at the Leipzig Book Fairs. The works of all authors, who have been dead twenty years, to be deemed public property, and they may be reprinted by any member of the corporation. An anonymous work may be reprinted by any member after a lapse of twenty years from the date of the last edition upon two months' notice of such intention being given. A number of minor regulations are proposed, but as they are merely conducive to the better accomplishment of the objects here declared, their recapitulation would be uninteresting to a general reader.

The foundation stone of the new ' Exchange for German Booksellers' was laid at Leipzig on the 26th of October last, by M. von Langenau, to whom the task was specially assigned by his Royal Highness, the co-regent of the kingdom. Mr. F. Fleischer, one of the leading booksellers, delivered an opening speech on the occasion, and was followed by Dr. Haase, the rector of the university, and other individuals of note.

Grants for the Promotion of Education and Science.—The ' Budget for Churches, Academies, and Schools, in the kingdom of Saxony' for the present year, contains the following among other items :—

For the University of Leipzig . . Doll.	34,001	or £4675
Protestant Churches and Schools	30,542	4199
Catholic ditto . . .	19,415	2669
Deaf and Dumb Schools in Dresden	300	41
Military Seminaries . .	34,285	4714
Completing the income of schools for the education of soldiers' children	9,130	1255
Mining Academy at Freiberg .	10,032	1379
Forest Academy and Agricultural Institution at Tharaûd . .	8,772	1206
Academy of Arts in Dresden .	20,043	2756
Maintenance of the Galleries and Collections in Dresden . .	20,666	2841
Support of several Societies of Arts, &c.	2,800	385
Academy of Medicine and Surgery	16,995	2337
Botanical Garden, Dresden .	850	117
		£28,574

WÜRTEMBERG.—*Examination for Admission into a University.* —The regulations for this examination were made public on the 14th of June last, and are to the following effect:—'Every individual, without exception, is required to give proof of his knowledge of the Latin language both by oral and written translations; to answer questions in pure and applied logic, as well as in ancient and modern history and geography; to solve questions in arithmetic, elementary algebra, and geometry (the latter in so far only as the questions are comprised in the First Three Books of Euclid); and to write a paper on given points in religion and morals; the paper to be written in German, and to be taken as evidence of the student's power of composition in his mother-tongue. Such students as intend to devote themselves to the study of theology, jurisprudence, or medicine, are to undergo an examination likewise, both orally and by written answers, in the Greek language. Candidates for the Church are in addition to pass an examination in Hebrew.'

Tübingen.—During the summer session just elapsed, the number of students in this university was 746; and of these 101 were not natives of the Würtemberg dominions. The *divinity* classes contained 163 of the Protestant, 169 of the Roman Catholic, and 5 of the Jewish persuasion; the *law* classes, 82; the students in *medicine* and *surgery* amounted to 165; in *pharmacy*, 10; *philosophy*, 106; and *rural, &c., economy*, 44.

Nassau.—There is an institution for the education of teachers in our national schools at Idstein, and every individual who is desirous of admission is allowed to enter, let his faith be what it may, provided he is a Christian. The prescribed course extends over three years, and the pupils are divided into three classes. The subjects of study include the doctrines and history of religion, German grammar, mathematics, history, natural history, geography and popular astronomy, psychology, pædagogy, composition, elocution, gymnastic exercises, organ-playing, singing, simple book-keeping, writing, and drawing; besides husbandry, which is taught in the practical school of agriculture attached to this seminary. But instruction given here includes the theory of rural economy as well, together with botany and mineralogy, and the rudiments of zoology. Youths are admitted into the seminary, provided they are not under sixteen nor above eighteen years of age. The number of pupils in it last summer was eighty.—S***.

Jena.—It appears, from a communication made by M. de la Nourrais to the editor of the *Revue Germanique,* that in the interval between Easter 1558 and Michaelmas 1786, which comprises a period of 228 years, 90,689 students matriculated in this university: namely, in the sixteenth century, from 1558 to 1600—10,851; in the seventeenth, from 1601 to 1700—39,402; and in the eighteenth, from 1701 to 1786—40,436. The most flourishing periods in the last interval were the years 1711, 1712, 1715, 1717, 1733, and 1752; the least so were 1611, 1626, 1636, 1637, 1640, and 1656. In the beginning of the eighteenth century, there were at one time

4000 students in actual attendance; during the Seven Years' War, the number varied between 1300 and 1400; but in 1778 and the following year they declined to their present number of 500 or 600.

SAXONY.—There are fourteen gymnasia in this kingdom, which has a population of about 1,500,000 souls; in Prussian Silesia, where the population is about 100,000 more, there are seventeen; and in Ducal Saxony, where the inhabitants are about 100,000 fewer, there are twenty-two. Each high-school in Saxony costs, on the average, about 120*l.* a-year,' independently of buildings and fittings. The Catholic schools are 11 in number, four of which are at Dresden, and the remainder in Leipzig, Chemnitz, Pirna, Zwickau, and Freiberg. All but two of them admit pupils gratuitously, and some are wholly supported by individual benevolence and endowments. The state does not expend more than about 3200 dollars (480*l.*) a-year upon them. The number of pupils whom they at present educate is 1020.

HANOVER.

Constitution of the 26th September, 1833.—This important document which is become the fundamental law of his majesty's Hanoverian dominions, contains the following clauses to which we give insertion as coming within the immediate range of subjects comprehended in this Journal:—' Clause 25. The education of the king during his minority is, in case the preceding king shall not have made any other arrangement, to be directed by his mother, and in her default, by his paternal grandmother, provided they have not contracted a subsequent marriage in other countries; and in default of these, by the regent and adjunct-councillor (*beirath*) of the ministry. In like manner the regent is to aid and assist the persons in whose province a minor king's education lies, and, in case there should arise any differences between such persons and himself, with regard to the choice of teachers or the plan of education, his decision shall be binding.' The 30th clause enacts, that ' Every inhabitant of the kingdom shall be entitled to full liberty of faith and conscience. And he is therefore authorized, as well as every individual in his family, to hold religious exercises under his own roof. The members of the Evangelical and Roman Catholic churches shall enjoy equal civil and political rights in the state. The king enjoys the right of recognising other Christian creeds and sects. The adherents of such unrecognised Christian confessions and sects shall be allowed the enjoyment of civil rights and private worship. Their political rights shall depend at all times upon a special law; the direct sanction of the king is requisite for the public celebration of worship. The nature of the rights to which members of the Jewish persuasion are to be admitted shall be laid down by a special law.'

Finance.—The budget of the ministry for religious matters and education for the present year amounts to 98,000 dollars (about 31,500*l.*)

Schools.—It appears by official returns that the actual number of elementary schools in the Hanoverian dominions is 3426, and that 3085 of them belong to the Protestant and 341 to the Roman Catholic persuasion. The income of these schools, independently of allowances for lodging and fuel, amounts in the whole to 351,544 dollars, or about 49,750*l.* sterling. The incomes of 436 of them are less than twenty-six dollars each (3*l.* 12*s.*), and those of 736 between 26 and 60 dollars (8*l.* 8*s.*) each.—*Hanover Paper.*

PRUSSIA.

Examination before Matriculation.—The minister of public instruction issued a code of regulations in June last, which places the examination of young men previously to their matriculating at any Prussian university on a new footing. These regulations prescribe, that every youth desirous of devoting himself to any particular branch of study, for which a three or four years' course of university study is laid down, shall undergo a previous examination before a regular board of examiners at the gymnasium or high-school of which he is a pupil, with a view to ascertain whether he has acquired the requisite degree of scholastic knowledge. He is authorised to petition for examination during the last three months of the fourth half-year of his attendance in the first or highest class. Scholars, however, who distinguish themselves by diligence, good conduct, and maturity of acquirements, may be admitted to examination in the last three months of the third half-year of their attendance in the first class. Such as wish to enter a university are to be examined in the German, Latin, Greek, and French languages; but if they intend to become candidates for the theological or philological departments, they are to be examined also in Hebrew. Further, all of them are to be examined in divinity, history combined with geography, mathematics, natural philosophy, and the elements of natural history (*naturbeschreibung*), and philosophical analysis. The range of such examination is to be confined to those subjects which form the groundwork of the studies pursued in the first class, and it is to be so conducted as to afford evidence ' of the continued, persevering, and successful assiduity of the examined during the whole of his attendance at the school.' The examination is to be both oral and by written answers and theses. With respect to the latter, the candidate is to write a prose theme in his mother-tongue; an extempore essay in Latin, and a free version in the same language of some passages with which he ought to be familiar; a translation of some passage in a Greek poet or prose-writer, which has not been before him at school, though it comes within the range of study assigned to the first class; and a translation from his mother-tongue into French, of some didactic piece which is not too intricate in a grammatical point of view; and a mathematical paper which is to contain the solution of two geometrical and two arithmetical questions, corresponding with the degree of mathematical knowledge which he ought to have attained. Candidates intended for the departments of divinity and philology are, in addition, to translate some piece in Hebrew, out of the Psalms or the historical part of the Hebrew Bible, and to add a grammatical analysis to such translation. The period allowed for composing these written papers for the examiners is three days, not consecutive ; each of which days must be confined to 8 hours' labour ; the German paper to 5 hours, the Latin extempore essay to 2, and the Latin version to 5 ; the translation from the Greek to 3, the French to the same number, the mathematical answers to 4, and the Hebrew, including the time for writing the paper out in a clear hand (*reinschrift*), 2. No subdivision of these labours is to be permitted ; *i. e.* no candidate can write part of a paper in the forenoon, and part in the afternoon. No books or other help is to be allowed except dictionaries and mathematical tables. The number of candidates present at oral examinations is never to exceed 12 ; and these examinations are to embrace all the subjects mentioned above.

SILESIA.—In the year 1831, this province, which had at that time a population of 2,459,789 souls, possessed the following seminaries ; namely, 1 university (Breslau), 21 gymnasia, 5 schools for educating masters, and 5400 minor schools.

Bible Societies.—The Parent Bible Society of Prussia received contributions last year to the amount of 7969 dollars (1095*l.*), and circulated 7602 bibles and 371 New Testaments. Since its first establishment, this society, in conjunction with its branches, has distributed upwards of 630,000 copies of the Holy Scriptures. The Bible Society founded by Baron von Canstein, at Halle, has published altogether 2,754,350 copies of the Bible, of six different versions ; 120,714 New Testaments with psalters ; 22,000 separate psalters; 90,105 copies of the Book of Jesus the son of Sirach ; 10,350 of a Bohemian Bible, which is already out of print; and 15,250 copies of the New Testament in the Bohemian language. The institution at present possesses and employs 10 common presses and 2 worked by steam ; and has a regular establishment of between 30 and 40 workmen and 24 bookbinders.

BERLIN.—The king has granted 16,000*l.* (120,000 dollars), over and above the annual appropriation, for improving the interior arrangements of the university buildings ; it being understood that the grant is to extend over six years, at the rate of 20,000 dollars per annum.

Population.—Without including the number of individuals, who took up their residence in or emigrated from the Prussian dominions, and excluding also the principality of Neuchatel, the population of this kingdom amounted at the close of last year (1833) to 13,223,385 souls. But if the exceptions be included, it may be reasonably estimated at 13,250,000.

BAVARIA.

Examination for admission into High Schools.—If a youth is designed for a learned profession, it is requisite that he should have exhibited sufficient talent and information, at the examination which he must pass through between his fourteenth and sixteenth year, to enable the Board of Examiners, consisting of four or more teachers in a gymnasium, to ascertain how far he has given proof that he possesses such capabilities as will warrant them in anticipating that he will go through the rest of his studies with diligence and effect. The preliminary step to admission into our gymnasia is, that a youth has duly attended a preparatory course of four years. Boys generally enter the preparatory school between the ages of 10 and 14, and quit it between those of 14 and 18. They then pass into the gymnasium, after having undergone a rigid examination before a board of masters on all subjects comprehended in the preparatory course. The conditions of this examination are thus laid down in the instructions for the board :—" Whoever shall not afford proof, in translating from German into Latin, that he possesses sufficient acquaintance with the etymology and syntax of the grammar, and aptness in applying the rules; or, in translating from German into Greek, that he is deficient in purity of expression and choice of words, as well as ignorant of the leading principles of the syntax; or, in translating an easy piece of Latin into German, that he is not well-grounded in German grammar, especially in orthography and punctuation; and further, whatsoever youth, upon oral examination, shall not readily translate from the Classics and other books prescribed for the upper classes of the Latin school, and shall not evince a due acquaintance with such parts of religion, history, geography, and arithmetic, as are prescribed for the said school,—shall not be admitted into a gymnasium. The members of the board are one and all responsible for a rigid and impartial execution of these directions.' A youth incapable of passing the examination here prescribed is sent back to continue his studies in the fourth class of the preparatory school; but this is seldom known to occur, except where he has been idle, or labours under positive want of ability.

SWITZERLAND.

Freiburg.—At the very moment when the schools in Lucern and Soleure have undergone a diminution of one-third in their number of pupils, the Jesuits' academy here has one thousand pupils at least under its care. In fact, the college has this year been thrown open for youth of all descriptions, and without any exception; and most branches of study are taught in one or other of two living and popular languages, even some of them in both, French and German. Though the income of this seminary amounts, on a very moderate computation, to 1600*l*. (24,000 Swiss francs) a year, the Great Council has been induced by their Jesuit friends to vote them 238*l*. (3877 Swiss francs) more, and this at the very time when the Council of Education has not been able to obtain above 160*l*., say 2400 Swiss francs, towards the support of all the other establishments for public instruction existing in this canton.

BERN.—The third university in Switzerland was opened in this town in November last, and the arrangements for the Medical school have been completed by the appointment of Dr. Mohl of this place as Professor of Physiology and Botany, and Dr. Jahn, of Saxe-Meiningen, as Professor of Special Therapeutics and Clinical Medicine; they are to receive a salary of 160*l*. each. Dr. Theile, of Jena, has also been appointed Professor of Anatomy, and Dr. Brunner of this town Professor of Chemistry; both with salaries of 105*l*. each.

PAYS DE VAUD.—The 388 parishes in this canton, the population of which is 177,000 souls, are divided into 162 school districts, which contain 625 schools, attended by 29,651 pupils, or nearly 17 in every 100 inhabitants. The sum expended on public education is about 7600*l*. (115,000 Swiss francs), to which 3665*l*. (53,494 fr.) have this year been added for the purpose of raising the masters' salaries.

ZÜRICH.—This canton contained, in the scholastic year 1832-3, 162 school districts, 576 parishes with schools, 393 teachers, and 49,187 pupils. The total endowment of these establishments was 257,320 francs, or about 8570*l*. per annum.

Zürich.—In March last the number of professors and other teachers in this university was 54, and the number of students 164. The expenses attending it had amounted to 83,000 Swiss francs, or about 5500*l*.

ARGOVIA.—The number of elementary schools in this canton in the year 1832 was 275; they were conducted by 440 teachers, and attended by 33,241 children.

ITALY.

SARDINIA.—Independently of the University of Turin, which is one of the best attended in Italy, there is a university at Genoa, which has 29 professorships, and a school of the fine arts, as well as chairs of painting, sculpture, architecture, engraving, and the art of embellishment, a school of ship-building, another of navigation, and four public libraries. The chief towns in each province possess a college with from eight to twelve professors or teachers, who instruct their pupils in theology, canon law, civil law, surgery, mathematics, geography, rhetoric, and Latin. And there is scarcely a town without a college of an inferior description, conducted by two or three professors, and as many assistants. But the rural population is left almost to shift for itself; indeed no country in Europe has greater need of a well-devised system of national education than the Sardinian states. The schools, in the hands of the lay and secular clergy, are but so many nurseries for ignorance and superstition.

State of Education in Savoy.—(From a private letter.)—' Since the year 1814 the clergy have contrived to obtain exclusive posses-

sion of all the colleges and grammar-schools in the country, and to
eject every lay master or professor from them. There are altogether
six colleges in this duchy, to which professors, both of the classics
and philosophy, are attached at the public expense; but no more
nor any other sort of philosophy is taught by them than what is
sanctioned by a government which is content to leave education in
the hands of narrow-minded ecclesiastics. It really appears to me
as if the ruling powers conceived that ignorance, or at least the
smallest possible degree of intelligence, was the surest stay of government; and if matters go on much longer in their present train,
the natural result will be that none but the children of individuals
of a certain income will be permitted to study the higher branches
of knowledge. The first step towards such a consummation has
long since been devised; but the temper of the times has apparently,
and I am told, really withheld the government from venturing upon
it. The archbishop of Chambery is its avowed parent; it was not
only proposed by him to the late king, Charles Felix, but actually
embodied in a royal edict and sanctioned by the royal signature;
the interposition, however, of a somewhat more enlightened coun-
cillor happily prevented its promulgation. This precious document
expressly enacts, that no parent who does not possess a clear income
of 1000 livres shall be allowed to have his children taught any
branches of instruction, besides reading, writing, and common arithmetic. In the meanwhile, no opportunity of giving the minds of
the Savoyards a befitting tone is neglected; among other means
adopted, a missionary was sent on his travels through Savoy last
year, for the purpose of warning the people (and I use his own
words), that " any one who suffers his children to learn reading and
writing places the key to every secret sin in his hands," and that
" every parent guilty of so horrible an offence will for ever forfeit the
key to heaven." In connexion with this anti-intellect device, I observed that the country clergy endeavour to put down all public
amusements, particularly dancing, for which they entertain a special
aversion; and I know from the mouths of the Savoyards themselves,
that great pains are taken at the confessional to persuade them, that
there is scarcely a trespass or crime which does not emanate from
" the light heel and fantastic toe." But the priest is too wary to
give utterance to such doctrines in populous places or large towns.
The Roman government has already set the example by excluding
every young man not possessed of a certain monthly income from
their universities, and requiring, before matriculation, that some responsible party should be bound for his good conduct.'—A. G. S.

Naples.—' There are few countries in Europe over which knowledge is less generally diffused than Naples, although it is not deficient in the machinery of education; for it contains, Sicily included, the three universities of Naples, Palermo, and Catania, 5
lycea, 11 royal colleges, 708 grammar-schools, in which a smattering
of Latin is generally acquired, and 2130 elementary schools; but
the majority of them are wretchedly attended, and the situation of

a master is almost become a sinecure. Hopes are, however, entertained that the present active-minded monarch will not lose sight of the intellectual slavery which presses upon his subjects, and that he will ultimately be enabled to break its fetters : but he has to wrestle first with ignorance in high places, and next with the contagion of bad example arising partly out of the idleness and partly out of the immorality of nearly one and twenty thousand pampered members of religious orders. He has done much to improve the financial state of his kingdom; he has infused a new spirit into mechanical industry and commercial enterprise; and has shown, on several occasions, that he considers learning and science entitled to his regard ; let him labour strenuously at overcoming the pride and prejudices of his nobles and clergy, who are almost the sole proprietors of the soil, and he may then become the blessed means of eradicating the moral and mental diseases which prey upon the vitals of this fair and favoured land.'—*Naples, 28th August.*

SPAIN.

There are schools in abundance in the Spanish metropolis, not excepting such as are suited to the capacities of the indigent portion of the community, though no one has yet ventured to introduce either the Madras or Pestalozzian system into them.   Nor is there any want of masters for teaching the accomplishments of more refined life in Madrid.   Mixed up with an occasional mathematician, naturalist, poet, or scholar, its learned society is deluged with theologians, though, long as I have resided there, I have never had the fortune to hear a good sermon.   An elegant observatory, too, is near, but for practical science or observations it is almost below zero.   The best part of the Spanish literature of the present day consists of translations from English and French ; the chief writers on medical science and pharmacy, chemistry, and natural history, the mathematics, and experimental philosophy, who are almost wholly of the French school, have been well translated in Madrid, and their works have been adopted as class-books in most seminaries.   There is no such thing in this metropolis as a regular academy of the arts and sciences, such as exists in almost every other capital in Europe, even in Lisbon; a partial substitute is, however, to be found in the special academies which have been instituted for the cultivation of history, philology, political economy, medicine, and the fine arts, from which last music, however, forms an exception.   Our medical practitioners are mostly brought up according to the French and English systems, though they are still warped by national prejudices.   The surgeons are divided into two classes ; Latin or educated, and non-Latin.   The latter, in fact, form the confraternity of barbers, blood-letters, and dentists, though they practise other branches of the profession which are not within their regular sphere of duties.   Medical police is more carefully looked after in Spain than in most countries, neither worm-doctors nor other quacks being allowed to dispense their art or drugs in public. Madrid is superabundantly provided with churches and monastic buildings; of convents and monasteries, indeed, it possesses no fewer than sixty-four: and yet there is not a really handsome or spacious place of worship in the whole town, nor a single steeple or tower of any pretensions to architectural beauty. The interior of the churches is equally destitute of taste: they are overloaded with old-fashioned embellishments, but without bench or sitting; the whole congregation stand or kneel, except ladies, who are permitted to squat down on mats: there are hosts of organs and organists, but few fit to be heard, and the bells are not rung by means of ropes, but by cumbersome machinery, which carries the bells and their clappers completely round the circle. The present school of painting is indifferently good, the painter, as compared with Murillo, Velasquez, or Mengs, holding much the same station as the present state of Spanish literature does when compared with the times of Cervantes, Calderon, or Lopez de Vega. We have a few decent engravers, but no first-rate engraver, nor much employment for any. There are printing-presses in abundance, but scarcely one of them affords a decent livelihood to its proprietor. A foreigner has also established a press for printing music; as yet, however, he has not met with much encouragement. We have some excellent mechanics here, particularly gold and silversmiths; but their charges are so excessive that, if you lose a key, it is cheaper to buy a new lock and key at once, which can be obtained of foreign make for less than the cost of a native key. I remonstrated once with my locksmith on his overcharge: ' I'll tell you the reason,' was his reply; 'abroad, everything is made with machinery, but here everything is extravagantly dear, and I have to pay my men enormous wages.' The commonest bricklayer or carpenter, in fact, earns his dollar a day; yet a poor creature of a female drudge in-doors scarcely gets three a month.—(*Communicated by a many-years' Resident in Madrid.*)

Public Instruction.—The following copy of a royal decree is from the *Madrid Gazette* of Sept. 28 :—' With a view to the formation of a general plan of public instruction, which may extend the sphere of learning and contribute to the propagation of knowledge most immediately useful, I deemed it proper to appoint, on the 31st of January last, a commission, composed of learned men zealous for the advancement of the public welfare; but considering that the labours of the said commission ought to have for their foundation a practical knowledge of the present state of public instruction in the kingdom, of the literary establishments, of the effects produced by the existing plan of study, and of the means which may be relied on for realizing beneficial reforms in this important department,—that these indispensable requisites are alone to be found in the board of general inspection for public instruction and its subordinate officers; and that, without the aid of the said requisites, it would be hardly possible to form a new system of education adequate to the present wants of the nation, and calculated to exercise a sufficient influence on the solid instruction of youth and the progress of knowledge, I have decreed, in the name of my august daughter, the Queen Donna Isabel II., as follows :—

' 1. The board of general inspection for public instruction is abolished.

' 2. A general directory of studies will be established in its stead, composed for the present of five regular and two supplementary members.

' 3. Regulates the precedency of members of the commission.

' 4. The general directory will immediately propose to me, through you, the authors whose writings, in their judgment, should be employed as text-books in the universities, in order that the course which is to open in October next may be read according to them, following in all other respects the system and direction of the existing plan of studies.

' 5. The general directory will take cognizance of the state of the universities and other literary establishments which have been maintained at the charge of the board of inspection, and supported by its revenues and dues, in order that they may accurately calculate on ulterior reforms, and on the possibility of carrying them into effect. From this inquiry the schools for primary instruction are for the present excepted.

' 6. The general directory will investigate what has been effected by the individuals who were charged with the formation of the system of study, on 31st January, and, aided by the knowledge and information which the existing state of education may afford them, they will form that plan which they may consider the most convenient and practicable, in conformity with the rules of experience, transmitting the same to me through you for my examination, and for the sanction of my royal approbation.

' *To Don J. M. Moscoso de Altamida.*'

The following ' Royal Order' was published in the *Madrid Gazette*, during the month of September :—' Most Excellent Señor,— Her Majesty the Queen Regent, being informed of the happy results which have been, and continue to be, produced in the greater number of European states, by the great encouragements extended by the governments thereof to the Lancasterian mode of public instruction, and being convinced that the adoption of this method cannot fail to spread primary instruction throughout the whole of Spain, and at the same time economise the time of the pupils, and save the people a considerable portion of the vast funds employed for this purpose, has been pleased to resolve that the commission (of primary instruction) should propose, with the shortest possible delay, whatever may be thought necessary by them, for the establishment in this city of a normal school of mutual education, in which a certain number of professors of primary instruction belonging to the provinces, or such as aspire to that situation, having made themselves practically acquainted with the plan, may establish the same method in the remaining capitals, and cause every town gradually to partici-

pate in its indisputable advantages. Her Majesty also desires that
the commission should at the proper time accompany their project
with an estimate of the funds requisite to carry it into effect, formed
with a view to economy, but without omitting the consideration of
any expense which may contribute to the better organization of the
establishment, and thus secure the immediate benefits which it must
produce, and which her Majesty considers as the origin of many
others of the highest importance for the promotion of civilization,
and the consequent improvement of the moral condition of Spa-
niards.'

Schools at Menars.—We are glad to have it in our power to
gratify the interest excited by an article in No. 13 of this Journal,
respecting the schools established at Menars, by the active exertions of the Prince Joseph de Chimay. Recent accounts state
that the enlightened and arduous labours of the prince have,
within the past year, been attended with many happy results. The
late director, M. Sauriac, has been replaced by M. Froussard, cheva-
lier of the legion of honour, and ex-director of the normal school of
the academy of Paris, than whom a more able man could not have
been selected for such an appointment. The Prytaneum now contains one hundred and twenty pupils, and possesses resources which
amply assure its independence ; and it is hoped that the school of
arts and trades will be soon in the same position. The organization,
also, being more perfect, the system of the institution has been more
completely developed, and it now comprises a school of commerce
and of agriculture, a superior school for girls, the school of arts and
trades, the school of pioneers, an infant school, and primary school
for girls. The two last are gratuitous, and the whole are connected
with the Prytaneum, of which they form the first, second, third, and
fourth divisions. It is in contemplation to publish a statement of
the progress of the institution, in which will be detailed the results
of past experience, and the defects which it is necessary to avoid.
This will be circulated at a cheap rate, and will be calculated not only
to serve the cause of education generally, but to satisfy the public
interest more particularly as to the system pursued at Menars.

GREECE.

NAUPLIA.—(*From private Notes.*)—This town is built in the form
of an amphitheatre ; the streets are regular, and by no means destitute of handsome dwellings, many of which might pass for minor
palaces ; and it is lighted at night by hundreds of lanterns,
which are kept blazing even when the moon is high and bright.
In comparison with the rest of Greece, Nauplia is well provided
with literary establishments ; they consist of a military academy, a
school for the middle classes, five printing-houses, a circulating
library, several book societies, two lithographical establishments, and
a bookseller's shop, which does not appear, however, to overflow
with customers. The ' Sotir,' or Saviour, a political and literary
paper, is published in Greek and French at this place, and much

read in every quarter. One of the printing-houses is the property of the government, and employed exclusively in printing the government paper; but of the remaining four, one is by no means at full work, though possessed of Greek, French, and German types: the other three are employed in printing school and religious books, none of which are very good. The expense of printing here is enormously high, at least double as much as in France or Germany. The Greek teachers lay particular stress on teaching boys to pronounce correctly, according, at least, to their own notion of correctness, and exhibit a degree of patience at their task which I never met with elsewhere.

National Schools, &c. (Syra, 17th July.)—The groundwork of a system of general elementary instruction has just been laid by the enactment of a law, which obliges every tithe-district in Greece to establish and maintain a school at its own expense; the masters are to be appointed by the government after a preliminary examination, and are to give gratuitous instruction in reading, writing, the rudiments of modern Greek, arithmetic, geography, history, and natural history. The same law establishes also a normal school for the education of masters for these national schools, and other teachers. Another law has appeared, which directs that, in the Greek metropolis, (Athens) there shall be formed an academy of science and the fine arts, a university, museum of antiquities, cabinet of coins, natural history, and scientific instruments, an athenæum and an observatory; besides other institutions for the encouragement of science and the fine arts in general. Establishments of a similar description are, in the course of time, to be instituted in the capitals of each department. The same law likewise orders that a director-general and local boards shall be appointed in the several departments to superintend and keep up all these establishments, as well as to watch over the preservation of national antiquities. It also prohibits the exportation of such antiquities in the strictest manner, and lays down certain measures to be adopted in this respect which are likely to prove very efficacious.

We regret that we became acquainted but a short time since with a little pamphlet entitled ' Zur Topographie Athens. Ein Brief aus Athen und ein Brief nach Athen, von Dr. P. G. Forchhammer und K. O. Müller, Gött. 1833,' which contains some very valuable and original observations on the chorography of Attica; and, although these letters are no novelties in Germany, we think our readers will not be sorry to hear Dr. Forchhammer's ingenious method of restoring the name of Lycabettus to a more dignified mountain than that which has been hitherto honoured with the name. Dr. Forchhammer tells Mr. Müller that it occurred to him, as he went up from the Peiræus to the city, that the ἅγιος Γεώργιος, which has hitherto gone by the name of Anchesmus, must be the ancient Lycabettus, both on account of the N.E. position with regard to the Acropolis, suggested by his very probable etymology of the word,

and also because Strabo calls the Lycabettus one of the ὄρεα, ἃ ἐν ὀνόματι μάλιστά ἐστι, a remark which would hardly apply to the little
elevation hitherto known by that name; and then proceeds to adduce the ancient authorities which are in favour of the new, and
against the old, supposed site of the mountain. In the first place,
when Plato in his ' Critias,' p. 112, A., talking of the boundaries of the
Acropolis, makes the Lycabettus the boundary ἐκ τοῦ καταντικρὺ τῆς
Πυκνός, he clearly means by that name the ἅγιος Γεώργιος. For, had
he intended to add another boundary on the same side as the Pnyx,
he would certainly have mentioned the hill of the Museium, rather
than an insignificant elevation hardly separated from the Pnyx.
Again, Antigonus the Carystian (de Mirabilibus, c. xii. p. 22,
Beckmann) tells us, that ' as Athena was bringing Lycabettus from
Pentele (or Pallene) as a protection for the Acropolis, she was informed by a crow that Ericthonius was ἐν φανερῷ, whereupon the
goddess, unfortunately too soon, set down the mountain where
it now stands.' Hence it appears, that Mount Lycabettus was
east of the Acropolis, and just so far off that it was not, indeed,
a protection for the Acropolis, but excited a wish that it had
been near enough to be one. Dr. Forchhammer's next proof is, we
think, conclusive. It is founded on Theophrastus (de Signis Vento-
rum, c. i. § 4. p. 788, Schneider), who says, that Matricetas in Methymna used Lepetymnus—Cleostratus in Tenedos, Ida—and Phaeinus in Athens, Lycabettus, as gnomons to obtain a knowledge of the
summer-solstice, which Meton received from Phaeinus, and so set
forth the cycle of nineteen years. Now, Ida lies in respect to Tenedos just in the direction where the sun must rise, with regard to that
island, at the time of the summer-solstice; and Lepetymnus, as appears from Theophrastus, was necessarily E.N.E. from Methymna:
consequently Lycabettus lay E.N.E. from the Pnyx, where stood
Meton's observatory; and, therefore, must be the ἅγιος Γεώργιος,—
an inference which is confirmed by an etymology suggested by
Dr. Forchhammer and approved by Mr. Müller, p. 18, who calls
Dr. Forchhammer's derivation of the word from λυκάβας, not only ingenious but self-evident. Besides, Strabo not only makes the Lycabettus one of the five mountains, τῶν ἐν ὀνόματι, but also (X. 2) sets
in juxtaposition Ἰθάκην καὶ Νήριτον, Ἀθήνας καὶ Λυκαβηττὸν, Ῥόδον καὶ
Ἀτάβυριν, and Λακεδαίμονα καὶ Ταΰγετον : and the little hill north of the
Pnyx was surrounded with buildings; whereas, it is said in the
second Dialogue of Æschines (Plato, Bekkeri, pars iii. vol. iii. p. 556),
that the house of Polytion would be as useless a possession among
the Scythians, as Mount Lycabettus is at Athens. If we add to these
testimonies the remark in Xenophon's Œconomics, (xix. 6), and
the words in Aristoph. Ran. 1056 (1084),

> ἢν οὖν σὺ λέγῃς Λυκαβηττούς
> καὶ Παρνασσῶν ἡμῖν μεγέθη,

we shall feel quite convinced with Mr. Müller, p. 17, that Dr. Forchhammer has beyond all doubt placed Mount Lycabettus on the site
which belongs to it. With regard to the now displaced Anchesmus,

Dr. Forchhammer thinks that, if it is to be sought for on the Athens' side of the Hymettus, it can hardly be any other than the little mountain which has hitherto borne the name of Brilessus.

The other observations in the Doctor's letter, and the very sensible remarks in Mr. Müller's reply, are well worthy the attention of the student, whom we must, however, refer to the letters themselves for these the less important part of their contents.

RUSSIA.

Russian Conversations-Lexikon.—An association of native Russians, comprising the most eminent literary and scientific persons in the country, has been formed for the purpose of translating the German Conversations-Lexikon on a very extended plan, as to every subject connected with the Russian empire. With this view, the members of the association, who are said to be sixty in number, have divided themselves into twenty sections, each of which is to undertake some separate branch of the work. They entertain an expectation, that this valuable addition to Russian literature may be completed in six years.

The Oriental Languages.—The celebrated Armenian Institution in Moscow for teaching the oriental languages, which was founded by John and Joachim Lasarew in 1816, has formed upwards of three hundred orientalists, and up to the present time has cost altogether 900,000 roubles, or about 41,200*l.* sterling.

University of Kiew.—The solemn inauguration and opening of the new University of St. Vladimir took place on the 27th of July last, and the first members admitted were so admitted on this occasion by the conferring of diplomas of honour: they were Eugenius, the metropolitan of the diocese, Field-Marshal Prince von der Osten-Sacken, and Count Levatscheff, the governor-general of the province. The second of these high personages then rose and presented swords to the students, who had entered their names for matriculation. The sum assigned by the government for covering the yearly expenses of the university is 248,390 roubles, about 11,400*l.*, and the remuneration to be paid the professors and others has been placed on the following footing :—a professor in ordinary for salary and lodging, about 205*l.* a year (4500*r.*) ; a professor extraordinary, 155*l.* (3400*r.*) ; an adjunct professor, 106*l.* (2300*r.*) ; a lecturer, 91*l.* (2000*r.*) ; and each of the two professors of divinity and ecclesiastical law, 106*l.* (2300*r.*) ; towards establishing a fund for allowing pensions to professors, lecturers, and teachers of drawing, their widows and children, a sum of 10,000 roubles (about 457*l.*) is to be appropriated. The following chairs are to be instituted, namely, in the Faculty of *Philosophy*,—' Section 1.' Philosophy, Greek Literature and Antiquities, Roman Literature and Antiquities, Russian Literature, General and National History, and Statistics ; ' Section 2.' Pure and Mixed Mathematics, Astronomy, Physics and Experimental Philosophy, Chemistry, Mineralogy and Geognosy, Botany,

Zoology, Technology, Husbandry, Forest Economy, and Architecture. And in the Faculty of *Jurisprudence*,—General Systematic Review of the Science of Law, or what is called Encyclopedia of the Laws; the Constitutional and Administrative Laws of the Russian Empire, and Social Law; Russian Civil Law, including the laws respecting credit, trade, and manufactures, as well as the provincial laws of particular governments; Russian Criminal Law, Police Law, Laws concerning the Expenditure and Finances of the State, Roman Law in connexion with its history. For these several series of lectures it is intended that 15 professors in ordinary, 4 professors extraordinary, and 6 adjuncts shall be appointed. Lecturers will be nominated for the Polish, French, German, and Italian languages. The lectures are divided into half-yearly courses, but a full course of study requires four years for its completion, the last of which, particularly with reference to the crown students, (young men educated for the civil service or intended for the profession of public teachers at the expense of the crown,) may be devoted to the study of any special branch of knowledge. There is to be a yearly examination of the students, and at the close of the full course a final examination, the details of which are to be laid down by the Minister of Public Instruction. The degrees which the university is empowered to grant are those of Candidate (or Bachelor), Master, and Doctor; and the student who is desirous to take a Doctor's degree will be required to defend a dissertation, previously published by him, in open hall. If it concerns any ancient literature it must be written in Latin. All crown students (of whom there are to be 50 at Kiew, 26 for the department of education and 24 for the civil service) are required, upon quitting the university, to serve six years in those stations to which they have been appointed. The Board of Schools forms a section of the University Council, and this board is to direct and control the studies pursued in the various seminaries within its jurisdiction, which, by a recent ukase, embraces the districts of Volhynia, Podolia, Kiew, and Tshernigoff. The general superintendence of the university is vested in the Curator, whose duty it is 'to watch vigilantly that all parties subordinate to him perform their duties conscientiously; to direct his particular attention to the capabilities, zeal, and private conduct of the professors and other officers, and to adopt instant measures for the suppression of disorders of any kind whatsoever. His place of residence must be Kiew, and whilst he is absent for the purpose of inspecting the schools in the districts, or if he be indisposed, the rector of the university is to act in his stead.'

Travelling Scholars.—There are at present 27 young men, who have been educated in Russia, now travelling in various parts, at the expense of the Russian government, for the purpose of completing their education. Of 5 philologists, 4 are at Berlin and 1 at Leipzig; of 3 Orientalists, 1 is in England and 2 in Constantinople; of 8 medical students, 6 are in Berlin, 1 at another German university, and 1 in England; 1 is studying history and another the mathematics at Berlin ; 2 are studying botany at Vienna; 3 are studying diplomacy and the political sciences, and 2 the law at Berlin ; and 1 is studying painting in Italy.

The Kubatshine Republic.—The four villages of Kubatsha, Surärkilly, Shirilly, and Amisgally, with the lands pertaining to them, form the little republic of Kubatsha (improperly called Kabusha) in the regions of the Caucasus. This petty state lies between the two circles of Saragi and Kabadaria, in the Akushan dominions, the government of which is at present in the hands of Kadi-Machmed, a Mohammedan ecclesiastic. According to the tradition prevalent among the Kubatshans, their ancestors came from Frankistan, that is to say, the west of Europe, many centuries ago, and made extensive conquests in the countries about the Caucasus ; but their descendants have been stripped of all of them except the three villages which we have mentioned ; and, in fact, they are still treated as a conquered people. About six hundred years ago the Kubatshans embraced Mohammedanism, and have ever since continued to be zealous followers of the Prophet and his doctrines. This little commonwealth was not tributary to any foreign power until the year 1821, when Prince Madatoff, the Russian general, imposed a yearly tribute of four hundred ducats upon it, in consequence of the secret aid it lent to the Kasikumückish rebel, Surchai-Chan. In this way it is partially become a dependency of Russia ; but in every other respect, the people are in the full enjoyment of their own customs and usages, and, notwithstanding their Mohammedan tenets, have rigidly preserved their earlier habits, which bear evident trace of an European origin. The inhabitants of Surärkally, Shirilly, and Amisgally, though not positive slaves, are excluded from all popular assemblies. Those of the first of these villages employ themselves in making earthen vessels of all kinds ; the Shirilly men are agriculturists, and the people of Amisgally manufacture excellent steel ware. The females assist in the various labours performed by the men ; there are about fifty families in each village, of the Lesghis tribe; but whether they pay any tribute or not to the Kubatshans it has not hitherto been possible to induce them to say. The village of Kubatsha contains between four and five hundred families, divided into twenty-five clans. Ten elders, whose station answers to what we should term senators (or oligarchs), and is hereditary, form a standing body of nobility ; they assemble once a year, and elect as many judges as there are clans, on whom the task of giving judgment in all contested cases devolves. In cases of importance, or on any occasion where either party is dissatisfied with the judgment given, the ten elders meet, and their award is irrevocable. In the event of dissensions in the three vassal villages, the whole twenty-five judges or heads of clans repair to the spot, and pronounce their decision after inquiry into the circumstances. The proceedings are oral, but the decision is framed according to certain ancient dicta and customs, which are recorded in a large book. The language spoken by the Kubatshans is perfectly unintelligible, not only to any of the Caucasian tribes, but even to the people of the three villages. It has imbibed, it is true, many of the qualities peculiar to the mountain dialects, but appears to be of easier flow than the language spoken either by the Avari or Lesghis of Daghestan. It is a guttural language even in its softer intonations. The code of laws seems to be written in their own tongue but in Tartar characters ; and their intercourse with the neighbouring Tartars has introduced several of their words into the language. The following words and phrases are taken from it :—' *allah sah*,' for God ; ' *the adamé*,' man ; *gall*, a man ; *chünûl*, a woman ; *ussû*, a girl ; *kaaka*, a stone ; *schin*, water ; *tulud*, bread ; *mûch*, iron ; *shin*, water ; *outshâ*, water ; *ssa*, one ; *qua*, two ; *av*, three ; *aug*, four ; *chu*, five ; *eck*, six ; *va*, seven, pronounced almost like *ua ; ka*, eight ; *utshu*, nine ; *wig*, ten ; *witkusa*, eleven ; *witkuqua*, twelve, &c. ; *ha*, twenty, almost like *ga ; aw-zahl*, thirty ; *aug-zahl*, forty ; *dâsh*, a hundred ; *asü*, a thousand ; *gall wa schian*, come here, servant ; *thsi na okullin*, where art thou going ? *oda mi vi kuldé*, I love thee ; *oda mi autsha*, I do not love thee ; *bequisi saaka*, bring me some food ; *shin deitshi hacka*, bring me water to drink ; *kaaka saaka*, bring me a stone. They usually lay the accent on the last syllable, and in conversation dwell with a drawling emphasis on the last word in a sentence. The males employ themselves in manufacturing iron, and the females in domestic labours and weaving cloth. The Kubatshan muskets, pistols, and daggers are in great request ; nor is their cloth of bad quality. If a male has learned no mechanical art, and is not rich or adventurous enough to engage in trade, he sits the whole day long in the mosque, and gives at least a tinge of piety to his indolence. His wives, of whom the Koran allows him to possess four, are bound to feed him.—[The length of the details transmitted to us on the subject of this hitherto unknown commonwealth compels us to postpone the remaining portion of them to our next Number.]

DENMARK.

Establishments for Education.—Denmark cannot have less than 2,000,000 inhabitants at the present day, among whom the number of children of all ages fit to be instructed may be estimated at 300,000. It possesses 2 universities, Copenhagen and Kiel, the former attended by 800 students, and the latter by 300 ; 27 grammar schools, containing 1400 pupils ; and 4600 elementary schools, of which about 3000 are on the principle of mutual instruction, attended altogether by 278,500 pupils. Besides these establishments there are 2 asylums for the deaf and dumb (in Copenhagen and Schleswig), 2 seminaries for the education of teachers, and 2 academies for cadets. A general code of regulations for schools has existed since the year 1817. It appears also that the various school-houses are in general in a satisfactory condition, and that the remuneration paid to masters is on the whole sufficiently liberal.

Returns of the Population of Denmark (the Duchies of Schleswig, Holstein and Lauenburg excepted), according to the Census taken by order of the Danish Government, on the 8th February, 1834, as compared with the Population in 1831.

Districts.	Superficies in Geographical Square Miles.	Census of 1801.	Census of 1834.	Increase of Population.	Increase per Cent.
I. District of Zealand, including the Islands of Moen and Samsoe.	133.6260	100,975 } 22,938 } 361,523 218,103 } 19,507 }	119,292 } 32,791 } 464,607 287,879 } 24,645 }	103,094	28 per Cent.
a. The City of Copenhagen.					
b. In the Townships of the District.					
c. In the Rural Parishes.					
d. In the Island of Bornholm.					
II. District of Funen, comprising the Islands of Funen, Langeland, and Thaasing.	61.2183	16,059 } 121,378 105,319 }	25,176 } 167,062 141,886 }	45,684	38 per Cent.
a. In the Townships.					
b. In the Rural Parishes.					
III. District of Laaland and Falster.	30.0584	5,918 } 52,980 47,062 }	8,667 } 66,186 57,519 }	13,206	25 per Cent.
a. In the Townships.					
b. In the Rural Parishes.					
IV. District of North Jutland.	448.4203	39,076 } 389,093 350,017 }	57,575 } 525,952 468,377 }	136,859	35 per Cent.
a. In the Townships.					
b. In the Rural Parishes.					
	683.6372	924,974	1,233,807	298,833	32 per Cent.

TURKEY.

Education.—The study of philosophy, so far as regards metaphysics and logic, is by no means neglected among the Turks, but it is pursued to a very limited extent; this must be obvious when we come to consider that the pursuit has always been rendered subordinate to a religious code which materializes the intellectual world, not only with respect to the world which we inhabit, but even the enjoyments of Paradise itself. As to logic, which they figuratively term the 'science of balancing,' their good sense teaches them, however well they may be acquainted with its subtleties and resources, to lay but slender stress upon the use of it. On this subject the Turk broaches a maxim, which might come into common use with much benefit to ourselves : ' *Do good to all the world, and avoid disputing with the ignorant.*' Though metaphysics and logic are held in slight esteem among Eastern nations, the science of morals on the other hand, or rather its precepts, is raised to the skies. In no other quarter is it arrayed in so splendid, attractive, and insinuating a garb. One cannot read the Turkish poets and historians, or the delightful outpourings of a Djami, Saadi, or Hafiz, by whom Persia has been raised to immortal fame, without concluding that lessons of so sublime a nature, as those which they inculcate, must be the type of a state of society which has attained to the highest degree of virtuous principle; but—I need not tell you what these Easterns actually are. The Turkish system of instruction is divided into three degrees. The 'mekteb,' or primary schools, are spread throughout the empire. There are about twelve hundred of them in Constantinople, and in some parts of the town you will find as many as twelve or fifteen in a single quarter. Every one of these schools owes its origin to some pious endowment; for it is not the ruling powers, but religious fervour which provides in Turkey for the exigencies of public education. The 'medressés' or colleges are similarly maintained at the expense of the Mosques. The instruction which is given in them being gratuitous, the children of the poor as well as the rich are enabled to receive those elements of knowledge which society owes to every member of it. It were much to be desired that, in this respect, we should not allow the Turks to be so much beforehand with us. At a more advanced age the distinction of classes depends, naturally enough, upon the wants and means of families themselves. But no better beginning or introduction to life could be devised than these primary schools, where all classes are intermingled, where every child's mind receives a religious impress which does not wear away, and where each pupil gains something by contact with his neighbour. The Turk is so sensible of the advantage thus acquired, that the wealthiest among them would feel repugnant to admit a ' kodja,' or master, under his roof ; in this matter, indeed, he adheres as inflexibly as in many others to the adage which is accepted amongst all his brethren, ' One must do as the rest of the world does.' As no instruction is to be found elsewhere than in the mekteb and medressés, and the whole system is subordinate to the religious code, it produces complete harmony of mind and action in the community at large, and imparts a uniform aspect to the whole nation. They know nothing of an academical clique, nor of what is extravagantly called amongst ourselves ' freedom of education.' Whoever has the means at his disposal is at liberty to set up as teacher. The Turk does not pretend to make philosophers and philanthropists of his children ; but he makes them Turks, and this it is which has hitherto preserved them as a compact whole. If it be asked, whether the spirit of reform will find its way into the Turkish schools, it may be replied, that it is indisputably the Sultan's interest that it should ; otherwise his labours will perish with him and be buried with the existing generation. Hitherto the mekteb and medressés have succeeded tolerably well in warding off all innovations.—(*Michaud et Pouzelat, Correspondance de l'Orient*, 1830—1831, 2d and 3d vols. publ. 1834.)

AMERICA.

University of the City of New York.—The present term of the university commenced on Monday last, previous to which fifty-seven applicants for admission had presented themselves. Others, we are told, are still to be examined ; and from present appearances the accession at the commencement of this year will be much greater than at any previous time since the university has been opened.

Among the young gentlemen received is Mr. Christopher Oscanean from Constantinople. Mr. Oscanean is an Armenian by birth, is already well versed in several languages, and has come out to complete a liberal education in the university. We hope he may be the forerunner of many others who may hasten to our shores on a like errand.

We congratulate the friends of learning on the highly prosperous condition of this noble institution. By looking over a list of the officers, it will be seen that the several professorships are filled by talent of unusual excellence and variety, and that the council are extending the means of instruction, not only in general literature, but in arts and sciences, with much spirit and liberality. The officers are as follow :—Rev. J. M. Mathews, D.D., Chancellor ; Rev. H. P. Tappan, Professor of Belles Lettres, and Lecturer on Moral Philosophy ; R. B. Patten, Professor of Greek ; Rev. John Proudfit, Professor of Latin ; C. W. Wackley, Professor of Mathematics ; W. A. Norton, acting Professor of Astronomy and Natural Philosophy ; Lewis C. Beck, Professor of Chemistry and Botany ; D. B. Douglas, Professor of Architecture and Civil Engineering ; S. F. B. Morse, Professor of the Literature of the Art of Design ; L D. Gale, acting Professor of Geology and Mineralogy ; Rev. George Bush, Professor of Hebrew ; Rev. William Ernenspeutch, Professor of German ; C. L. Parmentier, Professor of French ; Charles Rabadan, Professor of Spanish ; L. L. Da Ponte, Professor of Italian.—From the *New York Commercial Advertiser*, Oct. 9, 1834.

AFRICA.

ALGIERS.—Three schools on the system of mutual instruction, and as many classes in Arabic, are at this moment in full activity within the circuit of the regency. There are a number of Moorish children from Oran and Bona, who also attend the elementary schools. Professors, chosen by open competition, will very soon be appointed to the three chairs of Arabic. The education of the natives forms, indeed, a leading point in the system laid down by the French government, and it is but justice to say of the local authorities, that they lose no opportunity of seconding the impulse given from headquarters. Besides these establishments, some private individuals have, with the full consent of government, set on foot several Moorish and Jewish schools, in which the reading of the Holy Scriptures and the Koran, and instruction in writing Arabic, are all that is at present attempted. Surely these beginnings are a favourable omen for this new theatre of European exertion. In addition, it has been settled, that classes are to be opened next year in mathematics, Greek, and Latin; besides a course of practical geometry and design, adapted to the comprehension of mechanics, &c. It is also said to be in contemplation to found a superior seminary in Algiers, on the plan of the Royal Colleges in France. A complete and accurate alphabet of the Mogrebin characters in use upon this spot has been collected, and it is intended to have a fount of types cast from it at Paris. A fount cast from the most perfect manuscript letters, such as are employed in every-day writing, is also to be prepared at the same time.

Children's Friend Society.—In our Number for April last, we noticed the Annual Report of this Society, then conducted under the name of the Society for the Suppression of Juvenile Vagrancy; the office of which is at Exeter Hall, Strand, and the establishment at Hampton-Wick. The Society have since that time received returns from the Cape of Good Hope communicating the establishment in that colony of the boys and girls since sent thither. These returns, which they have printed, give a total of 204 boys and 18 girls comfortably settled in that colony, independently of those sent to the Swan River and to Canada, from whence the returns have not yet been received. The experiment appears to have been very successful, as will appear from the following extract from the *South African Commercial Advertiser*, published at Cape Town, July 2, 1834.

'We feel much pleasure at being able to inform our fellow Colonists that the Scheme for supplying them with young Apprentices as Agricultural Labourers, Domestic Servants, &c., of which we have so often spoken, is now fully matured, and the inhabitants of this Colony have it now in their power to obtain any number of such Apprentices of both sexes, by applying to the "Committee for Apprenticing Juvenile Emigrants in Cape Town."

'The Society in England, from which this Committee receives these Juvenile Emigrants, having enlarged its plan, so as to embrace destitute children of every age, and formed establishments in which they can be educated and trained in habits of industry, order, and virtue, has adopted the title of the " Children's Friend Society."

' In these Asylums a *mild* system of discipline has been adopted, from which, so far as it has been tried, the happiest effects have resulted. Youths who were found to be utterly immoveable by severity of demeanour and corporal punishment, have in many instances been shaken, and completely subdued by kindness and sympathy.

' When the first divisions of these Emigrants were landed here last year, an opinion was entertained by some, originating in the former title of the Society—" For the Suppression of Juvenile *Vagrancy*"—that most, if not all, of them had been guilty of, some crime or delinquency. And it is true that, of many of them, the Society in London could only say that they knew nothing, except that they were found in a state of destitution. Their future conduct was therefore a subject of deep anxiety with the Committee in Cape Town, and they pressed on the attention of the Society in London the superior advantages likely to be secured to the public, both at home and in the Colonies, by receiving destitute children into their Asylums, if possible before they had been forced by their unhappy circumstances into vicious courses, and to send none to the Cape beyond the age of fourteen years for Boys, and twelve for Girls, unless particularly applied for by individuals, and that a certificate of character should be transmitted with such as had been for any time under their protection. With these views the Society have signified their cordial concurrence, and the most satisfactory testimonials of character and behaviour have been received along with the last division which has just been distributed.

' It is but justice to these Children, however, to add, that though no fewer than 174 have been apprenticed during the last twelve months, *not a single case of theft, violence, or outrage, on the part of any one of them, has been brought under the cognizance of the Magistrate.* During the first two or three months a few cases of desertion occurred ; but this was easily checked, as it seems to have arisen entirely from the novelty of their situation, and a want of sympathy with the strangers among whom they were thus suddenly placed ; and from all we have seen and heard on the subject, we are able to say that their conduct has been not only blameless but exemplary.

' With a view to their further improvement, the Committee have engaged a Teacher to give instruction to such of them as their masters can spare for that purpose for one hour in the evenings of Monday, Wednesday, and Friday each week, from eight till nine o'clock. This School will be opened this evening.

' As we consider this method of introducing Labourers and Domestic Servants into the Colony the most likely to prove beneficial in every aspect in which it can be viewed, that has yet been suggested, we offer no apology for the length to which our remarks upon it have run whenever we have had occasion to refer to it. To relieve the distress of those who are suffering for the faults or in consequence of the misfortunes of their parents—to snatch from the jaws of a cruel death by cold, want, and hunger, or from the gulph of moral perdition, more to be deplored than the cruellest of deaths, the orphan or deserted children of an over-crowded population—is an undertaking to which none can be indifferent; and when, by thus affording exercise to the best feelings of the heart, we see the certain prospect of securing an incalculable sum of good to our fellow colonists, we contemplate the whole scheme with unmingled satisfaction and delight.'

South African College.—This institution has been placed under the protection of the British government by the admission into the council of two directors, who are to be appointed by his Majesty.

BRITISH.

UNIVERSITY INTELLIGENCE.

Oxford, Oct. 8.—This day the Rev. George Rowley, D.D. and Master of University College, having been re-nominated by the Duke of Wellington as Vice-Chancellor of the University, took the oath of office in convocation.

Nov. 29.—Nomina Candidatorum Termino Michaelis, A.D. 1834, qui honore digni sunt habiti, in unaquaque classe secundum ordinem alphabeticnm disposita.

In Literis Humanioribus. Classis 1.—Barnes, Carolus, e C.C.C.; Dale, Henricus, e Coll. Magd.; Daman, Carolus, e Coll. Magd.; Godfrey, Daniel R. e Coll. Reg.; Hussey, Gulielmus, e Coll. Ball.; Hyman, Orlando H. B. e Coll. Wadh.; Woolcombe, Henricus, ex Æde Christi.

Classis 2.—Brancker, Thomas, e Coll. Wadh.; Bruce, Hon. Fredericus Gul. Adolp. ex Æde Christi; Davies, Nathaniel, e Coll. Pemb.; Govett, Robertus, e Coll. Vigorn.; Gunner, Gulielmus H. e Coll. Trin.; Morris, Joannes B. e Coll. Ball.; Owen, Lewis W. e Coll. Ball.; Pocock, Nicolaus, e Coll. Reg.; Stupart, Gustavus F. e Coll. Exon.; Ward, Gulielmus G. e Coll. Linc.; Wilson, Joannes, e C.C.C.; Wing, Joannes G. e. Coll. Univ.

Classis 3.—Allen, Thomas, e Coll. Ball; Black, Patricius, ex Æde Christi.; Blencowe, Thomas, e Coll. Wadh.; Boyce, Henricus Le Grand, e Coll. Vigorn.; Bright, Joannes E. ex Æde Christi; Dewar, Edvardus H. e Coll. Exon.; Faber, Joannes C. ex Æde Christi; Fortescue, Robertus H. e Coll. Exon.; Hanmer, Thomas, e Coll. Æn. Nas.; Jackson, Thomas, ex Aul. B. M. V.; Johnson, Jacobus T. e. Coll. D. Jo. Bapt.; King, Bryan, e Coll. Æn. Nas.; Kitson, Ellis P. e Coll. Ball.; Law, Georgius S. e Coll. Oriel;

Mozeley, Jacobus B. e Coll. Oriel; Pelly, Theophilus, e C.C.C.; Slight, Henricus, e C.C.C.; Talbot, Hon. Gul. C. ex Æde Christi; Vaughan, Jacobus, e Coll. Vigorn.; Waller, Stephanus R. e Coll. Æn. Nas.; Webster, Josephus, e Coll. Trin.; West, Washbourne, e Coll. Linc.; Woolcombe, Gulielmus W. e Coll. Exon.

Classis 4.—Austin, Robertus R. ex Æde Christi; Butler, Daniel, e Coll. Linc.; Cookes, Denham C. J. e Coll. Vigorn; Coxe, Henricus J. T. e Coll. D. Jo. Bapt.; De Salis, Gulielmus A. e Coll. Oriel; Domville, Jacobus G. ex Æde Christi; Emerson, Alexander L. e Coll. Pemb.; Hall, Henricus, ex Æde Christi; Jeans, Gulielmus e Coll. Wadh; Mayne, Henricus B. ex Æde Christi; Morris, Johannes, e Coll. Jesu; Newton, Gulielmus, e Coll. Ball.; Oswell, Henricus L. ex Æde Christi; Owen Jacobus R. e. Coll. Jesu; Pell, J. e Coll. Exon.; Radcliffe, Carolus E. e Coll. Æn. Nas.; Ryder, Gulielmus, D. e Coll. Exon.; Sidney, Johannes, e Coll. Æn. Nas.; Spry, Arturus, B. e. Coll. Trin.; Sykes, Josephus, e Coll. Oriel; Vine, Marshall H. e Coll. Univ.; Whatman, Jacobus, ex Æde Christi.; Wheeler, David, ex Aul. S. Edm., Wrench, Henricus O. e. Coll. Vigorn.

AUGUSTUS SHORT,
GUL. HAYWARD COX,
GEORGIUS MOBERLY,
E. W. HEAD,

}Examinatores in Literis Humanioribus.

Oxford, Dec. 15.—Nomina Candidatorum Termino Michaelis, A.D. 1834, qui honore digni sunt habiti, in unaquaque classe secundum ordinem alphabeticum disposita.

In Disciplinis Mathematicis et Physicis. Classis 1.—Anstice, Robertus Ricardus, ex Æde Christi; Jeffray, Gulielmus Lockhart, e Col. Ball.; Pocock, Nicholas, e Col. Reg.

Classis 2.—Ward, Gulielmus Georgius, e Col. Linc.; Woolcombe, Henricus, ex Æde Christi.

Classis 3.—Brancker, Thomas, e Col. Wadh.; Domville, Jacobus Graham, ex Æde Christi; Kitson, Ellis Puget, e Col. Ball.; Slight, Henricus S., e C.C.C.

Classis 4.—Vine, Marshall Hall, e Col. Univ.

A. NEATE,
G. R. BROWELL,
G. H. S. JOHNSON,

}Examinatores in Disciplinis Mathematicis et Physicis..

Dec. 4.—The convocation voted 50*l.* from the university chest, towards building ah scool-room at Bexley, in Kent, in which parish the university possesses an estate, and where a subscription is being raised for that purpose. The building is in progress, the foundation having been laid in September last, as mentioned in our former number.

CAMBRIDGE.—The death of the Duke of Gloucester, Chancellor, and that of the Earl of Hardwicke, Lord High Steward, having created vacancies in those offices, the Marquis Camden has been elected Chancellor, and addressed a letter to the Senate on the 16th December thanking them for the honour conferred on him; and at a congregation held on the following day, the Duke of Northumberland was appointed Lord High Steward.

The subject for the Norrisian Prize Essay for the present year is, —' The person, character, and actions of Jesus Christ, afford a satisfactory fulfilment of all the prophecies in the Old Testament which relate to the Messiah.'

Oct. 25.—The Seatonian Prize Poem was this day adjudged to the Rev. T. E. Hankinson of Corpus Christi College. Subject, *Jacob.*

Dec. 25.—*Prize Subjects.*—The Vice-Chancellor has issued the following notice in the university :—

I. The Most Noble Marquis Camden, Chancellor of the University, has signified to the Vice-Chancellor, his intention of giving, this year, a gold medal to such resident under-graduate as shall compose the best English Ode, or the best English Poem in heroic verse, upon the following subject :—' The death of his late Royal Highness the Duke of Gloucester.'

N.B. These exercises are to be sent in to the Vice-Chancellor on or before March 31, 1835 ; and are not to exceed 200 lines in length.

II. Sir William Browne's medals will this year be—

(1.) For the Greek Ode—*Delos.*

(2.) For the Latin Ode—*Belisarius.*

(3.) For the Epigrams—

——— Amphora cœpit
Institui, currente rota cur urceus exit ?

III. The Porson Prize for the present year is—Shakspeare, Third Part of King Henry VI., Act ii. Scene 2., beginning,

' CLIF. My gracious liege.'

And ending— ' To hold thine own, and leave thine own with him.'

Nov. 22.—The following is the number of residents in this University during the present term ;—

	In College.	In Lodgings.	Resident.
Trinity	231	250	481
St. John's	237	83	320
Queen's	47	74	121
Caius	57	48	105
Christ's	69	25	94
Corpus Christi	71	15	86
Catherine Hall	32	34	66
Pembroke	45	20	65
Jesus	56	8	64
St. Peter's	54	9	63
Magdalene	51	12	63
Emmanuel	56	1	57
Clare Hall	39	0	39
Sydney	35	1	36
Trinity Hall	32	3	35
King's	28	0	28
Downing	13	2	15
Total	1153	585	1738

Matriculations (Mich. Term) . 396

Dec. 4.—A grace passed the senate, proposing, ' that in future the examination of the candidates for mathematical honours, shall commence on the Wednesday (instead of the Thursday) preceding the first Monday in the Lent term.'

The Lalande medal, which is every year adjudged by the French Institute to the author of the most important service in astronomy, has just been assigned to Professor Airy, for the benefit rendered to physical astronomy by his observations. It was last year given to Sir John Herschell for his discoveries respecting double stars.

Sydney Sussex College.—The Masters and Fellows have given notice that, in the week after the admission of the commencing Bachelors, 1835, there will be an examination open to candidates from any college in the university, for two mathematical exhibitioners on Mr. Taylor's foundation. One exhibitioner will be elected from those under-graduates who, in the ordinary course, would become commencing bachelors of arts, in January, 1836; the others, from those who would become commencing bachelors in January, 1837. The exhibitioners are to receive, *at least*, 50*l.* per annum each, and to have rooms in college rent free ; if elected from another college, they will be required to remove to Sydney on their election. The examination will be confined to Mathematics.

CAMBRIDGE PHILOSOPHICAL SOCIETY.—At a meeting of the society, on Monday, Nov. 24, Professor Airy gave an account of the calculations which he had caused to be made, in order to determine the apparent disk of a star and the rings which surround it, when seen through an object-glass with a circular aperture. He also stated that corrections had been recently discovered to be necessary in the results of the trigonometrical survey of this country, by which the difference which had previously appeared to exist between the astronomical and geodetical determinations of the latitude and longitude of Cambridge observatory are greatly diminished. Mr. Stevenson, of Trinity College, read a memorial on the establishment of certain geometrical properties, by the combination of the infinitesimal method with the doctrine of projections. Professor Sedgwick and other members then communicated some observations illustrative of the geology of Cambridge. It was stated that the relations of the successive formations are very obscurely exhibited, in consequence of the strata and their junctions being marked by diluvial masses; and it was requested that all persons who might obtain any additional information from excavations, borings, or fossils, would communicate it.

MEDICAL PROVINCIAL SCHOOLS.—Most of the large towns now possess one or more of these institutions, at which lectures are delivered, and opportunities afforded to medical pupils of studying the various branches of their art. The circumstances to which they owe their origin, and the probable consequences of their establishment, are briefly described in the following extract of a speech made at the anniversary dinner of the Sheffield Medical Institution, by Dr. G. C. Holland:—

' We live in a restless and spirit-stirring age—an age distinguished by improvements, and especially by the vigorous march of mind. In times past, year succeeded year with scarcely any perceptible changes, but now each succeeding year is fraught with important changes—the evolution of new principles—the recognition of new rights—and the outpouring of general knowledge. One of the numerous consequences flowing from this altered state of society is a sense of the imperfections of the educational establishments of the country; this, indeed, has been acutely felt by the medical profession, and hence, in every large town in the kingdom, one or more medical schools have been established for the purpose of giving to the rising generation abundant means of improvement. Schools of this description have the highest possible claim on the countenance of society, their aim and tendency being to relieve the bodily sufferings of humanity. To effect this with success, something more is necessary than a mere smattering of professional knowledge. An excellent professional education raises, as it were, a series of steps, by which the understanding ascends to a favourable position for receiving in the clear light of day everything around it; and without this education the steps are few, and the elevation extremely limited, and consequently the view is circumscribed to a comparatively small number of objects. He reasons best who reasons from the greatest number and best established data. Provincial medical schools exert a beneficial influence on the feelings, tastes, and pursuits of the profession at large. By promoting the interchange of thought and sentiment, by bringing the mind to the consideration of liberal and general subjects—narrow and selfish prejudices are gradually dissipated; and in their place ennobling feelings, enlightened views, and social regards spring up, giving to the profession respectability and dignity.'

ETCHILHAMPTON, WILTS.—On the 2nd of December a new and commodious school-room, built by subscription, for the use of the poor children of the village, was opened by the clergyman and a considerable number of visitors. The attention of the children to the addresses made to them on the occasion is stated to have been very gratifying.

CORRUPTION OF CHILDREN IN THE GIN-SHOPS.—By the subjoined extract from the Report of the Temperance Society our readers may form some estimate of the number of children who are in the habit of frequenting gin-shops. To prove how pernicious the habit of indulging in ardent spirits is, more particularly among children, we need but direct the attention to the squalid looks and dwarfish forms of the children who crowd St. Giles's, and other low neighbourhoods in the metropolis, whose countenances are deeply marked with lines, and disfigured by an expression, which betray the working of passions that belong to a more advanced period of life.

A Statistical Account of the Number of Persons who visited Fourteen Gin-shops in the Metropolis in One Week, showing the Number of Men, Women, and Children respectively.

MONDAYS				MIDDLE OF THE WEEK				SATURDAYS				SUNDAYS				Grand Total
Men	Women	Children	Total each day	Men	Women	Children	Total each day	Men	Women	Children	Total each day	Men	Women	Children	Total each day	
731	305	110	1146	819	443	113	1375	1268	651	141	2060	820	348	80	1248	5829
1121	706	137	1964	946	608	143	1697	1230	1029	201	2460	749	453	132	1334	7455
1150	659	121	1930	873	675	147	1695	1769	1368	181	3318	1048	546	159	1753	8696
1637	1042	161	2840	963	457	116	1541	1746	1545	126	3417	1278	1083	81	2442	10,240
1216	1014	190	2420	1395	1342	125	2862	1314	1107	190	2611	1331	1252	147	2730	10,623
1497	1518	173	3188	1104	920	235	2259	1710	1504	231	3445	919	819	147	1885	10,777
1718	1367	158	3243	1660	1332	149	3141	1558	1498	188	3244	1040	1051	163	2254	11,882
1671	1088	176	2935	1496	1103	169	2768	2272	1494	314	4080	1600	958	160	2718	12,501
1534	1684	217	3435	1361	1722	274	3357	1498	1711	218	3427	1101	1148	111	2360	12,579
1912	1305	155	3372	1932	1477	217	3626	1955	1580	179	3714	1493	1172	259	2924	13,636
1848	1194	200	3242	1929	1223	325	3477	2510	1589	219	4318	1959	1401	306	3664	14,701
1697	1626	279	3602	1544	1428	222	3194	2558	2293	538	5389	1532	1165	195	2892	15,077
2880	1855	289	5024	2590	1420	242	4252	2853	1894	255	5002	1487	1032	201	2720	16,998
3146	2189	686	6021	1858	1305	285	3448	2764	2336	369	5469	1440	836	189	2465	17,403
23,758	17,552	3052	44,362	20,475	15,455	2762	38,692	27,005	21,599	3350	51,954	17,795	13,264	2330	33,389	168,397

	Men.	Women.	Children.	Grand Total.
Totals for four days of the fourteen houses	89,033	67,870	11,494	168,397
Totals for three days, deduct one-fifth	53,420	40,723	6897	101,040
Totals for one week of the fourteen houses	142,453	108,593	18,391	269,437
Average of each house per week	10,175	7756	1313	19,244
Average of each house per day	1453	1108	187	2748

It is not surprising that the keepers of these houses should allow children to be served with spirits, for it is all in the way of trade ; but it is seriously worth consideration if any direct legislative enactment could be framed which might restrain this pernicious practice. The improvement of the poorer classes by a good education is, we are aware, the only effectual restraint ; but if anything could be done, in the mean time, in the way of direct prohibition, it might have the effect of diminishing the evil. Those who have once found their way to the gin-shop are very likely to go again ; but if the first visit can be deferred, or rendered more difficult, or at least less inviting, possibly the evil, in the case of children, might be partially diminished.

Mr. Smith's Garden Allotments to Children.—Among the various plans for rightly influencing the character of youth, which have of late been adopted, there is a very simple and efficacious one pursued ¡by Mr. Smith of Southam, in Warwickshire. This gentleman has neither erected a school nor hired a schoolmaster, but has let a small quantity of land to the children in his neighbourhood to be cultivated in gardens. The following is his own account, extracted from a recent publication :—

' It is not a school—it is simply three rods and ten poles of land, divided into twelve gardens, occupied by boys from twelve to eighteen years of age in the cultivation of garden vegetables, peas, carrots, cabbages, kidney-beans, celery, parsnips, &c. I allow only one-fourth to be cultivated for potatoes, and wheat not at all ; they pay all prices, from sixpence per month to one shilling per month, according to the size. The rent for the whole amounts to about 4l. 17s. per annum.

' The seventeen shillings I expend in one rent dinner and a cup of ale monthly, when they bring their rent, which I am glad to tell you, my dear little tenants have hitherto done to an hour. It is a glorious sight, or rather was a glorious sight in the summer, to see all the gardens clean and full of stuff—I could have challenged it for produce and cleanliness against any acre of ground in the country. The moral advantages, too, have been very great ; if it could be copied and extended in a small degree, all tendencies to sedition and anarchy might be neutralized and suspended. For instance, in this town we have 1200 inhabitants, the greater part of whom being agricultural labourers, have been fully and fairly employed the whole summer. There are about 40 boys or young men who have been at the national school, but who are not yet old enough to go out into service.

' In the summer evenings, if unemployed, they are very apt to be in mischief ; *but my boys, since they have had a garden to resort to, have forsaken the streets,* and are acquiring that sort of knowledge which is likely to be serviceable to them when they become men. Their fathers and mothers, especially the latter, are made very happy ; their cottages have been filled with good vegetables all summer, at no expense to the father's strength or mother's care ; *for the boys, whilst they work hard to procure the rent, are very willing to let their parents have the produce.* This they sometimes pay the poor boys for and sometimes not; whichever they do amounts to the same thing. If the boys sell their vegetables to their mother, the money is laid out in clothing, so that saves the father's purse. If four acres of land could be given up and procured for every 40 boys (which is about the number for 1200 inhabitants), we should have the whole country smiling with health, activity and content.'

SOUTHWARK LITERARY SOCIETY.—This institution now consists of about 500 members. Classes have been formed for the study of mathematics and astronomy. A reading-room has been provided, and a very extensive library formed both for reference and circulation, partly from the subscription funds, and partly from donations: and lectures are to be given.

BRITISH AND FOREIGN SCHOOL SOCIETY.—A speech of Lieut. Fabian (the Society's representative) at a meeting at Derby, states that the society is 1400*l.* in debt, and a deputation has been making exertions at different places throughout the country to obtain the means of diminishing the incumbrance.

BATH FREE GRAMMAR SCHOOL.—The date of the Bath Free Grammar School is July 12, 6th Edward VI. It was endowed with land that belonged to the dissolved Priory of Bath. It was 'for the education, institution, and instruction of boys and young men in grammar,' and the master was to be 'a fit person to serve in the said school, meet and learned, and at least well-instructed in the Latin tongue.' The mayor and citizens of Bath were to be the trustees, and were empowered, with the advice of the bishop of the diocese, 'from time to time' to make statutes and ordinances touching the order, government, and direction of the school, and of its revenues.

How long the school was well conducted is doubtful. The corporation was possessed of its funds, and was guilty of so scandalous a misappropriation of them as to excite inquiry. In the 10th Geo. II. a Decree was made, by the charity commissioners under the Act of Elizabeth, for its regulation. It states that the corporation 'having so notoriously mismanaged and misapplied the revenues of the lands given to their predecessors by King Edward VI., for the support and continuance of the Grammar School, and the relief and comfort of ten poor persons, paying interest sometimes 30*l.*, sometimes 20*l.*, and sometimes 10*l.* a year to the master; although the income thereof had amounted to a much greater yearly sum, and had not disposed of any part thereof for the relief of the poor persons aforesaid, but applied the same to their own private uses; nor having kept any account, at least not producing any, of the receipts or disbursements of the said revenues; and having so mixed the said lands with other lands of their own, or aliened or granted them away, that much the greatest part of the said lands could not be found or distinguished, and leaves being cut out of the account books, and having been guilty of other breaches of trust, should be for ever absolutely removed and displaced from the said trust.'

The Decree directs that the school shall for ever continue a ' Free Grammar School ' for the instruction of youth, subject to such rules, orders, limitations, and appointments as were thereinafter mentioned for its conduct and management for the term of thirty-five years, as the utmost time for which the tenants of the described premises could hold the same at existing rents. It orders that the master of the school shall instruct, gratis, ten boys, children of freemen or inhabitants of Bath, to be, from time to time, elected by the governors or trustees for the time being, to be nominated or recommended by twenty of the chiefest and most substantial inhabitants of Bath, who paid most to the rates, levies, or assessments of the said city. It directs the removal of the corporation as trustees, and that they shall pay two sums of 5000*l.* and 450*l.* for their misappropriations of the trust funds. It then orders that, upon the expiration of the said term of thirty-five years, or as soon before or after as the trustees should be enabled by the receipt of the said sums of money; or income of the said premises, a piece of land should be purchased; whereon should be built a school-house and house and conveniences for the master, and also an hospital (St. Catherine's) for the habitation of as many poor persons as could be maintained out of the revenues of the said charity lands, after the deduction of the allowance thereinafter directed to be paid to the master. And that after the expiration of the said term, or so soon as they should be enabled by the expiration of any of the said leases, the trustees should allow and pay the schoolmaster 50*l.* a year, who should then teach more boys, according as the trustees should direct.

By this Decree a conveyance was to have been made of the charity funds to trustees named in it, who were afterwards to govern the school. The corporation remained in possession, and there is no evidence to show that the conveyance was made. The school continued to be badly managed, and no free scholars were admitted.

The Parliamentary Commissioners investigated the affairs of the charity in 1820. In consequence of their interference, the corporation in 1822 passed certain resolutions which were afterwards signed, according to the terms of the original trust, by the Bishop of Bath and Wells. By these resolutions ten free scholars only are to be taught, and on each nomination the various conditions required by the Decree on the nomination of the first ten scholars are in future to be observed. The salary of the master is fixed at 84*l.* a year, and exhibitions or scholarships are to be founded upon the increase of the charity funds.

The school was originally open to all, and it was in consequence only of the mismanagement of its property that it ever became less useful than its founders designed. How far the Decree could limit the number of free scholars is doubtful: if they could be limited to ten, they might be limited to two; the principle in both cases is the same. But the Decree orders that the number of free scholars shall be ten, so long as the salary of the master is 20*l.*, and it distinctly directs an increase in the number of free scholars when the salary shall be raised. The members of the corporation, in 1822, fixed the salary of the master at 84*l.*, and limited the number of free scholars to ten, with the old Decree before them, perfectly aware of its directions, and fully acquainted with the orders it contains. Had they been desirous to provide for the interests of the population, they would not have been insensible to the importance of education; every mode by which it might have been extended would have been an object of solicitude. Occupying a public position, with great means of doing good, it was a portion of their duty to render public institutions under their control more useful and efficient, and in this instance, more strongly than in any other, their public duty and that of humanity coincided. Having the power to do so, they ought to have thrown the school open.

The master at present receives, in addition to the fixed salary of 84*l.* a year, the advantage of a good school-house and the rectory of Charlcombe, which was granted by a Mr. Robins to the Corporation, in order to present the master, if in holy orders; the profits of which amounted, in 1820, to 140*l.* a year, and in 1834 to about 300*l.* a year, and he is permitted to take private pupils. The master is not, by the terms of the foundation, required to be in holy orders,— but if he is in holy orders, the Corporation of Bath must present him to the rectory of Charlcombe.

The present mode of nominating the free scholars is offensive and unjust. The rule of the Decree relating to nomination was to continue for 35 years—not for ever. Had the elective franchise of the city continued limited, its operation might have been confined. It is now capable of being perverted to the worst species of political favouritism. The Decree states, ' that whereas, at the expiration of the said term of 35 years, or thereabouts, the leases of the said ascertained tenements will be expired, and the revenues of the same will be greatly increased; the said governors and trustees shall lease all the said tenements, except the said mill, for any term or terms not exceeding 21 years, upon small fines, reserving as large rents as possible for the more certain maintenance of the said charity,' and the mill ' shall be leased on lives, or years determinable on lives, reserving a large chief rent.' Monks Mill, the mill referred to, was then demised for 42 years, paying a rent of 32*s.* a year. The last lease was made in 1817, when it was demised for 99 years, determinable on lives, in consideration of 263*l.* and a chief annual rent of 41*s.*

The whole property is badly let. The leases are renewed upon fines, and small annual rents are reserved. The recommendation of the Decree, if acted upon, would be every way advantageous. A portion of a celebrated hotel called the White Hart, belonging to the charity, is valued at 286*l.* a year; Monks Mill is occupied by a sub-lessee at a rent of 200*l.* a year; Fountain-buildings (formerly Wanborough Chapel) is valued at 475*l.* a year, making, with other property of the charity, if let at annual rents, 1238*l.* a year. By the present mode of letting, the property produces to the charity nothing equal to this amount.

. The Decree directs 'That no lands whatsoever belonging to the charity shall at any time be let or set without public notice of such letting or setting, to be affixed to the Market-house or other public places in Bath, at least a fortnight before such setting or letting; and that such estate shall afterwards be let and set publicly to the best bidder, upon the best terms and considerations that can be gotten for the same, preference being always given to the tenant then or last in possession.' This rule is not observed, and no attention has ever been paid to it.

This case affords a very fair example of the insufficiency of the returns of the income of endowed schools, which profess to exhibit the amount of funds in England devoted to Education—(See *Journal of Education*, No. XVI. p. 335). The income of this school of Bath is set down in the returns at 86*l.* 13*s.*—a little more than the salary of the schoolmaster—while the annual *value* of the property, deducting all possible payments to St. Catherine's Hospital, is more than 1100*l.* a year.—T. F.

Bath Education Society.—This society has engaged extensive premises, and the schools for both sexes will commence in the early part of the present year. The necessary expenses will be defrayed, partly by the scholars, and partly by means of voluntary subscriptions. The principle, that people value most those objects for which they pay, is therefore judiciously brought to bear upon that which is the most important of all. The utility of this plan is clearly pointed out by the Bishop of London, in his evidence before the Select Committee on Education. His Lordship says:—'I am quite clear that it is desirable in all cases, and for the following reason, that the poor set a value on that for which they pay; and although perhaps a penny or twopence a week may be no exact value of the learning their children acquire, yet they do not like them to lose any part of that which they pay for; and the consequence is, that they are much more punctual and regular in their attendance, not to mention the general principle that it promotes a proper spirit of independence in them to let them purchase what is valuable when they can, rather than give it to them quite gratuitously. Where education is given quite gratuitously to the poor, I have almost invariably found that they consider themselves as conferring a favour on the clergyman by letting their children go to school; but where they pay for it themselves, they all seem to set a greater value upon the education so purchased. Another advantage of course is, that the payments form a very considerable addition to the funds which are otherwise raised.'

BRIGHTON.—A plan has been some time in agitation in this town for founding an establishment for educating the daughters of poor clergymen as governesses: to be, in fact, a normal school for females. It is proposed that each pupil shall pay 20*l.* per annum, for which sum they are to be educated in a manner to fit them for situations as governesses, their education having particular reference to their future avocation; and to be clothed, lodged, and boarded. Similar institutions, it is said, have succeeded in Westmoreland and Gloucestershire; and if a proper system of instruction be adopted, there is little doubt but that it may be productive of beneficial results. Far too little pains have been hitherto taken in the education of teachers, particularly of female teachers. The number of pupils is to be limited to one hundred.

CANTERBURY PHILOSOPHICAL AND LITERARY INSTITUTION.—On Tuesday, Nov. 18, the anniversary of the foundation of this institution was celebrated by a public dinner, at which upwards of 100 noblemen and gentlemen attended. We learn from some remarks made by Mr. Wilkinson, that the museum has recently received several valuable contributions; the library has very considerably increased in almost every department of literature; the public records have been presented to the society by his Majesty's commissioners; lectures have been delivered of a satisfactory and instructive nature, and the friends of the society are satisfied that it is gaining strength, and is daily acquiring that estimation in public opinion which it deserves.

BIRMINGHAM INSTITUTION FOR THE DEAF AND DUMB.—At the annual meeting in October, a report was read congratulating the friends of the establishment on its improved state and prospects. A new and very commodious apartment has been opened as a school-room, the cost of which, including the furniture, amounts to 301*l.*, and has been defrayed by means of a distinct subscription. During the year 10 children had been admitted into the asylum, 8 had left it, and there were 10 out of 12 children to be balloted for. In order to increase the pecuniary resources of the institution, branch societies have been established in some of the most important towns within the midland districts. By the labours and influence of friends, the accessions to the annual subscriptions in the town and neighbourhood of Birmingham amounted to 151*l.* 4*s.* 6*d.*; and the donations during the year to 480*l.* 16*s.* 1*d.* It is hoped that the establishment will soon be enabled to receive a larger number of pupils, and that, in consequence, the average cost of educating and maintaining each pupil will be considerably diminished. Pupils are not of necessity elected from any particular county or division.

SALISBURY MECHANICS' INSTITUTE.—A series of lectures has been for some time past delivered at this institution. The last general report shows the interest which is taken by its supporters even in scientific subjects, when explained to them in a pleasing and popular style; fifty-six new members having been admitted during the last quarter, and the receipts at the doors on lecture evenings having been nearly doubled. Among other subjects, optics, magnetism, chemistry, and 'galvanism have been treated by Mr. C. Tomlinson, and Pauper Lunatic Asylums by the Rev. J. R. Urquhart.

SILKSTON, YORKSHIRE.—This parish contains the town of Barnsley, which, in 1831, had a population of 10,330. The school endowed by Thomas Keresforth in 1665, is at present free to children of the name of *Keresforth* for *every* kind of instruction; and to all from the parish of Silkston for Latin and Greek. It exists as a pay-school for everything except Latin and Greek. The pay is about one guinea per quarter, exclusive of books, &c. Geography is a separate charge, and, we believe, accounts. The present master is Mr. William Gilbanks. There is a good house, garden, and school-room belonging to the charity, and about 18*l.* per annum, arising out of fee-farm rents charged upon lands in Barnsley, Silkston, and Dodworth, one of which amounts to 4*l.* 4*s.*; and there are some as low as 4*d.*, which makes the collection of them rather a tedious business. The donation is for '*the encouragement of a suitable and proper master,*' not for the *support.* Mr. Gilbanks does not take boarders; the number of children taught varies from fifty to sixty; his last return amounted to sixty, but he has not at present more than fifty pupils.

ST. DAVID'S COLLEGE, LLAMPETER.—It is stated that the appeal made by the principal and professors in favour of this institution has been very successful. The Bishop of Durham has lately presented the college with 500*l.*, the interest of which the Bishop of St. David's, as Visitor of the College, has directed shall form one scholarship. Mr. Butler's legacy, the annual interest of which amounts to 54*l.* 10*s.*, he has also directed to be applied to the foundation of four scholarships of equal value, to be called the Butler Scholarships. The Burton scholarship is also now (Nov. 25) vacant, by the appointment of the Rev. Enoch Pugh to a curacy, but will be filled immediately. The elections for the other five scholarships, together with several others of 10*l.* each, will take place in the ensuing year.

SCOTLAND.

FEMALE UNIVERSITY.—At Edinburgh an institution of rather a novel character has recently been opened. It is for the education of females; and as every branch of female education will be taught within its walls, the necessity of going backwards and forwards to the residence of the different teachers will be avoided. Popular lectures on science are included in the plan, and Mr. Lees, Mr. D. B. Reid, and Mr. M'Gillivray, are engaged to deliver courses upon natural history, chemistry, and natural philosophy. It is a great step gained in female education that it is no longer deemed necessary to confine instruction to what are termed accomplishments, and this attempt has already given rise to the establishment of a second institution founded on much the same principles.

GLASGOW UNIVERSITY.—Lord Stanley has been elected Lord Rector of this University. The friends of Earl Durham had put that nobleman in nomination for the office.

IRELAND.

TRINITY COLLEGE, DUBLIN.—*Michaelmas Term Examinations.* The names are arranged in the order of standing on the college books.

Junior Sophisters.—Honours in Science. Senior Prizemen.— Mr. James W. Murland, Thomas Stack, William Chichester, John Ball, Robert Hopkins, Henry Vickars, James Glanville, George M'Dowell.

Junior Prizemen.—James Shaw Willes, Charles E. Baggot, James Keith, William Butler, Richard Geran.

Honours in Classics. Senior Prizemen.—Thomas Stack, Henry Owgan, Robert Hopkins, George L. Fenton, John C. Colman, Edward Trevor.

Junior Prizemen.—Mr. Stewart M'Naghton, John Ball, Joshua Bull, Richard Wilson, Vernon P. Drapes, Leslie Badham, William Morgan, Edward Treanor.

Senior Freshmen.—Honours in Science. Senior Prizemen.—Mr. George Augustus Shaw, Lewis Higgins.

Junior Prizemen.—John James, Matthew Lynch, Richard Biggs, John Harris Flynn, James Green, Robert King.

Honours in Classics. Senior Prizemen.—Mr. Robert Welsh, Mr. Marcus Synnott, John Walsh, Benjamin Wade, Henry W. Tibbs, Thomas R. Wrightson, Robert King, Frederick Howe Ringwood, James Eccleston.

Junior Prizemen.—Mr. Robert Johnston, Mr. James Verschoyle, Mr. Walter W. Lynch, Joseph Wilson Higginbotham, Edward Hallam, Thomas Rice Henn, James Wm. King Disney, John William Hallowell, Daniel Finney, George Fletcher, Gilbert M'Ilveen.

Junior Freshmen.—Honours in Science. Senior Prizemen.— Mr. Charles Kelly, Henry Connor, Robert Warren, Frederick Sidney, Michael Roberts, William Roberts, Robert Beere, John Hewitt Jellett, James Anthony Lawson.

Junior Prizemen.—Mr. Richard Herbert, Mr. Richard William Bayley, Samuel Merrick, Richard Maunsell Ardagh, Edward Ovens, Thomas Saunders, Hamilton Law, Edmund Meredith.

Honours in Classics. Senior Prizemen.—Mr. Thomas Francis Torrens, Richard Wrightson, William Roberts, John Hewitt Jellett, James Anthony Lawson, Andrew O'Callaghan, William Miller, George Graham, John Watson, Cornelius Percy Ring.

Junior Prizemen.—Mr. William Knox, Mr. Thomas Galway, Mr. James Douglas, Telford M'Donagh, George Francis Hodder, Carew Smyth, Michael Roberts, Edmund Maturin, John Perrin, John Minnit, Edmund Meredith, Henry Stewart, John Greene, John Macartney, George Wallen, Patrick Murphy, William O'Connor.

The Senior Moderators are placed in the order of Merit; Junior Moderators in the order of standing on the college books.

Initio Termini S. Michaelis, habitis Examinationibus pro gradu Baccalaureatûs in artibus, in Moderatores Seniores nominantur in Disciplinis Math. et Phys.—1. Carolus Graves; 2. Josephus Carson.

In Ethica et Logica.—1. Gulielmus A. Butler; 2. Harold. H, Sherlock; 3. Jacobus Peed, Soc. Com.

In Literis Humanioribus.—1. Georgius B. Wheeler.

In Moderatores Juniores nominantur in Disciplinis Math. et Phys, —Franciscus Beamish, Alexander Smith Orr, Gulielmus Mockler, Georgius Crampton, Robertus Finlay.

In Ethica et Logica.—Carolus Haukes Todd, Thomas Walsh, Carolus Sharman Crawford, Robertus Chattoe, Josephus Meade, Franciscus Meade.

WINCHESTER SCHOOL.—Since our article on Winchester school was in type, we have been informed that many important changes have been made of late years, and that the barbarous system which we have described is abolished. We shall endeavour to ascertain the precise nature of these changes, and give them in a future Number. The account of this school, at p. 84 of this Journal, is from the writer's own experience, and is no exaggerated account of what Winchester school was at the time of his being there.

QUARTERLY

JOURNAL OF EDUCATION.

NATIONAL EDUCATION IN IRELAND.

In the fifth and sixth Numbers of this Journal, our readers will find a considerable amount of information relative to the means adopted by Government, and by private societies, for the literary, moral, and religious instruction of the children of the poor in Ireland. At the time when the statements to which we have here referred were written, the Government, in which the present Lord Stanley then filled the office of Secretary of State for Ireland, had recently appointed a Commission to superintend a system of national education in that part of the United Kingdom. The motives which produced this appointment, and the objects which it was proposed to accomplish, are explained in the letter addressed in October, 1831, by Lord Stanley, to the Duke of Leinster, who was appointed President of the Board of Commissioners; and as we have already inserted this letter at full length (No. V., pages 189—192), it is unnecessary to repeat it here.

This plan, which was conceived in a truly Catholic spirit, and in favour of which it was proposed to withdraw from establishments less comprehensive in their principles the pecuniary aid which had before been largely afforded from the public purse, met with considerable opposition ; and predictions of its entire failure were confidently hazarded by the partisans of the old proselyting system, who could see nothing but anarchy and disappointment likely to follow from the appointment as members of the same Board of such discordant materials as the Protestant and Roman Catholic Archbishops of Dublin, the Senior Fellow of Trinity College, and the Presbyterian minister of the Scots Church in Dublin. Taking into the account the unhappy state of opposition in which the various religious sects had so constantly placed themselves in Ireland, it was certainly a very high compliment on the part of the Government to the members of the Commission, to give them credit for a spirit of active benevolence, which would render them superior to the prejudices of party, and which would unite them cordially for the attainment of a common object, by means of mutual concessions on points which zealots of all sides held to be indispensable.

It is satisfactory to know that the opposition to the design and labours of this Commission has failed; that the sinister predictions of which it was the object have proved unfounded; and that the system has done more for the cause of national education in Ireland during the three years in which it has been in operation, than had been effected in the previous century by all the lavish expenditure and extensive machinery which are described in the article of this Journal already referred to, (Vol. iii., pp. 235—260).

The first, and hitherto the only report made by the Commissioners appointed in 1831 to administer the funds granted by Parliament for the education of the poor in Ireland was presented to the House of Commons on the 3rd of March, 1834. This document states, very briefly, the result of the labours of the Commissioners up to the end of 1833; and gives an abstract of their receipts and expenditure, from which little information can be gained beyond what was given by us in p. 191, No. XV., of this Journal. Since that report was printed, however, the House of Commons has called for several returns connected with the subject, which were accordingly presented on the 13th of August, two days before the close of the last Session of Parliament, but which returns have not been printed.

These returns are:—

" 1. The particulars of the 789 schools to which the Commissioners of National Education in Ireland have granted aid, as mentioned in their Report to Parliament, specifying where such schools are situated, the number of scholars in each, the names of the patrons, managers, and visitors, the sum granted to each, the person or persons to whom paid, whether any and what sum has been paid or expended on account of any or which of said schools by local subscription or contribution, with the number of subscribers or contributors of the sum subscribed or contributed by each as far as known to the Commissioners, and in what manner the Board ascertains the fact of such payment or expenditure having been actually made.

" 2. A return stating the reports of their inspectors as to the 52 other schools mentioned in the report to Parliament of said

Commissioners, as to which schools they have discontinued their assistance.

" 3. A return of the names of the 199 schools to which they have promised assistance, where situated, the names of the patrons and managers thereof, and of the clergymen who have applied for assistance to these schools respectively, and the amount of local subscription or contribution promised for each.

" 4. A return stating how and in what manner the number of scholars (107,042) mentioned in their report as in attendance on their schools has been ascertained, whether by inspection, or by any other and what check; whether this is the actual attendance, or the number on the school rolls.

" 5. A return of the particulars of the expenditure of the sum 28,842*l.* in their said report mentioned.

" 6. A return of the names of the schools to which the sum of 12,664*l.* 2*s.* 4*d.* was granted, with the sum to each.

" 7. A like return as to the sum of 3110*l.* 11*s.* 8*d.* granted for fitting up.

" 8. Copy of their correspondence with the Synod of Ulster, or any person on behalf of that body.

" 9. A return of the names of such clergymen of the Established Church, and of such Presbyterian and Roman Catholic clergymen as have received grants from the Board in aid of schools, and the names of such schools, and where situate, and whether such schools, and which of them, are now in connexion with the Board, and if not, why not."

We shall notice the returns of the Commissioners to these heads of inquiry in the order in which they are here given.

The first of these returns has been drawn up without any apparent regard to order or arrangement. The schools established in the various counties are jumbled together in the greatest confusion, and without any reference either to the number of their scholars or the expense of the establishments. In the absence of dates, we can only conjecture that the schools are inserted in the list according to the order of time in which assistance was given. We have been at some pains to remedy this want of arrangement, and have drawn out a short abstract, exhibiting the amount of what has been done, as well as the expense at which it has been effected in each separate county. As regards this latter part of the return, however, we have in vain endeavoured to bring our abstract into some sort of agreement with the accounts furnished by the Commissioners. In the detailed account which they have given in compliance with the first part of the order of the House of Commons, and from which our abstract has been made, the sums set down against the individual schools for building, fitting, and salaries, amount to 18,349*l.* 7*s.* 6*d.*, namely,—

	£	*s.*	*d.*
Advanced for building . .	2,971	7	0
for fittings up . .	5,573	0	6
for annual salaries .	9,805	0	0
Together .	£18,349	7	6

But the sums stated in the return No. 5, under these respective heads, are—

	£	*s.*	*d.*
for building school-houses	£3,850	14	9
fitting up schools . .	2,835	8	0
salaries of teachers . .	7,391	11	0
Together .	£14,077	13	9

This difference probably arises from sums being included in the first return which were not actually paid; and yet this supposition is at variance with the fact that the sum stated as advanced for building is considerably under the amount for which the Commissioners take credit under that head in the return No. 5.

The sum of 2971*l.* 7*s.* comprehends the amount of forty-three grants, three of which are of 200*l.* each, two are of 175*l.*, and two of 150*l.* each; the remainder is made up of various sums from 84*l.*, down to 10*l.* 13*s.* 4*d.* Other grants made for the same purpose,—that of building school-houses, which were not paid at the time their accounts were given in, but for which the Commissioners were then liable, amounted to 12,664*l.* 2*s.* 4*d.* The number of these outstanding grants was 165, of which 6 were for sums of 200*l.* to 220*l.*, 40 were for sums between 100*l.* and 200*l.*, and the rest were for smaller sums, some of them being as low as 10*l.*

The information concerning local contributions, furnished by the statements of the Commissioners, is exceedingly scanty; and, in fact, they have stated their inability, from the want of documents, to comply with the order of the House of Commons in this respect.

TABLE showing the Number of Schools in each County of Ireland, under the management of the Commissioners appointed to superintend a system of National Education in that Country, and of Scholars taught therein, at the Close of 1833; together with a Statement of the Sums advanced by the Commissioners towards Building School-Houses, and for Fitting up the same, and for the Annual Salaries of Teachers. Also, a Statement of the Number of Schools in each County, to which assistance had at that time been promised by the Commissioners.

COUNTIES.	Population.	Number of Schools.	Number of Scholars.	Advanced for Building.	Advanced for Fittings-up.	Annual Salaries.	Number of Schools to which assistance has been promised, and Amt. of local contributions raised for the same.	
							No.	Contributions
				£.	£.	£.		£.
Antrim	316,909	84	7,272	376	273	899	4	82
Armagh. . . .	220,134	19	2,311	150	72	251	1	380
Carlow	99,353	25	4,543	200	134	369	11	997
Cavan	227,933	17	2,315	264	227	166	10	488
Clare.	258,322	8	1,336	284	51	108	4	208
Cork	810,732	47	9,119	..	285	723	13	1,364
Donegal. . . .	289,149	16	1,288	130	148	144	19	641
Down.	353,012	57	5,620	..	130	609	6	246
Dublin	380,167	44	9,497	350	360	1,184	6	826
Fermanagh . .	149,763	23	1,740	74	124	186	4	63
Galway. . . .	381,564	21	5,282	451	237	414	20	1,141
Kerry.	263,126	8	1,571	..	345	88	8	479
Kildare	108,424	22	2,710	..	204	273	5	432
Kilkenny . . .	193,686	9	1,653	80	99	96	6	405
King's County .	144,225	14	1,498	..	280	115	5	68
Leitrim	141,524	12	1,659	11	64	119	9	262
Limerick . . .	315,355	19	2,591	..	55	234	3	306
Londonderry . .	222,012	30	2,346	..	152	279	4	73
Longford . . .	112,558	4	678	..	26	25	1	204
Louth	107,481	19	4,202	..	417	319	3	184
Mayo.	366,328	40	4,943	..	190	396	7	206
Meath	176,826	21	2,611	..	254	197	2	97
Monaghan. . .	195,536	33	3,366	70	153	299	6	251
Queen's County	145,851	31	5,305	80	193	405	5	244
Roscommon . .	249,613	6	1,094	..	41	75	3	150
Sligo	171,765	16	2,533	275	102	179	8	456
Tipperary . . .	402,563	35	5,012	50	152	457	3	224
Tyrone	304,468	49	3,812	58	233	405	13	221
Waterford . . .	177,054	20	3,342	..	126	249	3	100
Westmeath . .	136,872	9	1,509	68	161	151	4	189
Wexford . . .	182,713	18	2,834	..	122	222	1	85
Wicklow . . .	121,557	13	1,531	..	163	169	2	168
Total . .	7,767,401	789	107,118	2,971	5,573	9,805	199	11,240

The return to which we have prefixed the No. 2, relates to schools as to which the Commissioners have at one time afforded, but have since withdrawn, their assistance. These schools are stated in the report to be 52 in number; 41 of them were deprived of assistance in consequence of the reports made concerning them by the travelling inspectors appointed by the Commissioners. As the order of the House of Commons applies only to schools so reported on, no reason has been given by the Commissioners for withdrawing their support from the remaining 11 schools. Among the causes of dissatisfaction assigned by the inspectors in their reports, we find a considerable admixture of the old leaven by which, according to the evidence given before a committee of the Irish House of Commons, the charter schools of Ireland were formerly so much disgraced. In some cases it is reported, that "the school was held in a wretched cabin, totally unfitted for the purposes of education, and that the master was irregular in his attendance;"—"that the teacher was absent, and the school-house used as a granary;"—"that the school was disgracefully neglected, and the teacher incompetent;"—"that the teacher was a man of immoral conduct;"—"that the managers had been induced to expel the teacher, and lock up the school-house." It is to be hoped that these and similar abuses will soon be remedied; and we think ourselves justified in believing that whenever a better order of things shall be established, under which such irregularities will be no longer possible, the amendment will be in a great degree owing to the efforts of the Commissioners whose report we have now before us.

With regard to the third head of inquiry, that relating to the 199 schools to which the Commissioners have promised assistance, we have embodied all the useful information that is given by them, in the table already inserted; in which will be found a statement of the number of additional schools in progress in each county, and the amount of local subscriptions and contributions raised for their establishment.

In answer to the fourth head of inquiry, the Commissioners nave stated, that with regard to the greater number of schools, the numbers of the scholars were ascertained from the reports of the inspectors. Directions had previously been issued by the Commissioners, to the effect that all children who might have been withdrawn from school during any half-year should be struck off the school-roll at the end of that half-year; the object of which regulation was as far as possible to establish an agreement between the school-rolls and the numbers in actual attendance.

The return to the fifth inquiry states the particulars of the expenditure of the sum of 28,842*l.*, as follows :—

	£	*s.*	*d.*
Expenses of model school and training department	2,196	9	1½
Grants of aid to schools, including contributions towards building school-houses and fitting them up, salaries of teachers, and school requisites .	16,088	18	6
Salaries and travelling allowances to inspectors .	2,165	18	2½
Expenses of compiling, printing, and publishing school books , ...	3,244	15	10
Secretary's salary, rent and repairs of house, and other general expenses	5,146	0	0
	£28,842	1	8

In their returns of the names of the schools to which, as mentioned in the report of the Commissioners, the sums of 12,664*l.* 2*s.* 4*d.*, and 3110*l.* 11*s.* 8*d.*, were granted for building school-houses, and for fitting them up, the order of the House of Commons has been literally complied with; but we must confess that our imperfect knowledge of Irish topography does not enable us to draw any useful information from the mere list which has been given of places and sums, or to distribute them according to counties. The number of grants in aid of building is 167, and the sums vary from 218*l.* to 10*l.* More than two-thirds are for sums below 100*l.* The grants for fitting up are 197 in number; 120 of them are for sums under 10*l.*, and only 4 exceed 100*l.*

The next subject upon which information was required by Parliament, relates to a correspondence between the Commissioners and a Committee appointed for the purpose of conducting that correspondence by the General Synod of Ulster. This correspondence took place between August, 1833, and February, 1834, relative to the regulations under which the Synod proposed to sanction the acceptance of aid from the Commissioners, on the part of schools in connexion with their body. Copies of the letters which passed on this occasion have been given by the Commissioners, and we cannot refrain from expressing the feelings of dissatisfaction caused by a perusal of them. It appears to us that the Synod has been actuated in the matter by a sectarian spirit, directly opposed to the comprehensive benevolence of the system in the benefits of which they have been invited to participate.

The Commissioners have laid down, as it was necessary they should do, certain regulations to be observed by all who apply to them for assistance; and in framing these regulations, they have been especially careful not to adopt any which should have the effect of excluding the children belonging to any religious sect or denomination. This object might have been accomplished by limiting the subjects to be taught, so as to include literary and moral instruction, but to exclude religious subjects and exercises. The adoption of this course would, however, have subjected the Commissioners to the imputation of indifference as to the religious instruction of youth; and in a country like Ireland, where the great mass of the people are in a state of ignorance, it might not have been safe or proper to have left that point to be supplied to children by their parents, or by other persons who might possibly convert it into an engine for party purposes. Instead of thus disembarrassing themselves of the most difficult part of their trust, the Commissioners have fairly met the subject, and by their judicious arrangements have converted that which has been too often a cause of the bitterest strife into a bond of brotherly union. In all previous attempts made by Protestants to instruct the children of the poor in Ireland, it had been made an invariable rule to enforce in every school the reading of the Scriptures, without note or comment, by which regulation the children of conscientious Catholics were effectually excluded, and the hostility of the Catholic clergy was excited; since they who deny even to adults the right of unaided private interpretation of the Bible with respect to the articles of religious belief, could never concede that point in the case of children.

With these difficulties in their way the Commissioners framed the following regulations:—

" 1. The ordinary school business, during which all the children, of whatever denomination they be, are required to attend, and which is expected to embrace a competent number of hours in each day, is to consist exclusively of instruction in those branches which belong to a literary and moral education. Such extracts from Scripture as are prepared under the sanction of the Board, may be used, and are earnestly recommended by the Board to be used, during those hours allotted to this ordinary school business.

" 2. One day at least in each week (independently of the Sunday) is to be set apart for the religious instruction of the children, on which day such pastors or other persons as are approved of by the parents or guardians of the children shall have access to them for that purpose, whether those parties have signed the original application or not.

" 3. The managers of schools are also expected, should the parents of any of the children desire it, to afford convenient opportunity and facility for the same purpose, either before or after the ordinary school business (as the managers may determine) on other days of the week.

" 4. Any arrangement of this description that may be made is to be publicly notified in the schools, in order that those children, and those only may be present at the religious instruction, whose parents and guardians approve of their being so.

" 5. The reading of the Scriptures, either in the authorized or Douay version, is regarded as a religious exercise, and as such is to be confined to those times which are set apart for religious instruction. The same regulation is also to be observed respecting prayer.

" 6. A register is to be kept in each school, recording the daily attendance of the scholars, and the average attendance in each week, and each quarter, according to a form to be furnished by the Board."

It might reasonably have been hoped by the Commissioners, when issuing these regulations, that while on the one hand they had been careful not to offend the religious scruples of any denomination, they had on the other hand fully and satisfactorily provided for religious instruction. If such a course of religious instruction, as must be understood to mean instruction in the peculiar doctrines of the Christian faith, as professed by some particular sect, had been allowed during the hours of ordinary school business, it is obvious that the children of the Irish poor would have been as much split into parties under the new system as they had been under the old; or rather, that the course of the Commissioners would have been no other than that which had already so signally failed in producing any good results to the country. We should not, as now, have seen the children of the Catholic and the Protestant learning from the same books, and in the same classes, their social and religious duties; the spirit of religious hatred would have been encouraged; and one fruitful source of the miseries which have for ages weighed upon Ireland would have been perpetuated. The Commissioners approached as nearly as they durst to this dangerous path, when, in their first regulation, they recommended the use of extracts from the Scriptures as a part of the ordinary school business; and that they were fully aware of this fact, is evident from the following explanation which they have given of their motives for that recommendation, and which is prefixed to the first volume of those extracts :—

" These selections are offered, not as a substitute for the sacred volume itself, but as an introduction to it, in the hope of their leading to a more general and more profitable perusal of the word of God. The passages introduced have been chosen, not as being of more importance than the rest of Scripture, but merely as appearing to be more level to the understandings of children and youth at school, and also best fitted to be read under the direction of teachers, not necessarily qualified, *and certainly not recognized, as teachers of religion ;* no passage has either been introduced or omitted under the influence of any particular view of Christianity, doctrinal or practical."

We are of opinion that enough would have been done by the Commissioners for the religious instruction of the children in the national schools, if they had omitted these volumes of extracts from the list of books recommended by them as proper to be used during the ordinary hours of instruction. One entire day in each week, exclusive of Sunday, together with other "facility for the same purpose, either before or after the ordinary school business on the other days of the week," would be sufficient for religious instruction. The complaint that has been made against the Commissioners on this head, by those opposed to the Government system of education is, that they design "to substitute extracts from the Scriptures for the sacred volume itself;" and to deny to children the benefits of religious instruction by keeping the Word of God from them.

The correspondence between the Commissioners and the Synod of Ulster, a copy of which correspondence has been given in compliance with the order of the House of Commons, is upon this subject.

The members of the Synod commenced this correspondence by insisting "that it shall be the right of all parents to require of patrons or managers of schools to set apart, for reading the Holy Scriptures, a convenient and sufficient portion *of the stated school-hours,* and to direct the master or some other person *whom the parents may appoint and provide,* to superintend the reading. That all children whose parents and guardians so direct shall daily read the Holy Scriptures during the period appointed; but that no compulsion whatever be employed to induce others either to read or to remain during the reading." If the members of the Synod were altogether sincere in the degree of liberality expressed in the concluding part of their stipulation, it is difficult to imagine what objection they could urge against the regulation proposed by the Commissioners, of setting apart a sufficient portion of time for reading the Scriptures either before or after the usual school hours. What possible advantage could arise from such an interruption to the school business as would drive away a part of the scholars during the ordinary hours of attendance, we confess ourselves altogether unable to comprehend; and we think the Commissioners have acted wisely in resisting such an interference with their plan. But the Synod did not limit their stipulation to this point: they proceeded to the further and still more objectionable length of requiring that on each day of the week, during the first hour of the regular school business, " such children as are so directed by their parents shall repeat a portion of the Westminster Catechism; and on Saturday they shall repeat all they have learned during the week." We do not wish to accuse the Synod of intending by such means to exclude from the schools all children except those of their own religious persuasion : there can be no doubt, however, that such would have been the consequence if these stipulations had been enforced.   The intention of the Government in the formation of the Commission was to put an end to these and similar means of exclusion; the adoption of these stipulations would, therefore, have been in direct opposition to the spirit of the instructions given for the guidance of the Commissioners.   It is not our business to find fault with the members of the Synod of Ulster for endeavouring to enforce the observance of any religious duty which they conscientiously deem necessary in the conduct of their schools; and if they think that the reading of the Bible and the repetition of the Assembly's Catechism during the ordinary school hours are indispensable, they are doubtless right in insisting on the observance of those points.   We will only say, that in such case they have no claim whatever for assistance from funds granted for objects which would be defeated by a compliance with their stipulations.   Before quitting this part of the subject, we must state, that the members of the Synod conceive it to be their duty not only to provide in the manner and at the times already stated for the religious education of the children according to their own belief, but also to prevent the giving of religious instruction in any other way, by protesting against that regulation of the Commissioners which provides for the setting apart of one day in the week, independent of the Sunday, for attending to the religious instruction of the children, through the means of such ministers as might be approved by their parents and guardians, according to the doctrines of the sects to which they respectively belong. We will not say that, with their peculiar views on such subjects, the members of the Synod are wrong in thus endeavouring to prevent the diffusion of what they conceive to be erroneous opinions, by pre-occupying the minds of children with a different set of doctrines; but we are quite sure that the Commissioners were right in not lending themselves to the attempt, and in resisting, as they have successfully done, the factious and fanatical opposition offered from other quarters to the working of their enlightened and comprehensive plans.

Of that successful resistance we find the best evidence in the documents before us.   The return of the Commissioners to the order of the House of Commons, requiring the names of the clergymen of the three persuasions who have applied for grants in aid of schools, is given in such a manner as enables us to see in what cases those applications have been made by clergymen of each denomination separately, and in what cases the clergymen of different sects have concurred in the applications. This list, as given by the Commissioners, occupies 49 folios; and it would be of little use to transfer to our pages so long a catalogue of names: the practical purpose for which the return was asked will be fully answered by the following abstract of the applications.

	Established Church.	Established Church and Presbyterians.	Established Church and Catholics.	Established Church, Presbyterians, and Catholics.	Presbyterians.	Presbyterians and Catholics.	Catholics.	Total.
Antrim	2	1	3	2	15	34	27	84
Armagh	..	..	..	..	2	8	9	19
Carlow	..	..	1	..	..	..	24	25
Cavan	1	..	9	..	..	..	7	17
Clare	1	..	3	..	..	..	4	8
Cork	2	..	6	..	..	2	37	47
Donegal	..	..	7	1	1	..	7	16
Down	1	1	5	1	5	29	15	57
Dublin	..	..	5	..	..	1	38	44
Fermanagh	1	..	1	..	..	..	21	23
Galway	..	..	3	..	..	..	18	21
Kerry	..	..	3	..	..	..	5	8
Kildare	..	..	4	..	..	..	18	22
Kilkenny	..	..	1	..	..	..	8	9
King's County	..	..	1	..	..	..	13	14
Leitrim	..	..	..	..	..	..	12	12
Limerick	..	..	8	..	..	..	11	19
Londonderry	2	..	5	..	6	7	10	30
Longford	..	..	..	..	1	..	3	4
Louth	..	..	..	..	..	3	16	19
Mayo	..	..	1	..	1	..	38	40
Meath	..	..	4	..	..	..	17	21
Monaghan	1	..	1	..	1	..	30	33
Queen's County	..	..	..	..	..	..	31	31
Roscommon	..	..	.	..	..	..	6	6
Sligo	..	..	1	..	..	..	15	16
Tipperary	..	..	4	..	..	..	31	35
Tyrone	..	..	14	3	2	8	22	49
Waterford	1	..	2	..	..	..	17	20
Westmeath	..	..	4	..	..	1	4	9
Wexford	..	..	6	..	..	..	12	18
Wicklow	..	..	2	..	..	..	11	13
Total	12	2	104	7	34	93	537	789

It appears from this abstract, that 583 applications for grants were made by individual ministers of the different sects, without the co-operation of ministers of either of the other sects. Of this number, 12 were made by clergymen of the Established Church, 34 by Presbyterian ministers, and 537 by Roman Catholics. The ministers of the Establishment concurred in only two applications with Presbyterians alone ; they joined in 104 applications with Catholics alone ; and only seven cases occur in which the ministers of the three sects joined in the demand. It will likewise be seen that in 93 cases applications have been made jointly by Presbyterians and Catholics.

It is pleasing to observe, on the part of the ministers of the Catholic Church, a body which has been often accused of wishing to keep its disciples in ignorance, so great a willingness to come forward and participate for their benefit in the advantages offered by Government through the Education Board ; and it must afford the best encouragement to all who are interested for the welfare of Ireland to know, that the system of education under the direction of the Commissioners has hitherto been gratefully received and approved by the public in general in that country. The result of their labours, even at this early stage, affords abundant proof of the sincerity of the Commissioners when they declare that "it shall be, as it ever has been, their constant object so to administer their trust, as to make the system acceptable and beneficial to the whole of his Majesty's subjects ; to train up and unite through it the youth of the country together, whatever their religious differences may be, in feelings and habits of attachment and friendship towards each other, and thus to render it the means of promoting charity and good will amongst all classes of the people." Should the system prove in any considerable degree, and lastingly, productive of this effect, we need not fear contradiction when we assert, that it will be the greatest blessing which the Government of the United Kingdom has ever conferred upon Ireland.

A very important part of the duty intrusted to the Education Board consists in the preparation of books for the use of the schools, and for school libraries. The attention of the Commissioners appears to have been hitherto confined to the compilation of books for schools only ; we are not aware of their having yet published any for the use of school libraries, but we trust the intention of doing so is by no means either abandoned or deferred.

The list of books produced up to a recent date comprises—

> Four progressive numbers of a series of reading books, to which it is proposed to add a fifth number.
> A Treatise on Arithmetic, in theory and practice.
> The Elements of Book-keeping, in a series of short examples.
> Key to the Elements of Book-keeping.
> Elements of Geometry, containing the first and second parts of Clairaut's Elements, translated from the French.
> Scripture Lessons, No. 1, Old Testament; and
> Scripture Lessons, No. 1, New Testament;

in all, ten volumes. All schools connected with the Board have permission to purchase copies of these books, and other school requisites, such as paper, slates, quills, &c., at half cost price. A first stock of the books is furnished by the Board, gratuitously, to each school; and it is expected that these books will be kept as a school stock, and used in teaching the pupils, but on no account are they to be taken from the school-room. The inspector requires to see them at every inspection. Children, whose parents wish them to bring their books home with them, will be supplied at the reduced price at which books are furnished by the Board.

The titles of all books which the conductors of schools connected with the Board intend to use in the ordinary business of instruction must be reported to the Board; and no other books may be used than those which have been reported to and are sanctioned by the Board. It is proper to explain, with reference to this regulation, that no books are prohibited by the Commissioners, " except such as appear to them to contain matter objectionable in itself, or objectionable as peculiarly belonging to some particular religious denomination." The Board does not grant assistance by furnishing at reduced prices any books which have not been prepared by them. By a further regulation, it is provided, that " if any other books than the Holy Scriptures, or the standard books of any Church to which any of the children belong, are to be employed in communicating religious instruction, the pastor or religious teacher who proposes to employ such book is expected to communicate his intention to any individual member of the Board, and consult with him as to its suitableness."

We have examined the volumes published by the Commissioners, and we can speak favourably of them. If they are compared with any of the elementary works which were employed twenty or thirty years ago in private schools of the best reputation in England, these little volumes, prepared for the instruction of the poor children in Ireland, must be pronounced excellent; and even if we take another standard, and compare them with the improved lesson books now in use in Great Britain, the works before us will bear the test of even this comparison.

Of the four books of reading lessons, the second is, we think, the least deserving of praise. There is a want of clearness and precision about some parts of it; qualities above all things necessary for books which are intended to form the groundwork of all future knowledge. Such books cannot be too plain. It is a difficult thing for an instructed person to write with a full feeling of the ignorance of those whom he wishes to teach, but still through the want of this feeling the minds of children are often confused, and false or imperfect notions are frequently impressed upon them. This remark applies less to those parts of the volume before us which are original, than to the lessons which are taken from other books. In some of these lessons too much use is made of metaphors, which are frequently forced, and must unavoidably convey indistinct impressions to the mind of a child. This fault may, it is true, be remedied by explanation on the part of the teacher, but it would be much better to leave nothing to the operation of a remedy, the application of which must frequently be doubtful. A very little trouble would serve to remove the defect of which we complain, and the opportunity for doing so cannot long be wanting, as the constant demand for these volumes, and particularly those which are the most elementary, must require them to be frequently reprinted. Notwithstanding these blemishes, the book contains much that is really valuable. It communicates in an interesting manner several facts in natural history, and details many of those simple, but useful processes of domestic economy which the class of children for whom the lessons are intended will most probably some time be called upon to perform. It likewise inculcates religious and moral principles, in a manner calculated to make a deep impression, and teaches the duty and advantage of cultivating feelings of benevolence towards our fellow-creatures.

The third and fourth books of reading lessons, which are intended for the use of scholars of a more advanced age, are deserving of all the praise which we have given to the second book, and are free from the blemishes which we have pointed out. The greater part of their contents consists of extracts from works of high repute in prose and verse. The subjects are sufficiently varied, and comprehend fables, lessons in natural history, religious and moral lessons, geography, political economy, useful arts, and miscellaneous lessons. The third volume commences with an extract from Dr. Mayo's " Lessons on Objects," a work which was noticed in the first Number of this Journal. We are pleased to see this adoption of a system of instruction which teaches the nature and properties of things in daily use, as to which children were formerly allowed to remain in perfect ignorance. In another part of this volume there are some conversations on the different common metals, taken from Dr. Aikin's admirable little volume " Evenings at Home," in which the properties and uses of each metal are familiarly described.

The miscellaneous selections of both poetry and prose, the object of which is to combine amusement with instruction, are made with a considerable degree of taste and judgment. The poetry, especially, is of a quality that can hardly fail to be interesting to children whose minds have been awakened to the perception of moral beauty, and whose hearts have been opened to the influence of benevolent feelings.

So far as we know, the volumes before us furnish the first example in our language of any attempt to convey directly to children instruction in political economy ; and considering that it is not long since a senator, in the British House of Commons, " thanked God that he was no political economist," it may be considered a bold attempt, to aim at instructing the children of the poorer classes in this branch of knowledge. The explanations given on the subjects of value, wages, capital, and taxes, are plain and satisfactory expositions upon what have been generally considered difficult subjects. It is evident that they have been drawn up by one who is thoroughly master of the subject, and who possesses the art of communicating knowledge in plain, concise, and perspicuous language. The class of persons for whose use these lessons are prepared are fully as much interested as any other portions of the community in having a clear understanding of the leading doctrines of political science. For want of that knowledge, how often have the labouring classes been led by the ignorant or designing to form opinions, and to embark in projects fraught with equal mischief to themselves and their employers. Knowledge of this kind, if generally spread, would deprive of their hurtful character the " Trades Unions," which have occupied so much of the valuable time, and absorbed so much of the hard-earned money of workmen, and would teach both the men and their employers (for the lessons are equally needed by both parties) how much their real interests are identified.

An appendix to the fourth book of reading lessons contains a copious list of prefixes, affixes, and of the principal Latin and Greek roots which occur in the volume. The object of this appendix, and the manner in which the author proposes that it shall be used, are thus explained in the preface* :—

"Masters will derive considerable assistance in teaching, and pupils in learning, the lessons from the list of Latin and Greek roots in the appendix. Those in the first section have been arranged according to the lessons in which they occur, and have been selected at the rate of six roots to each page of reading. It will be of advantage, therefore, to teach the first section by prescribing, for each lesson, a page to be spelled, read, and explained, and six roots to be committed to memory. In hearing the Latin and Greek roots, teachers will be careful to examine their pupils on the formation of English words from them, by joining prefixes, affixes, and other words; and they will also cause them to give, in addition to the examples in the book, as many English words formed from the same root as they can recollect. The object of this exercise is to accustom young persons to habits of combination and analysis, as well as to give them a command of expressions in their own language. When the teacher is examining on the reading lesson, he will make his pupils point out all the words of which he has learned the Latin and Greek roots, explain them according to their derivation, and show how they are formed. These directions will be made more intelligible by the subjoined example of the method in which the lessons are recommended to be taught:—

" ' Linnæus, the great Swedish naturalist, characterizes and divides the three kingdoms of nature, the animal, the vegetable, and the mineral, in the following manner:—stones *grow;* vegetables grow and *live;* animals grow, live, and *feel.*'

"The teacher having seen that his pupils can spell every word in this sentence, and read it with proper pronunciation, accent,` and emphasis, may examine them upon it as follows:—Who was Linnæus?—A Swedish naturalist. From what Latin root is *naturalist* formed?—*Natura,* nature. What is the first affix added to *natura?*—*Al,* of or belonging to. What part of speech is *natural?* —An adjective. What affix is then added to *natural?*—*Ist,* a doer. What part of speech is *naturalist?*—A noun. Why is it called a noun?—Because it is applied to a person. Applied to persons, what should it be?—*Naturalists,* in the plural number. Is it applied to males or females?—To both, and is therefore of the

---

* Some of the explanations in the Appendix are not good, some are so confused as to be useless, and a few are wrong. The following are instances of these three classes of explanations—*Stratus* (p. 337); *Rego* (p. 332); and *Stinguor* (p. 332). We are, however, far from being of opinion that these explanations in the Appendix are badly done. The attempt is highly creditable to the Commissioners; and a future revision will no doubt render the execution more complete.

common gender. What is the meaning of the word *naturalist?*—
A person who studies nature. What kind of a naturalist was Linnæus?—Great. What part of speech is *great?*—An adjective,
because it expresses quality. Where was Linnæus born?—In
Sweden. Where is Sweden?—In the north of Europe. Point it
out on the map. What is Linnæus said to have done?—He characterized and divided, &c. What parts of speech are these words?
—Active verbs, because they express what Linnæus did. Any affix
in *characterize?*—*Ize*, to make. The meaning of the word?—To
make or give a character or name to. Give me some of the derivatives of *divide?*—*Division, divisible, indivisible, dividend*, &c.
What did Linnæus characterize and divide?—Animals, vegetables,
and minerals. What are these called?—The three kingdoms of
nature. How did he characterize minerals?—They grow, &c., &c,
State to me, in your own words, what you have learned from this
sentence?—Linnæus was a great naturalist. He was born in
Sweden. He formed all natural objects into three great classes or
kingdoms; and he thus distinguished each of these kingdoms from
the other—' stones *grow*, &c." '

The advantage of such exercises as these are too evident
to require pointing out. To children who do not receive
instruction in the dead languages—and all for whom these
lessons are designed come under that description—it appears
highly necessary to make them acquainted with such words
in those languages as enter into the formation of many
words in their own. It is only by these means that they can
be enabled to acquire the habit of expressing themselves with
correctness and precision; while children whose education
embraces the study of Latin and Greek, will derive great
advantage from being exercised in a similar way. It should,
however, be observed, that this plan of questioning, unless
managed by a skilful teacher, is apt to degenerate, like all
other teaching, into routine. The only remedy for this is
to be constantly bringing up a new set of well-instructed
teachers, to supply the place of those who die off. In the
sample here given of questioning, we think that there is too
little order and connection, and that the child will be distracted by the variety of the questions, and confused by the
vagueness of some of them.

We cannot say much in praise of the Treatise on Arithmetic, which does not appear to be well adapted for teaching the elements of that science. At the very outset of
his task, the pupil is met in this work by a series of abstruse definitions, for the full comprehension of which a considerable effort of the mind would be required on the part
of children of average capacity, even if they should be some
years older than it is probable those pupils will at first be,
into whose hands this treatise will be placed. The reason-

ing employed is no doubt sound and conclusive, and the explanations would be convincing to pupils sufficiently instructed to admit their force ; but addressed as they are to children of a tender age, and who for the greater part have not had their reasoning faculties much cultivated, they are sadly out of place, and will, we fear, tend to create a distaste for the study of a science which would prove of great utility to the pupils through life. There is little, if any thing, which bears the mark of originality in this treatise, which appears to be a compilation, and in a great degree indebted to Gregory's 'Philosophy of Arithmetic.' The author is so little practically aware of the changes which are going on that may affect a work which professes to combine practice with theory, that he refers in his tables to the old wine gallon, the use of which was abolished several years ago in favour of the imperial measure. We have noticed some other inaccuracies, which should certainly not be allowed to disfigure a work designed as an introduction to the study of one of the exact sciences.

We strongly recommend the Commissioners to let at least the introductory parts of this treatise be re-written, and made both more elementary and more exact than they are at present.

Geometry forms a part of the course of instruction in the national schools of Ireland : the elements of this science are presented in a manner admirably suited to the purpose in the unpretending little work before us, which is a translation from the French of the 1st and 2nd parts of the 'Elements of Geometry,' by Clairaut. His work has been strongly recommended by Lacroix, as being "calculated to open the minds of children, and to prepare them, under judicious teachers, for higher studies." Geometry has hitherto been too jealously confined to the rigid rules of abstract reasoning ; the senses have not been allowed to assist, and it has consequently continued to be too difficult a study for very young persons, whose minds have been perplexed by theory before they could perceive the practical use of the truths laid before them, and the complete proofs of which can be obtained only by a chain of close reasoning. It is truly observed in the preface to the little volume now before us, that "there is scarcely a theorem in geometry which is not applicable to some useful purpose ;" why then should the mass of the people be excluded from a knowledge of this science, because there unfortunately "exists (in this country more than in any other,) a *professional* pride upon this subject, which degenerates almost into bigotry ?" Why should we persist in teaching the first rudiments of the science, exactly in the same manner as they were taught by their great master more than 2000 years ago ? Those who admire abstract reasoning, who delight in deducing one truth from a number of others which have gone before, will not, cannot be satisfied with the practical view here taken of the subject: but even they will admit that this little book will prove a good preparation for Euclid; while the generality of young persons thus taught, and who would otherwise know nothing of geometry, will receive great and lasting benefit from the study.

It is the great merit of Clairaut's work, that it excites the curiosity of the pupil, and interests his attention before it enters into any dry details. Distances are to be measured, land is to be surveyed—how is this to be done? The properties of triangles, and of other figures, are gradually explained with simplicity and clearness, and applied to practical purposes. There is no long array of definitions at the beginning, to be learned by rote, and to disgust the pupil. No definition is given until it is wanted, and something is to be *done* by the aid of every piece of knowledge, before the theorem in which it is involved is demonstrated.

We give the following as an example of the way of treating the subject which has been adopted from the French mathematician. It is proposed (page 14, part 2) to make a square equal to two other unequal squares. This is very ingeniously done ; and thence the property of a right-angled triangle, which is demonstrated in the 47th proposition of the first book of Euclid, is clearly made out. We are glad to see that it is the intention of the Commissioners to cause translations to be made of the other parts of Clairaut's 'Elements,' for the use of the schools under their management.

' The Elements of Book-keeping,' and the 'Key' to the same, are plain and practical explanations of a subject which is really very simple, but which is somehow considered, on the part of the uninitiated, as a very abstruse business. Any person of plain understanding, and with a moderate knowledge of the common rules of arithmetic, may be made to master the whole art and mystery of book-keeping and " double entry" in the course of one or two lessons. It is surprising that in this commercial country, the subject should be so little attended to in schools, that with a few exceptions, no attempt whatever has been made to explain it. Even in schools which profess to give what is called a commercial education, all that is done in that respect is to carry the pupils through a few more rules of common arithmetic than are considered to be necessary for youths who are not intended for counting-house employment, with perhaps a few exercises and calculations of exchanges with foreign countries, and causing them to copy into their ciphering-books entries from fictitious journals and ledgers. As to the principle upon which book-keeping should be conducted, we will venture to assert, that not one in twenty of the boys who receive their education in the so-called "Commercial Academies," have any clear idea about it; in fact, the whole matter is to be learned at the time when they are called upon to put it in practice. The disadvantage of this imperfect education is not, indeed, experienced by those who commence their career of active life in mercantile counting-houses, for the reason already given, that the whole affair is so simple when properly explained, as to be mastered at once and without difficulty. The real disadvantage of ignorance in the art of book-keeping is experienced by a different class of youths—those who fill the humbler classes of traders, and who are not likely to meet with instruction from persons with whom they are placed, because they themselves are unacquainted with the principles of the art. Under this view, we think the Education Board has done wisely in preparing these little books, and in making them form a part of the studies of the children educated in the national schools.

It is not necessary to say much about the two volumes of 'Scripture Lessons.' The objects with which they have been compiled are sufficiently explained by the Commissioners in their report, which we have already quoted. They appear to be executed in a way calculated to avoid offending the religious feelings or opinions of all the sects for whose use they are intended.

REPORT OF THE SELECT COMMITTEE OF THE HOUSE OF COMMONS ON THE STATE OF EDUCATION. 1834.

THE interest which has been excited with regard to education, by the conduct of governments on the continent, has at last led to a consideration of the subject by a committee of the House of Commons; and as persons of various opinions have been examined, many of whom are distinguished by their talents and consideration in society, we conceive that we shall be doing some service at this moment, by selecting the most important points on which the parties are at issue; and by confronting the opinions of each, accompanied by their several reasons for them in their own words. The public will thus be enabled to judge on which side the truth lies. Although we have been at some pains to form accurate judgments on the different heads, still as we have no cause to serve but that of truth, we trust it will be found that we have given due weight to every well-grounded objection that is started by one side, and not effectually met by the other ; for we feel an assurance that this is the only spirit in which subjects of great importance ever can be discussed with benefit to the public.

That the very religion which was sent to bring peace on earth and good will towards man, whose essence is brotherly love, should itself become the cause of endless dissensions and bitter hatreds, is a circumstance which must be lamented by all good men. But as these dissensions and hatreds proceed not from any exciting cause in the religion itself, but from human passions and human infirmity, it behoves all well-wishers to humanity to consider how the blessings and comforts of what they prize so highly may be enjoyed, without the evils which we have mentioned. And every plan for attaining this desirable object, devised in the spirit of kindness, should meet with that consideration which the importance of the subject entitles it to.

We shall, therefore, in the first instance, as being a subject generally considered of great difficulty, adduce the evidence with respect to educating the children of parents of various religious denominations together. In the first article in this Number we have endeavoured to show how this attempt has succeeded in Ireland ; and in a previous Number (No. XVI. p. 246), we have discussed this part of the question as to national education in England. The importance of it, in a practical point of view, since it is now almost universally admitted to be the chief obstacle to the establishment of a truly national system, renders it unnecessary to make any apology for recurring to this part of the subject.

The Right Rev. the Bishop of London.

' 2470. Is not the system of voluntary contribution more peculiarly suited to this country, where it has, as your Lordship states, been in operation, and where likewise there are great differences among religious sects, which are an obstacle to their meeting together in one school ?—My own experience has long ago led me to the conclusion, that any attempt to give a common education, which is to comprise sound and correct religious instruction to children whose parents are of different persuasions, will be likely to fail ; unless, as is the case in many of our parochial schools, the parents are content to let their children receive religious instruction according to the doctrines of the Church of England, which, up to a certain point, are not objected to by the great body of dissenters; but where that is the case, I think it more expedient for the interests of religion and peace, that they should be educated separately, by teachers of their own persuasion. And so far from looking upon this view of the subject as narrow or uncharitable, I am persuaded it is the most liberal mode of proceeding, because it is the most likely to avoid those disagreements and misunderstandings which always occur where different denominations are united in one insti⸬ tution for the purpose of instruction. I wish it to be understood that my observations apply simply to education, and not to any other kind of charity; because in almost every kind of charity, churchmen and dissenters may unite without difficulty.

' 2471. With respect to the education of children, is it, in your Lordship's opinion, impracticable that the children should be taught on the days of the week such lessons and explanations of the Bible as may inculcate the doctrines of Christianity, on which the church and the greater portion of the dissenters of this country agree; and that, on Sundays only, those doctrines should be taught which are peculiar to the Church of England, as distinguished from the opinions of dissenters?—To a certain extent that is the case in our schools: the religious instruction usually given in our national schools is not such as would shock the opinions of any denominations, except perhaps Unitarians and Roman Catholics.

' 2472. With respect to the Baptists, are there not parts of the catechism to which they would object?—Yes; and I do not think that a Church of England teacher could consent to sink that part as not being important.

' 2473. All the dissenters object to the question as to godfathers and godmothers?—Yes, that is a question of fact; there is a difficulty about that, but not a very important one; *there is no doubt the children might be taught the catechism on Sundays;* but we could not come to any distinct compromise that it should not be taught on the week days. A number of the children of dissenters were educated in the national schools in the parish of Bishopsgate; there were the children of Roman Catholics and Jews, and I never had any difficulty.

The Rev. W. Johnson, clerical superintendent of the schools of the National Society.

' 41. Are the schools of the society in any way confined to children and parents who belong to the established church?—They are open to all; and children of all descriptions, both Roman Catholics and dissenters of all kinds, and also Jews have been in our school, and some of them have risen high in it.

' 42. But always understanding, though the parents were Jews, that the children are taught the Church of England discipline and doctrine?—Yes; the question has never been once raised that I am aware of.

' 43. The society does not authorize any exceptions being made with respect to the children of persons who dissent from the doctrine of the Church of England as to the condition of teaching the

Church of England catechism?—No; that is a case which I think has never occurred for the last twenty-two years; and had it occurred, and been sanctioned by the committee, *I should have considered it very inconvenient to have two sets of children in the same class, under the same roof, learning different things.*

' 44. Do the committee understand you to say that no application has been made by parents of such children to make that exception or condition?—That is the case.

' 45. Is there any obligation on the part of the parents of such children to allow their children to go to attend the worship of the established church on the Sunday?—As regards our own school, we are certainly always most anxious to have the children with us on the Sunday; but there are continually some absent on that day; reasons are assigned for their absence, and those reasons admitted; but *I should not think myself justified, according to the understood principle and practice on which the directing committee of the society act, to allow children to go to a dissenting place of worship.*

' 54. In speaking of the central school, over which you have a sort of personal control, supposing, for example, that a child had attended during the whole week regularly, and that, on the next Monday morning, having absented himself from the place of worship of the established church, should be asked why he was absent, and had stated that he had gone to the place of worship that his parents usually attended, would that child in your school be excluded?—Certainly not. I should send for the parents, and say, such are my instructions, your child is expected to be here on the Sunday, and I can assure you, that in no place where your child can possibly go, will greater kindness be shown to the child than by me; and, occasionally, the parents have been overcome in that way.

The Rev. J. C. Wigram, secretary to the National School Society.

' 705. *Many dissenters send their children with a feeling that the influence of the parent at home will countervail anything that is done at school; and it is their firm intention, as many of them have told me, to keep their children in the practices of dissenters when they grow up.*

' 714. Do not you think it would be possible to frame a general system of religious instruction, directed to the formation of religious habits, without in any way disturbing the peculiar feelings of peculiar sects?—I do not; because no person who takes what a churchman would call a low view of religious doctrine, or who verges towards Unitarianism, can conceive of our method of teaching the doctrine of redemption and sanctification in the catechism, as conciliatory, or as endurable in fact; I mean endurable in the sense of being at all consistent with his own religious convictions.'

The Rev. W. Cotton, member of the committee of the National School Society twelve or thirteen years.

' 1891. Do you think that dissenters and Roman Catholics generally would object to the superintendence of the clergy; or, if some minister of religion must superintend the schools, would they object more to the clergy of the church than to the ministers of the various religious denominations who happened to reside in the neighbourhood?—I think that the objection is rather a theoretic than a practical one ; for, as far as my observation goes, I do not think that the dissenters generally have objected to their children coming to our schools. Those dissenters who have strong religious feelings on peculiar points of doctrine, will neither send their children to our schools, or any school except those of their own persuasion ; but the great mass of the parents (of the destitute children of the country—destitute of the means of providing for their own education) who are commonly called dissenters, have very little religious feeling on doctrinal points at all, and care very little on the subject, provided their children have the advantage of instruction ; and, therefore, I do not believe that any serious practical inconvenience has resulted ; and as we ask no questions when a child comes to a school, whether the parent is a dissenter or not, I do not think that among the great mass of dissenters any serious objection exists to their children entering our schools, or that they view the interference of our clergy with the same jealousy that they would the superintendence of the ministers of any dissenting congregation. They have an impression that there is not that anxiety among our clergy to make proselytes to their church (although anxious to diffuse Christian knowledge) which is manifested by many of the sectarian ministers to increase their congregations ; and, therefore, I think they look with less jealousy to the superintendence of the clergyman than they would to the superintendence of any competent dissenting minister.

' 1936. Do you think it impossible to conduct national schools in such a way as to admit persons of various religious creeds?—I think that you can teach religion upon one set of principles, without in a very serious degree destroying the efficacy of your schools.

' 1937. Have you ever considered the matter in this point of view, whether you might not afford education to a larger portion of the children of the people generally, without compromising in any degree that which is due to the children of the established church, by permitting those who conscientiously dissent from the use of the catechism and the creeds to be excused from attending those particular portions of education?—I should be afraid of the consequences, if such an exception were made in the schools for the lower orders of the people, because a great number of the parents that send their children to our schools have very little religious belief. If you ask them what their religious belief is, they will tell you that they attend Mr. so and so. The differences of religion among the poor may generally be reduced to an attachment to some particular teacher, rather than to any defined principles or doctrines of religion ; and, therefore, I apprehend that our giving the permission to children who dissent from the church to decline joining the class where the catechism is taught, would be entirely disorganising the discipline of the school, and would be an encouragement to other children to make out that their parents were dissenters, and probably disturb the general instruction, rather than do the individuals in question any practical good. I would much prefer, where necessary, to have a separate school for those who differ so essentially from me as not to submit to any mode of instruction; and I have acted upon this principle, by subscribing to a Jews' school.

' Do you think there are not many parents who object to send their children to national schools, who yet send their children to schools on the British system, where no peculiar doctrines are inculcated?—My own opinion is, that it is not so much the circumstance of no peculiar religious instruction being communicated in the British and Foreign Schools, but other circumstances, such as the influence of persons connected with those schools, or the circumstance of contiguity, which carry the children there, because *I have a firm persuasion that the poor do not look with great anxiety to the particular religious principles upon which their children are educated, provided they are taught what we all understand as the great principles of religious and moral duty.'*

The Rev. George Clark, chaplain of the Military Asylum at Chelsea.

' 1957. Are the scholars brought up in the service of the established church?—Yes; we have a chapel in the institution, and they all attend divine service there.

' 1958. And you use the church catechism?—Yes.

' 1979. Are many of them children of dissenters?—I do not know; we make no inquiries of that sort; some of them of course must be children of Roman Catholics, as there are a great many Irish boys in the school.

' 1980. You follow one system with them all?—Yes: many of the parents are Irish soldiers, or their wives, but they never make any objection to our mode of instruction.

' 1985. Have you ever known a single instance of a difficulty occurring on account of religious scruples?—No, I do not recollect any. I think there was once, many years ago, an application from one or two of the parents who were Roman Catholics; and I think one of the commissioners explained to them the great inconvenience that it probably would be to the school, if there was a difference of instruction, and that their children would lose many advantages by it; and I think they acquiesced.

Professor Pillans.

' 446. Are you aware what is the system in Germany in that respect (of religion)?—I should say the arrangements in Germany upon that subject are extremely liberal, and, with every anxiety for religious instruction, provide at the same time for the cases of different religion with the greatest attention, and with the most perfect impartiality.

' 541. Do you not suppose that a sufficient religious education could be conveyed, without the conveyance at the same time of any peculiar religious doctrine?—I am disposed to think so as regards children, both *because I think that the doctrines of our religion, as far as they have a tendency to influence the habits and practice of the young, may be separated, and kept distinct from the peculiar opinions of any one sect; and because such opinions, embodied in any school books, I should consider as nearly ineffectual for any purpose at all, turning, as they generally do, upon points which are altogether beyond the comprehension of the young mind;* and therefore it is that I think it most of all desirable to have a system of religious instruction for schools founded upon the scriptures, but directed only to those parts of the sacred volume which have a moral tendency, and which are likely to influence the conduct, cherish the best affections, and regulate the behaviour of the young. I am fortified in that opinion by the example of the German States, where the school instruction is founded on this principle, as well as of France, where the law on that head is very nearly a transcript of the German.

' *Has it ever suggested itself to you, in the matter of teaching religion, that teaching theology is one thing, and inculcating religious habits is another ?*—*Yes, I think that is obvious, though certainly not sufficiently attended to in practice.*

' In the creation of religious habits, do not all sorts of Christians agree, as far as you have had an opportunity of considering the subject of teaching ?—I think so.

' Supposing that we wanted to teach theology to pupils, the teaching of theology would be like the teaching of any other science ? —It certainly requires a matured understanding to deal with subjects so deep and difficult ; nor can it be a very profitable employment for the mind of a child, to be turned to points of doctrine upon which, from its very nature, it cannot be informed.

' So that, in fact, the business of a teacher of the people, considering the matter of national education, would be to form religious habits, and those might be formed in a national school which did not impose any dogmata upon the minds of the pupils ?—I should say so, certainly ; at the same time, I wish it to be understood that, by dogmata, I mean the peculiar tenets of any particular sect: the leading and distinctive doctrines of Christianity ought not to be omitted. It is these only, I conceive, that are within the province of the schoolmaster, his vocation being more of a literary than of an ecclesiastical character.

' Assuming that there is a general coincidence in all Christian sects, those truths might be taught in a national school, without trenching upon any religious differences that might exist between them ?—I think they might.

' And, therefore, if there were a spirit of forbearance among the Christian sects at this time existing in England, there would, in reality, be no objection on this score to the institution of a national education?—Not the least, I should think. There is in the present day, as far as I have observed, less of excitement and mutual hostility between the different sects in Germany and France than in England ; and, *accordingly, in the ministerial and official instruc-*

tions sent out to the prefect of the circle or department, as well as to the teachers themselves, they are strongly enjoined to encourage mixed schools, where the children may practically learn the principle of toleration and mutual forbearance; and, where that cannot be done, the authorities are invited to take every means to provide such religious instruction apart, as shall be thought necessary, or even to form separate schools. The last, however, they consider as a resource not to be resorted to, unless all means of uniting the two persuasions shall be found unavailing.

' 548. *Do you not suppose that the teaching of various sects in one school, under that system of Catholic faith, if it may be so called, would very much tend to promote general kindliness amongst the whole population ?*—I think so desirable an object most likely to be attained by such a joint and mixed system. *Judging both from reason and experience, I should say it is a result that could scarcely fail to take place.*

' 549. Do you not think a true Christian feeling would be created by such a system of national education ?—I do.

' 550. Do you consider that in any way the interests of religion would be injured by such a system?—On the contrary, *it appears to me that the amount of religious feeling and true Christianity would be increased very considerably by such an arrangement, inasmuch as we are all taught to believe, and cannot help believing, who are familiar with the scriptures and the New Testament, that brotherly love is the first of Christian virtues.'*

Mr. William Allen, the treasurer of the British and Foreign School Society, follows on the same side.

' 865. In the schools of the British and Foreign School Society, are questions asked upon various passages of scripture, and particularly the extracts of scripture which are read by the children ?—I consider it a valuable part of the system that in which the children are interrogated, so that we may know whether they really understand what they have been reading. But as far as my knowledge goes, we cautiously avoid everything which shall have a tendency to proselyte to any particular sect, or to any particular feeling, on the subject of religion.

' 868. Do you conceive that there is any danger in so doing of making the religion which is taught to them of too vague and general a nature, to produce an effect upon the conduct and character ?—On the contrary, in the extracts from scripture, which were prepared in the first instance by some friends of mine and myself, at Petersburg, in 1818 and 1819, for the Emperor Alexander, and which were adopted by the emperor, and made the reading lessons of the empire, and which is now printed in most of the languages of Europe, and in Arabic also : in those reading lessons we have dwelt particularly upon the great duties of man towards God and towards mankind in general. We have made them bear upon those duties in a very striking and prominent way, without any comment whatever, but merely in the words of scripture ; such as the duties of subjects to government, in the words of scripture ; the duties of servants to masters, in the words of scripture; the relative duties of husbands and wives, and parents and children, in the words of scripture. They were most anxiously calculated to bring out those great and important duties, and to engrave them upon the minds of the children, while at the same time we let the children have the whole scriptures, without limitation; but their attention was particularly directed towards some of the most important points, and the good effects that have resulted from this have been very striking in various countries.

' 869. Do you conceive that that plan of instruction tends to produce charity and harmony between different Christian denominations ?—I conceive that nothing is so much calculated to produce unity and harmony among Christians in general, as the education of their children together, avoiding all those little distinctions by which one sect is separated from another; but where they shall unite in all the great features of the Christian religion as taught in the Holy Scriptures, without note or comment, or as to any particular view or sect.

' 893. Are the committee to understand that you endeavour, as much as possible, to inculcate morality, but not any particular religion ?—Religion, in the most emphatic sense of the word, we wish to insist upon; and we think that, by teaching the poor to reverence the word of divine revelation and inspiration, we are assisting the cause of religion most materially, because upon that is founded all our hopes.

' 897. Then you would leave the minister of his own denomination to superadd further instruction upon that foundation ?—Certainly.

' 898. Is the child made aware of the different constructions put upon the different passages of scripture ?—We should think it very much out of our place to put into the minds of poor children that there were great diversities of opinion about these things, which we wish them to consider as sacred. We should be sorry to stir up any doubt in their minds about it, seeing that there is so much that is plain, and does not require any explanation.

' 900. Do you, then, expect that the child shall be able to make the application which is intended in the Holy Scriptures—for instance, the proper application of the prophecies ?—We think it quite right to let the child know that there are certain prophecies with regard to the coming of the Messiah, in which all religious sects agree. All that we avoid is, anything sectarian that relates to any view that is peculiar to one set of Christians, and distinguishes them from another.

' 901. If there were any prophecy, for instance, of which the application was disputed by various sects, you would not, in teaching that particular passage, state anything to the child with reference to that peculiar application ?—We should think it most prudent to say nothing about it.

' 902. But in those cases in which the application is plain and evident, and agreed upon by all sects, in those cases you make it known to the child that it is the Messiah that is spoken of?—Yes.

' 9£9. How do you deal with the explanation of texts which necessarily involve points of doctrine?—We do not deem it necessary to explain them; we consider that, in the Holy Scriptures, there is enough that is plain; that the path is so plain, that the wayfaring man, though a fool, shall not err in it.

' 933. With reference to the doctrine of the atonement, do you suppose that any child leaves your school without having that inculcated upon him?—He has what the scripture says of it, and that is abundantly sufficient.

934. Has he no explanation of it?—It is to be understood that these are not schools of theology; they are schools for teaching the elements and the means of acquiring knowledge, and we take advantage of that opportunity to imbue the mind with the great truths of Christianity and morality as contained in the scriptures, but we do not enter into nice points.'

The Rev. J. Wood, secretary of the school on the British system in Harp-alley.

' 2166. Is it your intention not to teach anything, in your reading of scripture, that should be inconsistent or at variance with the instruction that the boys may afterwards receive in the Church of England Sunday-schools, or any other Sunday-schools which they may attend?—Certainly. I should endeavour to avoid teaching anything at variance with what they may afterwards receive at their own school.

' 2167. Therefore, if they receive as much instruction in regard to the Bible as you should give, what would be learned afterwards would be the amplification, and not anything in contradiction with what you teach?—Precisely so; but I may be allowed the opportunity of stating that, speaking practically, I believe almost the whole Bible may be taught, and made the basis of instruction, without going into the peculiarities of sects. I believe that, to do this, is much more practicable than people, who have not turned their attention to the subject, generally suppose.'

The following is a portion of the examination of Dr. Henry Julius, who conducted a journal partly devoted to education in Prussia.

' 1782. Is it not the fact, that the clergymen, both Catholic and Protestant, take great pains to see that the children attend the school?—Yes.

' 1784. Do you know any instance in which a difficulty has arisen on account of the religious belief of the different parts of the community, to meeting in one school on account of religion?—No; they are quite separate in religious instruction: if they are united, as soon as the commune can afford the means they are separated into two schools; but where only one can be erected the religious instruction is given quite separately by different persons.

· ' 1793. You stated that the clergymen superintend those schools; supposing you have got a school which is of a mixed character, containing Catholics and Protestants, do both the Protestant and Catholic clergymen superintend it?—Yes.

' 1794. Do you find there is any difficulty?—No, in general not.

' 1795. They unite in their desire of promoting education, and in that way superintend the school?—Yes.

' 1800. The Protestant father would have no apprehension that the Catholic master would try to make a convert of his son, or *vice versâ?*—No; the children are always educated in the religion of the father.

' 1803. Are there any prayers used in the school?—Yes, always at the beginning and the end.

' 1804. Supposing the children in the school are of a mixed character, what is done in that respect?—The master would have a prayer equally approved by both.'

Mr. Henry Dunn, secretary to the British and Foreign School Society.

' 211. Is it the principle of the British and Foreign School Society to interfere in any way with the religious denomination of the scholars in the schools of their society?—Not in any way further than to expect that they shall attend some place of worship, leaving it to the judgment of the parents to decide what place.

' Are they required to give an account on the Monday morning that they have attended some place of worship on the Sunday?— They are.

' 340. Are the pieces in the book of extracts chiefly from scripture?—They are entirely selected from the scriptures, both of the Old and New Testament. The object of the selection is to obtain, in a small bulk, as introductory to the whole Bible, those portions of scripture which are best adapted to the capacity of children.

' 341. They are moral, and not doctrinal?—They are both; they are selected from the Old and New Testament, and from the Epistles as well as the Gospels.

' 342. Are they approved of by ministers of different denominations?—We believe, from their being extensively used, that they are thus approved. They are used in many schools conducted by members of the established church, and they are equally used in others conducted by dissenters; so that we do not find any practical difficulty in their introduction.'

Mr. J. T. Crossley, master of the Borough Road School.

' 1123. And in those cases in which it occurs in a sentence in the New Testament, wherein it involves a great theological difference, you do not raise in the child's mind any conception of the theological difference?—We keep to the obvious meaning of the text.

' 1124. And in carrying out your plan, you do not so lead his mind as to make him believe upon one side or the other?—We simply keep to the authorized version.

' 1125. Do not you so form and discipline the mind of the child by his previous education, that you give him a capacity of judging of the meaning of it?—We believe that if the child is daily questioned upon the meaning of the scriptures, together with the grammatical meaning of the words, inasmuch as scripture is its own interpreter, he cannot fail to arrive at the most important truths.

' 1126. Those matters of opinion which peculiarly divide Christian sects, you do not think it necessary to present before him?—We should not, for instance, go into a discussion of the meaning of the word " baptize ;" we should avoid it.

' 1127. Supposing, for instance, you were reading the text—-" This is my beloved Son," you would probably ask the child what God called the Saviour, and expect the child to say his " Son ;" but you would not ask him in what sense he called him his Son?—We should ask, " Who is called here the Son, and by whom is he called the Son ?"   And it requires no further question.

' 1128. In limiting yourself to that kind of teaching, do you think that that in any way limits your usefulness in framing what may be termed religious habits and moral habits ?—I am convinced that it does not, because I see the result in children coming out.   They go into life with a large knowledge of scripture, and with a great desire to gain more ; and we find them acting consistently with it. Of the youths that we have had who have been taught side by side in the same class, and have become monitors in the school, some have become Independents, some Wesleyans, and some of the Church of England.

' 1166. Is any public prayer used morning and evening in your school ?—No.

' 1167. Is any prayer taught to the children for private use ?—The duty of prayer is impressed, and questions of course occur on what they are to pray for.

' 1168. Is there any religious exercise in the school?—At the commencement and at the close of the school, daily, I read a chapter, and sometimes more, in a slow and impressive manner; the attention of the children is kept up to it, and a solemn quietness is observed before and after it.'

The Rev. James Carlisle, one of the Commissioners for Education in Ireland.

' 2554. As regards the great leading features of the scheme, that of educating the children of the Irish population under the management of a board, consisting of individuals of different religious persuasions, your experience does not show that the scheme is not one that may be acted upon extensively and usefully ?—I think we have got over all the great difficulties upon that subject, and that we are now, both as regards the country, and as regards the board, prepared to go over the length and breadth of the land, if we had the means of doing so.'

By the foregoing evidence, it will be perceived that the foundations upon which the conclusions of the parties opposed to each other on this important subject are grounded, are nearly as follows :—

The evidence of those who would not educate Christians of various denominations together in the same schools, without interfering with the peculiar religious opinions of the parents.

The evidence of those who would educate various denominations of Christians together in the same schools, without interfering with the peculiar religious opinions of the parents.

That it would be better for the interests of religion and of peace, that the children of various sects should be educated separately.

That any attempt to give a common education, which is to comprise sound and correct religious instruction to children whose parents are of different religious denominations, will be likely to fail, unless the parents be willing that they should be instructed in the doctrines of the church of England.

That there is no doubt that the children might be taught the catechism on Sundays, but the church could not come to a distinct compromise that it should not be taught on week days.

That it would be very inconvenient to have two sets of children under the same roof, learning different things.

That the national schools do receive the children of dissenters, Roman Catholics, and Jews, but they are required to submit to the usual religious discipline, and attend the service of the church of England on a Sunday.

That, by so doing, children would be taught the principles of toleration and mutual forbearance ; that a general kindliness and brotherly love (which is the first of Christian virtues) would be promoted; and the amount of religion and true Christianity would be very considerably increased.

That as the doctrines of religion, as far as they have a tendency to influence the practice and habits, may be separated from the peculiar doctrines of sects, and as all denominations of Christians are anxious to cultivate religious habits, and controverted points of theology are beyond the comprehension of children, the leading and distinctive doctrines of Christianity upon which all are agreed, need only be taught at schools.

That as the great mass of doctrine and morals which all Christians have in common, and nothing which is in opposition to the opinions of any sect should be taught, whatever instruction may afterwards be given by the clergyman of the particular sect to which the individual belongs, will not be in contradiction to, but an amplification of, what the individual has learned at school.

That the peculiar doctrines of the church of which the child is to be a member, may be inculcated on a Sunday.

That the schools of the British and Foreign Society have been conducted upon these principles with the greatest advantage to the children ; and also the mixed schools of the Catholics and Protestants and other sects in Ireland.

That in Germany no mischief has been found to arise from children of various denominations of Christians being brought up together, and listening to the same prayer.

In this evidence we have been forcibly struck by the circumstance of Protestant Dissenters, Roman Catholics, and Jews sending their children to the national schools, simply on account of the impossibility of their being educated elsewhere, and of those children being compelled, not only to attend the service of the church of England, but even to learn the church catechism. The manner in which the Bishop of London and other clergymen have spoken of this, convinces us that either they or we take a most erroneous view of the case. Mr. Dunn, in his evidence (395), says, ' Their (the dissenters) feeling is, that it is not the best mode of teaching a child morality, to require him to repeat that which is not true ;' and we cannot refrain from saying, that, according to our ideas, a more odious piece of tyranny never came before our notice. If the National School Society has arrived at the conclusion that it is not practicable (the interests of religion being attended to) to educate children of various religious denominations under one roof, they ought either to refuse to receive the children of dissenters, or to obtain the permission of the parents to proselyte them, with a distinct understanding that no attempt should afterwards be made at home to bring them back to their own way of thinking : but thus to abuse and tamper with the minds of youth, and partially overturn their belief in those doctrines which, from their earliest infancy, they have been taught to revere as the fountains of virtue and of truth, and partially to teach them what their parents do not wish them to learn, without at the same time attempting to insure their not being again shaken in the belief of what they have been taught at school, immediately upon their return home, is, according to our ideas, perfectly indefensible. The Rev. J. C. Wigram, secretary to the National School Society, says (705), ' Many dissenters send their children with a feeling that the influence of the parent at home will countervail anything that is done at school; and it is their firm intention, as many of them have told me, to keep their children in the practices of dissenters when they grow up.' In order to prove that the system pursued by the National School Society in this respect is deserving of severe reprobation, we think that sufficient evidence has been adduced—and evidence to which the Society cannot object, as it comes from members of their own body. As to the evidence on the general question—whether children of parents of different religious denominations ought or ought not to be educated together—we shall leave it, without further comment, to the reader.

INFANT SCHOOLS.

| EVIDENCE AGAINST INFANT SCHOOLS. | EVIDENCE IN FAVOUR OF INFANT SCHOOLS. |

' The bad singing learnt by the children is very difficult to unlearn; and the method of teaching in those schools is very prejudicial to simple and effective reading.'— *The , Rev. W. Johnson,* 193.

' Infant school tuition is so much of an amusement, that the children are not willing at first to work, so as to make a serious business of their studies.'—*Mr. Dunn,* 352.

' The children from infant schools are certainly better prepared than other children, but not to the extent that we once hoped.'—*Id.*

' The number of competent infant school teachers is very limited. It is very easy to open an infant school, and to introduce certain amusements for the children, but it is not easy to obtain a teacher who will laboriously instruct them.'—*Id.* 354.

' We find the minds of children who have been to good infant schools better prepared than others.'—*Mr. Dunn,* 354.

' There is abundant reason for being favourably impressed with the advantages of infant schools. When children from them are admitted into the national schools, they begin at another grade; their desire of knowledge, too, is increased by the pleasurable form in which the elements of it have been communicated to them in the infant school.'—*The Rev. W. Wilson,* 2194-5.

' There are some few things perhaps to unlearn in going from an infant school to a national school. Our national schools (at Walthamstow) are now nearly formed of those who have had previous instruction in the infant school. Before that was the case, children coming from the infant school soon rose to the first class.'—*Id.,* 2196.

' The question is between children passing their time at the school, and their living for a considerable part of the day almost neglected in the streets.'—*Id.* 2217.

' I have seen, and I have thought a little on the subject of infant schools. The result is, an intimate conviction that there is no instrument of national improvement more powerful—none more likely, if well directed, to have a beneficial influence upon the habits of the population, than establishments of this sort. *Salles d'asyle,* as infant schools are called in France, though not mentioned in the law on primary instruction, are strongly recommended in the circulars of the minister to the prefects of the departments and the other local authorities. In the year 1833 there were already ten in operation in Paris, and they were spreading among the provincial towns.'—*Professor Pillans,* 601.

To the question 602—' Have you ever heard it observed that the children who have been at an infant school are apt to consider that instruction should be made merely a matter of amusement, and are for that reason more difficult to be brought under the discipline of severer instruction ?' Professor Pillans replied : 'I never heard the observation made before, and cannot believe it to be founded in fact. Such result, where it does occur, I should take to be an infallible proof that the school the children were transferred to was ill conducted, or on a bad system. The nature of an infant school is, to render a child submissive and obedient, and not disposed to resist any of the authorities that are over him.'

The Bishop of London is favourable to infant schools. 2442 and 2483.

Lord Brougham is in favour of infant schools.

Dr. Julius states that infant schools are beginning to be established in Prussia ; there are three or four in Berlin.   1792.

With regard to the difficulty of finding a number of mistresses fit to conduct infant schools, however the circumstance may be regretted, still, when we consider that no measures have been adopted to prepare them for the task, it can hardly be a subject of surprise.   Let us consider what the mistress of such a school has to do.   She has to keep the attention of fifty or sixty very young children constantly alive while she communicates instruction.   There are certainly manuals to assist her in the performance of this duty ; but all who have made any attempt to impart instruction on any subject, know that the method of putting the matter must be varied with the individual ; and, to do this, the mistress must not only have a thorough knowledge of the thing to be taught, but also considerable tact and patience.   We had, not long since, the pleasure of visiting an infant school under the direction of a mistress who was competent to the task she had undertaken, and we can bear witness to the talent, temper, and personal exertion which were called forth in the performance of this duty.

The evidence on this subject only proves how necessary it is that persons should be fitted, by a regular course of instruction, for the situation of infant schoolmistress, and that none should be permitted to undertake it who are unable to obtain a certificate of competency.   There ought, in fact, to be schools for forming mistresses of this description. This conclusion is derived as much from the evidence of those who are less favourable to infant schools, as from that of those who speak so highly of them. If the friends of infant schools think them very useful, even under the present system, they must admit, that if there were always a sufficient supply of good teachers for them, the usefulness of these schools would be increased in a very great degree.

That normal schools, or schools for educating teachers, must form the basis of any good system of general public education, appears to be admitted by all who have given the subject their serious consideration. The circumstance of persons being taken at hazard to teach what, perhaps, they know but indifferently themselves, would of itself account for the very little consideration in which the office of schoolmaster is held, and the small advantage gained by those who attend the schools. But if schools for the instruction of schoolmasters were organized in various districts, and certificates, upon examination, given—without which they should not be permitted to undertake the office—not only would the rank of the profession of schoolmaster be raised, but the means of diffusing a sound and regenerating system of education would be secured. The following are such portions of the evidence on the subject as we consider important.

NORMAL SCHOOLS.

The Rev. W. Johnson, clerical superintendent of the National School Society.

' 19. The total number of masters and mistresses of both kinds, trained in the central schools up to the present time, is 2039 ; and in addition to this, 657 schools in the country have been organized, and provided with temporary teachers.

' The supplying schools with masters and mistresses is one principal object of the society.'

Mr. Henry Dunn, secretary to the British and Foreign School Society.

' 222. Has it been a habit with the Society to furnish schoolmasters wherever they are able to do so ?—It has been ; and one chief reason why the schools in London and the neighbourhood which I have referred to, have sometimes failed to meet our wishes, has been, that committees have too frequently elected a master rather from some personal influence which he may have had with themselves, than on account of his merits ; and when they have once elected, we find them extremely reluctant to remove inefficient teachers.'

' 224. Have you an establishment for preparing schoolmasters for the duty of teaching in the central school of the Borough Road ?—We have.

' 225. Can you tell how many there are, on the average, who are usually in the school with that view ?—There are twenty at this time training for boys' schools, and ten for girls' schools ; during the last year ninety-eight were trained.'

' 227. What is the usual age at which young men are received who are to be taught as schoolmasters ?—From nineteen to twenty-three or twenty-four is about the age that we prefer. In some cases we take them a little earlier, and in others when they are much older ; but we prefer to have them between the age of nineteen and twenty-four ; because we consider that, by that time the character is formed, and they are not yet too old to learn a new system, or to conform to any plan laid down for their guidance.'

' 229. How long do they generally remain in your central school in the course of preparation for schoolmasters?—The time which we fix as the minimum is three months ; but of late we have found it exceedingly difficult to retain them so long, on account of the number of applications we receive for teachers. We think *three years* nearer the time they ought to remain than three months; but we do the best we can under the circumstances.

' 230. Do you conceive that there would be any advantage, supposing your funds enabled you to do it, in preparing young men from the age of fourteen or eighteen, and keeping them in your establishment till they were of a fit age, and competent to act as schoolmasters? —I think that fourteeen or sixteen would be somewhat too young ; at that age it is not easy to ascertain what the character of the individual may be. We have in some instances been greatly disappointed with youths selected from our own schools, by their being taken so early; we have found that at nineteen or twenty years of age the young man has been induced to follow some more lucrative profession, or he has shown those dispositions which have rendered him unfit for the management of a school, although likely to prove a valuable member of society in some other department. We should, therefore, think that from eighteen to one or two and twenty would be better than from fourteen to seventeen or eighteen.

' 231. Is it the opinion of the committee, that if young men of the age of eighteen could be admitted upon the establishment, and could be retained till the age of twenty-one, a better class of schoolmasters than you can now afford would be afforded to the country? —Very much better indeed.

' 232. What is the nature of the tuition that is now given to those who are to act as schoolmasters?—They are required to rise every morning at five o'clock, and spend an hour before seven in private study. They have access to a good library. At seven they are assembled together in a Bible class, and questioned as to their knowledge of the Scriptures ; from nine to twelve they are employed as monitors in the school, learning to communicate that which thay already know, or are supposed to know ; from two to five they are employed in a similar way; and from five to seven they are engaged under a master, who instructs them in arithmetic and the elements of geometry, geography, and the globes, or in other branches in which they may be deficient. The remainder of the evening is generally occupied in preparing exercises for the subsequent day. Our object is to keep them incessantly employed from five in the morning until nine or ten at night. We have rather exceeded in the time devoted to study the limit we would choose, on account of the very short period we are able to keep them ; and we have found, in some instances, that their health has suffered on account of their having been previously quite unaccustomed to mental occupations.

'233. Are many of them obliged to leave the school from proving incompetent to the tasks which are assigned them?—Comparatively few who are once admitted, because we take them, in the first instance, for a fortnight on trial; experience enables us to form a tolerably correct judgment as to a young man's capabilities, after we have seen him teaching in the school for a fortnight; we can then generally judge whether he has the elements of a teacher in him.

'240. When you speak of three years as being a desirable period for such persons to be in preparation for the profession of schoolmaster, what part of that three years, speaking generally, would you wish to be applied to the experimental teaching by such teachers of a large school?—The first three months, and the last three; the first three months, in order to ascertain previous to any large expenditure of time and money, whether the candidate possesses native aptness to teach, and ability to govern numbers; the last three months, to impart a readiness in communicating what he has acquired. I speak merely of actual practice in the school-room. The science of teaching is a branch of study to which attention should be directed during the whole of the third year.'

'251. I have myself taken especial care to impress upon local committees, that their school will be precisely what their teacher is; that every thing will depend on their selection; for a good teacher is the only real security for a good school.'

Professor Pillans:—

'501. No system would work well without a good master, and it is upon that account that I conceive the institution of schools for masters to lie at the very foundation of all improvement in national education.'

'428. I look upon it as quite indispensable, that those who are in the process of training as schoolmasters, should be tried in some large school, with a view of seeing whether they have a capacity of communicating the knowledge they have acquired. It is part of the law in Germany and in France, that there shall be an elementary school attached to every normal school, and during the two years devoted according to the French law, (the German law allots three,) the last six months are to be devoted almost exclusively to instruction in practical teaching, after being previously instructed in the theory. In France, as well as in Germany, sixteen is the lowest age at which they can be admitted, unless in some cases of extraordinary talents and acquirements.

'Are you aware whether in France many in the course of this tuition are rejected as unfit?—There are rejections numerous enough to prove the perfect efficiency of the commission which examines those candidates. That examination which is necessary in order to entitle a pupil of those schools to what is called a *brevet de capacité*, is a very serious one, and, as far as I have seen, cannot be passed without very considerable acquirement, both as to the quantity of knowledge possessed and the power of communicating it. They have three degrees, No. 1, 2, 3; a small proportion obtain the highest; a larger number get No. 2; and I think I may venture to say, there is scarcely any examination upon a large scale in a school of that kind in which some are not remitted at least to their studies.'

' 471. You stated that, not considering the peculiar circumstances of Great Britain, you thought the French and German system nearly approximating to a perfect one; what are the peculiar circumstances of Great Britain which in your opinion would prevent the introduction of that system here ?—The one that strikes me as most likely to prevent any project of that kind being gone into, is the necessary expense of these normal schools; last year there were already in full operation in France I think fifty-four normal schools, and sixteen in progress.   The law indeed declares one to be necessary in every department, and those *élèves maîtres* are maintained within the walls of the establishment with a considerable number of teachers, who are also boarded and lodged, or, if they come from an adjoining town,-must be paid.   The necessary expense of such an establishment, to be effective over the whole country, would, I am afraid, lay it where you will, be somewhat difficult to raise.'

' 492. Do you not think a great portion of the expense in England might be met, in a great measure, by the application of funds which it is well known have been left by private individuals for the purpose ?—I have no doubt of it; there can be very little doubt that if those funds so left were applicable to such a purpose, they would be ample, and we should be able to erect a machinery quite as complete, perhaps more so than France.'

' 510. In any of the schools in Prussia or Austria, in addition to the reading and writing, is there any kind of manual industry or any labour of any kind ?—Not in the schools ; there are particular institutions for perfecting young men in particular employments which go by a particular name, what the French call *écoles des arts et métiers;* and it is a question whether these should be united under the general superintendence of the university, or whether they should belong to the department of *arts et métiers.* They are quite separate at present, except that the young schoolmasters of the normal schools are taught to cultivate the ground, as I found them doing on a farm attached to the *Ecole Normal* at Rennes.

' 511. Do you think it desirable, as the greater mass of the population are to earn their livelihood by labour, that early habits of labour should be inculcated in conjunction with teaching reading and writing ?—I should think such a conjunction an object of the utmost importance.'

' 578. Do you not think that by making the schoolmasters public functionaries as it were, you would exalt their condition, and give them a power of influencing the education of the people, which at present they have not?—Certainly.'

' 613. You stated in one of your former answers, that you thought it quite essential in a system of national education, that every master who could not pass a certain examination, and obtain a *brevet de oapacité,* should be prohibited from teaching ; do not you think that a good deal might be accomplished even without an absolute prohibition of uncertified teachers, by the simple establishment of authorized schools, and producing a good set of masters so as to supply the wants of the country ?—Perhaps that may be a more advisable plan under present circumstances.

' 614. But you think it essential to the perfection of the system that no teachers should be allowed to teach without a *brevet de capacité* ?—I certainly think so.'

With regard to the education of the schoolmasters at the Borough Road, Mr. Crossley states :—

' 1043. On the introduction of a young man to the school, we put him to superintend the lowest division in the school, the children learning their letters, and he goes from grade to grade up to that of superintendent of the school, so that no part of the school business is omitted. During that time he is constantly under my eye, and I have an opportunity of asking him questions, and of pointing out the best means of accomplishing his duty, and of giving him that knowledge of the system which renders him master of it at the end of three months.'

' 1059. Supposing you had a school or institution in which you could train young men to be good schoolmasters, in what way would you secure their continuance in that occupation, and their respectability in the eyes of the country as schoolmasters?—No means occur to me immediately but rendering the situation respectable in character, and annexing a competency to it. We have some instances of young men rather of a superior stamp of character taking our schools, and I find them invariably directing their attention to other things besides the school. The result is, that, as in two schools that I have now in my mind, they are very inefficiently conducted, though in these cases they are superintended by two of the cleverest and most competent masters we have in the system.'

Mr. H. Althans :—

' 1595. Are you of opinion that the number of young men who are found to take up education as a business is increasing ?—I think it would increase if a better remuneration were given to schoolmasters ; we should then get some of the best teachers from our Sunday schools to turn schoolmasters; but they can get better remuneration even as mechanics.'

The Bishop of London :—

' Would it, in your lordship's opinion, be desirable to have any institution, or to afford means to any of the existing institutions, by which schoolmasters might undergo a training of one or two years, instead of the three or six months they have at present ?—I know of no other objection to their remaining longer under instruction than the expense which is incurred. I should certainly say that a longer period and a more systematic training would be desirable.'

Lord Brougham :—

' 2831. I am of opinion that it is expedient to establish schools for the instruction of teachers, or what M. de Fellenberg did in 1809 under the name of a normal school, or what the Prussian and French systems have adopted.'

Although all who have considered the advantages of uniting labour with mental study in the education of the labouring classes, and of making what they do as children bear upon their future destinations as men, have with scarcely a dissentient voice arrived at a conclusion in favour of so doing; the evidence on the subject taken before this committee is meagre in the extreme, and by no means places it in that prominent point of view to which its high political importance at this peculiar juncture entitles it. Professor Pillans (511) considers.the union of labour with literary instruction as of the utmost importance; and (510) at the normal schools in France young schoolmasters are taught to cultivate the ground. The Bishop of London (2485) gives it as his · opinion that the introduction of works of industry would be in the highest degree beneficial in country and in town; but that the circumstance of the children remaining too short a time, and the expense, will be found obstacles to effecting it. To these objections of the bishop we do not attach much importance. With regard to children remaining too short a time, although this is found to be the case in schools now in existence, the very nature and character of a school in which industry should be introduced, and the children should receive the profits of their labour, would be such as to change those circumstances which create the evil of which his Lordship complains. The reason why children are permitted by their parents to remain but for a very limited period at school is, that while they are there, the children are unable to contribute anything towards their own maintenance, and what they do learn is found to have but very little reference to their future employment in life. With regard to expense after the first outfit has been incurred, there is no reason why a school into which industry might be introduced should be more expensive than any other. In fact, the accounts which have been given respecting the agricultural schools at Hofwyl and Carra go to prove the contrary; while Mr. Smith's allotments of land to children in Warwickshire, which we noticed in the miscellaneous matter of our last Number, show that the system may be adopted with pecuniary advantage. The following is a question put to Professor Pillans, and his reply (611):—

'Are you at all acquainted with the views of M. de Fellenberg with respect to agricultural schools, and the effect of some of those agricultural schools in Switzerland?—I have a general idea .of the objects that he proposes to himself, and I have no doubt that those are institutions which might very safely and profitably be imitated. I may mention more fully, in answer to that question, what I think I alluded to on the former day, that there is attached to the *Ecole Normale* at Rennes a farm of some extent, if I recollect right about eight acres, which is worked by the *élèves maîtres* under the super-intendence of a person well acquainted with the management of ground, and who was kind enough to furnish me with an account of the objects to which he directs the attention of his pupils. The object of the government in making the grant for this is, that the masters should be acquainted theoretically and practically with the subject of agriculture, so as to fit them for spreading the best me-thod over the country. In others again, as at Versailles, there is a garden in which the pupils have tasks assigned to them, and the professor goes round with them explaining the nature of the plant, and every thing that respects its culture, training, and properties.

Ecole d'Agriculture annexée à l'Ecole Normale Primaire de Rennes.

PLAN DU COURS D'AGRICULTURE.

Etude de la Nature des Terres.

AMELIORATION DES TERRES.

Amelioration de la Nature Physique du Sol.
Au moyen des Amendemens.
Au moyen des Engrais Mixtes.
Au moyen des Engrais Vegetaux.
Au moyen des Engrais Vegetaux et Animaux.
Au moyen des Engrais Animaux.

INSTRUMENS ASSOLEMENS.

Culture des Céréales.
    ,,   des Plantes Sarclées.
    ,,   des Plantes à Cones.
    ,,   des Prairies Artificielles.
    ,,   des Prairies Naturelles.
Bétail, Attelage.
Laiterie.
Animaux Nuisibles et Utiles.
Pépinières, Arbres à Fruit, Vignes, Jardinage.
Economie Rurale, et Domestique.

Mr. William Wright, the master of the Hackney-Wick School, under the care of the Children's Friend Society, an institution which we have several times had occasion to notice, replies to the query :—

'2665. Do you find the children learn better when employed partially in industry, than when employed solely in the school ?—I think they do ; the exercise in the open air gives them both vigour of body and mind.'

At a school in Gower's Walk, Whitechapel, founded by William Davis, Esq., in conjunction with a few friends, the children are taught to print, and the most industrious at this work are generally at the head of the literary department of the school (2908). In this evidence it will be observed, that not a word is said with regard to giving children a share in the product of their labour. It is, however, of vital importance that this should be the case. The labourer is worthy of his hire, and a child of the working classes should be taught to look upon his labour as his own peculiar property— property of the highest and most valuable description. But how can he be so taught, unless the earnings of his industry, or at least a part of them, be delivered into his own hands to deal with as he pleases? Having worked for his money, he will know its value, and be tenacious of his right to it, and thus, from the circumstance of duly appreciating his own right, he will learn to respect the rights of others, will be just in his dealings with his fellows, and a defender of the rights of property in general. At this important juncture, when the poor-laws have, in a great measure, undermined these principles, nothing should be neglected that can assist in bringing up the young with accurate and well-grounded opinions about the nature of property and the necessity for the institution.

But schools of the description under consideration are not only useful for the inculcation of habits of industry, and a knowledge of the value of property; but to a cottager they will be also of advantage in actually increasing his resources, and means of comfort. How valuable will be a quarter of an acre of land, if he knows practically how to cultivate it to the greatest advantage, and to collect and prepare his manures! How many comforts may he not be able to collect around him by employing his long winter evenings in turning his carpenter's tools to account, the use of which he has learned at school!

SINGING AND DRAWING.

Professor Pillans:—

' 594. In Prussia is there any provision made for the education of the children in dancing and music?—For singing universally. I conceive that regulation to be one which it is most desirable to transfer into any system of national education that may be thought of for this country. I am disposed to estimate very highly the humanizing and improving influence of music, as a part of popular instruction. It should be taught, however, not by mere vocal imitation, but on scientific principles; and not confined to hymns and sacred songs, but extended to airs associated with simple rural ideas, and with kindred and country.'*

'598. Would not your principle extend to teaching them to take a pleasure in the arts generally; for example, painting and design? —I think it would be desirable if the means existed of doing so. It is a portion of the Prussian system to teach their children to sketch and draw, or design, without going the length of painting in colours.

'599. Would not that give the population a source of pure and unalloyed pleasure from looking out upon nature generally?—I think it has that tendency very much; above all, if it were coupled with training children from the very outset of life to the use of their senses in observing attentively and discriminating the different properties of objects around them; a habit which cannot be too early nor too earnestly encouraged, but which has hitherto been shamefully neglected.'

This is good. It is for want of innocent recreations that the gin-shop and ale-house are frequented. Unemployed man requires some stimulant; he cannot work all his time, and if for want of instruction he has not the power of enjoying pleasures of an innocent description, tippling, as it needs no talent or training, is invariably resorted to. It excites and stimulates. And what if health be impaired? The passing of his time in the enjoyment of even this low pleasure is to him preferable to that weariness of mind which proceeds from vacancy.

Whether or not a uniform system of national education, under the immediate superintendence of government, and partly supported by public money, could be adopted with advantage, is a subject which has not been fully considered in the volume of evidence before us. The Committee has confined its inquiries, and we think wisely, to certain questions, such as those of religion and the education of masters, which opposed *in limine* very serious difficulties to the adoption of such a system; but which, if removed, would make a subsequent consideration of the system itself, and of the minor objections to it, a task comparatively easy. We should not, therefore, in this article have taken the subject into consideration, had not Lord Brougham spoken somewhat at length with regard to it; and even now, while we give certain extracts from his Lordship's evidence, we must beg our readers to bear in mind that the question still remains to be investigated by the Committee, which we trust will be appointed during the present session of Parliament.

* The teaching of singing was often provided for in the old endowed schools of this country.

Lord Brougham's evidence against a national system of primary education.

' 2821. Those who recommend it on account of its successful adoption on the Continent, do not reflect upon the funds it would require, (his Lordship calculates the annual expense at 2,000,000*l*.) and upon the exertions already made by individual beneficence. ...... If the State were to interfere, and oblige every parish to support a school or schools sufficient for educating all children, the greater part of the funds now raised voluntarily for this purpose would be withdrawn. ... ;. That the funds now raised by subscription, and which amount to near a million a year, would be withdrawn, I take to be the inevitable consequence of establishing a school-rate. ......
But supposing the expense provided for, I am clearly of opinion that one great means of promoting education would be lost, namely, the interest taken by the patrons of schools supported by voluntary contributions. At present, when well-disposed persons subscribe to keep a school, they do all they can to make the poor send their children ; and, unfortunately, in many parts of the country there is not such an eagerness for instruction as to render this superfluous, although it is certainly increasing ; and by degrees, as the parents themselves become better educated, the indifference to the advantage of schooling for their children will disappear.'

Lord Brougham's arguments in favour of a national system of primary education.

' 2830. There are revenues of more than half a million sterling devoted to endowing charities. It is difficult not to repine at the silly use which well-meaning, but ill-informed persons have so often made of the funds which they have designed for charitable purposes.
' The funds now raised by subscription amount to near a million per annum.'
' 492. Pillans :—Do ´you not think a great portion of the expense in England might be met, in a great measure, by the application of funds which it is well known have been left by private individuals for the purpose ?—I have no doubt of it ; there can be very little doubt that if those funds so left were applicable to such a purpose they would be ample, and we should be able to erect a machinery quite as complete, perhaps more so, than in France.
' 2826. Lord Brougham says: —In Scotland, when the Act was passed, there were hardly any schools of any kind, and the benefit was incalculable, which made it necessary to have one in every parish. In Scotland there would be but a miserable provision for education, if nothing more were done than the Act requires; in fact, the great benefit of that Act was its effect in making education more thought of and desired, and in exciting the voluntary efforts of the inhabitants, who, however, went far beyond what the enactment required.'*

* See the history of the various Acts for schools in Scotland, and the effects of these legislative measures.—Journal of Education, No. XVII., p. 1, &c.

His Lordship again says :—'One proof among others of the
same excellent spirit (of promoting education) still subsisting in the
community, is afforded by the number of applications made for grants
out of the vote of 1833. The British and Foreign School Society received applications from 169 quarters, with offers to raise 25,000*l.*, provided government would issue the rest of the sums required to establish those 169 schools : viz., between 23,000*l.* and 24,000*l.* ; and
between 9000*l.* and 10,000*l.* was granted towards establishing 59
schools to educate nearly 13,000 children, the applicants raising the
sum of about, I believe, 15,000*l.* themselves. I presume the National Society had an equal number of applications.'

Lord Brougham apprehends that if government were to aid
the schools with public money, the greater part of those
ample funds now furnished by voluntary subscription would
be withdrawn. We believe, on the contrary, that if the
government would contribute a certain share, either by
authorizing direct local taxation, or from the public purse,
or by both means combined, the amount raised by private subscription would increase instead of diminish.
The experience of the new education system for Ireland,
and the experience of the Northern States of the American
Union*, are both in favour of our opinion. We assume that
the money granted by government must be granted judiciously, and must be given *in aid* of local exertion, that is,
on condition of other sums being raised by each school district. As to its being necessary for subscribers to urge
parents to send their children to school, we may state a fact
with regard to a garden school lately established at Ealing,
in the neighbourhood of London, in which labour is blended
with instruction. No prospectus was ever put out with respect to this school, but so much do the children delight in
the variety which alternate labour and study afford, that they
have themselves been the advertisers of the school, which,
although it has been established only a few months, is already
attended by between 50 and 60 children.

LORD BROUGHAM'S EVIDENCE ON COMPULSORY EDUCATION.

' 2822. Do you consider that a compulsory education would be
justified either on principles of public utility or expediency?—I am
decidedly of opinion that it is justifiable upon neither ; but above
all, I should regard anything of the kind as utterly destructive of
the end it has in view. But even if measures far short of decided

---

* See a subsequent article of this Number on Woodbridge's American Annals
of Education. Also an article on the New England Free-Schools (Journal, No.
IV., p. 253) :—' In almost every part of these six states whatever may be the
injunctions of the law, the popular demand for education is so much greater,
that the legal requisitions are generally or constantly exceeded.' On the
taxation system in the State of New York, see Journal XVII., p. 56, &c,

compulsion were taken to induce the poor to educate their children, such as holding out advantages or imposing disqualifications, my opinion is, that the same consequence would follow, namely, making education unpopular, and so retarding its progress incalculably.

'2823. It has been suggested that the government which has a right to punish crime for the sake of prevention, has also a right to take the surest course of direct prevention, and thus to force the people to educate their children with this view; does your Lordship agree with this position?—I think it wholly fantastical and unsound, and I can hardly say to what lengths it might not lead. Indeed, mere elementary education will not of itself prevent vice, unless the means which it furnishes be usefully employed towards improving the feelings and understanding. What can tend more to prevent crime than sobriety, temperance of all kinds,—nay, economical habits? Then is it intended to maintain that the legislature should prohibit the use of fermented liquors, and pass sumptuary laws? But there would be infinitely more reason for this, than for compelling men to educate their children, that is, to teach them reading and writing, in order to prevent crime. That the character and habits of men will be improved, and the amount of crimes greatly lessened by education, I confidently expect; but it is a wild imagination to fancy that crime ever can be extirpated. This actually supposes the nature of man to be changed by reading, and that though still inhabiting the body, his mind has obtained a complete ascendant and mastery over his senses.'

'Dans ces états, un bon législateur s'attachera moins a punir les crimes qu' à les prévenir; il s'appliquera plus à donner des mœurs, qu' à infliger des supplices.'—*De l'Esprit des Loix,* Liv. vi. c. ix.

But M. de Fellenberg has shown that primary education may be directed to higher objects than bare reading and writing, which are mere instruments that may be turned to good or to ill according to circumstances.—In imitation of that noble philanthropist, the school for poor children has been established at Ealing, in which it is attempted to give a knowledge of the value of property by letting out gardens of the sixteenth of an acre to each child, for which they pay a rent; a knowledge of the value of labour, by paying them for what they do; a habit of industry, by keeping them constantly employed; and such a skill in carpentry as will enable them to provide many little conveniences in their own homes by their own ingenuity, which perhaps their means would not enable them to purchase. Besides this, the school instruction is not only interesting, but adapted in a peculiar manner to develope the moral and intellectual faculties.

Education cannot with propriety be compared to reading, in its operation upon character: a book may inform us what any habit ought to be; but right education insures a number of acts in accordance with the principle laid down in the book, and thus by degrees forms the habit. In a book it may be written that early rising is good for the health; the master, however, takes care not only that the boy knows this, but that he does rise early. In this way a habit is formed, which may in the greater number of cases, though not in all, continue through life. The formation of good habits is the main business of education.

'2825· Are there any other objections to a national system of education besides those you have stated?—I do not well perceive how such a system can be established, without placing in the hands of the government, that is, of the ministers of the day, the means of dictating opinions and principles to the people.'

In a despotic government jealousy may be reasonably entertained of education being placed entirely under the control of the government; but in a country where a watchful House of Commons narrowly scrutinizes every act of the executive there cannot be the same reason for apprehension. If a reformed House of Commons is not more honest, and better informed than an unreformed house, the object for which the recent change was made is not attained, and the change, so far from being an advantage, is a great evil. If a reformed House of Commons is not wise enough to second the government in all measures tending to the improvement of the people, active enough to watch how the government uses the power with which it is intrusted, and strong enough to change the members of government when their administration is pernicious, then there is no hope left for the future, and our social condition, instead of improving, will certainly grow worse.

In the volume of evidence which we have been considering, although we have seen that much inquiry has been made respecting the nature of the theological and literary instruction given to the children, but few questions have been put respecting the methods pursued in order to form moral character, and to give the children of the poor an accurate knowledge of their true position in society, and such a training as will insure their good conduct and consequently their happiness. All who have in any degree mixed with mankind know that the circumstance of committing to memory, or grammatically understanding a number of texts of scripture and rules of conduct, unless some method be taken to deeply root them in the conviction, and to form habits in accordance with them, is of little use. Virtue is not merely the knowledge of what is right, but a correspondent habit of action. De Fellenberg caused his scholars to keep books in which they daily registered their actions and their reasons for them, in order that they might continually test them with reference to the various heads of Christian duty. We, therefore, think that it would be desirable to inquire whether any and what methods are adopted at the various schools, in order to ascertain the peculiar character of each individual child beyond the superficial observation of the children as a mass, in order that the assistance which each requires for the formation of his character may be rendered. It will, perhaps, be replied, that the master after a short period becomes as a matter of necessity acquainted with the characters of all the children; but unless he pays an accurate attention to the conduct of each individual, keeps a written account of this conduct to which he can at any time refer, and converses confidentially with him upon the subject of it, we are not disposed to admit that this can be the case. We ourselves when at school were never favoured with a confidential conversation with any of our masters during the long period we were there, and never received the least assistance in correcting errors in character beyond that which the rod could give. Indeed, we feel an assurance that, upon leaving school, the masters in a great majority of instances are ignorant of all the motives and reasons which actuate the conduct of their scholars, with the exception of those which lie immediately upon the surface. The preaching and teaching of general doctrines and rules of morality, although it has no doubt its weight with those already disposed to a right course, and who are themselves seriously bent upon the improvement of their own characters, has but little influence upon such as have not the habit of thinking upon the matter, and whose conduct and opinions are a reflection of the general tone of the school. To such it is not only necessary to say that falsehood or any other vice is wrong; but it is also necessary to point out the particulars in which their conduct has been deficient, calmly to hear the reasons, if they have any, by which they support what they have done, and then to show in what respects these reasons are insufficient or fallacious. Nor ought a short time to obliterate the recollection of an offence: it should be noted down with all its particulars, both by the master and the child, in order that it may be recurred to at a future period. It is only by accuracy such as this that a master can hope to be well acquainted with the character of those committed to his charge, and to render them that assistance which their inexperience and tender years demand at his hands.

Beyond the few remarks which it has occurred to us to

make upon the evidence here quoted, we shall not at present enter further on the subject. We hope that a Committee of the House of Commons will take the subject up again during this session, and consider the whole matter; and that they will more particularly investigate the points that have been as yet but lightly touched on, so as to be enabled to agree to a report which shall induce the legislature to take some decisive step in providing a sound and practical education for the poorer classes of this country.

ON TEACHING SINGING.

SINGING is an acquirement which perhaps gives more general pleasure than any other accomplishment, since it affords gratification even to those who are ignorant of the art, and does not, like instrumental music, require a practical audience in order to be appreciated, nor, like painting, a particular education in order to perceive its beauties. The love of sweet sounds seems a part of our nature ; and these, when connected with poetry, address themselves to the understanding and to the sensibility, as well as to the ear.

Music, and vocal music especially, forms a valuable addition to domestic enjoyments, and, as a female accomplishment, deserves cultivation upon this ground, as well as upon the principle that women should possess as many rational resources as possible both for their own happiness, and that of those who look to them for solace and amusement. While we urge the expediency, and in some sort the necessity, of acquiring the art of singing, we must allow, that it already often engrosses a large portion of female education, to the exclusion of many more important attainments; and we regret to add, that, after much application of time and labour, the result is frequently either entire failure, or at least partial disappointment—for which we account in the following manner.

Singing is properly regarded as a part of female education; yet the necessary organic formation is not generally considered in the outset, neither is the end proposed precisely ascertained, nor the best means of attaining it determined. Parents wish their children to be musicians, and yet it often happens that they are themselves entirely ignorant of the real meaning of the term, and unable to decide what constitutes excellence in the art, or how that excellence may be obtained. On the other hand, many persons of uncultivated ears and indifferent education imagine that singing is a gift of nature, and requires no training; but this is a mistake. In the art of speaking, defects are to be overcome, and particular kinds of excellence acquired by a proper training: so is it with singing; both arts alike require discipline.

It has been often said, that nothing is worth learning that is not worth learning well. This maxim applies to music equally with other things; and for this reason we would endeavour to show how an acquirement, which contributes so largely to individual and general happiness may be best attained, and with the least expenditure of time. We shall here confine ourselves to singing, the highest branch of the art, which more completely calls into exercise the sensibilities of the performer than any other branch of music. We do not propose to treat of professional education, and we are also speaking of female instruction only, though most of our remarks are generally applicable.

We presume that the pupil has some knowledge of music; that she plays the piano-forte as well as is usually judged necessary to accompany herself, and understands musical terms. It is first necessary to ascertain whether the voice and the ear promise any results, and when parents are not themselves qualified to determine this point, they must consult disinterested and competent judges. The cultivation of a feeble voice requires time and labour on the part of the pupil, and probably the result will be only mediocrity.

In determining the natural capabilities, there are two points to be examined, first, whether there is any power of imitation, since it is evident that all singing must be resolved into an imitation by the voice of sounds heard by the ear. If the pupil is totally incapable of repeating the sounds of an instrument, or another voice, all attempts to learn singing are hopeless.

Secondly, presuming the imitation to be made, it must be next ascertained whether the notes be strictly in tune, and if they be not, whether the imperfection arise from a density of hearing, or from weakness in the voice itself; and also (which a few trials will decide) whether the natural defect in formation is likely to be overcome by practice.

If these points be determined unfavourably, we conclude that no rational person would contend against nature in a matter which does not concern the moral welfare of the pupil; and that, where organic capability does not exist, the attempt to learn will not be made.

Those who do not possess the qualities which are essential to a singer have other sources of gratification, which, when judiciously cultivated, will be productive of equal pleasure. We would therefore earnestly recommend persons who are not so gifted to waste no time on a pursuit the failure in which 'will inevitably produce great disappointment, and something like disgrace, since a want of success will be put down by the world to general natural incapacity, ignorance, idleness, or insensibility.

We next consider how the pupil whose natural organs are worth cultivating may be best trained. The object of vocal art is to produce agreeable sounds, and, at the same time, to modify those sounds to the expression of the words which are uttered in connexion with them, and which are presumed to have dictated the sentiment of the melody to the composer. The word *tone** comprises all the elements of the art; and the power of varying the character of tone constitutes expression. However sweet, rich, or powerful a voice may naturally be, cultivation and practice alone can confer the power of modifying its quality to suit the sentiment or passion which the words and the music express.

Purity of tone (which necessarily implies perfect tune) is the first object to be attained in learning to sing; and to acquire this, the practice of the diatonic scale, ascending and descending, beginning on C natural (the C on the first ledger line below the lines) and ending where the compass of the voice ceases, ought to be steadily pursued.

By *pure tone,* we mean that the notes emitted by the voice are free from the guttural, thick sound which shows that they are formed in the throat—from the snuffling which indicates that the nose is not performing its proper function—and from the muffled, indistinct sound, which indicates the improper action of the tongue and lips. Some one of these defects is generally perceptible in amateur singers. The Italian method of instruction is the only system which makes pure tone the basis of vocal instruction, and it is this that we would here recommend and explain. Nothing is more difficult than to describe *sound;* but a good model may always be selected, either among the profession or amateurs, whose tone may be imitated with advantage, and this without any fear of degenerating into a mere copyist, for singing, like speaking, is necessarily, in the first instance, purely imitative.

The diatonic scale, ascending and descending, ought to be executed in the following manner. Let the pupil pronounce the Italian letter *a,* which is uttered like the *a* in the English word *father,* and begin the note very soft, swelling it gradually to the full power of the voice, and then as gradually diminishing it to the softest sound. The mouth must be opened wide, but a little elongated, and kept steadily in the

---

* It must be observed that *tone* and *intonation* are distinct things: the former refers to the quality or character of the sound, the latter to its tune or pitch.

same position till the note is ended ; for it is evident that the size of the aperture through which the sound issues must alter the character of that sound, even if it do not affect its tune or pitch, and a variation in the tone during the production of a note is always bad ; the *quantity* but not *quality* may change. This method ought to be applied to every note in the scale, going on to the second octave, and descending as soon as the voice has reached the extent of its compass, taking care not to strain it beyond that compass.

In all voices the upper notes are formed by using what is called *falsette*, or *voce di testa*, which we may translate by the words *head voice*. This term seems to imply that the voice comes from the head ; but the fact is, that all falsette notes are produced by an action in the upper part of the throat, and the tone is sensibly felt in the head. High notes can also be formed by the chest voice, or *voce di petto*, but they are loud, strained, and harsh, incapable of flexibility, possessing neither sweetness, richness, nor brilliancy, and wholly unfit for chamber singing ; indeed they ought to be employed only occasionally even on the stage, in the expression of strong passion.

The singer, in practising the scale, should discover where the chest (or natural voice) ends, and learn to unite it to the falsette, so that no breach or striking dissimilarity between the two voices may appear. The falsette will require to be strengthened, and at the same time the cultivation of a sweet and pure tone carefully attended to ; indeed the agreeable quality of all high notes depends upon cultivation, since there are few voices which produce them naturally.

Particular attention should be paid to taking the breath. A long note cannot be held unless the lungs are fully inflated, and this is equally important in a succession of short notes, because a frequent inhaling disturbs the smoothness of the performance, and gives an idea of exhaustion which is both painful and destructive of effect.

In practising, the pupil should open the chest by throwing back the shoulders and raising the head, so that the action of the throat, as well as of the lungs, may be unimpeded. The breath should be very deeply inhaled *before* the note is commenced, and should not be emitted rapidly with the sound, but gradually, and in a restrained way, rather than exhaled quickly. By this means a command of the breath will be acquired, and the singer will never be, or appear to be, distressed, but will have the power of duly apportioning the quantity of force she may be called upon to use, and of applying it where and when it will be required. When the voice has become tolerably steady, and the tune certain, it will be necessary to learn to unite notes; and this may be done by proceeding from one note to the next in a breath, or at intervals of a second, third, fourth, fifth, and so on.

The first note should be commenced soft, gradually swelled, and when it nearly reaches the loudest point, the next note taken, and the voice diminished. In passing from one note to another, whether slowly or rapidly, that union should invariably be observed which the Italians designate by the term *legato, tied.* This quality is essential to a singer. It may best be attained by the practice of the diatonic scale, pushing the voice from note to note, in ascending throughout the octave, and increasing in loudness; in descending, by sliding the voice from note to note, and decreasing the sound : the rapidity should be increased in proportion to the progress of the student, but all first essays must be slow. The times for breathing will also vary in the like proportion. And here we would caution the singer against changing the syllable, or altering the position of the mouth when executing rapidly ; it is a defect which commonly obtains either from carelessness, or from an idea that the execution is thereby facilitated. It may be imagined, that as, in singing words, a constant change of syllables occurs, it is therefore needless to guard against an event which must necessarily take place : every finished singer, however, knows that words may be made articulate, and yet be kept subservient to tone, and that the latter is first to be steadily acquired. For this reason the voice should be first practised on one and the same syllable.

When the pupil can execute a slow scale, in which each note has the same character of tone (allowing for the modifications caused by a difference of pitch or height) and in perfect tune, with the power of beginning and ending it either loud or soft, and a quick legato scale, possessing the same characteristics of unvaried tone and correct tune, much has been done towards the formation of a singer ; at least, the chief mechanical difficulties are overcome. Half an hour a day, regularly and well employed on the best means, will be sufficient for the amateur, but we would earnestly recommend that the voice be used in no other way until good habits have been firmly fixed, otherwise the process of learning to sing will not be unlike the process of Penelope's web, all making and unmaking.

Exercises for the voice (and among the best are Ferrari's) form the next step. These also should be practised on the syllable *a*, with the same cautious attention to the purity of tone, correct intonation, and legato execution; taking the breath without effort or noise, never suffering it to be exhausted, yet, when inhaled, being careful not to break the accent of the music, selecting a rest, or the unaccented part of the bar, for the purpose, and filling the lungs before a long note or a passage of uninterrupted execution.

Attention should also be paid to the increase or diminution of sound, whether upon one or a succession of notes, giving the loud parts without violence, and the soft with the distinctness of an audible whisper. Contrast is as necessary in singing as in painting, but it is seldom required to be violent : this character belongs to the expression of strong passion rather than sentiment, and is more suitable to the theatre than a private room. The gentleness and strength, softness and firmness, which combine to form the basis of an admirable female character, are also the best characteristics of her vocal efforts ; and the same good sense and judgment which are necessary in her general conduct, must also be applied to singing.

In the acquisition of rapid execution, the student must be guided by the time which she can devote to practice. It is decidedly an ornamental part of the art, and, when properly applied, a valuable and powerful adjunct of expression. But it is not, like tone, an essential. Voices which are naturally flexible, acquire execution easily, while thick and heavy voices move with difficulty, and demand more labour. While we advocate singing as an ornament to domestic life, and as a means of enjoying and bestowing pleasure, we admit that it ought not to engross the time which is due to higher employments or necessary duties, and that the pupil must determine upon how much time she can properly devote to singing, and regulate her studies accordingly. The mode of practice, and the energy of the learner, will convert minutes into hours : half an hour daily will scarcely be deemed too great a sacrifice ; and we boldly assert that this is time enough when coupled with regularity and ardour, to produce an agreeable, and, where nature has been bountiful, an accomplished singer. The quantity of the attainment being so regulated, the pupil must attempt no more than it is probable she can acquire : the ornamental part of the art must therefore be the last considered. The essentials are tune, tone, the expression which results from the singer's capability to make the voice perform her intentions and conceptions, and the power of producing the precise quality of tone which will best express the various emotions of joy, sorrow, love, anger, disappointment, or calm delight. In plainer language, we may say that the pupil must learn the simple means of expression, and then the power of applying them. Until these are acquired, she has no pretension to be styled a singer at all; and when they have been obtained, it depends upon opportunity and other circumstances whether the acquisition ought to be carried any farther.

A certain quantity of practice is necessary to retain all knowledge; a little more than that quantity will enable us to extend our knowledge or attainments. All things either retrograde or advance, and those persons only who understand the value of minutes actively and rightly employed can conceive how much may be done by the regular application of a short time daily; and most particularly is this the case in singing. We say this to encourage those whose wishes go beyond their apparent means, and whose natural powers are good.

Having thus described the course of study necessary to acquire the first principles of the art, we proceed to the adaptation of words to sound. It is a rule that pronunciation must be distinct, and free from vulgarity or affectation; the inaccuracies of dialect are even more disagreeable in singing than in speaking. It must be perceptible to every one that there is a melody that belongs to each county, as well as a peculiarity of pronunciation: this character of speech will also impart itself to the tone of a singer, if not guarded against.

Though distinct utterance is essential, the pupil should be on her guard against that sharp pronunciation which separates the speaking from the singing, so that the words appear to come upon the ear unconnected with the tone of the voice. If words be clearly begun and perfectly finished, they will fall distinctly upon the ear, and will neither impede nor be impeded by the tone. A clear and finished enunciation, when not carried to excess, also imparts a general finish to tone and manner. The tongue must be held rather back in the mouth, and the lips not suffered to hang loose, or they will make the pronunciation, as well as the tone, thick and indistinct.

Attention should also be paid to the meaning of the words, to their accent, and to the rhythm and sentiment of the poetry; for unless the sense be ascertained, the right expression will be wanting, and every singer is expected to unite her own conceptions with those of the composer. As an actress studies her part, adapts her voice and action to the emotions described by the language, so should the singer comprehend and feel the poetry, and apply the tone which is her vehicle of expression to convey the sentiment of the words which she utters.

Recitative, as the term itself implies, approaches more nearly to speaking than to singing: it is commonly so written that one note falls to each syllable: it requires more of striking enunciation, and less of singing, than the performance of an air; and some compositions (Handel's more especially) call

upon the performer for the feeling and elocution of an orator,
rather than the qualities of a singer, since she is neither limited
by time nor rhythm, but solely by the accent of the words themselves. It is therefore in recitative especially that the elocu-
tionary defects of the singer are detected; and it is consequently the best exercise for the attainment of articulate and
finished pronunciation. But in singing an air, the speaking
must blend so entirely with the tone, that although the audience may be able to hear every word, yet the speaking must
be only as an adjunct. The poetry ought not to be the prominent part of a song; the pronunciation, as in reading, should
be articulate and free from vulgarity or affectation. There is
a standard which all educated persons are supposed to possess
in speaking, and to this they must refer in singing. In taking
breath, the singer must endeavour not to breathe in the middle
of a word, (unless it be before a passage of execution), and
also not to break the sense of the words, or the accent of the
melody. The singer should not change the vowel or syllable
upon which she may have to hold a note or execute a passage, since it will detract from the beauty of articulate speaking, as well as from correct tone.

As to the ornamental part, professional singers are expected
occasionally to alter or add to the notes set down in a melody,
for the sake of novelty and variety, and also for the purpose
of exhibiting their peculiar attainments, or their invention and
imagination. The nearer an amateur approaches professional
excellence, the more highly is she estimated; and this custom
is consequently practised by the former where music is highly
cultivated. It is obvious that, in order to create new combinations of notes, the mind must be stored with examples,
and possess the power and habit of invention; and in order to
apply them tastefully and appropriately, there must be a perfect understanding of the style of the composer, and of the
character and expression of the composition. All this information and ability presumes an acquaintance with the science
of music, an intimate knowledge of style, or a wide and extensive reading in the works of various masters. There are,
however, some persons with retentive memories, quick apprehension, and refined feelings, who can remember and apply
ornaments appropriately and effectively. But these are exceptions, for this capability is generally the result of study,
and requires more time and labour than singers can commonly bestow. There are some graces which are indispensable, and call for no such exertion, nor such expenditure of
time, but only patience and industry. The shake is one of
these. It should be first practised on the middle of the voice,

beginning slow, and gradually increasing the velocity. A perfect shake is rapid, but distinct, liquid, smooth, and full of tone. In old English music it almost invariably terminates every composition; the Italians use it more as a passing grace, either very slow or very quick. The singer ought to be able to make a shake on every note of the voice; but though essential in the middle, it is not often required at the extremes of the compass. It demands some labour and more patience on the part of the pupil, but is an indispensable ornament to an English singer, and well worth the trouble of acquiring.

The mordente and the turn, both plain and inverted, are other necessary graces, requiring liquid tone, and distinct, but legato execution. Their application, where not designated by the composer, must be regulated by the sentiments of the passage to which they are affixed; and their expression may be varied, and a new character given by the employment of different accentuation and tone. A slow inverted turn, though composed of the same notes, bears a totally different expression from a quick turn; and the accent falling upon any one of the four notes will again change its meaning. Excellence in these minor points is derived from the mind: it is the intellect working with mechanical means which raises artists of every description above the mass. We cannot, therefore, urge too strongly upon the young vocalist to exercise her understanding at the same time that she practises her voice and her fingers.

We will endeavour to describe a more modern ornament of Italian origin for which we know no name, but which is full of elegance and feeling. It is generally used at the end of a musical phrase where the same note is repeated, and it consists in a gentle glide to the third above, which last note is just touched, and the next note descending dwelt upon more at length, ending upon the second note of the original phrase, for instance, *g, b, a, g*: when properly executed, it resembles a sort of gurgling sound; and when applied in pathetic passages, requires little effort to imagine it a sigh or gentle sob. When given with more boldness it confers dignity, and when lightly executed it imparts a playful character.

The appoggiatura is another addition, the use of which calls for the discretion and judgment of the performer. It is too common to need description; it requires legato execution, and may be varied in rapidity, accent, and tone, according to the expression required. The Italians almost invariably introduce the appoggiatura, when the same note occurs twice in succession: this frequently happens in recitative, when the rule is that the singer instead of taking the first note as it is written introduces the note above, or the half note below as an appoggiatura.

Another modern application of this ornament consists in repeating the appoggiatura a second, or even a third time before taking the note which it precedes. The execution of the repetition should be soft, like a throb of the voice, if we may be allowed the expression.

The portamento, or carrying the voice from one interval to another, comes perhaps under the head of legato execution. It consists in sliding the voice through the intervening notes. Italian singers rarely omit so to connect the notes : in English music it must be employed with caution, and under all circumstances it ought to be used without violence; otherwise, it has a ludicrous effect, and resembles a caricatured imitation of the Italian manner.

It has long been the fashion to conclude English songs with a cadence, why we know not, unless it be to give the singer further opportunity of displaying his execution and invention. The Italians have better taste, and although they may be justly accused of ending all their arias alike, yet this is a less obvious absurdity than commencing a long roulade upon a word of no meaning, when the sentiment has drawn to a close, and passion has vented its fervor. The singer has every opportunity in the course of an air to show her taste and ability, and these are not unfrequently best displayed by a sparing rather than a redundant use of ornament. It is desirable to possess the power of execution, but equally so to employ it judiciously.

We have now treated of tone, execution, elocution, ornament, and expression. We come next to style, or the peculiar mode in which all these means are employed. It seems impossible that a succession of notes arranged to certain words should be so performed by two or more persons as to bear a different character, and yet that each performance should be equally successful. This is undoubtedly the case in acting. Actors give the same passage different readings, and accompany it by different action, yet each may claim equal excellence ; how else indeed should there be variety or novelty, the two great charms of life? So is it with singers. No two voices have the same character, and although trained by the same master and in the same method, yet they are totally dissimilar ; and as no two minds are alike, the nature of the intellect gives other varieties which are manifested in conception, imagination, and feeling. For instance, one singer will be distinguished for tenderness, another for dignity, a third for pathos. One will employ mere beauty of voicing, another great power, a third will adopt contrast, a fourth delicate or powerful execution. Some will introduce appropriate, but far-fetched ornaments; others, when the character of the words is not decided, will alter the time of a composition from quick to slow, or the contrary, so as to surprise by novelty, or to gain the opportunities of displaying some acquirement or natural gift peculiar to herself. It is also to be remarked, that different kinds of compositions have each their peculiar character. The music of the church in all its subdivisions, chamber music in all its varieties, such as the canzonet, the air, the bravura, the ballad, &c., are distinct species which call into action the same qualifications, but demand an application fitted to the particular nature of the composition. There is also some regard due to the age and country of the composer. Attention to these points implies a general knowledge of the art, and its history, and requires more than mere mechanical excellence. All these differences constitute style ; for as they belong to mind, or the attainments resulting from long and diligent study, they will manifest themselves in every attempt, however extensive the field upon which they are exerted. It follows, therefore, that style is a consequence of sedulous practice united to a good understanding, and the experience which comes of hearing and observing; and hence it is that amateurs seldom acquire style. It is lamentable how little the reasoning powers are exercised and cultivated in female education ; were it otherwise, the time and money now wasted upon accomplishments would be employed to the advantage and pleasure of the pupil, and of all who expect from her the fruits of those long years which she has expended on her studies.

Those parents, then, who desire their daughters to become singers, must first ascertain how far nature has lent her aid; next, what degree of excellence it is probable they may attain, and whether the talent is to be employed as a means of profit or of mere amusement; and, finally, how much time they can rationally spare from duties and studies of more importance. The next step is to adopt the methods most likely to secure the ends proposed. An honest and capable instructor is essential; but an explanation, such as we have endeavoured to convey of the best method, although necessarily general, will materially assist the pupil, because she will understand why that method is desirable, and being thus led to reflect upon the subject, she will be more likely to apply it advantageously. When some progress in the art has been made, hearing the best models frequently, listening with the mind, as well as with the ears, will do more than many lessons carelessly given and thoughtlessly received,

GRAMMAR SCHOOLS.

West Riding Proprietary School, Wakefield, Yorkshire *.

THE establishment of a proprietary school in one of the most
fertile and wealthy districts of England, under the patronage
and with the support of the neighbouring gentry, is an event
which we hope and expect will be highly favourable to the
improvement of education in the north of England.

Various causes have contributed to the formation of proprietary schools in different parts of the country, and though
the experiments have not in all cases been equally successful,
we are inclined to think that these schools have, both directly
and indirectly, tended to improve the schools for the middle
and richer classes. On looking at the number and localities
of the endowed schools in various parts of the kingdom, we
are inclined to think that about the time when the most
recent of them were founded, nearly every large town and
populous district was provided with its school. But in course
of time many of these schools fell into decay, some have
entirely disappeared †, and a new or an increased population has arisen in many places where no endowed schools
exist. Owing to the great development of the mineral and
manufacturing industry of the kingdom, there has been a
great increase in the national wealth, and its distribution among
the population of the manufacturing districts has formed a
large body of pers ns who are able and desirous to give their
children the advantage of a good education. Twenty or thirty
years ago, or even much less, many of these persons would
probably have sent their children to the nearest school, public
or private, or to some public school then in repute, without
much troubling themselves as to what the school was, provided it was generally said to be good. But at present it is
an undeniable fact, that parents inquire much more particularly about the character of schools than formerly; and this
attention is the very best indication that our education is in
the way of improvement. Indifference on the part of parents
will always be accompanied with inertness or carelessness on
the part of teachers; and the surest way to urge the teacher

* The proceedings at the opening of the West Riding Proprietary School,
August 5th, 1834; to which are added, the Rules and Regulations adopted by
the Directors for its government; a list of the Shareholders and Pupils of the
Establishment, and a Catalogue of the Library of the Institution. London:
Longman, Rees, &c., 1834.

† For instance, Banbury, in Oxfordshire, where the school-house only remains,
and is let for 4*l*. per ann., which is now paid to the national school. There is
no trace of any lands belonging to the school.

to activity and zeal is for the parent to show that he examines into and can appreciate the faithful discharge of his duty.

As a general rule, parents in the middle classes have now to decide whether they will send their sons to one of the endowed grammar schools, or to a private school. Both alternatives often present difficulties. Most of the grammar schools which have a high reputation are very expensive—the course of instruction is generally limited to Latin and Greek—and there is no reasonable security that a youth will be protected against the tyranny of the older boys, or that he will escape the contagion of bad example. The best private schools are also very expensive; and, indeed, it must necessarily be the case that private schools, as a general rule, cannot avoid charging more than public schools. Each individual, however small his number of pupils may be, is compelled to make certain large outlays for a house, school-room, &c., which in most endowed schools are already provided. Besides this, it is, in most cases, a pure speculation, which may entirely fail. The private schoolmaster begins with only a few boarders, and must work the number up to the paying point;—an endowed school already contains a number of scholars, and, if it has been tolerably well managed by his predecessor, a new master steps at once into an adequate income. He is also secured against any risk of the numbers falling off, provided his own conduct is not the cause of it, by the force of habit, which makes many parents send their children to the same place where they received their own education.

The price of good education, therefore, at an endowed school, ought to be less than in a private school of equal character, for the profit is more certain, and the chance of absolute loss is almost removed; but, as we have already remarked, the charges at many of the endowed schools in high repute are very heavy. The expense, therefore, of the grammar and private schools in highest repute, and the indifferent character of many grammar and private schools where pupils are boarded at lower rates, combined with the opinion that few of these schools furnish all the kinds of instruction that are now requisite, have led to the foundation of various proprietary schools. The general object of these schools, as well as that of the West Riding Institution, is to give a good classical education, and with it a competent knowledge of mathematical and, in some cases, physical science, with instruction in the most useful European languages. It cannot be denied that in many of the pure grammar schools little Latin and Greek is learned, and this little is all the instruction that a boy receives. With improved methods and better masters, more Latin and Greek may be learned than is acquired at many grammar schools, and sufficient time will remain over for the study of other branches of knowledge of more immediate utility to a large portion of the children of the middle classes. The defenders of the pure Latin and Greek system have often urged that, however good many of the new systems of education may be, and however useful the other branches of knowledge which are introduced into these schools, Latin and Greek will not be well taught; and that in these respects boys who go from such schools to the Universities will be inferior to those who are specially trained for University examinations at some of the best grammar schools. The proprietary schools have hardly existed long enough to settle this question, which, however, if settled against the proprietary schools, will by no means disprove the great and obvious advantages of such institutions in other respects. It is, however, in the power of the masters of these institutions to show, as they do in the German Gymnasia, that some boys will not learn the less Latin and Greek because others devote themselves more particularly to other pursuits; or that because the students of Latin and Greek devote a reasonable portion of their time to mathematics and the modern languages, they must therefore make less progress in Latin and Greek. But on this we shall say a few words presently.

The property of the West Riding School consists of 240 shares, we presume of 100*l.* each, but this is not stated: no proprietor must hold more than four. With the money advanced a school has been built, and so far finished as to accommodate above one hundred boys. It appears from the report that the expenses of the building have exceeded the fund in hand by 1000*l.*, but hopes are entertained that this debt will soon be redeemed.

Many people are perhaps not aware that similar associations have given origin to some of our old endowed schools, and that we are only imitating the example of our ancestors, who, after the suppression of the religious houses, colleges, and chantries, to some of which at least schools were attached, endeavoured to supply the defect by their own exertions. Though some of the lands of the religious houses, here as well as in Scotland, were reserved for purposes of education, the larger part fell into the hands of laymen, and the funds for education were diminished *.

' In the year 1563, the mayor, jurats, and principal inhabitants of Sandwich agreed to raise a sum of money by subscription, for the purpose of erecting a building for a free-school, under a promise from Mr. Roger Manwood, then a barrister,

* See Strype's Memorials, ii, ch. viii,

to endow the same with lands of sufficient value to support the building and maintain a master. Accordingly, the sum of 286*l.* 7*s.* 2*d.* was immediately collected, and other measures were taken to forward the work. It happened fortunately that Archbishop Parker was then in the neighbourhood, and approving the design, he became eminently instrumental in founding the school. He made application to the Dean and Chapter of Canterbury for a grant of some land belonging to their church, which was judged to be a proper site for the school; and moreover he wrote to his friend Secretary Cecyl for his interest with the Queen to procure her license for the foundation and endowment. The license in mortmain issued the 1st of October, 1563, by which Roger Manwood of Hackington, Esq., is empowered to erect a free grammar school in Sandwich, by the name of the Free Grammar School of Roger Manwood in Sandwich; and the Queen grants that the mayor and jurats of Sandwich, and their successors, shall be governors of the school, and be one body incorporate in deed and name, by the title of Governours of the Free-School of Roger Manwood in Sandwich; that they may sue and implead by that name in all the Courts, may purchase estates in fee to the value of 40*l.* a year, and have a common seal; and she further gives special license to the said Roger to give and grant to the said governors the particular estates recited in the subsequent deed of feoffment, with other grants usual in instruments of that sort *.'

There seem to be at present two difficulties in the way of following up the principle of founding new schools in districts where there are either no grammar schools existing, or where these schools are unsuited to the wants of the present population. Neither of these difficulties involves the want of money,

---

* From ' Collections for an History of Sandwich, in Kent,' by William Boys, Canterbury, 1792. The author gives the following curious extract from the Records of the Corporation :—21st May, 5th Elizabeth. ' It was moved by the maior, what a godly acte and worthie of memorye yt shuld be, to make and fowend a free schoole within the towen, for the godly educacion of children in the knowledge and feare of God, and that God therefor wold blesse the towen the better; and required therefore, that euery inhabitante within this towen wold consyder so good an acte, and to knowe what euery man wold willingly give therto; and that he and his brethern as they dyd judge that a very godly worke, so thei wold largely give of their porcions, that the same might be stablished ; which said mocion liked well all men. And so with one consent they offeryd to guive every man for the same worke accordinge to their abillytye, as followythe,' &c.

It is probable that the want of a school was felt at Sandwich, owing to the suppression of the chantry. Roger Manwood received the first rudiments of his education in a school belonging to Thomas Ellis's Chantry, in Sandwich, which was suppressed and sold, the 2nd of Edward VI. (Boy's *Sandwich,* p. 186.)—Strype speaks of schools also having been suppressed under the act of 1 Edward VI. Schools were often connected with the old chantries : see the case of Blackburn (Charity Commissioners' Reports), and Barnstaple.

which is the least difficulty that the friends of education have to contend against.

The first difficulty is the tenure of the school property. Under the proprietary system we believe that all the subscribers are joint proprietors, and individually liable for the debts of the institution in which they are shareholders, whatever arrangements among themselves they may make to the contrary. This is a great inconvenience, which can only be remedied by an act of incorporation. Besides this, if such schools could assume a legal character with permission to hold property of a limited amount, they would at once have a higher rank in the estimation of the public, and be established on a secure foundation. What is wanted, therefore, is something analogous to the letters of license which were granted by Edward VI. and Elizabeth. All schools for which a certain amount of money has been raised, and vested in a piece of land and a school building, should be entitled, on fulfilling certain other conditions, to an act of incorporation. These conditions should be, a certain amount of fixed property, secured for the maintenance of the school; an adoption of a certain course of instruction, leaving the mode of instruction free to the managers and masters; the granting to government a visiting power, and the making of periodical returns to the government. One absolute condition should be, that all money should be actually given, without any stipulation for profit in the shape of interest, but with the right of transfer by will, or by sale subject to the directors' approbation of the purchaser. Such conditions would tend to secure these schools against the decay into which many grammar schools have fallen, owing to mismanagement of the trustees: and this security would be further increased by the periodical election of managers or directors by the proprietors out of their own body, as already provided for in the rules and regulations of the proprietary schools. Whenever we shall have a government sufficiently wise to comprehend the question of education in all its extent and importance, we may expect to have legal provision made for the improvement of all existing endowed schools, and the establishment of others where they are wanted. One strong argument in support of such a measure is, that it will cost the government nothing.

Another difficulty which has been experienced in the proprietary schools, has arisen from dissensions among the directors, and from their injudicious interference with the masters. The first difficulty is inherent in endowed schools also, and has only not been felt of late years to any amount, because the directors of them often take very little interest in their management. Such disputes, when not settled by the rules of the school, might be decided most promptly by a reference to the visiting authority. This principle appears in the rules of many of the old schools. Some person, such as a bishop, archbishop, or some other public and always existing personage, is named as the arbiter in disputes. We would modify the principle so far as to have one arbiter instead of many, for the purpose of giving consistency to decisions, and this arbiter must be the State, or those to whom the State delegates the power.

As far as we can judge from the Report on the West Riding School, the proprietors are well aware of the danger that must arise from interfering with the internal conduct of the school. The first and most important duty of directors is to choose good masters, to whom, when chosen, they must give their confidence, which will seldom be abused, if they have taken due pains in the first instance. Nor is this surrender of the internal direction at all incompatible with a vigilant superintendence, which it is the directors' business to exercise.

Among the regulations of this school we find the following (p. 70.)

' The funds of the institution shall be appropriated to the payment of the salaries of the several masters, the wages of servants, the repairs and other necessary expenses of the institution, and to paying the interest upon the capital advanced by the proprietors.'

To the last clause we have a decided objection. No interest is likely to accrue in such schools, if every thing is done for the advantage of masters and pupils that ought to be done ; and to hold out a distant expectation of it is a lure to the greedy and a bait to the ignorant. Should the school be filled with pupils, and its income consequently increase, we think the masters should be so well paid as to make them unwilling to leave, or to accept another place ; additional masters should be procured, and no expense spared in the way of books, models, maps, and other aids of instruction. A good library also should be formed for the use of the proprietors, masters, and pupils. If there is any incidental circumstance which would weigh more strongly than another in inducing a well-educated man to take a mastership in a provincial proprietary school, it is the access to a good library, which would put him on an equal footing as to literary advantage with those who live in London and the Universities. The West Riding School has already begun to form a library by donations.

The two following regulations differ in some respects from those of several proprietary schools :—

s 2

'The following masters shall be appointed :—A head master and a second master, who shall be graduates of one of the Universities, and of approved academical merit; an assistant master, a French master, and a German master, with such other assistance as may be found necessary.

'The head master shall not take any private pupils or boarders, and, if a clergyman, shall not serve any church where weekly duty is required.'

Both these rules are good ; but the last would be better, if the head master and all other masters who happen to be in orders were excluded from serving any church at all. Education will never become a distinct and acknowledged profession till it is separated from all others: nor do we understand how a clergyman can serve a church in any way, either on Sundays or week-days, who must be, or ought to be, *every* day engaged in attending to his pupils. It is, however, gratifying to see that the directors have not followed the rules of some schools of this kind, in which all but clergymen are excluded from the head-mastership. Till this error is rectified such schools will labour under the disadvantage of choosing their master out of a limited number, instead of out of the whole number of those who are competent for the duty. The wisdom of the Directors of the West Riding School, in retaining all that is good in the old grammar schools, and adding to their scheme whatever is requisite to render it fully adapted to present wants, cannot be too highly commended. Old institutions were well suited to the times and places in which they were established ; and we act more in conformity to the spirit of these institutions, when we adapt them to our present wants, than if we adhere rigidly to the letter of their rules. The second regulation as to clerical duties very nearly resembles one in the rules of Sandwich School made by Roger Manwood.

"Item. I ordeine that the master and vsher be at libertie either to remaine single or to marie, or to take priesthoode, so he trouble not himself with any benefice of cure or worldly business, in such wies that shall hinder his office and dilligent attendaunce in the schole.*"

As to the principles on which it is proposed to conduct this school, we think, as far as they are explained in this publication, that they are sound. Flogging, as a general rule, will not be used ; and fagging, with all kinds of tyranny practised in many large schools by the older upon the younger boys, will not be allowed. The statements as to the intended system of

* See also Dean Colet's rules about St. Paul's School, London. Journal of Education, No. XVI., p. 241. The rules of Sir Anthony Judde for Tunbridge School, Kent, contain a rule to the same effect, and nearly in the same words.

instruction are necessarily expressed in general terms. We learn, however, from the speech of the head-master, that it is his intention to adopt a plan of instruction and discipline in close accordance with that which was introduced, and has been successfully pursued, by Dr. Jerrard at the Bristol College, and with the working of which Mr. Butterton became well acquainted during the time that he held the office of vice-principal in that institution. One thing, however, disappointed us, which was that the reverend gentleman has not resolved to banish the rod in the case of moral as well as all other offences. It appears from the reports of the council which are now before us, that it has been found possible at the Bristol College to dispense altogether with the aid of that instrument of punishment; and that a system of discipline based upon an appeal to 'the reason and best feelings' of the students, has raised up among them a 'tone of feeling' and a degree of 'mutual courtesy' such as we believe do not exist in any flogging establishment.

To remove from these proprietary establishments an objection above alluded to as sometimes made, and also to render them efficient places of instruction for all boys who go there, we think that there should be a division of the youths into two classes, after the age of twelve, thirteen, or fourteen, as it may be. Up to this time, most, if not all the boys might receive the same kind of education in Latin, arithmetic, geography, French or German, or both, with such other knowledge as is now indispensable for all well-educated people. But from the age or ages above mentioned, it is clear that some division must take place between those intended for the universities and learned professions, and those who are not. The boys intended for the universities will now require a regular discipline in the more difficult Latin authors, in Greek, in the writing and the translating of both languages, together with the elements of algebra and geometry, and the branches of mixed mathematics studied at the universities. For the other boys we conceive Greek to be quite unnecessary. Having no strong motive for prosecuting it vigorously, it is probable that they would learn little; and they would often leave the school before it were possible that much proficiency could be made, even if they were diligent. The time of these boys then should be employed from the ages above mentioned, more particularly with reference to their future pursuits : and a knowledge of mathematics, of some of the branches of physics or natural history, and the ability to write and speak the French or German languages, or both, will be much more useful to this class of boys than anything else.   By such a principle of division, we believe that the proprietary schools may send youths to the university better prepared than they are in general from either grammar schools, or private schools; and those who are not intended for the universities, will get that sound and useful education, which at present can rarely be procured at any expense.

ON WRITING LATIN AND GREEK EXERCISES.

It does not now need to be shown, that setting to learn is not teaching, or that the art of instructing is something different from the art of puzzling.   But this principle, though now generally admitted, is not generally acted on.   Many teachers doubtless adopt or conform to practices which, in theory, they condemn.   We confess we are at a loss how else to explain the common adherence to the Latin-Latin and the Latin-Greek grammars of our forefathers, and the manner in which boys are flogged for not learning what they cannot understand. But these inconsistencies are now becoming more rare; and, if allowance might be made for the play on the word, we would say, that the studies of humanity are beginning to be pursued on principles of humanity.   These, however, are by no means the only customs in which the convictions of a teacher must often be at variance with the practice which he has adopted from imitation, and in which he perseveres from habit.   Exercises, both Greek and Latin, seem to have been used for little else than to puzzle the pupil, both on points which he has studied, and on points which he has not studied; at all events, to show him rather what he does not know, than what he does know; to show him rather his weakness than his strength.   Whether from accident or design, the fact has been, that, on seeing his exercise corrected, even the diligent pupil has been far more discouraged at the amount of the mistakes, than encouraged by the correctness of the rest.   He has very seldom felt that he could do his exercise without a single mistake, and that he has been able to avoid the traps laid to catch him.   The system of setting exercises appears to have been (it certainly has had the effect of) a struggle between the master and the pupil; the one to avoid mistakes, the other to give opportunities for making them.   In this struggle, nothing but the severe infliction of the rod, or some other equivalent punishment, could prevent a boy from giving up the contest in despair.   We are not ignorant that it may, with some show of reason, be replied, that such a system is calculated to form valuable habits of attention and perseverance, as well as to impress the knowledge so attained more firmly on the mind. Doubtless, habits of attention and perseverance may be formed no less by a severe corporal discipline than by a strict mental discipline; but we conceive, that the application of the former means is limited to that class of teachers who do not understand the latter; and we hope presently to show, that the knowledge so acquired is not, after all, impressed on the mind so firmly or so easily by this as by a different method.

In the case of exercises as they are ordinarily managed, in which mistakes can hardly be avoided, the pupil remembers his own error as much as the master's correction; but he does not, at the same time, acquire an accurate discrimination between that which is right and that which is wrong. His eye, as well as his ear, are habituated to a sort of jargon, and the error having made the first impression, will probably be found to have made also the more permanent impression. We believe the pupil's knowledge of any language thus acquired, is more injured by the constant errors to which his eye and ear are familiarized, than benefited by all the corrections which he receives. We learn modern languages with ease in the countries where they are spoken; not by hearing bad French, bad German, bad Italian, with a running commentary of emendations, in which case our memory would be the common lumber-room of errors and corrections, the former claiming as much importance as the latter, but by habitually hearing and reading good French, good German, and good Italian. A beginner will always make mistakes in speaking a language which he is learning; and, consequently, when many are learning together, each must frequently hear errors; but there is not the same necessity for him to see errors, much less to be constantly writing errors. It will readily be admitted, that if these observations are correct with respect to men, they apply with double force to boys. Teachers themselves may frequently, in their remarks upon an exercise, find themselves repeating the errors of their pupils, from having seen them so many times on paper: it cannot then be surprising, that boys find it difficult to divest themselves of errors to which they have been familiarized. A plan, not inferior in absurdity to that to which we have adverted, has been adopted, pretty generally we believe (more, however, in girls' than in boys' schools), for teaching orthography and orthoëpy, correct writing and correct speaking. Whether it originated with Mr. Lindley Murray or not, we are unable to decide; but it is a method which in principle fully coincides with the superficial and absurd system which he diffused so widely. Our experience convinces us, that the most effectual way to teach a child to spell the word *always* correctly is not to give him the sentence : 'That, which is sometimes expedient, is not *allways* so,' and then the rule, 'Words taken into composition often drop those letters which were superfluous in their simples.' A child, who understood the rule would not need the exercise, and to one who did not understand the rule, it would be worse than useless. We cannot be persuaded that good grammar will be best taught by the exhibition and correction of bad grammar. A boy is not brought to say, 'we were,' by constantly hearing 'we was:' he does not learn to say, 'It is I,' by constantly hearing, 'It is me;' nor will he, after having waded through all the vulgarisms in Murray's Exercises, have a very nice ear for idiomatic English. It will be well if he ever succeeds in unlearning the greater part of what he has learnt. Whatever other argument may be alleged in defence of theatrical representations, it will hardly be pretended that they are very effective in promoting moral improvement. The exhibition of vice has never proved the best means for enforcing the practice of virtue. We never knew the principle of teaching by negatives applied so boldly to a matter of practice as by the venerable dancing-master, under whom we made our first essays in the art. He would commence his lesson by the performance of some simple step, saying, 'Look at your copy;' and when he had finished, would add, 'Now that is the way in which you should not do it. My son will show you how you should do it.' He would then, with a pathetic complaint that his pupils could not appreciate his services, call forward his son to administer the antidote : and as he began, so he ended. The result was what might be expected ; we walked and danced, if possible, more awkwardly than before : and if such was the effect, in a matter of bodily dexterity and aptitude, it would be equally so in one of mental discipline. If it is true in morals, it is no less true in the cultivation of the understanding, that example is more powerful than precept, that is, than mere rule.

We repeat, then, that, *cæteris paribus*, the best plan is that which least exposes the eye and ear to error. Let it not be supposed, however, that we entertain any chimerical expectation of being able to communicate knowledge, especially in the dead languages, without difficulty to the learner. Nothing that is worth having is got without labour ; but we know no reason why art should increase that labour. There is indeed no such thing as a funnel through which knowledge may be poured into the mind, nor, if there were, would the infusion be as useful as if the knowledge were acquired in a more laborious way : and we are fully aware of the benefit to be derived from the process of learning, and that the habits acquired by such discipline are perhaps the most valuable effects of the study, inasmuch as they remain when the knowledge itself is forgotten. But though we make this admission, we contend that the pupil should not have tasks which he is unable to perform, or which he is not likely to perform well ; for, if the exercise be too difficult for the pupil, it does not furnish that proper employment for his understanding which is the true discipline of the mind. It is impossible to give boys the judgment of men, and therefore to impose on them tasks which are fit only for men, which boys cannot be expected to perform correctly, is highly injurious. Should it be urged, that the best plan is that which affords the most exercise for the powers of the mind, we would reply, that to give a boy a weight to carry which he cannot lift, may be exercising his temper, but cannot be called exercising his strength. We assent pretty nearly to the following observation by Dr. James Robertson : ' Fatemur nos totos fuisse in hoc ut studium hujus linguæ magis magisque facile redderemus, immo, si possemus, decuplò facilius reddere, nos non omissuros.' *

No argument, we conceive, beyond the notorious failure of the methods usually pursued, is needed to show the reasonableness of trying any plan which promises less vexation and more profit. It is almost unnecessary to condemn the practice of translating Ellis's, or Neilson's, or any other exercises without any explanation or illustration being given by the teacher, where the quantity is more regarded than the quality of the performance ; although we have heard of such being written, and never corrected or even examined when brought up. Little less preposterous is the plan of examining the exercises, and administering reward or punishment without explaining the nature of the difficulties and correcting the errors. But these are practices which, of course, cannot obtain in any well-regulated school. Our immediate object is to state what are the unavoidable bad consequences of the plan generally adopted, even where the system of exercises is best administered, and to suggest a few hints for the prevention of these consequences. Into the merits or defects of the existing books, it is not within the scope of our present purpose to inquire. We have only to do with the manner in which they are used.

The plan which we wish to recommend may be stated in very few words ; let no exercise be written which has not first been translated orally to the master from the sentences proposed as the exercise. Any one who has been accustomed to the arduous duties of teaching will readily allow, that no aid,

* Præf, ad Clav. Pentateuchi,

however apparently trifling, should be overlooked. Amidst the excitement of a class, teachers themselves think of many things which would never occur to them in solitary study ; and boys may be supposed to be, in a much greater degree, affected by this collateral aid.   Instead, then, of leaving the pupils to their own unaided, unexcited labour, let the sentences be translated by them orally as a part of the day's lesson : errors, of course, would be made in this oral translation, but they would be comparatively few.   It may be objected that written exercises, under this system, would not furnish a sufficient test of the positive and relative merits of each pupil.   But the real trial of each pupil's knowledge will be made during the previous oral examination ; while the activity of mind, which must be kept up to some extent, in order to remember the sentences when rendered correctly, will give to all the pupils a sense of power and mastery over the language which is rarely gained by the ordinary methods, but which will be a highly beneficial stimulant.   To show the necessity of giving to boys this encouragement and confidence, we would refer, not to instances of exercises in which every declinable noun is declined wrong, and scarcely a verb is conjugated right, but to instances in which diligent and able boys have brought up exercises of twenty lines, containing ten mistakes, when they expected they had made none, and have very naturally been discouraged at the result.   Courage is one of the most powerful instruments in the hands of the teacher for the advancement of his pupil, and, without it, there can be little hope of success.   We can imagine nothing more likely to make a boy a blockhead than to call him a blockhead : few means could be devised more likely to prevent a boy from learning than to tell him that he is stupid and cannot learn, or to give him such exercises as he cannot possibly do well.   We are not unacquainted with the large demand frequently made on the patience and temper of the teacher ; but we are also acquainted with the bad effects of pettishness and petulance in the instruction of boys, and of imposing labour above their strength to perform, and then rating them for their blunders.   Boys should never be robbed of their self-respect, never be allowed to entertain a low opinion of what they can do, however badly they may actually do.   Let a boy see that he is suspected of lying, and he will soon verify the suspicion : he has no longer a character to lose ; he has no longer any regard for himself.

.   The importance of this principle, we conceive, it is hardly possible to overrate.   We believe that it has been little attended to, and that the feelings of the pupil have been held in far too light estimation for his own improvement or his teacher's credit. That there should be no stupid boys it would be unreasonable and useless to expect ; but, we are persuaded, there would be many fewer, if their courage and dignity were consulted more, and their feelings outraged less. Why is a boy to be told that he is an ignoramus ? It may be his own fault, but it may also be, and is quite as likely to be the fault of his parents in not having provided better early instruction, for which the schoolmaster is not to be expected to find an immediate remedy : it is his business to devise the most rational, easy, and speedy method of supplying deficiencies and imparting knowledge. If other methods fail, abuse is not likely to succeed. Independently of the consideration of insult, what would be so discouraging, so fatally damping to an adult pupil, as to tell him he is stupid or to call him hard names ? We say, independently of the insult offered, what would be more likely to dispirit the learner and to dash his energies ? There can be little doubt, that the abusive epithets lavished so freely by many teachers on their pupils, have rather caused stupidity and nourished ignorance, than been originally provoked by their existence. Nor are we wandering from our point in making these observations; for, if as will be generally allowed, the errors committed in exercises given on the usual methods are so numerous as we have described, it is manifest that some animadversion is called for, and that some expression of anger or displeasure will certainly escape the master ; if not, the pupil thinks he is considered to be doing well, and yet he finds so many mistakes that he has no hope of ever attaining a respectable knowledge of the language. It is true that after a long course of years he does learn something, and in a construing sort of style is able to hammer through a Latin author; but, were it not for the apparent paradox, we would say that, if he had been learning less, he would know more. His courage is gone, his zeal is gone, the attraction of novelty is lost, and he regards his studies with indifference or even disgust.

On the strength of first impressions, and on the difficulty of correcting errors acquired in early instruction, it is needless to remark : we will only observe generally, that in language this difficulty is perhaps greater than in any other study. Mis-pronunciations, or peculiar pronunciations, to which we have been first habituated, we seldom or never get rid of. This is particularly observable in foreigners, who invariably contract the oddities and provincialisms of those natives in whose society they first mix, and can never remove the impression originally made. In the same way, if we have been early accustomed to blunders in writing exercises, it is long before we can restore our original correctness of eye and ear. It is not enough to

say that errors are corrected after the exercise has been examined ; the original impression is not so easily erased, and,
after a week's interval, a boy will have a more vivid impression of what he himself originally wrote, than of the
after-correction of the master. If it be said, that he must
write out the exercise again fairly (although this will by no
means remedy the evil,) why, we ask, was he at first exposed
to the commission of error, and then obliged to have recourse
to this tedious process of correction? Why was not the exercise first translated orally to the master, and afterwards
written by the pupil, in which case there would have been far
less liability to error, and yet sufficient scope for activity and
vigilance, and sufficient employment for all the powers of the
mind ? The error which is made in an oral translation and
is corrected on the spot, has not time to settle into an impression. But that which is considered and reflected on, and
then deliberately put down on paper and slept over, is often
permanent.

Exercises have been, and we fear still are regarded as a
very subordinate part of the system of instruction in Latin
and Greek. It would generally be thought little better than
a waste of time to devote the hours usually given to the day's
lesson to the explanation and correction of an exercise : it would
be said that nothing had been done, because a given number
of paragraphs or pages had not been read. Instead of being
deemed one of the most efficient means for impressing what is
learnt on the mind, exercises have been looked on rather as an
expedient for filling up the pupil's time out of school, and of
puzzling him on particular rules of construction. Much of the
neglect or misuse into which exercises have fallen, may, we apprehend, be attributed to the usual custom of putting a new book
(as it is called) into the hands of the pupil every half-year or
year, so that the inquiry has not been—what can he do ?—
what does he know ? But, what is he reading ?—when did he go
into Virgil, &c. ?—he will soon, I suppose, be going into a new
book, &c. ?—while some authors have been called lower, and
others dignified with the name of higher, all arranged according to a fanciful scale of degrees, which boys regard with a
sort of mysterious veneration. The object has been to drag a
pupil through the greatest number of these authors, rather
than to enable him to read any of them with ease and pleasure.
As soon as a pupil finds that he can do something himself, he
takes courage and is certain of success ; but as long as he reads
much and writes but little, there can be no great improvement
in any language, and no well-grounded feeling of confidence.
Whoever wishes to read a language with ease, should write

much. This principle has long been acknowledged; but the old prejudice of reading a given number of books as the best means of learning languages, seems to be not yet entirely removed. That no books should be read, it would be absurd to maintain; but we contend, that in the early stages of instruction at least three times as much should be written, as is read. It is not necessary that all that is translated into Latin or Greek orally should be written; but it is important that none should be written which has not first been translated orally. With respect to the best kind of exercises, we may refer to some remarks in the last Number of this Journal (Review of 'Elegantiæ Latinæ'). A similar plan to what is here recommended has been, and still is adopted, in the course of instruction pursued at the London University.

It is easy for the diligent teacher to make exercises as they are wanted. One example will explain our meaning. From the first passage in the twenty-seventh chapter of the Gallic War of Cæsar—Helvetii, omnium rerum inopia adducti, legatos de deditione ad eum miserunt—we may form the following sentences for translation :—

Orgetorix, induced by the want of everything, sent an ambassador to them (to treat) concerning surrender.

The Eburones, induced by the want of corn, send an ambassador to him (to treat) concerning surrender.

The Carthaginians, induced by these things, sent ambassadors to him (to treat) concerning peace.

Cicero, induced by this thing, sends a messenger to the generals (to treat) concerning surrender.

Twice this number of sentences might very advantageously be given for oral translation in class, when the original passage is well understood. A good variation of the plan is to have a chapter of Cæsar committed to memory, after it has been translated and explained, and then to give short English sentences constructed upon the model of phrases contained in it, while each boy has a slate in his hand, and writes down the correct Latin corresponding to the English sentences. When the whole exercise is thus written, it should be read aloud by the pupils in order. This plan requires a different and perhaps a greater effort of memory, than the plan of translating sentences orally in class, and writing them down after the whole is done; and, therefore, it should not be adopted till the pupil is sufficiently familiar with the sounds and inflexions of the language to remember the original and apply it with ease. We cannot agree with the recommendation of Mr. Kenrick in the Preface to his Greek Exercise-Book, that sentences when corrected should be committed to memory.

We think it would be a gratuitous tax on a pupil's patience formally to learn by heart so many short and unconnected passages ; and, we conceive, the end would be better answered by each pupil in the class reading them over aloud. The sentences would in the first place be given under every possible advantage, and (any mistake being corrected at once) they would then be written almost without an error, and would afterwards be impressed on the ear, as well as on the memory, by being read aloud.

Some small variations of the plan will occur to the intelligent teacher. He will always, however, bear in mind that his object is not to see how many mistakes his pupil will commit, but to diminish as much as possible the causes and chances of error. By thus impressing early and strongly on the mind all the necessary inflexions of words, and all the various forms of the simple sentence, the teacher will have laid the foundation of a sound and comprehensive knowledge of the language. On this foundation, not weakened or impaired by the admixture of improper materials, he may erect the superstructure with safety, and with the satisfaction of seeing that each addition, instead of weakening or rendering more incongruous what has been already built, will be so much gained towards the completion and perfection of his work.

An objection may be made, that, though the importance of writing exercises is not here over-rated, the value of reading classical authors is under-rated ; that the practice of writing exercises composed of very short sentences is an excellent way of fixing inflexions in a boy's memory ; but that when he has mastered the mere etymological part of the language, and has to learn the collocation of words and the construction of involved sentences, he must read largely ; and he cannot write exercises with *this* object, till he has read pretty largely. A few words will show how far we assent to the truth of these remarks, and wherein we dissent from them. It is not only to teach the pupil the inflexions of words that short sentences should be given for translation ; the object is to teach him at the same time what are the component parts of all simple sentences however long and however apparently involved, and to make him fully comprehend the logical connexion of such parts, and the order which they generally take in the language that he is studying. We believe that this knowledge, which is the true introduction to the study of language, considered as a means of expressing connexion of ideas, is best attained by writing short sentences according to given models, and by analyzing and reducing to the general form of all simple sentences the examples which occur in the course of reading a Latin author.

In order to teach fully the mode in which two sentences are connected, when one is subordinate to the other, it is certainly necessary to read, but perhaps not largely, though to this there can be no objection, if at the same time we read accurately. But here also we conceive it necessary for the master to frame short exercises, in order to show the principle of connexion between the different parts of a complete sentence : and we think that a logical exposition of this principle of connexion, when explained by examples and impressed on the mind by suitable exercises, is the best means of teaching the pupil how to analyze the involved complex sentences which will frequently occur in the course of his reading. No pupil certainly can acquire a good Latin style without reading both much and well : and no pupil can learn a language completely without a careful analysis of good authors. But as one end of learning the Greek and Latin languages is to enable a boy to read with tolerable facility and as soon as possible, the books written in those languages, the question thus limited is,—how may this end be best accomplished? In the opinion of the writer of this article, a boy will best attain the power of reading Latin and Greek authors with pleasure and advantage, by going through a systematic course of exercise-writing from the time that he commences the study of the language till the time when he can construct sentences, both simple and complex, of all forms that occur in the best writers. While going through this course of exercises, he must certainly read Latin and Greek authors with great care, and must be continually applying what he has learned to the analysis of sentences in these authors, and at the same must be increasing his stock of words and his facility in the use of them : but we think that the quantity read during the early stage of his instruction in either language should not be much. He may read as much as he can, or as much as his own time and that of his teacher will allow, when there is a certainty that he has fully mastered the principles, without which no language can be successfully studied. The logical connexion of ideas depends on general principles, which principles we should propose to make the basis of the scientific study of all languages.*

* Compare the superior manner in which Bekker has handled the syntax of his German Grammar, with that of Matthiæ in his Greek Grammar, vol. ii.

ON THE ELEMENTS OF ARITHMETIC.

By the methods ordinarily used in teaching numeration, the pupils seldom acquire anything approaching to a correct idea of the value of figures. This remark may be attested by examining the children of any of the common schools, public or private. On visiting one of the schools for the poor, in an enlightened provincial town, one of the head-boys was found to be engaged in arithmetic. This boy was desired to write down the value of a short row of figures 26316, which he expressed correctly. On being asked what number was represented by the second figure, he replied *one ;* the third? *three ;* the fourth? *six ;* the fifth? *two.* When required to put down the value of the second figure on another part of his slate, he wrote 1 ; the third, he wrote 3 ; the fourth, he wrote 6 ; the fifth, he wrote 2. The experiment having been repeated at various schools, and with a similar result to the one now mentioned, leads to the supposition that it is a common error ; and it is undoubtedly one which a little attenton would correct. A teacher of long practice recommends the following method, as one which has never failed in producing a clear idea, even in a young pupil's mind, of the value which figures acquire from their situation. After having given a correct notion of the cardinal numbers as high as 100, by beads, pins, peas, marbles, or by other objects (during which time the pupils learn to express the numbers on their slates, both by writing and by figures), a course of analytical exercises is commenced, which is found so satisfactory that it may be recommended with confidence. Though there is nothing new in the principle, yet as it is not generally practised, it is presumed that it may not be generally known. A number of figures being placed before the class, 26316 for example, are analyzed individually, as follows :—

$$6$$
$$10$$
$$300$$
$$6,000$$
$$20,000$$

As each figure is separately written down, a pupil writes, to the right of it, its value. The appearance of the example is then, as given below :—

6	six
10	ten
300	three hundred
6,000	six thousand
20,000	twenty thousand.

The example may next be presented to the pupils in another shape, beginning with the highest number instead of the lowest, thus :—

20,000 twenty ~~thousand~~
6,000 six thousand
300 three hundred and
10 ten ⎫
6 six ⎭ sixteen.

This being done, the pen is drawn through any superfluous words as above, the sentence is made complete, and the figures are written in one line, with their value in words. It is a good practice to cover the analysis in figures, leaving the words only visible, when it is wished that the whole may be expressed in one line of figures ; and the reverse, to cover the words, &c. A longer example will perhaps more fully elucidate the mode :—

560,043,007
———

500,000,000 five hundred ~~millions~~ and
60,000,000 sixty millions
0,000,000
000,000
40,000 forty ~~thousand~~
3,000 three thousand and
000
00
7 seven

Five hundred and sixty millions, ⎫ 560,043,007
forty-three thousand and seven. ⎭

Much time is finally saved by this method of numeration, by the satisfactory knowledge which is imparted of the value which figures acquire from their situation.

A black board, four or five feet square, or a slate of the same size, to be written upon with chalk, is a valuable help in teaching various subjects. If the characters written upon it are large, they will be seen by the class to be taught, or by the whole school, at a considerable distance. Such a tablet serves to receive examples or lessons for the pupils, as well as to exhibit diagrams and other needful explanations. It should incline upon a firm easel with four legs, or be used in any other way that is convenient and cheap.

The system of analysis ought not to end with numeration. In addition, we find school-boys, not only adding up tens, hundreds, thousands, &c., as if they were units, but also considering them as such. First impressions, in teaching, are certainly lasting ones. The first examples, then, on any subject to be taught, should be well considered, and conveyed to the pupils with great care and precision. These tend more to the correct development of such subjects than future examples, though future ones may be more intricate. After learning to add units, in which the bead-table, or other objects will be found very serviceable; an example similar to the following may be given, and explained in the manner which will be described :—

$$
\begin{array}{r}
5347 \\
6673 \\
8297 \\
6054 \\
8868 \\
\hline
\end{array}
$$

The unit line being added up is found to amount to twenty-nine;—nine is the unit, to be placed under the unit column. The twenty is to be added to the tens. Twenty and sixty are eighty, and fifty are one hundred and thirty, &c. The tens column amounts to three hundred and thirty. The thirty is to be placed under the tens column, and three hundred to be carried to the hundreds column. The pupil will now understand that the figure *three* in the tens line represents thirty. Proceeding with the next column, we say three hundred and eight hundred are eleven hundred, or one thousand one hundred, &c. The whole line amounting to two thousand two hundred. The digit representing two hundred is to be placed under the hundreds line, and the two thousand to be carried to the thousands line, &c. After some examples of this kind have been gone through under the eye of the teacher, the pupil may be left to pursue the usual method, *naming the figures as if they were units;* but it must be explained to him, and kept constantly in his mind, that though in thus adding he does not call the numbers tens, hundreds, thousands, &c., yet that such value is to be implied and understood.

We hope not to be deemed mere fault-finders, if we allude here to the absurd practice which frequently obtains in schools, of not allowing the pupils to count their fingers in the common operations of arithmetic. This is the intelligent and rational mode which naturally presents itself to the beginner. While pupils are thus practising they are making themselves acquainted with the powers and combinations of numbers. Let the practice then be encouraged, even extensively. It would be little less than miraculous, if a child could tell, without some such process, that 8 added to 4 makes 12; that 4 subtracted from 12 leaves 8; or that four fours are equal to sixteen.

Subtraction is always a difficult operation with young arithmeticians. So long as the examples are confined to simply taking a less number from a greater they are aware of the principle, and with the knowledge they have acquired of the nature of numbers, in the preceding rule, they will commonly give correct answers if allowed time, and their own way of arriving at the result. But when they have to *borrow* and *pay again*, the operation becomes mysterious, and above the comprehension of the generality of pupils. By dint of continual and persevering· practice, and by hard labour, both of pupils and teacher, the former will at length learn to go mechanically through the examples set before them ; but they will generally know nothing of the principle on which the borrowing and returning is founded *. The ordinary method of teaching subtraction has been very successfully superseded by a practice now to be detailed; we give the following example :—

$$7430746$$
$$2379627$$

We say to the pupil, as we cannot take seven from six, we will take ten from the forty : this ten added to the six will make sixteen, and of the forty only thirty will be left, or, in other words, instead of calling the two last figures in the upper line, forty-six, call them now thirty and sixteen; take seven from sixteen and nine remain. Set down the nine, &c. Remember that as we have taken ten from the second figure, it is only thirty ; take twenty from thirty, and ten remain. Set

---

* We are indebted to a friend for the following note :—'The writer of this note has found from experience that these difficulties are most readily overcome by making the examples in the early stages relate to sums of money. Thus, a man had 27*l*. 12*s*. 8*d*. in his possession, and was called upon to pay 19*l*. 15*s*. 4¼*d*., what would he have left when he had paid the debt ? The sum 27*l*. 12*s*. 8*d*. should be described as consisting of two notes (10*l*. each), seven sovereigns, one half-sovereign, two shillings, and eight pence. If the sum can be actually exhibited in that state, so much the better. It is further necessary to suppose, that the means of changing any of the pieces of money are at hand, or, what is better, let change be actually exhibited. As a matter of convenience to the present purpose, the operation begins with the lowest pieces of money. The man has first to pay the ¼*d*. The pupil will perceive that this requires that one penny must be exchanged for four farthings; and here it should be pointed out to him that the quantity of money is as yet unaltered, 7*d*. and ¼*d*. being worth just as much as 8*d*. When the man has paid ¼*d*., he will have ¾*d*. left; he next pays the 4*d*. out of the 7*d*. and has 3*d*. left. To pay the 15*s*., a sovereign must be taken from the 7 sovereigns, and exchanged for 20*s*., which being added to the 12*s*. makes 32*s*. (leaving 6 sovereigns), and 15*s*. being paid from 32*s*. leaves 17*s*. To pay the 9 sovereigns, one of the ten pound notes must be taken from the two, and exchanged for 10 sovereigns, which added to the 6 sovereigns make 16 sovereigns, and after paying 9 of them there are 7 left. One ten pounds is to be paid, and there is one note to pay it with. The money, therefore, which the man retains, is 7*l*. 17*s*. 3¾*d*. This process, though long in description, is simple in practice ; and that it is much better understood than one in which abstract numbers are used, is a matter of experience to the writer.'

down the ten. Take six hundred from seven hundred, and one hundred remains. Set down the one hundred. In the next operation, we cannot take nine thousand from nothing, we will therefore take ten thousand from the thirty thousand; take nine thousand from ten thousand, and one thousand remains. Set down the one thousand. The thirty thousand is reduced to twenty thousand by our having taken ten thousand from it. Now, we cannot take seventy thousand from twenty thousand, we will therefore take one hundred thousand from the four hundred thousand, which will make one hundred and twenty thousand, from which we have to take seventy thousand. This leaves us fifty thousand, which is to be set down. The four hundred thousand is now only three hundred thousand, from which if we take three hundred thousand nothing remains. Set down a cipher. The next number to be subtracted from is seven millions, from which we take two millions, and five millions remain.*

Few pupils will fail to understand these operations, especially if every new subtraction is illustrated before them by the digits on the black board. They are supposed to have become familiarized with the right names of the numbers from their having been taught numeration in the manner suggested at the commencement of this paper. The operation of each subtraction will appear on the board, or on the pupil's slate in some such form as the following; each result being conveyed to its own place in the example as it is produced:—

---

* In explaining the operation of subtraction, we have, at the suggestion of a friend, not used the word *borrow*, which he considers, and we believe correctly, to be the source of much confusion to learners of subtraction.

$$\begin{array}{ccccccc} 7 & 4 & 3 & 0 & 7 & 4 & 6 \\ 2 & 3 & 7 & 9 & 6 & 2 & 7 \end{array}$$

5 | 0 | 5 | 1 | 1 | 1 | 9

16
7
—
9
=

30
20
—
10
=

700
600
—
100
=

10,000
9,000
—
1,000
=

120,000
70,000
—
50,000
=

300,000
300,000
—
000,000
=

7,000,000
2,000,000
—
5,000,000
=

In teaching the multiplication table, the practice of saying or singing it, as in infants' and other schools (some of the British schools, for example,) is bad. Every method by which thought is rendered unnecessary ought to be avoided. Rote-learning tends not at all to the development of the reasoning faculties, but rather to stultify and oppress them; and though we would not pretend to say that there is any one way which is better than all others for teaching any one thing, we would condemn learning by rote as the worst of all methods ever practised under the name of instruction, in training up a rational being. Modes of conveying knowledge must be varied according to the disposition and the intellect of the pupil. The first lessons in multiplication should doubtless be given upon the bead-table, or with other portable objects. Two-twos, five-sixes, three-tens, &c., should all be shown by objects, so long as there is any reason to suppose that the pupil continues to be unacquainted with the principles of the process of multiplication. Similar examples may then be shown by the digits on the slate, or on the black tablet before mentioned, beginning with,

$$\left.\begin{array}{l}1\\1\end{array}\right\} 2 \times 1 = 2$$
$$\overline{2}$$

which should be continued to $9 \times 1 = 9$, and proceeded with to,

$$\left.\begin{array}{l}12\\12\end{array}\right\} 2 \times 12 = 24$$
$$\overline{24}$$

and so on to $12 \times 12 = 144$, and as much further as may be thought advisable. Should the example proposed be 7×17, it may be shown as follows :—

$$7 \times 17 = \begin{array}{l} 7 \times 7 = 49 \\ 7 \times 10 = 70 \end{array} \qquad \left\{\begin{array}{l}17\\17\\17\\17\\17\\17\\17\end{array}\right.$$

$$119 = \qquad \begin{array}{r} 17 \\ 7 \\ \hline 119 \\ \cancel{4} \end{array}$$

If it be thought necessary, the seven-sevens above may be shown separately, by addition, to produce 49, and in the same way, the seven-tens to produce 70. We will now take a single example in long multiplication, in which the necessary reasoning is shown in so clear and obvious a manner, as to speak at once to the mind and the eyes of the pupil. Its superior claim to attention over the ordinary method of drilling children into such combined operations, will at once recommend it to notice, and we hope to adoption. Example, $4239 \times 5064 = ?$

$$4239 \times 5064 = \begin{cases} 9 \times 5064 = & 45576 \\ 30 \times 5064 = & 151920 \\ 200 \times 5064 = & 1012800 \\ 4000 \times 5064 = & 20256000 \end{cases}$$

$$4239 \times 5064 = 21466296$$

$$
\begin{array}{r}
5064 \\
4239 \\
\hline
45576 \\
151920 \\
1012800 \\
20256000 \\
\hline
21466296
\end{array}
$$

In teaching division, details similar to those already recommended in multiplication should be exhibited before the pupil, for example :

$$2684 \div 4$$

$$
\begin{array}{l}
2000 \div 4 = 500 \\
600 \div 4 = 150 \\
80 \div 4 = 20 \\
4 \div 4 = 1 \\
\hline
2684 \div 4 = 671
\end{array}
\qquad
\begin{array}{l}
4 \mid 2684 \\
\hline
\quad 671 \\
\hline
\quad 20
\end{array}
$$

A similar process may easily be applied to the teaching of long division, as it is called, which is one of the great difficulties to students in arithmetic.

$$21466296 \div 5064$$

$$
\begin{array}{ll}
21466296 & \\
20256000 & = 4000 \times 5064 \\
\hline
1210296 & \\
1012800 & = 200 \times 5064 \\
\hline
197496 & \\
151920 & = 30 \times 5064 \\
\hline
45576 & \\
45576 & = 9 \times 5064 \\
\hline
\end{array}
$$

It will be clearly seen from the course recommended in various parts of this paper, that even the simple example in division should not be attempted till more palpable methods have been first taken to explain the elements; thus 2 is contained in 2, once; in 3, once, and one over; in 4, twice, and so on :—the teacher not only proving these examples by reference to objects, but also requiring a variety of mental calculations from the pupils.   It is perhaps unnecessary to lengthen this article: the writer has endeavoured to illustrate some modes in which numbers may be analysed with much advantage to pupils; under a judicious course of instruction children may be made aware that arithmetical operations are dependent on principles which, if correctly developed, must produce interesting and correct results.

ON THE DISCIPLINE OF PUBLIC SCHOOLS.*

To the Editor of the Journal of Education.

Sir,
      As the sentiments contained in this Article will differ materially from those which have appeared from time to time in your Journal, it appears to me most proper to address them to you as coming from a correspondent; and therefore, as in no way pledging you to agree with them, you will not perhaps object to receive my views on a very important subject connected with education, although they may not agree with your own.

Liberal principles and popular principles are by no means necessarily the same; and it is of importance to be aware of the difference between them. Popular principles are opposed simply to restraint—liberal principles to unjust restraint. Popular principles sympathise with all who are subject to authority, and regard with suspicion all punishments—liberal principles sympathise, on the other hand, with authority, whenever the evil tendencies of human nature are more likely to be shown in disregarding it than in abusing it. Popular principles seem to have but one object—the deliverance of the many from the control of the few.   Liberal principles, while generally favourable to this same object, yet pursue it as a means, not as an end ; and therefore they support the subjection of the many to the few under certain circumstances, when the great end, which they steadily keep in view, is more likely to be promoted by subjection than by independence.   For the great end of liberal principles is

---

* As it is both the professed and real object of this Journal to endeavour to improve education, it is hardly necessary to remark, that both sides of all difficult questions should be examined. The opinions expressed in this communication are not those which have been maintained in this Journal; but, for the reason just stated, it is thought useful to give to them the same publicity that opposite opinions have received through this Journal.

indeed 'the greatest happiness of the greatest number,' if we understand that the happiness of man consists more in his intellectual well-doing than in his physical; and yet more in his moral and religious excellence than in his intellectual.

It must be allowed, however, that the fault of popular principles, as distinguished from liberal, has been greatly provoked by the long-continued prevalence of principles of authority which are no less illiberal. Power has been so constantly perverted that it has come to be generally suspected. Liberty has been so constantly unjustly restrained, that it has been thought impossible that it should ever be indulged too freely. Popular feeling is not quick in observing the change of times and circumstances: it is with difficulty brought to act against a long-standing evil; but, being once set in motion, it is apt to overshoot its mark, and to continue to cry out against an evil long after it has disappeared, and the opposite evil is become most to be dreaded. Something of this excessive recoil of feeling may be observed, I think, in the continued cry against the severity of the penal code, as distinguished from its other defects; and the same disposition is shown in the popular clamour against military flogging, and in the complaints which are often made against the existing system of discipline in our schools.

The points which are attacked in this system are two—flogging and fagging; and we will first consider the question of flogging. We have nothing to do with arguments against the excessive or indiscriminate use of such a punishment: it is but idle to attack what no one defends, and what has at present hardly any real existence. The notion of a schoolmaster being a cruel tyrant, ruling only by the terror of the rod, is about as real as the no less terrific image of Bluebeard. The fault of the old system of flogging at Winchester, alluded to in your last Number, was not its cruelty, but its inefficiency; the punishment was so frequent and so slight as to inspire very little either of terror or of shame. In other schools, eighty or a hundred years ago, there may have been a system of cruel severity, but scarcely, I should imagine, within the memory of any one now alive. But the argument against *all* corporal punishment applies undoubtedly to an existing state of things; and this argument, therefore, I shall proceed to consider.

'Corporal punishment,' it is said, 'is degrading.' I well know of what feeling this is the expression; it originates in that proud notion of personal independence which is neither reasonable nor Christian, but essentially barbarian. It visited Europe in former times with all the curses of the age of chivalry, and is threatening us now with those of Jacobinism. For so it is, that the evils of ultra-aristocracy and ultra-popular principles spring precisely from the same source—namely, from selfish pride—from an idolatry of personal honour and dignity in the aristocratical form of the disease—of personal independence in its modern and popular form. It is simply impatience of inferiority and submission—a feeling which must be more frequently wrong or right, in proportion to the relative situation and worthiness of him who entertains it, but which cannot be always or generally right except in beings infinitely more perfect than man. Impatience of inferiority felt by a child towards his parents, or by a pupil towards his instructors, is merely wrong, because it is at variance with the truth : there exists a real inferiority in the relation, and it is an error, a fault, a corruption of nature, not to acknowledge it.

Punishment, then, inflicted by a parent or a master for the purposes of correction, is in no true sense of the word degrading; nor is it the more degrading for being corporal. To say that corporal punishment is an appeal to personal fear is a mere abuse of terms. In this sense all bodily pain or inconvenience is an appeal to personal fear; and a man should be ashamed to take any pains to avoid the tooth-ache or the gout. Pain is an evil; and the fear of pain, like all other natural feelings, is of a mixed character, sometimes useful and becoming, sometimes wrong and mischievous. I believe that we should not do well to extirpate any of these feelings, but to regulate and check them by cherishing and strengthening such as are purely good. To destroy the fear of pain altogether, even if practicable, would be but a doubtful good, until the better elements of our nature were so perfected as wholly to supersede its use. Perfect love of good is the only thing which can profitably cast out all fear. In the meanwhile, what is the course of true wisdom ? Not to make a boy insensible to bodily pain, but to make him dread moral evil more; so that fear will do its proper and appointed work, without so going beyond it as to become cowardice. It is cowardice to fear pain or danger more than neglect of duty, or than the commission of evil ; but it is useful to fear them, when they are but the accompaniments or the consequences of folly and of faults.

It is very true that the fear of punishment generally (for surely it makes no difference whether it be the fear of the personal pain of flogging, or of the personal inconvenience of what have been proposed as its substitutes, confinement, and a reduced allowance of food,) is not the highest motive of action; and therefore, the course actually followed in education is most agreeable to nature and reason, that the fear of punishment should be appealed to less and less as the moral principle becomes stronger with advancing age. If any one really supposes that young men in the higher forms of public schools are governed by fear, and not by moral motives; that the appeal is not habitually made to the highest and noblest principles and feelings of their nature, he is too little aware of the actual state of those institutions to be properly qualified to speak or write about them.

With regard to the highest forms, indeed, it is well known that corporal punishment is as totally out of the question in the practice of our schools as it is at the universities; and I believe that there could nowhere be found a set of young men amongst whom punishment of any kind was less frequent, or by whom it was less required. The real point to be considered is merely, whether corporal punishment is in all cases unfit to be inflicted on boys under fifteen, or on those who, being older in years, are not proportionably advanced in understanding or in character, who must be ranked in the lower part of the school, and who are little alive to the feeling of self-respect, and little capable of being influenced by moral motives. Now, with regard to young boys, it appears to me positively mischievous to accustom them to consider themselves insulted or degraded by personal correction. The fruits of such a system were well shown in an incident which occurred in Paris during the three days of the revolution of 1830. A boy of twelve years old, who had been forward in insulting the soldiers, was noticed by one of the officers; and though the action was then raging, the officer, considering the age of the boy, merely struck him with the flat part of his sword, as the fit chastisement for boyish impertinence. But the boy had been taught to consider his person sacred, and that a blow was a deadly insult; he therefore followed the officer, and having watched his opportunity, took deliberate aim at him with a pistol, and murdered him. This was the true spirit of the savage, exactly like that of Callum Beg in Waverley, who, when a 'decent gentleman' was going to chastise him with his cane for throwing a quoit at his shins, instantly drew a pistol to vindicate the dignity of his shoulders. We laugh at such a trait in the work of the great novelist, because, according to our notions, the absurdity of Callum Beg's resentment is even more striking than its atrocity. But I doubt whether to the French readers of Waverley it has appeared either laughable or disgusting; at least the similar action of the real Callum in the streets of Paris was noticed at the time as something entitled to our admiration. And yet what can be more mischievous than thus to anticipate in boyhood those feelings which even in manhood are of a most questionable nature, but which, at an earlier period, are wholly and clearly evil ? At an age when it is almost impossible to find a true, manly sense of the degradation of guilt or faults, where is the wisdom of encouraging a fantastic sense of the degradation of personal correction ? What can be more false, or more adverse to the simplicity, sobriety, and humbleness of mind which are the best ornament of youth, and offer the best promise of a noble manhood ? There is an essential inferiority in a boy as compared with a man, which makes an assumption of equality on his part at once ridiculous and wrong ; and where there is no equality, the exercise of superiority implied in personal chastisement cannot in itself be an insult or a degradation.

The total abandonment, then, of corporal punishment for the faults of young boys appears to me not only uncalled for, but absolutely to be deprecated. It is of course most desirable that all punishment should be superseded by the force of moral motives ; and up to a certain point this is practicable. All endeavours so to dispense with flogging are the wisdom and the duty of a schoolmaster; and by these means the amount of corporal punishment inflicted may be, and in fact has been, in more than one instance, reduced to something very inconsiderable. But it is one thing to get rid of punishment by lessening the amount of faults, and another to say, that even if the faults are committed, the punishment ought not to be inflicted. Now it is folly to expect that faults will never occur ; and it is very essential towards impressing on a boy's mind the natural imperfectness and subordination of his condition, that his faults and the state of his character being different from what they are in after life, so the nature of his punishment should be different also, lest by any means he should unite the pride and self-importance of manhood with a boy's moral carelessness and low notions of moral responsibility.

The beau-ideal of school discipline with regard to young boys would appear to be this—that whilst corporal punishment was retained on principle as fitly answering to, and marking the naturally inferior state of, boyhood, morally and intellectually, and therefore as conveying no peculiar degradation to persons in such a state, we should cherish and encourage to the utmost all attempts made by the several boys as individuals to escape from the natural punishment of their age by rising above its naturally low tone of principle. While we told them, that, as being boys, they were not degraded by being punished as boys, we should tell them also, that in proportion as we saw them trying to anticipate their age morally, so we should delight to anticipate it also in our treatment of them personally—that every approach to the steadiness of principle shown in manhood should be considered as giving a claim to the respectability of manhood— that we should be delighted to forget the inferiority of their age, as they laboured to lessen their moral and intellectual inferiority. This would be a discipline truly generous and wise, in one word, truly Christian—making an increase of dignity the certain consequence of increased virtuous effort, but giving no countenance to that barbarian pride which claims the treatment of a freeman and an equal, while it cherishes all the carelessness, the folly, and the low and selfish principle of a slave.

With regard to older boys, indeed, who yet have not attained that rank in the school which exempts them from corporal punishment, the question is one of greater difficulty. In this case the obvious objections to such a punishment are serious; and the truth is, that if a boy above fifteen is of such a character as to require flogging, the essentially trifling nature of school correction is inadequate to the offence. But in fact boys, after a certain age, who cannot keep their proper rank in a school, ought not to be retained at it; and if they do stay, the question becomes only a choice of evils. For the standard of attainment at a large school being necessarily adapted for no more than the average rate of capacity, a boy who, after fifteen, continues to fall below it, is either intellectually incapable of deriving benefit from the system of the place, or morally indisposed to do so, and in either case he ought to be removed from it. And as the growth of the body is often exceedingly vigorous where that of the mind is slow, such boys are at once apt for many kinds of evil, and hard to be governed by moral motives, while they have outgrown the fear of school correction. These are fit subjects for private tuition, where the moral and domestic influences may be exercised upon them more constantly and personally than is compatible with the numbers of a large school. Meanwhile such boys, in fact, often continue to be kept at school by their parents, who would regard it as an inconvenience to be required to withdraw them. Now it is superfluous to say, that in these cases corporal punishment should be avoided wherever it is possible; and perhaps it would be best, if for such grave offences as would fitly call for it in younger boys, older boys whose rank in the school renders them equally subject to it, were at once to be punished by expulsion. As it is, the long-continued use of personal correction as a proper school punishment renders it possible to offer the alternative of flogging to an older boy, without subjecting him to any excessive degradation, and his submission to it marks appropriately the greatness and disgraceful character of his offence, while it establishes, at the same time, the important principle, that as long as a boy remains at school, the respectability and immunities of manhood must be earned by manly conduct and a manly sense of duty.

It seems to me, then, that the complaints commonly brought against our system of school discipline are wrong either in their principle or as to the truth of the fact. The complaint against *all* corporal punishment, as degrading and improper, goes, I think, upon a false and mischievous principle : the complaint against governing boys by fear, and mere authority, without any appeal to their moral feelings, is perfectly just in the abstract, but perfectly inapplicable to the actual state of schools in England. I now proceed to make a few remarks upon another part of the system of public schools, which is even less understood than the subject already considered, I mean the power of fagging.

Now by ' the power of fagging,' I understand a power given by the supreme authorities of a school to the boys of the highest class or classes in it, to be exercised by them over the lower boys for the sake of securing the advantages of regular government amongst the boys themselves, and avoiding the evils of anarchy,—in other words, of the lawless tyranny of physical strength. This is the simple statement of the nature and ends of public school fagging—an institution which, like all other government, has been often abused, and requires to be carefully watched, but which is as indispensable to a multitude of boys living together, as government, in like circumstances, is indispensable to a multitude of men.

I have said that fagging is necessary for a multitude of boys when *living together;* for this will show how the system may be required in the public schools of England, and yet be wholly needless in those of Scotland. The great Scotch schools are day-schools—those of England are boarding-schools. Now the difference between these two systems is enormous. In the Scotch schools the boys *live* at their own homes, and are under the government of their own relations ; they only meet at school for a certain definite object during a certain portion of the day. But in England the boys, for nearly nine months of the year, live with one another in a distinct society ; their school life occupies the whole of their existence; at their studies and at their amusements, by day and by night, they are members of one and the same society, and in closer local neighbourhood with one another than is the case with the ordinary society of grown men. At all those times, then, when Scotch boys are living at home in their respective families, English boys are living together amongst themselves alone; and for this their habitual living they require a government. It is idle to say that the masters form, or can form, this government; it is impossible to have a sufficient number of masters for the purpose; for, in order to obtain the advantages of home government, the boys should be as much divided as they are at their respective homes. There should be no greater number of schoolfellows living under one master than of brothers commonly living under one parent; nay, the number should be less, inasmuch as there is wanting that bond of natural affection which so greatly facilitates domestic government, and gives it its peculiar virtue. Even a father with thirty sons all below the age of manhood, and above childhood, would find it no easy matter to govern them effectually—how much less can a master govern thirty boys, with no natural bond to attach them either to him or to one another? He may indeed superintend their government of one another ; he may govern them through their own governors ; but to govern them immediately, and at the same time effectively, is, I believe, impossible. And hence, if you have a large *boarding*-school, you cannot have it adequately governed without a system of fagging.

Now, a government among the boys themselves being necessary, the actual constitution of public schools places it in the best possible hands. Those to whom the power is committed are not simply the strongest boys, nor the oldest, nor yet the cleverest; they are those who have risen to the highest form in the school—that is to say, they will be probably at once the oldest, and the strongest, and the cleverest ; and further, if the school be well ordered, they will be the most respectable in application and general character— those who have made the best use of the opportunities which the school affords, and are most capable of entering into its objects. In short, they constitute a real aristocracy, a government of the most worthy, their rank itself being an argument of their deserving. And their business is to keep order amongst the boys ; to put a stop to improprieties of conduct, especially to prevent that oppression and ill-usage of the weaker boys by the stronger which is so often ignorantly confounded with a system of fagging. For all these purposes a general authority over the rest of the school is given them; and in some schools they have the power, like the masters, of enforcing this authority by impositions, that is, by setting tasks to be written out or learnt by heart for any misbehaviour. And this authority is exercised over all those boys who are legally subject to it, that is, over all below a certain place in the school, whatever be their age or physical strength; so that many boys who, if there were no regular fagging, would by mere physical force be exercising power over their schoolfellows, although from their idleness, ignorance, and low principle they might be most unfit to do so, are now not only hindered from tyrannizing over others, but are themselves subject to authority—a most wholesome example, and one particularly needed at school, that mere physical strength, even amongst boys, is not to enjoy an ascendancy. Meanwhile this governing part of the school, thus invested with great responsibility, treated by the masters with great confidence and consideration, and being constantly in direct communication with the head master, and receiving their instruction almost exclusively from him, learn to feel a corresponding self-respect in the best sense of the term; they look upon themselves as answerable for the character of the school, and by the natural effect of their position acquire a manliness of mind and habits of conduct infinitely superior, generally speaking, to those of young men of the same age who have not enjoyed the same advantages.

What becomes then of those terrible stories of cruelty which inspire so many parents with horror at the very name of fagging; or what shall we say of that very representation of the fagging at Winchester, which appeared in the last Number of your Journal? It is confessed, indeed, in a subsequent page of that Number, that your correspondent's representation is not applicable to the present state of Winchester. Would it not then have been fairer to have inserted in the running title of the article, ‘Flogging and Fagging at Winchester,’ the words, ‘ as formerly practised ?’ But, indeed, even as describing a past state of things, there is surely some confusion in the statement. It is important to distinguish such acts of oppression as belong properly to the system of fagging, from such as arise merely from superior physical force, and consequently exist as much, I believe a thousand times more, in those schools where there is no legal fagging. For instance, your correspondent complains of the tyranny practised at Winchester at bed-time, ‘ tossing in the blanket, tying toes, bolstering, &c.' These, indeed, are most odious practices, but what have they to do with fagging? I have known them to exist at private schools, where there was no fagging, to a degree of intolerable cruelty. In college, at Winchester, where there were two or three præfects in every chamber, I scarcely remember them to have been practised at all during the period of which I can speak from my own experience. And this is natural; for the boys who delight in this petty tyranny are very rarely to be found amongst the oldest in a school, and still less amongst those who have raised themselves to the highest rank in it: they are either middle-aged boys, from fourteen to sixteen, or such older boys as never distinguish themselves for any good, and who, never rising high in the school, are by a system of fagging, and by that only, restrained from abusing their size and strength in tyranny. Other abuses which your correspondent mentions, such as toasting, lighting fires, &c., arise so far from a system of fagging, that this system, when ill-regulated, allows a certain well-defined class of boys to exact services which otherwise would be exacted merely by the strongest. But I said, what every one must be aware of, that the government of boys, like every other government, requires to be watched, or it will surely be guilty of abuses. Those menial offices which were exacted from the juniors at Winchester were only required of them because the attendance of servants was so exceedingly insufficient, and the accommodations of the boys in many particulars so greatly neglected. If you do not provide servants to clean the boys' shoes, to supply them with water of a morning, or to wait on them at their meals, undoubtedly the more powerful among them, whether the power be natural or artificial, will get these things done for them by the weaker; but supply the proper attendance, and all this ceases immediately. There will remain many miscellaneous services, such as watching for balls at cricket or fives, carrying messages, &c., which servants undoubtedly cannot be expected always to perform, and which yet belong to that general authority vested in the boys of the highest form. They belong to that general authority, and are therefore now claimed as rightfully due; but if there were no such authority, they would be claimed by the stronger from the weaker. For I assume it as a certain fact, that if you have two or three hundred boys living with one another as a distinct society, there will be some to command, as in all other societies, and others to obey: the only difference is, that the present system first of all puts the power into the best hands; and, secondly, by recognizing it as legal, is far better able to limit its exercise and to prevent its abuses, than it could be if the whole were a mere irregular dominion of the stronger over the weaker.

There is another thing, which to those who are acquainted with schools, will seem of no small importance. Leave a number of boys together as legally equal, and the irregular tyranny exercised under these circumstances by every stronger boy over every weaker one, has so far the sanction of the public opinion of the school, that any individual sufferer would be utterly afraid to complain of his ill usage to the master. But give one class a legal superiority over the rest, and an abuse of power on their part is no longer received with sympathy ; and the boy who were to complain of it to the master, instead of being hated as an informer, would rather be regarded by the mass of his companions as an asserter of their common liberties. Now to those who consider the difficulty of getting boys to complain of ill usage where public opinion condemns the complaining, it will appear an immense security against oppression, that it may be denounced without incurring general odium ; and such I fear is the Jacobinical spirit of human nature, that this can never be the case unless the oppression proceed from one invested with *legal* authority.

For my own part, however, I am not one of those who think it an evil that younger or less manly boys should be subject legally to those more advanced in age and in character. Such subjection is not degrading, for it is rendered not to an arbitrary, but to a real superiority ; it is shown to a power exercised in the main not for its own good, but for that of the society as a whole. Neither do I regard it as oppressive ; for the degree and kind of obedience enforced under a well-regulated system of fagging is beneficial to those who pay it. A strict system is not therefore a cruel one ; and the discipline to which boys are thus subjected, and the quickness, handiness, thoughtfulness, and punctuality, which they learn from some of the services required of them, are no despicable part of education. Many a man who went from Winchester to serve in the Peninsula in the course of the last war must have found his school experience and habits no bad preparation for the activity and hardships of a campaign ; not only in the mere power of endurance, but in the helpfulness and independence which his training as a junior had given him. When your correspondent talks of the servility encouraged by the system of fagging, and gravely imputes to this cause what he calls the characteristic servility of English gentlemen, the cause appears to me as wrongly assigned as I think the supposed result imaginary.

The real servility which exists in England, whether amongst men or boys, is not an excessive deference for legal authority, but a surrender of individual judgment and conscience to the tyranny of public opinion. This tyranny exists in schools to a fatal degree; but it is not exercised chiefly by those who have the power of fagging, and far less in virtue of that power; on the contrary, the boys of the highest form are the only corrective of it, and so far as they contribute to it, it is not owing to the power which distinguishes them from the other boys, but to that imperfection of age and judgment which, to a certain degree, they share in common with them. Great, indeed, is this evil; but it is one arising almost inevitably from the circumstances of a *boarding*-school, namely, that it is a society wholly composed of persons whose state, morally and intellectually, is, by reason of their age, exceedingly imperfect.

It is this which renders it so difficult to make a large school a place of Christian education. For while, on the one hand, the boys stand to their masters in the relation of pupils to a teacher, they form, on the other hand, a complete society amongst themselves; and the individual boys, while influenced by him in the one relation, are unhappily in the other more influenced by that whole of which they are members, and which affects them in a much larger portion of their lives. And how can this influence be of a Christian character, when the perfect impression of Christianity cannot possibly be received by any society which is not in the highest state of advancement? by all others it is either taken incorrectly, or repelled altogether : they can but exhibit that mixture of superstition and profaneness which characterized the semi-barbarous societies of the middle ages; a mixture as unfavourable to the development of man's highest excellence, as Christianity purely imbibed is favourable to it, and indispensable.

The stress of this remark, however, applies to a *society* in a low moral state, and not to an individual. Boys in their own families, as members of the natural and wholesome society of their father's household, may receive its lessons, and catch its spirit, and learn at a very early age to estimate right and wrong truly. But a society formed exclusively of boys, that is, of elements each separately weak and imperfect, becomes more than an aggregate of their several defects : the amount of evil in the mass is more than the sum of the evil in the individuals; it is aggravated in its character, while the amount of good, on the contrary, is less in the mass than in the individuals, and its effect greatly weakened.

Now this being the case, and the very fact of a *boarding-school* involving the existence of such an unfavourable state of society, he who wishes really to improve public education would do well to direct his attention to this point; and to consider how there can be infused into a society of boys such elements as, without being too dissimilar to coalesce thoroughly with the rest, shall yet be so superior as to raise the character of the whole. It would be absurd to say that any school has as yet fully solved this problem. I am convinced, however, that in the peculiar relation of the highest form to the rest of the boys, such as it exists in our great public schools, there is to be found the best means of answering it. This relation requires in many respects to be improved in its character; some of its features should be softened, others elevated : but here and here only is the engine which can effect the end desired ; and if *boarding-schools* are to be cleared of their most besetting faults and raised in all that is excellent, it must be done by a judicious improvement; but most assuredly not by the abolition of the system of authorized fagging.

I have the honour to be, Sir,

Your obedient servant,

A WYKEHAMIST.

January 22nd, 1835.

A TREATISE ON ALGEBRA. (No. II.)

A Treatise on Algebra. By George Peacock, M.A., F.R.S., &c., &c., Fellow and Tutor of Trinity College, Cambridge. Deighton, 1830.

In our last Number on this subject we gave some idea of the extensions by which the part of algebra hitherto called *impossible* has been (since the year 1805) shown by several writers to be capable of a general interpretation, on the same principle of extension by which the results of numerical arithmetic were made to assume a wider form, in the doctrine of positive and negative quantities. We left off at this question: How far is it practicable, or desirable, to introduce these extensions into elementary treatises written for beginners? By a beginner in algebra, we cannot agree to mean less than a young person who has studied arithmetic, both in principle and practice—to whom numbers and demonstration connected with numbers are both familiar. We should very much like to add logic in its most exact form; an easier science than algebra, and which, come by it how he may, the student must have in one sense, before he can ever become a mathematician. We mean that he must have certain perceptions with regard to proper use of terms, which, if not derived from actual examination of verbal arguments, he will have to learn at a much greater expense of time. See this Journal, vol. VI., page 238.

The desirableness of introducing the considerations of the last article depends entirely upon their utility. The latter, considering them as a mere addition to the *mechanism* of algebra, is not much (as yet). It is true that they suggest analogies of great beauty, and accustom the student to take views which cannot but make his inventive faculty more active; but this is incidental. It is the *reasoning* of algebra, considered as a pure science, which is improved by the considerations suggested. In whatever proportion then the benefit of mathematical studies is derived from the formation of deductive power, and in whatever proportion algebra is thus purified, the ratio compounded of those two ratios, to speak mathematically, will be the proportion of the whole benefit of mathematics, which the student may acquire by the considerations discussed in the last article. If there be a person who cares little for the applications of the pure sciences, and much for their methods, he will consider the introduction alluded to as materially increasing their value; if there be another who treats mathematics only as a proper instrument for obtaining and expressing physical truths, he will care but little for it. As a matter of education, we view mathematics almost entirely in the first-mentioned light, and we accordingly rate the extensions very high.

If arithmetic and pure arithmetical algebra could be well learnt together, there would be little difficulty in introducing the extensions afterwards, from any complexity of operations which they would require; but much embarrassment would arise from the new habit of mind required, namely, that of abandoning part of the definition of well-known terms, so as to extend their meaning, and of considering what previously established propositions remain true after the extension, and the contrary. Here is a dilemma: if the extensions be taught too soon, the student is not sufficiently familiar with the primitive meaning to make the change properly striking, or to enable him properly to distinguish between *arbitrary alteration* and *extension ;* if too late, the power which is to be formed is opposed by the fixed character which the signs have acquired in the mind. There will be too large a measure of reform, and the newly-enfranchised symbols will be apt to run riot. We can carry our simile still farther: to prevent excessive extension at a future time, we should propose ' bit-by-bit' modifications, as the demand arises. We suppose a student to have learnt arithmetic with a small portion of arithmetical algebra ; we should then immediately introduce him to those parts of the latter which do not require such complex operations as actual division by polynomials, or extraction of the square root. This is simply for convenience ; for the extensions, when they come to be explained, materially simplify and unite the various cases into which one process must otherwise be parcelled out. We have met with no writer on *arithmetical* algebra who completely dispensed with the appearance of an isolated negative sign, and, up to the time when this should be explained, we consider such a phenomenon as inadmissible.

Our method would be therefore to wait for every extension until the period when it becomes necessary, that is, until some result of arithmetical algebra appears, which is not explicable on arithmetical principles. Such results may be made to arrive as soon as a student is able to solve an equation of the first degree, and to deduce it from a problem. For it will very soon appear that problems looking rational enough, present results which are not arithmetical. It is evident also that if a problem which is not possible to be solved, be tried by just reasoning, one of two things must be true : either there is in the problem a *compensation of errors*, by which the effect of one error overturns that of another ; or the result must appear in some form which indicates an error. The first case has never been sufficiently considered, in our opinion ; it has been too much the practice to look upon a rational result as evidence of a rational process, which is neither necessary, nor as it happens, true. The extensions afterwards dictated by convenience may arise of themselves in every process where a general symbol is used ; and it is not the least of the arguments in favour of the extensions, that without them every process must be examined by its result, and verified by it. That is, the reasoning is not good until it has been shown to be so by using a result which depends for its validity upon that very reasoning. Suppose, for instance, a problem produced the equation

$$x - \frac{x-7}{2} = 6 \text{ which would give } x = 5$$

the equation then is not arithmetical, that is, in the language of the arithmetical algebraist, it is absurd. How then can the *arithmetician* prove this ? If he offers to make his first step, multiplying both sides by 2, he is reminded that his first step is not admissible, unless x be greater than 7, for what can be meant by multiplying a thing which is not a quantity ? So that when the result proves less than 7, the reasoning by which the result was derived falls, and with it the result. Therefore that result is not applicable. This seems sophistry, but in reality it is not so, because the arithmetician asserts and requires certain limitations according to which the preceding is strictly conducted. We cannot admit his right to say that an equation is absurd, because a result derived from absurd reasoning shows it to be so. The old fallacy of Epimenides* will strike every one as resembling this ; but let it be remembered that if he had said that *every* Cretan lied in *every* assertion he made, the objection would not have been sophistry, but perfectly good reasoning ;† and the original assertion would have been a contradiction in terms ; for no Cretan can *truly* say

* Epimenides said, all the Cretans are liars ; but he was a Cretan, therefore he lied, and the Cretans are not liars, therefore he may be believed, &c., &c., &c., *ad infinitum.* How to settle this we hardly know ; does $1 - 1 + 1 - 1 +$ &c., $= \frac{1}{2}$?

† If the arithmetician asks for a new convention, namely, that when x is less than 7, $x - \dfrac{x-7}{2}$ shall be considered merely as a way of representing $x - \dfrac{x}{2} + \dfrac{7}{2}$, he leaps the fence which separates him from the algebraist. It is true he does not go far from the hedge, but he is not on the side of it at which he intended to keep when he first set out.

that every Cretan always *lies*. The arithmetician makes his assertions in as perfectly general a form.

The student should be introduced both to cases of this kind, and the *less difficult* ones (we maintain them to be such) in which the impossible subtraction ($-a$) appears openly. Call them, if you will, misapprehensions, mistakes, or absurdities, but let them be examined and classified, so that the young practitioner may be well acquainted with all the *mistakes* incident to the equation of the first degree. In most of our elementary works, this is not done ; so that if the student venture out of the 'little collection' (see page 86 of the last Number) he finds -1, $\frac{0}{0}$, $\frac{1}{0}$, and other *êtres de raison*,* to contend with which his weapons are useless.

What we are here proposing is direct appeal to experiment, which we have advocated in laying the first principles of arithmetic and geometry. If there be any who have taught the decimal notation to a child who has never counted by his fingers, they will be the proper persons to do without experiment or experience, that is, the effect upon the mind of a large number of experiments. Care should be taken to remind the learner (of course in plainer language) that his results are only good for the cases he has investigated, and that he is in progress, not to methods, but to such a view of the subject as shall point out on what symbols it will be convenient to establish methods.

Such a plan never can be carried into effect while the present system lasts, for algebra cannot be thus taught by books full of rules, but must become a science of demonstration, in which the care of a tutor is more necessary than in geometry, simply because algebra is a harder science. But if any teachers will not take the trouble to teach algebra, they should at least return to arithmetical algebra in its simplest form, which, however defective, is a great deal better than ' + means addition, − subtraction ; subtract + a from − b.'

After the classification above described, the student may be put upon a new sort of operation, namely, a trial of the arithmetical absurdities which he has been led to discover, by the rules to which they would have been subject, had they admitted of being reasoned on as quantities : and this, not to produce trustworthy results, but to see what the consequences of using the symbols above named may be. By comparing the results of irrational processes, with those which arise from proceeding correctly from the beginning, the two following principles will appear, that is to say, on *experimental* evidence.

* A curious use of language found in French writers, meaning results of pure reasoning, as distinguished from *sensible* quantities. These symbols being properly considered, the phrase is a very good one.

1. That each of the absurd forms is the result of one particular class of misapprehensions, and of that only: for instance, — *a* springs from some quantity having been estimated in a wrong direction, $\frac{a}{0}$ from attempting to find a quantity from data which afford no criterion of distinction between one number and another, and so on. This is a remarkable difference between the *mistakes* (as we have called them) in question, and other mistakes. That 5 is wrong, is no evidence that 6, 7, or 8 is right; but $3 - 7$ is evidence that $7 - 3$ is correct, or would have been correct if the original conditions had not been misunderstood.

2. That certain simple rules, not differing from those which really apply to quantities, may be made to furnish corrections of the incorrect process in every stage of the whole. Or that a process known to be incorrect may be extended further, and corrected by the same rules at any subsequent stage of the process.

This is the point to which the student should be brought, in our opinion, before he is really introduced to any algebra, except universal arithmetic. That mistakes and absurdities should thus admit of being marshalled under simple laws, where it is said that truth is single, and error manifold, will hardly be believed by man or boy, and both would feel the absolute necessity of discovering some further relation. The primary reason of the errors is this. Operations are represented requiring limitations which they do not express. Thus $a + b$ is always a quantity, but $a - b$ is not a quantity, unless a is greater than b. But $a - b$ does not carry this limitation with it, which consequently is liable not to be attended to. The object is then to get rid of the limitation, which cannot be done without giving $a - b$ a universal meaning. On looking still further it is seen that a and b have in reality limitations, which being generally expressed escape notice. They do not carry their full meaning with them, for whatever *quantities* they may express, they do not express in what sense those quantities are to be taken, in what direction they are to be measured, and so on. The steps by which we are now led to the independent use of $+ a$ and $- a$ are in most works on the subject.

We now come to the book we have undertaken to review. It may not be known to every reader, that the author of this work is the gentleman to whom the University of Cambridge is in great part indebted[*] for the introduction of the continental mathematics. He took a share in the translation of Lacroix, which made them accessible, in the collection of examples which showed their practical superiority, and finally,

[*] In conjunction with Messrs. Herschel and Babbage.

took upon himself solely the responsibility of introducing them into the University examinations, during his year of moderatorship. How the innovation succeeded, and finally banished its predecessor almost from the historical reading of the student, is sufficiently well known. We mention these facts, because they give Mr. Peacock a claim to be listened to with attention, when he proposes any alteration or modification of the course of mathematical study, on the simple rule, that the forwarder of one good measure is very likely to be that of another. We may add also that the universal information which he has shown himself to possess upon what is actually doing, and has been done in analysis*, is precisely the sort of qualification which ought to be possessed by the proposer of an extension. We have elsewhere observed, that the self-taught usually fail in innovations connected with symbols ; we believe also that it is to those who have read most of the works of others to whom we must look for successful amalgamation of any new principle of algebraical language with those which have preceded.

We shall consider this work in three lights :—firstly, as connected with the elementary student ;—secondly, as connected with the more advanced student ;—thirdly, as an exposition of a novel view of algebra for the opinion of the mathematician.

It is but natural to suppose that Mr. Peacock would not have written for the mere beginner, considering what species of views he intended to develop. The Cambridge student about to enter on his career of competition for mathematical honours must have been the person to whom this work was particularly addressed, both from its size, price, and matter. By describing therefore this species of raw material, we have a ready method of letting any student know whether he is in a state to receive an addition of value from the process implied in reading our author's work.

Those among the students who *come up* (as the phrase is) with all the advantages of a previous education, specially directed to the attainment of University distinctions, have very frequently a knowledge of mathematics, which, if applied out of the University to some particular department of experimental philosophy, might gain considerable scientific reputation. Nor is this to be wondered at, when we consider that the average age of first residence is perhaps above eighteen†, and that the

---

* See the *Report to the British Association,* &c., cited in our last Number, page 90.

† Those who are intended for the Church frequently begin their course nearer to twenty, so as to obtain the B.A. degree only just in time for ordination. Probably the average age of those intended for other professions is something younger.

two preceding years are most valuable to a resolute student. And we may say that almost all who are intended for the University of Cambridge go there with a larger quantity of mathematical knowledge than is usually acquired by others. Thus, though the lectures commence *ab initio,* both in geometry and algebra, some students are permitted to attend the lectures of the second year; others attend merely to refresh their previous knowledge, and the subjects of the lectures are carried further than could be done in a class of mere beginners, those who find themselves deficient generally having recourse* to private tutors. In the next place, *reading* at Cambridge means *reading and writing.* The circumstance of the examinations consisting of written answers to printed questions, obliges the student to consider nothing as learnt, until he is competent to write the substance of it without the book. Hence he is quite sure of his previous ground, and requires no more from his author than that he should not make more chasms in his reasoning than can be filled up by one who perfectly knows all that precedes. And this constitutes the great difference between the works which are written for University students, or on the same model, and those which are intended for schools : all the Cambridge works are found difficult by other students, except by those who know the secret. It also accounts for the small amount of reference to previous articles, which would be useless to a student who should be (and many are, all more or less) able to write any of the previous part of the work. The Cambridge reading also differs from ordinary school study, in that the student is supposed to acquire facility of application. A great part of the examinations consists in problems which are given by the examiners, and which are not to be found in the books. This makes it even desirable, as far as the Cambridge student is concerned, that the elementary works should not lead him all the way, but should indicate points between which he may be expected to travel for himself. Every such step is a useful exercise ; and the student is very soon made to know (the college examination at the close of his first year will give a broad hint) that, until he becomes capable of original mental exercise, he has no chance of the highest distinctions at least. Consequently, whatever he may think about impossible quantities, he does not permit himself to believe in impossible difficulties : but considers, or should consider, that he *must* conquer whatever any one who knows the public examinations thinks it

---

* We would not be understood as approving of this indiscriminate mixture of students of different degrees of attainment, which is, we believe, now in course of alteration.

expedient to write. And hence it happens, that his progress depends less upon the works he reads, than in other places: for though much of what we have said is applicable to other Universities, we believe that there is no place of education in the world where the system is carried so far as at Cambridge, and certainly no place where original effort is so much the character of education. A better system of mental training for those who can bear it cannot be, in our opinion: that a better plan of making the most of the average student might easily be superadded to it, we have no doubt. But we have here nothing to do except with the facts, which must be borne in mind by every one, reviewer or not, who examines what is called a *high* book at Cambridge, such as the present must be considered to be.

This is all we have to say with regard to the elementary student; we think that any one who has read a little of algebra, say to the binomial theorem and its most usual applications, might read this work, if he determines not to proceed to any part until he has thoroughly mastered what precedes. He might sometimes be required to pay attention to what we have said in page 83 of the last Number.

With regard to the more advanced student, the principal difficulty which will lie in his way appears to us to arise from Mr. Peacock not having carried his own principle as far as he might have done. He properly rejects arithmetic as the foundation of algebra, considering the former science as a particular application, subject to certain limitations of the generality of the symbols. He considers algebraical symbols as representatives of concrete. as well as of abstract *quantity ;* and the meaning of the fundamental operations $+$ and $-$ as determined by the nature of the magnitudes affected by it, expressing to one another only this relation, that the one must be the opposite of the other : if $+ a$ be time *after* $- a$ is time before, or *vice versâ*. He then distinctly ' *assumes* not *proves*' that ' whenever by the incorporation or combination of two symbols two similar signs come together, they are replaced by the single sign $+$; but if the two signs are dissimilar, they are replaced by the single sign $-$.' On tracing the assumptions up to this point, we find,—first, that letters are symbols of quantity; second, the definition of $+$ and $-$ above noticed ; third, that there is an operation to be called *incorporation*, particular cases of which are multiplication and division in arithmetic. But of this operation we have no express definition : the first use of the word occurs in the following sentence (Art. 7) :—' Symbols may be incorporated into each other so as to represent a new quantity of the same or a different kind, as in the operations of *multiplication* and *division.*'

Now surely, as incorporation is not expressly defined, this is the definition of incorporation : namely, that (every symbol being considered as affected by + or −) incorporation is that operation which is expressed as follows, its meaning depending upon the particular application afterwards made : + *a* and + *b* incorporated (thus expressed + *a* × + *b*) is required to have such a meaning as shall be expressible by + *a b*, where the meaning of *a b* depends on the application in question.

But we also hold that the limitations of arithmetic are here not quite shaken off. We contend that all that is generally necessary is the following :—*Whichever* sign it is found convenient to give to the incorporation of + *a* and + *b*, that of − *a* and + *b* must have the other. It is only in arithmetic that + + and − − require +, and − + and + − require −. Take an instance from mechanics : the incorporation of a force and a line will be found to imply the taking of a distinct kind of force, known by the name of a *moment of rotation.* Now that a pulling force on one side of a point and a pulling force on the other produce *opposite* species of rotations round that point, is all that algebra needs to express when applied to mechanics ; either sort of rotation may be denoted by +, if the other be denoted by −. But in applying *arithmetic* to mechanics, this would be highly inconvenient, and that is all. We should consider it advisable to drop the preliminary definition that the symbols represent *quantities*, and the attempt even to make *arithmetical* algebra a prominent accompaniment of the *symbolical* science. For, in effect, the definition of algebra which we should collect from the preface to the work before us is as follows :—Algebra is the science which teaches how to use symbols according to certain fixed rules, and to deduce other rules from the first, in such manner that when any method of interpreting the symbols is found, which is consistent with the first fixed rules, all the deduced rules become truths of the science which suggested the method. And that this is Mr. Peacock's own view (to himself) is evident from the following quotation (Preface, pages x. xi.) :—

' If we should rest satisfied with such assumed rules, for the combinations of symbols and signs by such operations as are perfectly independent of any interpretation of their meaning, or of their relation to each other, we should retain in the results obtained all the symbols which were incorporated, without possessing the power of any further simplification : it is as a first step to effect such further reduction of the results, and in order to define the symbolical relation of pairs of those operations to each other, that we assume the operation denoted by + to be the inverse of that which is denoted by – , and conversely. Under such a form the fundamental operations of algebra are altogether symbolical, and we might proceed to deduce symbolical results and equivalent forms by means of them, without any regard to the principles of any other science; and it would merely require the introduction of some such sign as = in the place of the words *algebraical result of*, or *algebraically equivalent to*, to connect the results obtained with the symbolical representation of the operations which produce them, in order to supersede altogether the use of ordinary language. It is at this point that the essential connexion of algebra and arithmetic may be properly said to commence : for a science of mere signs and symbols must terminate in the consequences of their laws of combination, unless they can be associated by interpretation with real operations upon real magnitudes with specific representations : and it is with a view to such applications of this science that we have considered, even in the assumptions which we have hitherto made, arithmetic or arithmetical algebra as the *science of suggestion :* that is, as the science whose operations and the general consequences of them should serve as guides to the assumptions which become the foundation of symbolical algebra.'

That there is in the mind of every tutor or writer a *science of suggestion* must be indisputable. Usually it is the higher part of the subject in question : what is to follow* suggests what is to come before. Is it only in algebra, as thus stated, that the science of suggestion can possibly accompany the ideas which are suggested? Whether the two should be taught together is matter for grave consideration. The inconvenience is, that the pupil will be apt to confound the two ; so apt, from all we know of that class, that perfect success will be very difficult, if not impossible. The advantage is that the student will be applying his thoughts to investigations which have a prototype in his own ideas, and will not be merely employed in dry symbols arbitrarily put together, much after the manner of one of Milton's daughters reading Greek to her father. Between these arguments we feel it very difficult to form a decided opinion, nor do we feel ourselves able to do so without studying the results obtained by actual experience. The examiners at Cambridge† are the fittest persons to form an opinion on this point : and if we should imagine that rational curiosity would not lead them to put questions on the subject into their papers, we should remind them that a

* We should strongly recommend elementary writers to change *suggestion* into *adaptation*, that is, to write their works from the end to the beginning, instead of *vice versâ*.

† That is, those who examine the *third* and *fourth*, &c. classes in the Senate House, not those of the *first* and *second*.

very remarkable innovation has been proposed in a very matured form by the Senior Tutor of Trinity College, who has
not proceeded after the manner of Professor Woodhouse, by
writing a work for the graduates, to gain its end in ten years;
but has at once appealed to the undergraduate himself, by
taking the field with an elementary work. In this state we
must leave the question as to the Cambridge student; but we
should recommend it to every future writer of the *first* elements
so to model his work, by extending arithmetic in the manner
already described by us, that no student should be incapable
of taking a rational view of a science of pure symbols, the
interpretation of which should be subsequent to the results,
and, in Mr. Peacock's phrase, 'governed' by them.

And we here feel the want of a society to which teachers
might communicate the results of their own observations. It
is a sufficient proof of the little interest which is felt in the
subject, that while hundreds of really cultivated minds, in and
out of the universities, are engaged in the difficult task of instruction, we have no evidence that the advocates of any one
method must in all probability be acquainted with the arguments used by those who prefer another. We are not ignorant
of the great objections which would be held to exist against the
formation of such a society: we can only hope that they will
grow less every year.

We now proceed to the consideration of Mr. Peacock's work
in a purely mathematical point of view, as the exposition of
algebra in its most extended form. Throughout our last
article, we intentionally avoided describing what is peculiar to
this work, that we might put the reader in possession of the
order of investigation which has actually occurred.

The history of the extensions has been given at length by
the author of the work before us in the Report on Analysis
already cited. With this we have nothing to do here, except
with the introduction of the system into Cambridge, as the
latter is connected with the distinction which we must draw
between the work of Mr. Peacock, and that of his predecessor
Mr. Warren, late tutor of Jesus College. The last-named
gentleman published in 1828, under the humble title of 'A
Treatise on the Geometrical Representation of the Square
Roots of Negative Quantities,' a complete view of the extended algebra explained by us in page 94 of the last
Number. This work was executed in a purely synthetical
form, with a degree of exactness and elegance which are not
often equalled by writers who are combining their own ideas
upon a model of their own. Mr. Warren was the first who
combined the various hints which had been given that ' $\sqrt{-1}$

denotes *perpendicularity'* into a connected, demonstrated, logical system, distinguished, as Mr. Peacock justly remarks, ' for great originality and for extreme boldness in the use of definitions.' This work is now a very proper introduction to the new system, for any who may feel metaphysical or other difficulties in that of Mr. Peacock, in this point of view ; that those who may be embarrassed by the connexion of numerical and symbolical algebra will do well to add to the particular view called arithmetic, the geometrical view proposed by Mr. Warren, as they must certainly thereby get rid of the notion of the *necessary* connexion between algebra and abstract number. Mr. Peacock*, admitting that ' it must be allowed that Mr. Warren's conclusions, when viewed in connexion with his definitions, were demonstrably true,' is of opinion that ' the course followed leads almost necessarily to very embarrassing details.' We should make the same charge against himself, while we admitted the truth of his criticism, if we did not remember that both were writing elementary works *quatenus* the new algebra, for students who had some acquaintance with the old. Both have entered largely into special applications for the benefit of the reader, and with judgment : for it is only by turning a subject round and round again that the student can at last find in which way it fits his previous ideas. Had it not been for this we could not have allowed Mr. Warren 150 pages, or Mr. Peacock 700 ; but must have recommended a paper in the Cambridge Transactions for the first, and the 150 pages for the second.

The distinction between the leading ideas of Mr. Warren and Mr. Peacock is this : the first, by laying down such definitions as we have explained in the previous articles, shows that the equivalent forms of his own algebra are the same as those of the common system ; the second, by laying down definitions as we have seen in the first part of this article, which do not receive their determinate meaning until some particular application is contemplated, *shows that the interpretation of* $a + b \sqrt{-1}$ *is a necessary consequence of the relative interpretation of* $+ a$ *and* $- a$, or, in other words, this theorem : if it be admitted that (in geometry for instance)

$$a (\cos \theta + \sqrt{-1} \sin \theta)$$

is, in *any one instance* (or for any one value of θ), the representation of a line a units in length, inclined to an axis at an angle θ, that then it must be admitted that the same symbol is a representation of a similar line for every other value of θ. One obvious instance, to which the student is led in ordinary

* *Report*, &c., p. 229.

algebra, is that where $+ a$ represents a line drawn from a point in one direction, and $- a$ represents the line of the same length drawn in the opposite direction, or inclined at an angle of 180° to the first. But $- a$ and a (cos 180° $+ \sqrt{-1}$ sin 180°) are equivalent; whence the geometrical interpretation of impossible quantities is a consequence of the extension which gives positive and negative quantities.

This is a very great step; indeed it may be said to be the only admissible link between the extended and limited forms of algebra. For, as in common arithmetic, the student is led to the use of $- a$, by proof that the mistake (so long as limitation of definitions requires the use of this term) which produces $- a$ is the measurement of a line in a *diametrically* wrong direction, so it may be shown that the mistake (so long as it is such) which produces $a + b\sqrt{-1}$ is the measurement of a line in a wrong direction, but not in a *diametrically* wrong direction. Keeping more closely to Mr. Peacock's view (rejecting even the notion of quantity, if we please), we should state it as follows. He proves that if θ be m times the nth part of four right angles, and if $+$ and $-$ be considered as of directly opposite significations, then a and a (cos. $\theta + \sqrt{-1}$ sin. θ) have this connexion, that the repetition of the operation signified by cos. $\theta + \sqrt{-1}$ sin. θ upon a, n times in succession, must restore a.

We have throughout kept in view, and Mr. Peacock has done the same, that the rational interpretation of the *general* algebra is not a necessary consequence of its application to any particular case. Thus $- b$ has no meaning in pure arithmetic, or $\sqrt{-b}$ in a question in which concrete duration is made the subject of the symbol (see p. 88 of our last Number) though it is capable of explanation in geometry. Mr. Warren, who has in fact written the application of general algebra to plane geometry, has no need to consider any irrational case, because no such arises. Mr. Peacock seems to contemplate the possibility of rendering interpretation possible in a case of profit or loss, suggested by us in the last Number as not being possible. His words are as follows (p. 367):—

' If a denoted a sum gained by A, $- a$ might denote the same sum lost by A; in this case the affectation of a by $\sqrt{-1}$ would' (suppose we say *might*) ' transfer the gain from A to B: the affectation of $a \sqrt{-1}$ by $\sqrt{-1}$ would' (here would is strictly proper) ' convert the gain of B into a loss by A; the affectation of $- a$ by $\sqrt{-1}$ would transfer the loss from A to B; and the affectation of $- a\sqrt{-1}$

by $\sqrt{-1}$ would again transfer the loss by B to a gain by A; we then obtain a repetition of the same changes,' &c.

Again (p. 668) :—

' If a and b denoted property, and $a + b\sqrt{-1}$ denoted property whose absolute magnitude was $\sqrt{a^2 + b^2}$, but which was so constituted that a portion of it equal to a only belongs to me, or is available to my use, then we should arrive at, and be able to interpret, the results $a + b\sqrt{-1}$ and $a - b\sqrt{-1}$, &c.'

We cannot conceive such a modification ; but we will put the question in another form, as a first step to what is required. Can such an hypothesis be framed with regard to property, that the two extreme cases shall be, that when A gains all, B gains nothing, and that when B gains all, A gains nothing ; but that, in all intermediate cases, that is, where both A and B gain something, the sum of the squares of their gains (in pounds) shall be equal to the square of what either might gain in the extreme case ? If this can be found, the rest will follow by simple extension. But it appears to us that we must wait till the necessity for the supposition forces itself upon us, as it does in geometry and mechanics.

There is one class of readers which has been entirely left out of the question by Mr. Peacock, and still more by Mr. Warren ; namely, consisting of those who have read and are content with the extension of forms without the extension of definitions, which has been the failing of our usual algebraical works. To this class we may add those who, having established the negative sign upon satisfactory principles (which is now frequently done), would wish to see how common algebra, with all its defects, might be made to indicate at least the consistency of the interpretation of impossible quantities with that to which they are accustomed in relation to the negative sign. For these we shall endeavour to show, by common algebra, that the results in question may be attained ; and at the same time to show, that the common forms of algebra are not perfectly consistent without extension. If we admit that $-a$ or $(-1) \times a$ is equivalent to a line of equal length and contrary direction to that indicated by $+a$, we see that, ' multiply a by -1' is equivalent to ' make the line a revolve through 180°.' Hence $\sqrt{-1}\,a$ represents the line a after it has revolved through 90°, for $\sqrt{-1}$ twice introduced as a factor causes 180° of revolution, and therefore each $\sqrt{-1}$ indicates 90° of revolution. Similarly, $\sqrt[n]{-1}$ indicates revolution through the nth part of two right angles, and

$(-1)^{\frac{m}{n}}$ through m times the nth part of two right angles, or $\frac{m}{n}\pi$. That is,

$(-1)^{\frac{m}{n}}a$ is a line a inclined at angle $\frac{m}{n}\pi$ to α.

It only remains to give an analytical expression for $(-1)^{\frac{m}{n}}$, or, which will answer the purpose, for its logarithm, $\frac{m}{n}$ log. (-1). If we assume the universality of the well-known series

$$\text{Log. } x = x - \frac{1}{x} - \frac{1}{2}\left(x^2 - \frac{1}{x^2}\right) + \&c.$$

(which, correctly or not, is always done in common algebra), and substitute -1 for x, we have,

$$\text{Log. } (-1) = -2\left(1 + \frac{1}{3} + \frac{1}{5} + \&c.\right)$$

a useless result, because the analytical equivalent of the second side cannot be determined by ordinary means. But if we also assume the universality of log. $x = 2$ log. $\sqrt{x}$ (which is also commonly done), we find, by substituting $\sqrt{-1}$ instead of x in the above series,

$$\text{Log. } \sqrt{-1} = 2\sqrt{-1}\left(1 - \frac{1}{3} + \frac{1}{5} - \&c.\right) \text{ or } 2\sqrt{-1}\times\frac{\pi}{4}$$

and hence, log. $(-1) = \pi\sqrt{-1}$,

from which, by expanding $(-1)^x$, which gives

$$(-1)^x = 1 + x \text{ log. } (-1) + \frac{x^2 \text{ log.}^2 (-1)}{2} + \&c.$$

Substituting $\pi\sqrt{-1}$ for log. (-1), and making all necessary reductions, we find, by means of the well-known series for sin. x and cos. x,

$$(-1)^x = \cos. \pi x + \sqrt{-1} \sin. \pi x;$$

and calling $\frac{m}{n}$, x, we thus see that $(-1)^x a$, which denotes a line a making an angle πx with a, is analytically equal to

$$a (\cos. \pi x + \sqrt{-1} \sin. \pi x),$$

which latter, therefore, also represents the same line as $(-1)^x a$. We never can rely upon the preceding as any thing more than an indication of results analogous to those which might be expected upon stricter notions of what this process brings us to consider, namely, what Mr. Peacock calls the *principle of the permanence of equivalent forms.*

By this principle we conceive Mr. Peacock to mean that, in extended algebra, the propriety of putting the sign $=$ between two symbolical expressions is not dependent upon the specific values of the expressions, or of the symbols they contain. Throughout the work runs a constant reference to this *principle*, as it is called, and we find the definition in page 104, as follows:—

' Whatever form is algebraically equivalent to another when expressed in general symbols, must be true, whatever those symbols denote.

' Conversely, if we discover an equivalent form in arithmetical algebra, or any other subordinate science, when the symbols are general in form though specific in their nature, the same must be an equivalent form when the symbols are general in their nature as well as in their form.'

Now, we think that we here discover the traces of the method by which the mind of the author was led to the several views which he finally adopted, and that we have some of the loose earth dug out of the foundation, which has been neglected to be cleared away when the building was finished. For it seems to us, that the first part of the principle is that on which all the definitions are built. Their universality, and consequently the universality of the deductions legitimately drawn from them, is made the peculiar character of algebra. On any other supposition, we should hold this principle to be a taking for granted of a nature wholly inadmissible in a pure science. What more does the student of ordinary algebra want, or on what do the ideas depend, which have led Poisson, Cauchy, and others, to reason only on convergent series, except doubts upon the principle of the permanence of equivalent forms? But the difference between Mr. Peacock and the common algebraists is this, that whereas the latter assume the principle without giving their fundamental assumptions the necessary universality of meaning, Mr. Peacock constructs those fundamental assumptions with no other intention than to justify the use of the principle. And in the preface, where an author's last view is generally to be found, he does, cautiously, and with some hesitation, admit what we have said, in the following words (the italics are our own):—

' The principle of the permanence of equivalent forms which appears to me so important in generalizing the results of algebraical operations, *must* derive its authority from the view which I have taken of the principles of algebra and of their connexion with arithmetic considered as a science of suggestion: for, in the first place, *this principle assumes* the operations of algebra and their results as altogether independent of the specific value of the symbols and equivalent forms; as existing *therefore*, whatever values such symbols may *be supposed to possess, so long as they are general in form.*'

We should rather say that the *operations assume the principle.*

The converse of the principle, or the last part of the last quotation but one, amounts to this—that if, in a process of any subordinate science, the limitations which prevent the general application of algebra do not happen to be introduced, the result is also one of general algebra. It may be imitated thus: If in a proposition which, for a particular purpose, is necessary to be established for right-angled triangles, the limitation that the triangles must be right-angled is not found to occur in the demonstration, then that proposition, though only contemplated for its utility as regards right-angled triangles, must be true for all triangles.

What we are afraid of is this; that the *student*, seeing definitions accompanied by a principle, which appears to be used independently, will be led to imagine that the principle is assumed *of* the definitions, instead of *in* the definitions. But we, at the same time, admit, that considering the limited intentions with which the author began the work, as appears from the note to page 80, where it is said that the consideration of cos. $\theta + \sqrt{-1}$ sin. θ ' hardly comes within the compass of this work,' we might have expected to find many little inconsistencies of the same character; which does not appear to us to be the case.

The present work, and that of Mr. Warren, we consider as the most original which have appeared in England, in *pure* mathematics, since the 'Analytical Calculations' of Professor Woodhouse. It is some evidence of the confusion which an attempt to reconcile general theorems with limited definitions might produce, that the very inquisitive as well as learned writer last mentioned, whose book has made more Cambridge men think on first principles than any other, was obliged, in order to keep consistently by arithmetic, to suppose $x + 1$ and $1 + x$ different things, for every purpose of algebraic developement, and in some instances appears to have evaded impossible quantities by using impossible equations. The work of Mr. Peacock is difficult, but logical: the difficulties are in the subject, and arise from the necessity of reasoning upon a part of the meaning of terms, that is, drawing those conclusions which necessarily follow from certain parts of the meaning, without considering in what manner the remainder may limit their truth, until the time comes to apply the conclusions.

This is what we conceive Mr. Peacock expresses by saying, that the results govern the interpretation, though we are not sure that he would here coincide with us. But it is clear that $a - 2a$, as a result of arithmetic, is irrational, being a breach of the limitation required by that science, that in $a - b$, a must be *greater* (an arithmetical relation not considered in algebra) than b; but in geometry, &c. the result does admit of an interpretation, as before stated.

If we were to recommend any alteration, it should be to abandon, in a great measure, the *science of suggestion*, except in the very early part of the work, where the methods of the two should either be placed in double columns, or the application to arithmetic, as we should call it, made a corollary of each theorem. But whether this be done or not, the work before us is one which the student must look forward to reading, if he is really desirous of knowing the meaning of algebraical symbols in their widest sense.

We are not without hope that elementary works on algebra will undergo some modification, with a view to rendering the reading of the present work easier. The higher parts of algebra, and all the applications of pure mathematics, require such a continual knowledge of the metaphysics of algebra, and comparatively so little acquaintance with the details which occupy the half of most of our works, that much time may be saved to the student by giving the first principles in a very different shape. If algebra will be hard, it must be hard; nothing is gained by substituting a science which is only easier, because it substitutes operations of the fingers for those of the head, and calling it algebra.

In thinking over the various matters contained in this work, Mr. Peacock has gradually formed a number of phrases with which he has so familiarized his own mind, that he appears to have forgotten that the ideas of others, which have run in a different channel, will not easily accommodate themselves to his expressions. To speak of symbols as things invented to obey rules, instead of being representations of quantity from the notion of which rules follow, certainly will introduce a very new set of idioms. These produce difficulties which the proficient will avoid by helping himself to the meaning of the terms out of the algebraical context; but the student, who is to be introduced to the latter by help of the former, has no such resource. We mention this, which is more or less the accompaniment of all new expositions, to suggest the possibility of writing a treatise on the use of words in mathematics, and their connexion with symbols. Except perhaps Carnot, we know of no writer who has dwelt upon the meaning of his phrases. But we must perhaps wait until the general use of words, or logic, is considered as a necessary preliminary for mathematical studies: in the meanwhile, we can only assert our opinion, that to a pupil practised in logic, language is a vehicle of instruction as superior in kind to what it is to one not so skilled, as the decimal notation to the rule of finger and thumb, or the English language to the Caribbean.

In closing what we have to say upon this very remarkable work, we may answer the question why it has not been noticed before, seeing that it was published in 1830. The reason of this was, the very great difficulty of forming fixed opinions upon views so new and so extensive. At first sight it appeared to us something like symbols bewitched, and running about the world in search of a meaning. Accustomed as we are to see peremptory decisions written, printed, and published within the space of a few weeks from the appearance of a work which has cost the author years of thought, we yet could not reconcile ourselves to differ from thought accompanied by most extensive reading, without having a little of both on our own side. And as further consideration has induced us to admit the soundness of Mr. Peacock's general views, we think it probable that those who will adopt the same process will come to the same conclusion. We should hold him either more or less than man, who would not be much startled if led from common algebra to the system developed in this work. But ' great originality and extreme boldness in the use of definitions' and symbols are either of them enough to startle; and Mr. Peacock has fairly thrown the *onus* upon any opponent, of producing a better general view, and one more free from difficulties. If this be not done, we foresee the certain adoption of his system as the final resting point of the user of symbols.

EDUCATION IN AMERICA.

American Annals of Education and Instruction. Edited by
William C. Woodbridge. Vols. I., II., and III. Boston, 1833.

This is an American work, published monthly, with the same
general object as the Journal of Education. It is almost the
only publication in the United States exclusively devoted to
the subject of education. Numerous periodicals issue from
the press, in which the views of different parties are advocated
in respect to religious instruction; but these, for the most
part, have a local circulation, as well as a limited object. The
design of Mr. Woodbridge's work is more general. It enters
into the principles of universal education. The object appears
to be, to diffuse a knowledge of improvements, from whatever
quarter they proceed, and to expose errors wherever they are
found, without attaching itself to any exclusive system. To
disseminate what is good, and improve what is bad, in the educational institutions of his country; to ascertain what is their
actual condition in respect to internal and external management; to give publicity to new experiments and improved
methods of instruction ; to collect statistical details connected
with education in different parts of the world, and more particularly in America; to excite and concentrate public efforts
in behalf of schools, and to provide for every town and district
of the Union an efficient system of instruction, are the objects
to which the editor of the Annals has directed his labours, and,
in our opinion, with skill and success. That such labours
should not be adequately remunerated we are not surprised to
learn; but it does excite our astonishment, that a work of
such a nature, conducted with independence and ability, should
be allowed to want support in a country like America, where
the political institutions must owe their permanence solely to
the knowledge diffused among the people.

Though we have not space to notice separate articles in the
' American Annals of Education and Instruction,' we cannot
refrain from adverting to a series of letters, in the first two
volumes, entitled, ' Sketches of Hofwyl,' Fellenberg's establishment. Fellenberg's plans, so far as we know, have never
been so completely developed as in these letters. The principles on which they are founded, their operations and effects,
are described in such a manner as to present a complete view
of the highly perfected system of intellectual and moral edu-

cation pursued in that institution. These letters ought to appear in a separate publication.

Many of the articles in which improved methods of teaching are described merit attention, as well as several others on the deaf and dumb, on the blind, and on teaching music in schools. But what has most interested us in these volumes, and will be found, we think, to be most interesting to our readers, is the information relative to the system of instruction now prevailing in the States of America, exhibiting also the actual condition of the people in respect to education, and the efforts that are being made to render the immense resources of the country more available than at present to the organization and improvement of schools.

The Americans generally seem to be aware, that the security of their political and social institutions depends upon the unrestricted diffusion of education. There is little of that jealousy which, in older countries, obstructs the progress of information among the people. Some states in the Union are more careless than others, and, from the inefficiency of their measures, or from indifference to their operation, have suffered their youth to be neglected; but, with these exceptions, very considerable exertions have been made, by legislative and by other means, to promote the establishment of schools, and to discover better methods of conducting them.

Of late years, the extension of education upon systematic principles has occupied no inconsiderable portion of the public attention. So strong a conviction of its necessity prevails among the people, that earnest and repeated applications have been made to Congress to pass some general law by which the object may be at once secured throughout the Union. The general legislature having properly declined all interference, the same object is now sought to be attained by means of societies and associations framed with a view to accelerate the progress of education.

In North America there is no uniform system of instruction, as in Prussia and France. Having formed no part of the original constitution of the United States, the general government is unwilling to deviate from the course which it has hitherto followed, of non-interference on the subject of education, leaving it to the state legislatures to make such provisions as are adapted to the wants of the respective states. This mode of proceeding is probably the safest and best, in a country where the estimation in which knowledge is held is so high as to make it sought after for the advantages which it gives—a motive which at once supersedes the necessity for compulsory regulations. Something is lost of unity and strength by it, but a greater scope is allowed for the operation of public opinion.

The power of making a suitable provision for training their youth being vested in the separate states, the inequality in the condition of their institutions is not surprising. The ignorance that prevails in some of the south-western states, for instance, is a fact perfectly reconcileable with the fact of the intellectual superiority of New York and New England. Where there is activity in the government to extend instruction, there is a desire created among the people to receive it; where there is little or no legislative effort, the amount of instruction is as small as is compatible with any degree of diffusion of knowledge.

The present state of education in the different states of North America is, in several points of view, deserving of attention, especially from those who are undecided about the advantage of legislative interference. The problem is approaching its solution in a way which can hardly fail to work conviction in its favour. The facts already collected show, in the clearest manner, that, in those states where the superintendence of government has been most vigilant, the results have been, beyond all comparison, favourable to the establishment of schools and the diffusion of knowledge.

' The following table, derived from the best sources, shows the proportion of children who receive common school instruction to the whole population in several of the United States, and furnishes statistical evidence in corroboration of the above statement :

New York . . .	1 pupil to	3·9 inhabitants.
Massachusetts, Maine, Connecticut	1 — to	4 —
New England . .	1 — to	5 —
Pennsylvania, New Jersey .	1 — to	8 —
Illinois . . .	1 — to	13 —
Kentucky .	1 — to	21 —

Annals, vol. ii. p. 335,

The necessity of a public provision for schools, though not recognised by the general government, forms a distinct article in most, if not in all, of the constitutions of the States. Acting up to the letter of this instruction, the different legislatures have, by grants of land, or by taxation, by one or by both of these means united, created public funds which in some states of the Union are very considerable. Some idea of their amount may be formed from the following particulars, which we have collected from authentic documents which are given in the Annals of Education :

	Dollars.			
Connecticut fund	1,700,000;	annual revenuue about £20,000	sterl.
Maryland . .	164,363	. .	2,100
New Jersey .	240,000		3,000
Rhode Island .	10,000		140
New York .	1,661,081		15,000
Delaware . .	170,000		2,000
Mississippi .	2,000,000		15,000
Ohio . .	100,000	. .	1,200

Virginia, South Carolina, Louisiana, and Pennsylvania make an annual appropriation for the support of their free schools to the amount of about 60,000 dollars, equal to more than 12,500*l.* sterling. In Maine, New Hampshire, Massachusetts, and Vermont, the whole charges of education are defrayed by a tax for that purpose.*

' The provisions which have been made for the support of schools may be reduced to three; 1st, by means of funds; 2ndly, by taxation ; 3dly, by a combination of both.

' Connecticut and Rhode Island are examples of the first plan, although the fund is small in the latter place, amounting only to 10,000 dollars. Connecticut is an instance of the paralyzing effect of providing for gratuitous instruction without calling for any effort on the part of the people. New Hampshire, Vermont, Massachusetts, and Maine furnish ample evidence of the good effect of the system of taxation. Ohio is the only remaining state which has adopted the plan of taxation; and the character of the inhabitants affords none but good indications of its effects.

' New York has advanced more rapidly in the education of the youth than any other state in the Union, by a combination of both systems, which aids and rewards those who tax themselves, and precisely in proportion to their contributions.

' Most of the other states in the Union have adopted the plan of providing for education by means of funds, or annual appropriations from the state treasury. The western states generally have a section of land in each township appropriated to the support of schools, either by the state, or by the United States ; but we cannot learn that any important effect has yet resulted from this provision.'— *Annals,* vol. i. pp. 19—161.

The appropriations of land in the western states have not been quite so inefficient as might be inferred from this statement. In Alabama, for instance, a University was established in 1830, out of the funds arising from the sale of these lands ; the number of students at this University has averaged nearly a hundred. See Article ' Alabama,' *Pen. Cycl.*

From a survey of these multiplied resources, there is clearly

* On the New England Schools, see Journal of Education, No. IV. p. 251.

no want of legislative foresight, as far as funds are concerned. In one section of the country, Connecticut, the annual revenue from school-lands is sufficiently large to educate all the children of its inhabitants without any cost to the parents. In another, New York, the payment is reduced to six-tenths of the actual expense of education.

As the operation of these different modes of providing instruction involves a principle about which there is much difference of opinion, it may not be amiss to look a little further into their results.

Connecticut may be taken as a type of the tendency of the gratuitous principle; the other New England states (except Rhode Island) of the system of general taxation ; and New York of the effect of a low scale of charges. Each of these plans has its own class of advocates.

Were the comparative merits of each system to be tried by the results of the few past years, there is no question that the gratuitous principle could urge but little in defence of its continuance. It is allowed on all hands, that there is less education in Connecticut than there was before the fund was provided. Parents have been released, by the bounty of the state, from paying for the instruction of their children, and their sense of obligation has vanished with the habit of performing this duty. In those parts of the Union where the opposite principle has been acted upon, the number and condition of the schools have been regularly improving, more particularly in New York, where, within a few years, most extraordinary success has attended the efforts that have been made by the legislature and the public. We are bound, however, to add, in justice to Connecticut, that other causes, besides the one already pointed out, have materially contributed to the disadvantageous contrast which exists in the relative condition of the schools in the two states. There is a public functionary appointed by the government of New York, designated ' Superintendent of Common Schools,' who is the secretary of the state. On him it devolves to present to the legislature annually, a report of the actual condition of education throughout the state. The materials from which this important document is drawn up are obtained from the school-committees who are expected to make returns of the number of children educated in all the common schools of their district, their ages, their average period of attendance, their acquirements ; also respecting the competency of their teachers, their modes of instruction, their salaries ; and further, in respect to the amount of accommodation in the school-houses, and to give a general view of their internal and external arrangement. By means of these local reports, the superintendent is enabled to draw up a comprehensive account of the institutions under his charge, and, by a comparison of the different statements, he can perceive at once where the condition of education is improving, and where changes are required in the methods of teaching, or in those arrangements which devolve upon the committees. To notice these, and to describe any improvements which can be introduced with advantage into the general system, form the chief features of this yearly report. The office, whose duties we have but imperfectly described, was instituted, we believe, in the year 1831; and to the able manner in which it has been filled, first by Mr. Flagg, and since by Mr. Dix, must be ascribed much of that superiority which distinguishes the common schools of this state, not only from Connecticut, but also from New England itself, which has so long been celebrated for its attention to education.

The successful results of this experiment in the state of New York have already induced the governments of Maine and New Jersey to appoint superintendents of their schools—an example which will probably be followed by all the states in the Union.

We have long wished to see similar duties devolve upon a Minister of Instruction in this country. The establishment of a uniform system of education may be of questionable advantage; the organization of a graduated succession of schools upon the Prussian model, or of common schools upon the American plan, may be impracticable; the obstacles to the formation of any scheme calculated at once to reconcile the religious prejudices of the country, and to avoid the intermixture of the different grades of society, may be great, and perhaps insurmountable; but, in the absence of a national system of instruction, there is enough, and more than enough, for a public functionary to perform, if he were invested with similar powers to those of the French Minister of Instruction, or of the superintendent of common schools in the state of New York. Preliminary to a more official connexion with the various institutions for education, his public duties might commence with the preparation of a statement to be laid before Parliament, of the statistics of our schools, infant, national, Lancasterian, subscription or proprietary, and endowed schools, whether grammar-schools or not. Our Sunday-schools would form another section of such a document, the private schools a fourth, and the universities and dissenting academies a fifth. Under these or some other divisions might be included, in a succession of reports, a fund of information which could not be made public without being productive of ulterior measures, both in and out of Parliament, beneficial to the interests of education. Their influence upon the various institutions to which they related would be immediately corrective, and, eventually, they would lead to the establishment of a better, cheaper, more uniform, and more enlarged system of instruction throughout the country.

We come now to examine the actual state of education in the United States, according to the views which are given of it in the volumes under our notice. Mr. Woodbridge has not furnished us with very ample information as to the courses of study in the universities and theological academies of North America. The best information in reference to one of these seats of learning is contained in an Article taken from the Journal of Education, on the state of education in Virginia,* in which the course of study in the university of that state is fully detailed. Some additional statistical particulars are given in a note extracted from the American Quarterly Register, where it is stated, that ' the number of colleges in the United States is 59 (of which 12 are in the New England states, 13 in the Middle states, 15 in the Southern states, and 19 in the Western states and territories); theological institutions, 22; medical schools, 18; law schools, 4; whole number of instructors, 400.

Students in the classical department	4100
Medical . . .	1868
Law	88
Theological, at 18 of the Institutions	709
Total	6760

Annals, vol. ii. p. 334.

The editor of the ' American Annals' has directed his attention, primarily, to the improvement and diffusion of instruction among the mass of society. His work, though not confined, is evidently principally directed to that object; and this object ought to occupy a prominent place in such a publication; for the main feature of American education is its common schools. The buildings appropriated to their use are scattered throughout the several states in which they exist, like the school-houses over Scotland; and, though often humble in their exterior, they are the most powerful instruments that the states can use, for the formation of the character of their citizens. Education in the United States always has a reference to these institutions. The comparisons made between one state and

* No. VII. p. 49. This Article was written by Professor Tucker of the University of Virginia.

another only extend to their common schools. In these seminaries three-fourths of the American community begin, and complete their education. It would, therefore, be unjust to deprive them of that station which they hold among the educational institutions of the United States. There are higher and lower schools, especially in towns, but they are only appendages to the common school, which is *the school* of the country.

In these seminaries are found children of all ages between four and sixteen, and, as we presume, of both sexes. They are taught by female teachers during one part of the year, and by masters during the other. This arrangement is peculiar to America. There is a summer and a winter school; the former, taught by a mistress, is of a lower grade, and for younger children; it opens about May, and continues for three or four months: the latter is of rather a higher character, to which a master is appointed. Its duration varies from six weeks to three months. To these schools, not averaging, singly, a term of more than three months in the year, all the rural population are indebted for the instruction which they receive. Private schools are sometimes resorted to when these are closed; but this seems to be the amount of the public provision for education through nearly all the states. Another circumstance, which renders this arrangement still more objectionable, is, the constant change of teachers—male and female—instances being rare of the same master or mistress ever teaching the same school for more than one season. Several causes may be assigned for this; but the fact itself is a curious one. The custom is now so established, that a change in it would be neither agreeable to the teachers nor the taught. The persons who discharge these important duties are stated to be generally young men and young women, under twenty years years of age, who take up this employment, for a few years, before they are settled in life. The salary allowed to teachers is generally less than we pay to household servants; and it is not uncommon for them to board, for a week in succession, in the houses of the parents of their pupils, as a part of their remuneration.

Under such discouragements, it cannot cause any surprise that one of the great complaints in America is the want of competent instructors. Various plans are in progress to supply this deficiency; but every effort will prove ineffectual which is not based upon a more liberal rate of payment. Schools for teachers will only increase, instead of diminishing, the difficulties, unless an ample recompense is held out as an inducement to those who possess the requisite qualifications, to engage in the labour of tuition.

The appointment of school-teachers is vested in the district committees, who not unfrequently require proof of their proficiency in reading, writing, and arithmetic. To these is sometimes added geography and grammar, which comprise all that is taught in the common schools of the states in which this common school system prevails. On this limited range of acquirements is based that moral superiority which is claimed for the inhabitants of North America over most other countries. There is probably less intellectual acquirement above this point, than in many other nations confessedly behind them; but, to make up this deficiency, knowledge to this extent, small as it is, is unquestionably more widely disseminated in the northern states, than it is, perhaps, anywhere else out of Prussia. One of the striking features of this system is its levelling of rank. It brings together, under the same roof, boys of all classes. There is a simplicity about it suited to republican institutions. In some of the southern states, where there is a departure from this practice, and education is in a very languishing condition, the cause of it is ascribed to this circumstance, by the Secretary of the State of New York, who has devoted so much of his time to the correction of the American system of common schools. These are his words :—

' The radical difference between our school system (New York) and the provision for instruction in Pennsylvania and Virginia is, that ours embraces the whole population, and theirs only the poor. To this, more than to any single cause, may be ascribed the success of our plan, and the failure of theirs.'—*Annals*, vol. i. p. 162.

The Virginia and Pennsylvania common schools receive the same class of scholars as our Lancasterian and national schools; while the common schools in the other states exhibit a similar admixture of ranks to what is found in our free grammar schools. In New England states, particularly in Massachusetts, there are primary, grammar, and high schools, all provided by the government. Sunday and infant schools are supported by subscription, when they are not taken under the protection of the states. Under similar auspices, agricultural and farm-schools, on the plan of Fellenberg, have been established, chiefly with a view to render instruction accessible to those who are unusually destitute. In these institutions it is customary to require, from each pupil, three hours' manual labour in the course of every day ; by which means, the expense of board and education is half defrayed. Mechanical as well as agricultural employments are introduced into some of these asylums. At Philadelphia it is one of the regulations of the State Manual Labour School—at which instruction and board are gratuitous, with the exception of the three hours' daily work—that persons who are educated there shall engage themselves as teachers, for at least a year after they leave the institution.

That unfortunate class of persons who are deprived of sight or of speech have asylums provided for them in several of the states, at the public expense. A private institution for deaf-mutes was established in Virginia by a descendant of the celebrated Braidwood. In 1817, the first public American asylum was opened in Hartford (Connecticut), within whose walls more than a hundred pupils are educated. Other asylums have been subsequently founded in Philadelphia, at Canajoharie, in the state of New York, in Ohio, and in Kentucky, which, altogether, provide instruction for about three hundred more—making a total of four hundred provided with instruction, out of a population of upwards of six thousand deaf-mutes.

The accommodation provided for the blind is very inadequate to the number who must stand in need of instruction.

' According to the last census, the total number of blind in the United States, whites and coloured, is 5444. What proportion of these are of an age for instruction is not ascertained, but if we take it at one-fourth, we shall not exceed the truth. Until a year ago, there was provision only for sixty; and thirty of these were in the institutions of Boston. Since that time, asylums have been founded at New York and Philadelphia; which still leave the south and western states destitute of suitable accommodation for that class of beings who labour under this privation.'

Notwithstanding these various provisions for all classes of the community, education in America is yet in its infancy. Much remains to be done even in those parts of the Union where it has made the greatest progress. Its universality is the main recommendation of it. The organization of the states into districts and sub-divisions of districts—all of which are more or less directly connected with their own legislatures—facilitates the operation of the common school system, by placing, within certain definite limits, the responsibility of making a suitable provision for all who are of an age to require instruction.

The amount of education gained under this system may be small for each individual, but it is, collectively, great; and we think that the state-governments act wisely in restricting their efforts, for the present, to this point. When arrangements for securing instruction to this extent are complete, and the organization of the common schools is so improved, as to produce the greatest amount of instruction which can be conveyed under the present system, then the demand for a higher scale of attainment will render further improvements comparatively easy, and lead to the introduction of those superior branches of learning which, as soon as practicable, ought to find a place in a well-arranged course of popular instruction.

At present, it would appear that, in all parts of the Union, with few exceptions, classical and mathematical knowledge, along with other of the higher branches of education, can only be obtained in the private schools, and in the colleges or universities, which are more numerous than might be expected, in all parts of the Union. In these schools those young men are prepared who finish their studies in the colleges or universities,[*] and who fill the learned professions. It is not well known in what condition these private academies are, compared with the corresponding class of schools in this country, but there is no reason to believe them inferior to our own in any other than the classical department; and even in that department, we are inclined to think that the character of those schools, in the northern states, is improving more rapidly than the condition of schools of the same description in England. It is an object deserving of more particular attention than it has yet received, to ascertain the methods of teaching, the books used, and the degree of general improvement, in these establishments. Although they act a less important part in America than in England, in the formation of the intellectual character of the country, the extent of their influence must be very considerable upon the higher classes of society, and more particularly so in the southern states, where public education in schools is confined to the lower classes.

It would convey a wrong idea of the condition of education in America, were we not to show a little of the other side of the picture. Though her institutions are essentially popular, there is a number incredibly large, growing up without those advantages which are in many districts so easily procured. It is calculated that, in Pennsylvania, more than 200,000 children are without the common means of instruction; that in Kentucky there are more than 100,000 in the same condition; and in New Jersey, besides 11,742 children, there are 15,000 adults unable to read. Pennsylvania contains a large German population, by no means well instructed; and the Germans, who are numerous in western Virginia, are very ignorant as regards all scholastic knowledge. They are good farmers, and generally honest men, but with little or no book instruction.

[*] Some incorporated institutions in America are termed colleges, others universities. All that are termed universities have the power of conferring degrees, and when the incorporated colleges possess the same power, which is the case in most instances, there is no difference, except in name, between such colleges and universities.

' The whole number of children,' says a writer in the ' Annals' (vol. iii. p. 367), ' exclusive of New England and New York, is 2,000,000. If we suppose the whole as destitute as Pennsylvania and Kentucky—each of which has only about one in three of their children at school (and this, we suspect, is by no means an unfavourable average), it will follow, that there are not less than 1,400,000 destitute of common instruction !'

Notwithstanding this set-off against the amount of education diffused in America, she is yet entitled to a place among those nations who hold the highest rank in the scale of diffusion of school instruction. The proportion of pupils to her inhabitants is about 1 to 11; in Bavaria and Prussia it is 1 to 7; in Scotland, 1 to 10; in Austria, 1 to 13; in England, 1 to 15; and in France and Ireland, 1 to 18.

In turning over the ' American Annals of Education and Instruction,' we have endeavoured to ascertain the effect of the interference of government in the common schools. The different degrees of assistance extended to education by the various states present a favourable opportunity for estimating the operation and comparative advantages of the two principles. From the statistical reports already given, it appears that, in precisely the proportion in which the legislatures take an interest in their schools, the condition of them is improved, and the amount of instruction increased. So far from paralyzing popular exertions, nothing acts as a stronger stimulus to it than legislative assistance and control. None of those evils which are so confidently predicted by individuals in this country, who are opposed to it, are known in America. The only evils that exist in the American school system arise out of the want of it. From one end of the Union to the other, the friends of education, not satisfied with urging more efficient measures on the part of the governments, are striving to procure the appointment of some person, in every state, invested with official power, to superintend the general interests of the public schools. Nothing is better attested than the fact, that legislative interference augments instead of diminishes that interest in the public mind, which some people are in the habit of supposing could be preserved by no other means than by desultory exertions, founded on what is designated ' the voluntary principle.' The state of popular feeling in America, in reference to education, compared with what it is in England, furnishes a complete answer to that objection. The contrast is striking and instructive. In England, where the government has no official connexion with the institutions for instruction, there is little or no public interest among the community at large on the subject. There are numerous

Y 2

individuals who persevere in their exertions, amidst every discouragement, to rouse the nation in behalf of education; there are members of school committees who are desirous of making their institutions more extensively useful; there are teachers, here and there, who are willing to introduce improved methods of instruction; and, probably, a considerable portion of the community, who are at present inactive, would cheerfully promote any general measures to render education more accessible, systematic, and effective, than it is at present. But all this amounts to little. It offers no plan of reform or improvement. It leads to nothing but the establishment, perhaps, of a national or an infant school—which, indeed, is the extent of our notions, generally speaking, of what is implied by the diffusion of education. There is none of that enlightened spirit of inquiry which, in the United States, assisted by the legislatures, is in active operation in many of the states. Our transatlantic neighbours are not satisfied with merely establishing schools; they watch the working of them, improve their system of superintendence, and their plans of tuition, and extend their sphere of action to the very limit of their means. Associations exist in almost every state for promoting improvements in education. Under the different names of ' Lyceums' and ' Institutes,' they seek to accomplish the same general object; and enrolling, as they do, among their supporters, the names of the most enlightened and influential portion of the people, they cannot fail to render most important services to education. Some idea of the objects and workings of these associations may be formed from the following outline of one of them, viz., ' the Illinois Institute of Education.'

' The constitution which was adopted, requires that the members of the institution shall consist—1. Of such persons as subscribe the constitution, and pledge themselves to aid personally in obtaining and diffusing information on the subject; to aid in getting up and sustaining a school, other than the one in which they are personally interested, as parents or guardians; or to contribute annually in money towards the incidental expenses of he institution. 2. Of delegates, chosen by county, district, or branch associations or schools, and who shall be appointed to attend the meetings of this institution. 3. Of all teachers of primary and other schools, who will correspond with the institute, and furnish annually, or oftener, a report of the schools with which they are connected.

' Friends of education, teachers and preachers of the gospel *throughout the state*, are requested to correspond with the secretaries, and to furnish such information as may be in their power, on the topics involved in the following questions :—

' 1. What kind of school-house have you? 2. How many months in a year is a school taught? 3. What is the cost of your school-house per annum, including payment of teacher, books, fuel, and repairs of school-house? 4. What is the cost per scholar? 5. How many different scholars attend? 6. What is the average number of scholars? 7. How many children need aid from public funds? 8. How many schools in the county? 9. What branches are taught in your schools? 10. What books are used in spelling, in reading, in arithmetic, in geography, in grammar? 11. Are the elements of natural history taught? 12. Does your teacher lecture the scholars on branches of science? 13. Does he ask questions on every reading lesson? 14. How many adults in your settlement who cannot read? 15. Have you a public library; and, if so, how large, and under what regulations? 16. Could not a small library of useful books be had for the use of your school, and loaned to the scholars, as rewards for proficiency in study and good behaviour? 17. Would you like to have a good teacher permanently settled with you, and would the school support him? 18. How would a circuit teacher do, who should conduct four or five schools, visiting these once a week, as teachers of singing do, and lecturing and explaining the branches taught? 19. What measures, in your opinion, or that of the people around you, should the state adopt in relation to the school funds? 20. Can you get up meetings of the people on the court day, or any other convenient time, on the subject of education? 21. Will any gentlemen make public addresses, or deliver lectures to the people on the subject of education and schools? 22. What proportion of families take newspapers, or any other periodicals?'—*Annals*, vol. iii. p. 185.

If the general sentiment of the country is at all represented in the proceedings of the Illinois Institute, and that it is we are inclined to believe, it may be safely predicted that the people of America will rapidly advance in education, and it may be as safely affirmed that voluntary efforts are not superseded by legislative assistance. The existence of such societies as the one described is not confined to one or two states. They extend into the western territory, as we see in the case of Illinois, and are penetrating into the slave-holding states of the south. They are influential from their number and their various localities, but this influence is greatly extended by their radiation to a common centre. Unity and vigor are thus given to their proceedings. The National Association, with which the others communicate by delegates or otherwise, holds a convention for three days, annually, at New York. At this meeting, the information collected from the branch associations is incorporated into one general report, by which means a complete view is obtained, not only of the measures adopted for the promotion of education, but also of the obstacles which retard its progress in the various portions of the United States. The object of this important national association, which is designated 'The American Lyceum,' is thus described in its own words : ' to secure a representation from every state of the Union, and with it a collection of *facts* relating to the condition and wants of schools, and to provide and execute measures by which their wants may be supplied, and a uniform and improved system of education introduced and extended throughout the country.'

Through these various channels, aided by the more obvious sources of information, the real condition of its schools will soon be better known in North America, than in any other country in the world, and being better known, will lead rapidly to the establishment of a complete and efficient system of instruction. It might alarm some of the opponents to popular education, or those whose nerves are yet shaken by the thought of the taxes upon knowledge being removed, to hear what are the results of early instruction and of cheap publications in the United States. In an institute at Philadelphia, which is accessible to all the young men in the city, there are no fewer than *sixteen* daily papers, besides *eight* monthly and quarterly periodicals.

It is a striking fact in favour of legislative interference in the school institutions of a country, that in the United States, so far from any evil being found to result from it, or any prejudice being raised against it, the popular voice is loud and general for its extension ; the evils which really exist are ascribed to the supineness and inactivity of the constituted authorities.

In the only two points in which a state connexion with schools has been admitted to be assailable, namely, 1st, in its being ineffective ; and 2nd, in its tendency to paralyze and supersede individual and voluntary exertion, the evidence is clear and satisfactory. The objections on both grounds are completely disproved by the experience of America. The state of New York, in which the influence of government is in the fullest operation, is universally admitted to have the best organized system of general instruction. And in respect to the effect of this arrangement upon the individual efforts of the friends of education, it is only necessary to appeal to the lyceums, and associations, supported in the same state, to prove that, wherever legislative exertions are wisely directed, instead of checking, they encourage, in an eminent degree, a corresponding effort on the part of the community.

The time is not perhaps so near as we could wish, when our own government will be induced to appoint a public functionary with duties such as we have described in a former page, which would be the first step towards the establishment of a system of general instruction. Much, however, might be done for the promotion of the same object, by an association established in the metropolis, but spreading itself into all parts of the country, for the advancement of education. If it were, at first, little more than a statistical society, its services would be of great value; but if it would assume the more important office of investigating and comparing the merits of different methods of instruction, classical as well as common, and of diffusing a knowledge of the plans pursued in those schools where the results are most favourable, we might look forward with something like confidence to progressive improvements in our institutions for education, if not to some scheme of universal instruction.

The utility of such an association would be greatly increased by occasional meetings, with lectures and discussions upon subjects connected with its leading object, according to the plan of the American Lyceum, or the British Association. The public would thus be addressed with more effect; the state of our own endowed and private schools would be brought prominently forward, and compared with the condition of similar institutions on the two continents; and, what is by no means of the least importance, the fact would then be as well known to ourselves as it already is to our neighbours, that in few countries of Europe are the elements of sound and useful instruction so scantily diffused as in England and the sister island.

ETYMOLOGICAL RESEARCHES.

Etymologische Forschungen auf dem Gebiete der Indo-Germanischen Sprachen, mit besonderem Bezug auf die Laut-Umwandlung im Sanskrit, Griechischen, Lateinischen, Littauischen, und Gothischen, von Dr. August Friedrich Pott, (Professor in the University of Halle.) Lemgo, 1833. lxxxii. and 284 pp. 8vo.

Etymological Researches in the Department of the Indo-Germanic Languages, with particular reference to the Interchange of Sounds in the Sanscrit, Greek, Latin, Lithuanian, and Gothic, &c.

'The present volume,' says Mr. Pott in his preface, 'only contains materials: the author found himself compelled almost altogether to forego the merit of properly arranging them. Even while preparing his work for the press, new remarks crowded upon him so thickly, that it became difficult to assign a convenient place to each: and with the certain prospect that, on entirely recasting the work, a further increase of matter, equally difficult to be disposed of, would present itself, no alternative was left to the author but, however reluctantly, to close the account for the present.'

We have placed this frank avowal at the head of our notice of Mr. Pott's work, because it shows that the author himself is well aware of what we consider to be its principal defect. The great difficulties attending the proper arrangement of a mass of remarks, which from their very nature will often descend to the minutest details, and the number of which, as Mr. Pott observes, seems almost to increase under our hands while we try to put them in order, will be readily acknowledged by every one who has at any time made etymological inquiries on an extended scale. But it will at the same time be as generally allowed, that clearness of design, and perspicuity in the execution, are requisites of the first importance in any work upon etymology which is intended to impress its reader with distinct and improved notions regarding the nature and essence of the languages inquired into. Coincidences between words and families of words, as well as certain analogous principles in the formation, derivation, and inflection of words, will occasionally present themselves to every one who is conversant with two or more cognate languages. But whoever makes these coincidences and analogies an object of special research, ought, we think, to exhibit the result of his investigations in a manner calculated to afford us a clear survey of the information which he has collected, and to place us at once on the eminence which he has reached, without imposing upon us the necessity of following him through all the windings of the path that brought him thither : our position would then command a view of the entire field of inquiry, and enable us to do justice to the skill of our guide in exhibiting the primitive stamp and character of the family of languages to which his researches refer, and the modifications of that universal character in the individual members comprised in it. The merits of Mr. Pott's work, and the amount of his claims to our gratitude, it is not so easy to appreciate. From the style in which it is written, it is often extremely difficult ; and it requires the greatest attention, while attending to the variety of novel and striking matter in which it abounds, not to lose sight of the leading principles by which we ought to steer our course. The smallness and closeness of the type in which the book is printed, the scarcity of occasional breaks and paragraphs, and the want of an alphabetical index, or good table of contents, all contribute to render the perusal of the book a task of great difficulty ; and this is the more to be regretted, as it will appear, from the following remarks, that much new information may be derived from it.

The volume before us comprises an Introduction and two principal divisions : the first on vowels ; the second on consonants ; the latter are considered, 1st, as occurring in nouns and suffixes; 2dly. in verbal roots, under which head the author gives a list of the Sanscrit verbal roots, reduced in number according to his own views, and compared with words sprung from apparently the same etymological elements in the cognate languages.

The Introduction sets out with some general remarks on the comparative study of languages, in the greater part of which we entirely concur. Mr. Pott lays it down as a rule that the affinity of languages should above all things be established by a comparison of their mode of forming and deriving words, and the system of their inflections.

'Comparisons of detached words,' says he, 'frequently yield but a single point of coincidence, which is always liable to the suspicion of having been transferred from one language into the other; while the actual coincidences in the expression of some grammatical relation, which is not so easily transplanted, and in the roots as found by careful grammatical analysis, often present a hundred or thousand points of approximation. Even languages of the same family sometimes diverge widely, owing to the diversity of pronunciation which gradually estranges them as dialects no longer intelligible to each other. But this diversity of pronunciation, although from a higher point of view it must be considered as accidental, stands under the control of certain natural laws, especially that of the physiological affinity of sounds; and these laws we ought to discover and to establish. *Kindred languages* are those which either, in consequence of the internal development and the geographical spreading of a language, or the effect of external influences, have lost their original identity, and have become varied and manifold; while *languages not akin* are those which, from the outset, have originated under principles of formation altogether different, and have grown up conformably to those principles. If languages not akin concur in any particulars, such concurrences must be accounted for either through the intercourse of the nations to whom they belong (even if that intercourse cannot be traced in history), or by the general sameness of the human mind and senses, or of the object designated; or finally by assuming an accidental coincidence which is not altogether to be excluded. No small proportion of the words collected by Klaproth, in his Asia Polyglotta, in support of his theory of an antediluvian uniformity of languages, show an external similarity of sound; but this similarity vanishes as soon as we come critically to investigate these words, and to dissect them into their component elements, conformably to the rules of their respective languages. The number of simple articulations in language (though liable to many intermediate shades of difference) is comparatively small, and their number (which however may be determined variously according to different points of view) may be estimated at from forty to fifty at the highest. Out of these primary elements the wonderful fabric of so many as yet uncounted languages is erected; and I doubt whether any language ever raised the number of its roots beyond one thousand, if properly investigated and exhibited in their greatest attainable purity.'

To the last observation we are quite willing to subscribe: and we concur entirely in Mr. Rückert's opinion, that the great majority of those assumed Sanscrit roots, which according to the Hindu grammarians form verbs of the tenth conjugation, are only the themes partly of causative and partly of denominative verbs, which may be resolved into still simpler elements; but yet we must withhold our assent from the principles on which Mr. Pott in some instances proceeds, in reducing the number of roots usually received as such in the Indo-Germanic languages. To the Greek verb πιέζειν, for instance, in Sanscrit, corresponds a verb of the tenth conjugation (*pídayati*, 'he vexes'), the root of which is registered by the native Hindu grammarians under the form *píd*. To this stem Mr. Pott will not accord a place in the list of roots; he considers *pídayati* as a verb sprung from the substantive *pídá*, 'vexation, pain,' and this substantive again he supposes to be a derivative of the genuine verbal root *sad*, 'to sit,' with *pi*, instead of *api*, prefixed to it. According to what law *api-sad* or *pi-shad* could have been contracted into *píd*, Mr. Pott does not explain; the analogy of the Sanscrit word *nida*, 'a bird's-nest' (the Latin *nidus*), to which he refers us, and which he considers as an offspring of the same root *sad* preceded by the preposition *ni*, whence *ni-shad*, 'to sit down,' seems at all events insufficient to establish such a contraction. That in Greek, independently of the Sanscrit, the verb πιέζω could not, consistently with the general rules of derivation, have arisen out of a composition of ἐπί and ἴζω, or ἕζομαι, is evident, and is further shown by the compound verbs ἐφέζομαι and ἐφίζω, which are met with in the earliest monuments of the Greek language. We are therefore compelled to assume that the Sanscrit verb *píd* and the Greek πιέζω are the common property of both, and existed before the languages, or the nations speaking them, separated; and is it probable that at so early a stage in their development as that to which this assumption brings us back, corruptions like that of *api-shad* into *píd*, should have taken place?

Another instance in which we cannot agree with Mr. Pott's analysis of a verbal root, is that of the Sanscrit *subh* (written with a palatal *s*), 'to shine,' of which he observes that it corresponds to the Persian *khúb*, 'beautiful, good,' and the Greek κόμψος,* but which he nevertheless considers

---

.* We would add κόμπος, the Pindaric use of which word (Isthm. i. 43. iv. 43. Nem. viii. 49.) in the sense of 'praise, honour, glory,' agrees well with the acceptation of 'decorating by praise,' in which the verb *sumbhati* is used in the Hymns of the Rig Veda.

as a compound of the root *bhâ*, (the Greek ΦΑ in φάος, φαίνω, &c.) 'to appear, to be visible, to shine,' and the prefix *su* (written with the dental *s* and answering to the Greek εὖ) 'good, well.' Out of *su-bhâ*, 'to appear well,' he supposes a new verb to have arisen, in which the palatal sibilant was substituted for the initial dental *s*, and which subsequently followed its own mode of inflection independent of that of its supposed primitive ;* for whilst *su-bhâ* would form the third person sing. of the present tense *su-bhâti*, and that of its reduplicated preterit *su-babhau*, we find from *subh*, in the present, the forms *sôbhate* and *sumbhati*, and in the reduplicated preterit *susubhe*, *susôbha*, and *susumbha*. But what we chiefly object to, is the supposed substitution of the *palatal* for the *dental* sibilant, at so early an epoch as we are obliged to assume, in order to account for the initial *x* and *kh* in the cognate Greek and Persian words standing in the place of the palatal sibilant in the Sanscrit. There is no example (as far as our knowledge extends) of a transition from a Sanscrit dental *s* into a Greek or Persian guttural sound, whereas there are numerous instances of such transition from the Sanscrit palatal sibilant. We are told that the present Hindus (the natives of Bengal at least) make hardly any distinction in the pronunciation of the three sibilants (the palatal, lingual, and dental), sounding them all like *sh*,† and this remark may explain the unsettled orthography of some words, which we find occasionally spelt with either a palatal or a dental *s* in carelessly written manuscripts; but are we justified in supposing that a similar confusion should have prevailed at the early epoch which preceded the separation of the Indian from the Persian and the Greek branch of the original language? We do not think that much is gained by reducing the number of our roots, if it is to be effected by assumptions apparently so much at variance with those simple principles of formation, which we find to prevail the more consistently in language the nearer we approach the stage of its infancy.

In a subsequent part of his Introduction, Mr. Pott makes some observations on the relations between the Greek and Latin, the substance of which we here extract, as they inculcate a truth which cannot be too often repeated :—

'The Latin language has long been called a daughter of the Greek ; and there are still philologists who look upon the Latin as a mixture of different elements, chiefly Greek. If we set aside the number of manifestly borrowed Greek words in the Latin, which

* In the Greek adjective *λαμπρός* we find united the same two elements, which Mr. Pott supposes to have coalesced in the Sanscrit verb *subh*.
† Haughton's Bengali Dictionary, col. 2455.

certainly is greater than that of Latin words transplanted into the Greek, we may with just as much reason assert that the Greek language is Latin, with a residue of words peculiar to itself. Or will it be said that the Italic language only had the pliancy to adopt and appropriate to itself accessions from abroad, and that the Greek was not so receptive?* I fear the number of Greek words naturalized in the Latin has been greatly overrated. It will be objected that the Greek, especially that of the Æolian dialect, is of a more antique character than the Latin, so that the latter must be a daughter of the Greek, we being informed, moreover, that colonists from the East settled in Italy. I should not object to grant such a conclusion, if the antecedent propositions could be established. But there is much more truth in the contrary assertion, that the Latin, though poorer than the Greek, has yet preserved an air of greater antiquity in its · forms and structure. And besides, who were these emigrants from the East? The Grecian settlers in Magna Græcia can hardly be meant. Or were they Trojans? I think there is good reason to suspect that the tradition which would make the Romans the descendants of emigrated Trojans has no foundation, except in Grecian and Roman vanity. The extant genuine monuments in the Etrurian language can be but indifferently explained by means of the Greek: and what do we know of the Tyrrhenian, or Pelasgic language? But suppose that both were Greek . is it admitted that the Tyrrhenians and Pelasgians were the ancestors of the inhabitants of Latium Do not the Oscan, Umbrian, and Sabine dialects, even in their scanty remains, show many words and formations which belong to the great family of the Indo-Germanic languages? And again, was the number of the Pelasgian colonists large enough to have exercised so great an influence over the language of the prior inhabitants of the country, as we must suppose them to have exercised, in order to account for the great proportion of what is originally akin to the Greek in the Latin? The Latin, as well as every other language, has received foreign words; but its structure and organism is *Latin*, just as much as that of the Grecian language is *Greek*.'

The family of the Indo-Germanic languages may, according to Mr. Pott, be divided into five branches, two of which belong to Asia, and three to Europe, and through European colonies to other parts of the world. They are enumerated by Mr. Pott in the following order :—

I. The *Indian branch*, in which the *Sanscrit* takes the lead, and is followed by several derivative dialects, comprised under the name of the *Prácrit* languages, and deviating more or less in their structure from the Sanscrit. Among them the *Pali* deserves to be particularly mentioned, which is almost altogether Sanscrit, only softened in its pronunciation.

II. The *Medo-Persic*, or *Arian branch*, at the head of

---

* This we suppose to be the import of the passage, which in the German original is not very clear. The words are :—*Oder ist die Uebereinstimmung etwa nur einseitig auf Seiten der Italerin, auf der anderen nicht ?*

which stands the *Zend*, the language in which the ancient sacred writings of the Parsees are composed. A critical investigation of the structure of this language has but just commenced, and we are therefore not yet enabled to define with precision the relations subsisting between the Zend and the other ancient languages of the country, the *Pehlvi* and the *Deri*, and also the *modern Persian*. The Armenian language, as is evident from its system of inflections, does not form part of the Medo-Persian, nor of any other branch of the Indo-Germanic languages.

III. The *Teutonic* branch, with the Gothic at its head, and comprising the different *German* dialects, the *Anglo-Saxon*, the *Icelandic*, the *Swedish*, the *Danish*, &c.

IV. The *Greco-Latin branch*, comprising the two ancient classical languages.

V. The *Slavonic branch* should, according to Mr. Pott, be subdivided into three divisions : the first comprises the Lithuanian, with the ancient Prussian and Lettic ; at the head of the second stands the Russian ; the third comprehends the Polish and Bohemian, and the languages of the Slowaks in Hungary, and of the Wends and Sorbs in Lusatia and Saxony.

It will be observed, that the different Celtic languages are not comprised in this enumeration : Mr. Pott does not consider them as belonging to the Indo-Germanic family. It is to be regretted, that he has not stated in detail the reasons that induced him to exclude them from his arrangement : there are many circumstances connected in particular with the grammatical structure of the Welsh language, which have given us a strong impression that the Celtic does belong to the same family as the other languages considered in Mr. Pott's work. The subject is of high interest, and well deserves to be fully investigated, which, as far as we know, has not yet been done.

Mr. Pott concludes the introductory part of his work by assigning the etymology and import of a number of proper names in ancient oriental history and geography : some of which we submit to our readers.

The name of the Persian noble Otanes ('Οτάνης, Herod. iii. c. 68, &c., 141, 144, &c.) is, according to Mr. Pott, equivalent to the Sanscrit compound adjective *sutanu*, 'having a beautiful body,' from *tanu* (the modern Persian *tan*), 'body, frame,' with the prefix *su* (the Greek εὖ) put before it. The initial sibilant of the Sanscrit adjective is dropped in the Persian name, as it is in the Greek (and Persian) name of the river 'Ινδός, which in Sanscrit is *Sindhu*. Mr. Pott sees in these examples a confirmation of the remark made by others in the investigation of the Zend language, that the Persians must at an early period have begun to change into a soft aspiration, or entirely to drop, the initial *s* of words which in the Sanscrit have retained the sibilant; and as in the correspondent Teutonic words the same *s* is likewise often preserved, this circumstance may be adduced as a further argument against the formerly very prevalent opinion that the Germans were descended in a direct line from the Persians. A few examples will make Mr. Pott's remark clearer :—

Sanscrit.	Zend.	Modern Persian.	Gothic.	Modern German.
saptan (seven)	*hapta*	*haft*	*sibun*	*sieben*
sd (she)	*hâ*		*sî*	*sie*
sam (with)	*ham*	*ham*		*sammt*
santi (they are)	*henti*	*end*	*sint*	*sind*

The name of the brother-in-law of Darius Hystaspis, Γωβρύας (Herod. iii. c. 70. 73, &c.), Mr. Pott explains, as equivalent to the modern Persian adjective *khûb-rûi*, 'of beautiful face;' that of the Persian admiral Βάδρης (Herod. iv. c. 167) he supposes to be the Sanscrit *Bhadra*, "fortunate:" we perceive, however, that the same individual is in another passage of Herodotus (iv. c. 203) named Βάρης.[*] Another Βάδρης is mentioned (Herod. vii. c. 77.) but he does not appear to have been a Persian.

Mr. Pott proceeds to comment upon a class of names in different languages of the Indo-Germanic family, which signify either *given* or *gifted* (for that, in some instances, remains undecided) *by the gods*. At the head of the list stand ancient Sanscrit names such as *Devadatta, Haradatta, Indradatta, Somadatta*, &c. (*i. e.* given by the gods, by Hara or Siva, by Indra, by Soma or the Moon, &c.) and Greek names such as Θεόδοτος, Διόδοτος, Ζηνόδοτος, Ἡρόδοτος, &c. follow next. On this occasion the author expresses his belief, that in compounds such as Θεόσδοτος, Θεοσεχθρία, Θέσφατος, Θέσκελος, the former part is the abridged form of what once was a dative case in the plural number: so that Θεόσδοτος would be = Θεοῖς δοτός, *a Diis datus;* Θεοσεχθρία, the abstract of Θεοῖς ἐχθρός,[†] 'hated by the gods;' Θέσφατος = a Diis effatum;

<hr />

[*] The Sancroft MS. has in the latter passage Μάρδης, and in iv. c. 167, Μάρδης.

[†] Has the derivation of the word ἰχθύς ever been satisfactorily explained? As long as no better etymology is to be had, we propose to consider it as identical with the Sanscrit *satru* 'an enemy,' the initial palatal sibilant of which word is observed in numerous instances to correspond to a guttural letter in Greek and Latin. *Satru* properly signifies 'a destroyer,' being a derivative of the verbal root *sad*, 'to perish,' in the causative conjugation, (*sdtayati*) 'to cause to perish, to throw down' (see Colebrooke's Sanscrit Grammar, p. 327), with the *Unâdi* affix *ru :* the word is thus explained by *Bhattôji, Siddh. Kaum.* fol. 202, *a.*

Θέσκελος = Θεοῖς ἴκελος ‘ like the gods ;’ Θεσπρωτός = Θεοῖς πεπρωμένος, ‘ decreed by the gods.’ To these we would add the Æschylean word Θεόσσυτος or Θεόσυτος, ‘ sprung from the gods,’ (ἐκ Θεοῦ ὁρμηθεῖσα as a scholiast explains it, Prometh. v. 116.) The word Θεσπιέπεια also belongs to this class, the latter part of which, according to Mr. Pott contains the root of εἰπεῖν twice over, and therefore properly signifies ‘ pronouncing what was said [to her] by the gods :’ it is a compound of Θέσπις and ἐπ (ἔπος), and the former word is again a compound of Θεός and the root of εἰπεῖν.

Among the ancient Persian names which are formed on the same principle as those mentioned above, Mr. Pott explains the ‘ Οϱμισδάτης of Agathias as ‘ given by Ormuzd ;’ the *Madates* of Curtius (v. c. 3.), which name is perhaps the same as the *Mĕdáthá* (מְדָתָא) of the book of Esther (c. iii. v. 1), as ‘ given by the moon ;’ the Φαρανδάτης and Φερενδάτης of Herodotus (vii. c. 67, ix. c. 76.) as ‘ given by Behram.’ Mr. Pott conjectures that as in the ancient calendar of the Persians every day in the month was sacred to, and called after, a particular deity, and as the Persians were in the habit of celebrating their birthdays (see Herod. i. c. 133), many of the names so formed may have been given in honour of the deity presiding over a person's birthday. But some celebrated names remain yet to be noticed. The Μιτραδάτης of Herodotus (i. c. 110), or, as the name is likewise written, Μιθριδάτης (Xenoph. Anab. vii. c. 8. near the end), or Μιθραδατης (Septuagint, Ezra i. 8; iv. 7, in the Hebrew text *Mithrĕdath* מִתְרְדָת), and in a more modern corrupted form *Meherdates* (Tacit. Ann. xii. c. 10.) Mr. Pott explains ‘ given by Mithra (the sun).’ Many other compounds with *Mitra* or *Mithra* occur, e. g. Μιτροβάτης (Herod. iii. c. 120); Ἰθαμίτρης (*id.* ix. c. 102) and Ἰθαμάτρης (*id.* vii. c. 67.); Σιϱομίτρης (*id.* vii. c. 68) &c., besides several names which appear to be derivatives, e. g. Μιτραῖος (Xenoph. Hellen. ii. c. 6.), Μιθρίνης or Μιθρήνης (Arrian Exp. Al. i. c. 17; iii. c. 16.), &c. The Μητραγαθής in the Persæ of Æschylus (v. 43) is, we suspect, a fictitious name.

The signification of the name *Spendadates* in Ctesias (Pers. c. 10.) is, according to Mr. Pott, ‘ given by the Amshaspands :’ the complete name of these deities is, in the Zend language, a compound term, *Amesha-spenta :* Mr. Pott

---

* Professor Bopp (*Vergleichende Grammatik*, p. 244.) interprets *Amesha-spenta* ‘ non conniventes sancti :’ and *amesha* is, according to his translation, of the same import as the Sanscrit epithet *stabdhalóchana*, ‘ having fixed, not twinkling eyes,’ which occurs as an attributive of the Hindu deities, (Nalus, v. 25.) The Sanscrit word etymologically corresponding to *amesha* would be *animisha*.

supposes the latter element of this term to have been used as equivalent to the whole, in forming the name *Spendadates ;* in the same manner as, in the Zend adjective, *mazda-dháta,* ' given by Ormuzd,' we find the latter portion only of the Zend compound name of Ormuzd, *Ahuro-mazdáo.*

The Persian names beginning with *Arta-* and *Ario-* give rise to an interesting series of remarks. After an attentive perusal of the information upon the subject, collected by Mr. Pott, we venture to suggest that *Arta-* might be taken as identical with the crude form of 'Αρταῖοι, the ancient national name of the Persæ, * and *Ario-* as identic with that of Ἄριοι or Ἄρειοι, likewise an ancient designation of the inhabitants of the table-land of Persia. (Herod. iii. c. 93 ; vii. c. 62.) The latter name is, according to the concurrent opinion of several Orientalists, etymologically the same with the Sanscrit word *Arya,* by which, in the ancient writings of the Hindus, the followers of the Brahmanical law are designated. This word is a participle of the future in the passive voice, and properly signifies ' honourable, entitled to respect.' † A word strictly corresponding to the Persian theme *Arta* is not found in Sanscrit : but we are confident that we cannot be far from the truth if we regard it as the passive participle of the preterite, ending in *-ta* from the same verb *rĭ,* of which *Arya* is the passive participle of the future. ‡ Should this conjecture be correct, *Arta* will signify ' honoured, respected.' The sense thus assigned to the two words seems to agree tolerably well not only with their independent use as the name of a nation (Ἄριοι or' Ἄρειοι, and 'Αρταῖοι), but also with the manner in which we see them employed as component elements of proper names. If we are right in thinking with Mr. Pott that Ξέρξης is the Zend word *ksathra* (Sanscrit,

---

* Ἐκαλέοντο δὲ πάλαι ὑπὸ μὲν Ἑλλήνων Κηφῆνες, ὑπὸ μέντοι σφέων αὐτέων καὶ τῶν περιοίκων Ἀρταῖοι. Herod. vii. c. 61.

† From the verbal root *rĭ,* ' to go or approach.' *Pánini* (iii. 1. 103.) observes that the participle of this root may be formed either with the change called *guna,* or with *vriddhi* of the radical vowel : with the former (*árya*) the word is applied to men of the agricultural and military (*swámin ?*) caste ; with the latter (*árya*) to Brahmans.

‡ The only difficulty which seems to arise against this assumption is, that the preterite participle of the passive is in Sanscrit formed without modifying the radical vowel of the verb *rĭta.* But this objection may, in some degree, be removed by the observation that in numerous instances the Sanscrit vowel *rĭ* appears represented in Zend words by *ĕrĕ,* e. g.

Sanscrit, *sakrĭt,* (once)	Zend, *kahĕrĕt,*
krĭnôti, (he makes)	*kĕrĕnoit,*
mrĭtyu (death)	*mĕrĕthyu.*

According to the analogy of these examples, the Sanscrit *rĭta* would in Zend become *ĕrĕta,* which approaches at least one step nearer to *arta.*

kshatra) ' a king,' 'Αρταξέρξης will be either ' the honoured king,' or ' king of the Artæi ;' perhaps, like the Indian *mahárája* (great king), a regal title rather than a proper name confined to one individual * ; 'Αρταπάτης (Xen. Anab. I. c. 8), perhaps the same name as 'Αρταβάτης (Herod. vii. c. 65) will be the ' honoured lord, from *arta* and *pati*, which in Sanscrit signifies 'a master or lord ;' 'Αριόμαρδος (Herod. vii. c. 66. Æschyl. Pers. 38.) ' vir honorandus, from *arya* and *mard*, in modern Persian ' a man ;' 'Αρτασύρας (Ctes. Pers. c. 9.) ' heros honoratus,' from *arta* and *súra*, in Sanscrit ' a hero;' &c. 'Αρταῖος the honoured, the noble,' occurs as the name of a person, (Herod. vii. c. 22.)

We regret that the limits of our article do not allow us for the present to give an analysis of the remaining, and in fact the principal, portion of Mr. Pott's work. With a view to ascertain the transitions of sounds in the various branches of the Indo-German family of languages, he goes through their alphabets, taking that of the Sanscrit, as being the most complete, for his basis, and he endeavours to determine what are in other languages the sounds corresponding, as etymologically equivalent, to each Sanscrit letter. That in a field of so great extent no transition of sounds should have escaped the author's attention, or that no variety of opinion should exist on any of the transitions assumed by him, will not of course be expected. But we confidently say, that such as it is, Mr. Pott's book contains a mass of new and valuable information, and that it will fully repay the task of perusing it with attention.

Progressive Exercises in English Composition. By R. G. Parker, A.M. London, John R. Priestley, 47, High Holborn.

In the Fifteenth Number of this Journal, appeared a review of ' Parker's Exercises in English Composition.' The writer of that article considered that Parker's Exercises would be a useful book, if certain alterations were made in the arrangement, and certain defects were supplied. The reviewer, at the same time, observed that much of Mr. Parker's work was

---

* Mr. Pott draws our attention to a passage in Ctesias (Pers. c. 49. conf. 53. 57, βασιλεύει δὲ 'Αρτάκης, ὁ μετονομασθεὶς 'Αρταξέρξης) and another in Curtius (vi. c. 6. *Bessus veste regia sumpta, Artaxerxem appellari se jusserat*) which seem to warrant us in considering the word *Artaxerxes* as a mere title of sovereignty.

This etymology would agree tolerably well with the remark occurring in Herodotus, (vi. c. 98,) according to which Ξέρξης signifies 'αρήιος, and 'Αρταξέρξης, μέγας αρήιος. The passage is considered by some editors to be spurious ; but whoever wrote it knew something of the Persian language.

taken from Walker's ' English Themes and Essays ;' and he says (p. 136) " we are obliged to add, for the most part,* without acknowledgment. Even the models, the themes, the skeletons, the subjects, are all appropriated with only very slight alterations. We must, however, do Mr. Parker the justice to say, that his alterations are improvements," &c. Then follow some remarks, condemnatory of the practice of taking from other books without proper acknowledgment.

We are happy that it is in our power to do justice to the author, the reviewer, and the publisher. The following is a letter sent by Mr. Parker to Mr. Coates.

Boston, Massachusetts, United States of America.

Dear Sir,   *January 4th*, 1835.
The 15th Number of the ' London Quarterly Journal of Education' contains a review of a little book of mine, entitled ' Progressive Exercises in English Composition,' which was first published in this city in August of 1832, and passed to a second edition in the course of two months. It was stereotyped in a third edition in the following January, and in December of 1833, was republished in England ; and, as I perceived by Bent's ' Literary Advertiser,' was in a second edition in the month of August of 1834. The Number of the ' Quarterly Journal ' containing the review of the book is dated July, 1834. The first London edition I have never seen ;—the second is now before me. As the publisher has stated in an advertisement to this last edition, that " no alteration has been made either in the matter or the arrangement," it is not material whether the review was made of the first or second London edition. But as the British publisher has made no allusion to the trans-atlantic origin of the work, and has taken the liberty to omit a portion of my preface and substitute something of his own, which has subjected me to the charge of plagiarism, from the reviewer, I deem it a duty to myself to ask of you, the acknowledgment of the injustice done to me by the publisher, in the suppression of that portion of my preface which is not embraced in the English copy. The passages suppressed are as follow :

' The author is encouraged to believe that the plan will be favourably received, if it leads the pupil to think, or removes any of the difficulties which lie in the way of those who are just turning their attention to composition. Justice requires the acknowledgment that some hints have been derived, and some extracts have been taken, from Walker's ' Teachers' Assistant,' Booth's ' Principles of English Composition,' and Jardine's ' Outlines of a Philosophical Education ;' but the plan and the general features of the work are believed to be new.'

' The book is designed as the sequel to a grammar, which will be

* The only acknowledgements made in Mr. J. R. Priestley's first edition, which we can find, are in foot-notes, pp. 64, 69, 84. [This note is not in the Review, No. XV., p. 136 : it is added here by the editor to make the statement as complete and accurate as he can.]

shortly published, on a plan in some respects different from any now in use. It therefore presupposes some acquaintance with syntax, although the practical exercises under most of the lessons, can be performed with tolerable facility by those who have but a slender knowledge of any part of grammar.

'*Boston, June,* 1832.'

In lieu of the above paragraphs the English preface contains the following passage:

'Among the best works on Rhetoric, the author has availed himself of several extracts from Booth's ' Principles of English Composition ;' for which, as not being noticed in their respective places, this general acknowledgment is made.'

This unjust substitution has led the reviewer to make the following assertion : (p. 136th of the review.)

' Nearly the whole of these three lessons, (35th, 36th, and 37th,) as well as lessons 20th, 21st, and 23rd,' (he means the 22nd instead of the 23rd, for the 23rd is wholly original, and even the 22nd is indebted to Walker for the model only ; which, *en passant*, is a very indifferent one,) ' are taken from Walker's ' English Themes and Essays ;' and we are obliged to add, for the most part without acknowledgment. Even the models, the themes, the skeletons, the subjects, are all appropriated with only very slight alterations. We must, however, do Mr. Parker the justice to say that his alterations are improvements, for Mr. Walker's language is often inelegant and occasionally incorrect. We strongly disapprove of the principle of taking piecemeal from another work; but when such a thing is done, without being properly acknowledged, it is what we feel ourselves called upon to condemn.'

If the reviewer is sincere in this last assertion, he will not be unwilling to render to me the justice which I ask ; for he must see by the preceding statements, that the English publisher has taken my preface ' piecemeal,' without its ' being properly acknowledged.' He will likewise perceive that I have given credit to Mr. Walker, and to others also,—and that the charge of appropriating without acknowledgment, is wholly unfounded.

The reviewer asserts (p. 136th of the ' Journal,') that ' the only portion of Mr. Parker's book which can be considered new is comprised in the early lessons.'

To this assertion I have only to reply, that nine out of the forty lessons, into which the book is divided, are derived from hints given or extracts taken from the authors whose names are mentioned in my preface. The remaining thirty-one lessons are entirely original; or if ever suggested by others, I did not know it when I wrote them, and am still ignorant of the fact.

Again, the reviewer says (p. 133rd), ' had the title of Mr. Parker's book been ' Exercises in Rhetoric,' we should have had less to say about its defects. We have no objection to rhetoric being included in an elementary work on composition, but it should undoubtedly occupy a subordinate place to grammar.' To this I reply, that my preface states that ' the book is designed as a sequel

z 2

to a grammar which will shortly be published.' &c.—and in the se·
cond part of this grammar (the first part of which I have very
recently published) he will find that I have endeavoured to render
grammar subservient to rhetoric, and that all his suggestions
(see pages 131 and 132 of the review,) with regard to the lessons
'illustrative of the etymological changes in words, and of the general
principles of Syntax,' of the 'structure of sentences,' &c., in which
he says ' Mr. Parker's Exercises are very defective,' have been anti-
cipated and are embraced.

The reviewer says (p. 127,) that the use of the active participle
is 'erroneously called the case absolute.' My authority for the use
of that term is Murray's fifth note to his first rule of Syntax. The
suggestion with regard to the addition of 'a lesson on punctuation,'
(p. 137th of the review) is embraced, as it ought to be, in the plan
of the second part of the grammar, which is now in the press.

I trust that the editors of a highly respectable Journal, 'published
under the superintendence of the Society for the Diffusion of Useful
Knowledge,' will have the magnanimity to endeavour to undo the
act of injustice of which that Journal has been guilty toward me in
the unfounded charge of plagiarism contained in the review of my
little book. I cannot conceal the pride that I feel, in the high commendation bestowed upon my book in the fourth paragraph of the
124th page of the review ; but I regret that the subsequent statements required me in self-defence, to state how little I am indebted
to others for the merits or defects of the work.

Before I had seen the review or the English edition, I addressed
a copy of the stereotype edition published in this city, to Mr. John
R. Priestley, 47, High Holborn, near Brownlow-street, who, as
Bent's Advertiser informed me, is the English publisher. My
object in sending it to him was, that he might avail himself of the
last additions, &c. With it I sent to Mr. Priestley a copy of the
first part of my grammar, entitled ' Progressive Exercises in English
Grammar,' containing the principles of Analysis, or English Pars-
ing. Part 2nd will contain the Synthesis, or construction of English
Sentences ; and part 3rd, the Prosody of the Language. These two
parts are now in the press.

To return to the Exercises in Composition, I would observe, that
the English copy is an exact reprint of the American, with the exception of the omission of my title as Principal of the Franklin
Grammar School, Boston, and the substitution in the title-page of
an extract from Whately's Rhetoric, for what I consider the more
appropriate motto in the American copy, namely, "Ordo et modus
omnia breviora reddunt." A few verbal changes, of a merely national character occur in several pages, such as the substitution of
the name of Mr. Curran, an Irish orator, for that of Mr. Otis, an
American (p. 48th of the English, and 52nd of the American copy.)
The difference of the paging arises from the fact that the former
commences at the first lesson and the latter at the title-page.

You will excuse, I trust, the liberty I have taken in thus address-
ing you at such length ; and permit me to hope that in some future

Number of the Journal of Education, some notice may be taken of the communication with which I have troubled you.

Very respectfully, yours,

Thomas Coates, Esq. R. G. PARKER.
Sec. Soc. Diff. U. K.

Neither the reviewer nor the editor knew that Mr. Parker's Exercises was an American work : in the English reprint this fact is entirely suppressed. The *first* English edition is that which was reviewed, as will appear from Mr. Parker's dates. All that is quoted by Mr. Parker from the preface of the American edition, is omitted in the preface to this first English edition. Nor does the preface to this first English edition contain a reference to Mr. Booth's Principles of English Composition, which reference Mr. John R. Priestley has inserted in the Preface of his *second* edition, as we learn from Mr. Parker's letter. We have not seen Mr. John R. Priestley's second edition.

Mr. John R. Priestley, we take it for granted, saw the article in the Journal, in which Mr. Parker was blamed for taking from others without acknowledgment. We assume that he saw it, because the book was forwarded by him to the editor, in the same way that works are often sent to the editors of other periodicals; and because publishers in such cases have generally curiosity enough to see what is said of their books. Mr. J. R. Priestley has inserted, in the preface to his *second* edition, an acknowledgment, so far as Mr. Booth's work is concerned. From this fact we infer that his attention had been directed to the circumstance of Mr. Booth's name being omitted, and to the propriety of inserting it. It is rather singular that Mr. J. R. Priestley, while amending his preface in part, did not amend it altogether, by inserting the whole, or at least, the substance of the original preface ; especially as he must, we presume, have seen the Number of the Journal which contained the review of Parker's Exercises, before his own second edition was fairly out. When Mr. J. R. Priestley mutilated the American author's title-page, suppressed his preface, and put one of his own in its place, it is very probable that he did not foresee the consequences of this act. We are very willing to suppose that he did not intend to do the author any injury ; and we take it for granted, that he did not wish to do anything that might impair the character or injure the sale of his own book. Still we think that Mr. J. R. Priestley, in his eagerness to get rid of the American preface, lost sight of his own interest ; for he laid his book open to the charge of being rather exercises in rhetoric than anything else, which objection could not have been made, at least without qualifications, had the

American author been allowed to speak for himself. It would appear that the English publisher's original design in making certain changes and omissions, was simply to pass off the work as an English publication, either because he conceived that under this assumed character it might circulate more widely and so do more good ; or, it may be, that it was thought advisable to give it the appearance of an English book, with the view of preventing any reprint or any new edition of the work in England. Accordingly, we find the author's designation omitted in the title-page, and a quotation from Whately's Rhetoric (a well-known English work) placed there ; his preface struck out to make way for one entirely different ; and further, the name of Otis, an American, (which occurs in the body of the work,) replaced by that of Curran, an Irish orator.*

But the act of Mr. J. R. Priestley assumes a very different character, when we find him allowing a charge of plagiarism against Mr. Parker to circulate uncontradicted for more than half a year, through Great Britain and the United States, when he, Mr. J. R. Priestley, was one of the few persons who could disprove the charge,—when he was the sole cause, by his own deliberate act, of the charge being made. Instead of confessing his fault, and doing all he could to make amends, the English publisher has remained silent, and left the American author to make his complaint to the Journal in which he was accused. In making the charge, we went upon the evidence furnished by Mr. J. R. Priestley, which on any future occasion we shall certainly be less ready to receive. We hope that the present statement will, as far as it is possible, make reparation to the author for any injury which we may have done him ; and we hope, too, that it may tend to check such offences as that which Mr. J. R. Priestley has committed. Mr. J. R. Priestley may indeed say, that as to suppressing † American authors' names, and garbling prefaces he has not set the example, at least, if the present is his first attempt in this line ; he has only improved upon it.

* We have just discovered a passage in Mr. J. R. Priestley's edition, which we did not notice before, and which we believe the English publisher either overlooked, or did not understand ; either supposition may be true. If he had seen and understood it, we have no doubt he could have changed an American revolution into an Irish rebellion, as dexterously as he has transformed an American into an Irish orator. The example is in p. 20, No. 6 : ' I have seen, in different parts of the Atlantic country, the breast-works, and other defences of earth, that were thrown up by our people during the war of the Revolution.'

† See one instance given in this Journal, No. I. p. 170, in the case of Richard Priestley, High Holborn ; and another in this Journal, No. IV. p. 331, in the case of Mr. Whittaker.

Universities of Belgium, Holland, Germany, Switzerland, Austria, Russia, Sweden and Norway, and Denmark.

Universities.	State in which situated.	Date of Institution or Renovation.	Year:	Total Number of Students.	MATRICULATIONS.			
					Divinity.	Law.	Medicine and Surgery.	Philosophical Sciences, &c.
Bâsle	Canton of B. Switzerland.	1459 R.1582	..*	..	..	..	..	..
Berlin	Prussia	1814	1814	640†	..	..	..	..
			1817	608	340	173	52	143†
			1819	689	..	..	..	..
			1828	1752	..	..	..	..
			1829	1706	566	628	299	203
			1831-2	1469	474	508	258	229
			1832-3	1732	569	585	320	258
			1833-4	1801	528	611	341	321
			1834-5	1800	553	571	368	308
Berne ‡	Canton of B. Switzerland	1834	1834	208	..	..	..	..
Bonn	Prussia.....	1780 R.1818	1819	45	..	..	..	..
			1820	402	..	..	..	..
			1825	749	..	..	..	..
			1828-9	1002	437	236	262	143
			1829-30	977	..	..	..	..
			1832	904	383	249	140	118
			1832-3	774	..	..	..	..
			1833-4	874	314	269	152	114
			1834-5	877	306	273	164	116
Breslau	Prussia.....	1702	1818	500	..	..	..	..
			1829	1147	541	365	104	137
			1831	1114	526	316	114	158
			1832	1013	470	249	109	175
			1833	941	463	263	106	109
			1834	875	429	238	102	106
Brussels§	Belgium....	1834	..	..	..	..	..	..
Charkoff	Russia	1803	1830	308	..	..	..	..
			1831	313	..	..	..	..
			1832	320	..	..	..	..
			1833-4	464	..	..	..	..
Christiania ..	Norway	1811 R.1818	1818	149	..	..	..	..
			1832	500	..	..	..	..
Copenhagen .	Denmark ...	1438	1815-20	..||	..	..	..	..
			1828	578	..	..	..	..
Cracow......	Republic of C.	..	1833	270	..	..	..	..
Dorpat......	Russia	1632 R.1803	1815	310	..	..	..	..
			1829	628	91	84	207	227

* No returns published ; students believed not to exceed 100.
† Besides in each year non-matriculated students attending special courses. In many foreign universities the students are not required to matriculate for any particular faculty ; and hence the discrepancies in many instances between the matriculations and the total numbers. ‡ Opened the 15th Nov. 1834.
§ Opened the 20th Nov. 1834. || Averaged by Stein at 700.

Universities.	State in which situated.	Date of Institution or Renovation.	Year.	Total Number of Students.	MATRICULATIONS.			
					Divinity.	Law.	Medicine and Surgery.	Philosophical Sciences, &c.
Dorpat *cont..*			1830	529	..	..	..	..
			1831	619	..	..	..	..
			1832	590	55	64	252	219
			1833	539	49	44	287	159
			1834	549	48	45	302	154
Erlangen....	Bavaria ...	1743	1815	227	..	..	..	..
			1817	abt.200	..	..	..	..
			1834	413	..	..	..	..
Freiburg	Baden	1456	1818	273	..	..	..	..
			1829	627	203	96	182	146
			1830	865	387	232	134	112
			1831	559	202	110	146	101
			1833	484	175	79	133	97
			1834	434	137	68	138	91
			1835	445	115	82	155	93
Ghent .,....	Belgium ...	1816	1823	395	..	..	..	..
Giessen	Hesse-Darmstadt	1607	1818	241	..	..	..	..
			1829	558	..	..	..	..
			1832	402	..	..	..	..
			1834	362	94	91	69	91
Göttingen ...	Hanover ...	1734	1812	1165	..	..	..	..
			1828	abt1500	..	..	..	..
			1831	920	235	354	206	125
			1832	847	227	321	167	132
			1834	860	58*	93*	59*	58*
			1835	878	..	..	..	..
Grätz	Austria	1586 R.1826	1828	321	..	..	..	..
Greifswald .	Prussia	1456	1818	55	..	..	..	..
			1827	160	..	..	..	..
			1829	183	..	..	..	..
			1833-4	219	..	..	..	..
Gröningen ..	Holland....	..	1830	284	..	..	..	..
			1831	314	..	..	..	..
Halle	Prussia	1694†	1816	500	..	..	..	..
			1829	1330	..	..	..	..
.. ..	.. ..		1833	868	530	168	89	81
.. ..			1834	842	521	162	95	64
Heidelberg ..	Baden	1386	1819	603	..	..	..	..
.. .			1823	587	55	340	47	95
..			1831	923	71	499	250	103
			1833	828	75	406	256	91
..			1834	518	..	..	..	..
Helsingfors‡.	Russia	1828	1832	420	..	..	..	..
			1833	422	..	..	..	..
Jena	Weimar	1587	1818-19	669	..	..	..	..
			1832	583	..	..	..	..
			1833	485	221	141	67	56
			1834	441	196	130	68	47
Innsbruck ...	Austria.....	1672 R.1825	1828	352	..	..	..	..

* New matriculations.   † University of Wittemberg united with it in 1817.
‡ Transferred from Abo after the fire in 1827.

Universities.	State in which situated.	Date of Institution or Renovation.	Year.	Total Number of Students.	MATRICULATIONS.			
					Divinity.	Law.	Medicine and Surgery.	Philosophical Sciences, &c.
Kasan or Oson	Russia	1803	1816	130	..	..	..	..
			1830	113	..	..	..	..
			1831	146	..	..	..	..
			1832	100	..	..	..	..
			1834	209	..	..	..	..
Kiel	Denmark ...	1665	1819	111	..	..	..	..
			1833	294	110	100	70	14
			1834	321	110	123	76	11
			1835	293	95	99	73	26
Kiew*	Russia	1833	1835	300	..	..	..	..
Königsburg..	Prussia.....	1544	1818	300	..	..	..	..
..	..		1829	452	..	..	..	..
			1830	416	215	114	19	63
			1831	471	..	..	..	..
			1834	480	..	..	..	..
Leipzig	Saxony	1409	1819	1000	and up	wards	..	..
			1831	1436	..	..	..	..
			1832	1400	..	..	..	..
			1834	1307	..	..	..	..
Lemberg	Austria.....	1784 R.1817	1833	1311	485	242	185	399
Leyden......	Holland....	1575	1830	684	..	..	..	..
			1831	791	..	..	..	..
			1834	745	..	..	..	..
			1835	647	212	250	131	54
Liege	Belgium ...	1816	1828	511	..	..	..	..
Louvain	Belgium ...	1426	1828	651	..	..	..	..
Lund	Sweden	1666	1794	360	..	..	..	..
			1819	600	..	..	..	..
			1829	640	148	108	34	145
			1833	639	103	101	59	138
			1834	596	108	130	50	160
Malines.....	Belgium ...	1834	..	..	..	..	..	..
Marburg	Elect. Hesse	1527	1818	200	..	..	..	..
..	..		1827	350 to 370	..	..	..	..
			1832	362	..	..	..	..
			1833	422	..	..	..	..
Moscow	Russia	1755	1829	716	..	..	..	..
			1830	754	..	..	..	..
			1833	900	..	..	..	..
Munich	Bavaria	1826†	1826	1369	..	..	..	..
			1830	1854	..	..	..	..
			1831	1915	493	525	275	562
			1832	1585	..	..	..	..
			1833	1592	344	469	342	437
			1834	1502	234	450	365	364
			1835	1433	218	415	385	385
Münster	Prussia	1631	1827	399‡	..	..	..	..
			1829	361	..	..	..	..

* Opened 1834.   † Transferred from Landeshut and Ingolstadt.
‡ Principally Roman Catholic Divinity, and Medicine.

Universities	State in which situated.	Date of Institution or Renovation.	Year.	Total Number of Students.	MATRICULATIONS.			
					Divinity.	Law.	Medicine and Surgery.	Philosophical Sciences, &c.
Olmütz	Austria.....	1581 R.1827	1833	682	..	..	..	..
Pesth	Austria	1633	1815	812	75	205	172	360
			1833-4	1666	33	224	930	387
			1834-5	1610	72	184	885	409
Petersburg ..	Russia.....	1819	1827	177	..	..	..	..
			1830	202	..	..	..	..
			1832	310	..	..	..	..
			1834	206	..	..	..	..
Prague......	Austria	1348	1817	879	..	..	..	..
			1825	1449	..	..	..	..
Rostock	Mecklenburg-Schwerin	1419	1820	80	..	..	..	..
			1830	abt.110	..	..	..	..
Tübingen....	Würtemburg	1477	1821	740	..	..	..	..
			1829	874	..	..	..	..
			1830	887	396	103	166	222
			1833	822	..	..	..	..
			1834	756	342	72	173	169
			1835	734	289	82	166	181
Upsala	Sweden	1478 R.1595	1768-77	534	..	..	..	..
			1820	1297*	..	..	..	..
			1829	1443*	315	386	111	354
		·	1831	830†	..	..	..	..
			1833	1381	269	304	159	368‡
			1834	1303	245	331	150	328‡
Utrecht	Holland....	1634	1818	198	..	..	..	..
			1830	476	..	..	..	..
			1831	519	..	..	..	..
			1834-5	553	154	73	53	273
Vienna§	Austria.....	1365	1817	1103||	..	..	..	..
			1825	1954	..	..	..	..
			1832	1619	309	332	519	459
Würzburg ...	Bavaria	1403 R.1582	1831	605	159	99	230	117
			1832	521	118	109	244	50
			1834	402	..	..	..	..
			1835	408	..	..	..	..
Zürich¶	Canton of Z. Switzerland.	1833	1834	164	..	..	..	..

* On the books.   † Present.

‡ The remaining students had not entered to any particular faculty.

§ In the year 1832 the eight Austrian Universities were attended by 20,603 students, inclusive of students of the fine arts, in the ecclesiastical seminaries, &c., not matriculated.

|| In Italy--Pavia, 1831, 1300 ; Padua, do. 410.

¶ 54 professors and lecturers ; yearly expense 5870*l.*

Proportion between the Number of Students in each State and the Population, 1834-5.

States.	Population.	Number of Universities.	Matriculated Students.	In every 17,000 souls.
Russia	52,000,000	7	3050	about 1
Switzerland	2,100,000	3	470	— 3 $\frac{80}{100}$
Mecklenburg-Schwerin	464,000	1	110	— 4
Austria	35,000,000	9	9000	— 4 $\frac{37}{...}$
Prussia	13,400,000	7†	5500	about 7
Belgium	4,100,000	5	1700	do. 7
Denmark	2,000,000	2†	870	— 7 $\frac{39}{...}$
Würtemburg	1,620,000	1†	730	— 7 $\frac{44}{...}$
Grand Duchy of Hesse	740,000	1†	360	— 8 $\frac{27}{...}$
Bavaria	4,200,000	3†	2300	— 9 $\frac{30}{...}$
Hanover	1,600,000	1†	880	— 9 $\frac{35}{...}$
Sweden and Norway	4,100,000	3	2400	nearly 10
Holland	2,482,000	3†	1520	— 10 $\frac{44}{...}$
Electorate of Hesse	650,000	1†	420	nearly 11
Baden	1,230,000	2†	960	— 13 $\frac{21}{...}$
Saxe-Weimar, —— Coburg Gotha, —— Meiningen H.	542,000	1†	440	— 13 $\frac{80}{...}$
Saxony	1,580,000	1†	1300	nearly 14
	127,901,500	52	32,280	Average 4$\frac{21}{100}$

N. B. In all the Universities which have † affixed to their names, there are many German students and others who are not subjects of the States to which those institutions belong. The average proportion may be estimated at one-tenth of the respective number of students.

MISCELLANEOUS

FOREIGN.

FRANCE.

Paris.—Rapid progress is making in the education of the lower classes. The principal object proposed to be attained in the infant asylums is to accustom the inmates from their earliest years to industry and obedience. There were not more than seven of these establishments in the year 1833; but at present there are nineteen of them, which are attended by 3500 children. The documents laid before the municipal council of Paris give the subequent view of the statistics of education in its public institutions for the year 1834, beginning with the lowest class, and closing with the colleges attached to the University of Paris.

Asylums founded and supported by the administrators of the hospitals 19 ; number of children received 3500.

Schools for Children maintained by the city of Paris 49 ; and by the hospitals 71 ; total 120 ; number of pupils 25,035.

Adult Schools, maintained by the city of Paris 19 ; and by the hospitals 7 ; total 26 ; number of pupils 1898.

Independently of these establishments, the authorities have founded 29 schools of industry (*ouvroirs*), in which 1595 girls, between the ages of twelve and fifteen, are taught to work at the needle.

Colleges, 7 in number, attended by 4932 pupils, of whom 1873 are boarded and lodged in the colleges, and 3059 are day-scholars.

The whole number of these several establishments is 172, and that of the individuals attending them 36,960.

Lyons.—The Academy of this town, a branch of the University of France, has opened a faculty of science, which began its courses in January, in the Palais de St. Pierre, where the lectures are delivered until a definitive site is fixed upon. The classes in chemistry and experimental philosophy will not be opened before a laboratory and other requisite means are provided.

Rouen.—The Society of Emulation in this town has established three gratuitous courses for young men engaged in trade or mechanical pursuits. The subjects at present taught are commercial law, book-keeping, and mechanics. Other courses, which will complete a system of instruction adapted to the pupil's station in li'e, will hereafter be set on foot.

French Academy.—The members have been placed in a singular situation by a clause in the will of their late colleague, M. Arnault. It is dated on the 18th of February, 183 t, and is to the following effect: ' I entreat the French Academy, which has so much honoured me by the constant and intrepid interest it has evinced towards me during my exile, and which has restored me with the least possible delay to that station among its members of which I had been deprived by a contemptible stretch of power, to accept this last expression of my respectful gratitude. It would set the last seal to my aspirations if it met my liveliest and most ardent wish, by granting the seat which will become vacant by my decease to the author of Regulus, Peter of Portugal, Catherine of Medicis, and the Death of Tiberius. It may be possible that these works, which have often earned the applause of good taste, and have never done violence to good sense, may be considered sufficient grounds for justifying this testimony of its regard, which I solicit from the depth of my grave. I will not add to these considerations, that I solicit it in behalf of my own son.' M. Lucien Arnault, the son here named, transmitted a copy of the clause to every individual of the Academy, and Dupaty, one of the candidates for the vacant seat, was in consequence induced to withdraw. In spite of the appeal, however, Lucien did not prove successful at the ballot of the 22nd January last.

University Budget.—The budget of the Minister of Public Instruction, for the year ending 1836, includes the same items of expenditure as those for 1835, which amounted to 12,291,629 francs, or about 491,665*l.* There is an addition to the budget for the former year of 28,000*l.* (700,000 fr.), which are applicable to the purposes of national education (*instruction primaire*). In all other respects, the budgets for the two years are precisely similar. It appears by a report to the king, which is attached to the present budget, that the minister is desirous of a grant of 6000*l.* (150,000 fr.) towards the establishment of district colleges (*collèges communaux*); but the legislature decline to vote this sum until they have first decided upon the system to be pursued with regard to the class of secondary instruction: the primary, it will be remembered, forms the elementary education, and approximates in character to that of our national and Lancasterian schools. M. Guizot has also added his report to the king on the measures prescribed with a view to investigate and publish the most valuable inedited records illustrative of French history : and he closes the‐appendices with a return of the functionaries and other official persons who are resident in the several buildings and establish‐ments within the cognizance of the Minister of Public Instruction, or under the roof of the University buildings themselves. This return shows that 58 individuals reside in the public libraries in Paris; 78 in the Museum of Natural History; and 29 in other literary and scientific establishments, such as the Institute, the College of France, the Royal Academy of Physic, and the Board of

Longitude. The residents in the buildings belonging to the University consist of 7 rectors or inspectors of academies, 10 professors of the faculty of law at Paris, 9 deans or professors of the other faculties, 21 secretaries or apparitors of academies and faculties, and 44 persons otherwise employed in the service. The whole number gratuitously housed is 91.

STRASBURG.—*School for the Children of Beggars.*—The Anti-Mendicity Society in this town have very wisely included schools for gratuitous instruction in their arrangements ; and we are gratified to learn that they have already done much good. These schools consist of

2 schools of a superior class, attended by .	69 pupils.
4 intermediate schools for boys . .	447
1 evening school for young mechanics .	89
4 girls' schools with a needle-work school	361
	966
The Society has likewise opened	
8 receptacles or asylums, containing .	1113
1 school and asylum in the citadel .	89

In all 20 establishments, containing . . 2168 pupils.

A meeting of this active society was held on the 28th of December last, when prizes were given to 305 boys and girls, principally as a reward for their good conduct, application, and general assiduity. The prizes consisted of articles of clothing, which were almost exclusively contributed by the benevolence of female friends to the institution. The ladies who act as patronesses and inspectors on the several committees, and have come forward to assist the teachers in their schools, got the little bundles of clothing together, and adjusted their contents in such a way, that their value was as nearly proportioned as possible to the merits of the candidates.

Jewish Schools.—From an account given by M. Cahen, the director of the Jewish seminary at Paris, it appears that no Jewish school was regularly organized in France before the year 1817; they were at that time mere private speculations, mostly in very unqualified hands, and not subject to any superior control ; and nothing was taught in them but the Bible and Talmud. Metz, in the first place, and Paris next, established public schools for the indigent children of Hebrew parents ; and the example has since been followed by several other French towns, particularly in Lorraine and Alsace. Nearly 2000 boys attend these establishments in the last mentioned provinces; and we may add to these 2000 those Jewish children who attend private schools kept by masters of their own persuasion, Christian seminaries, and institutions of a superior class.

Munificent Bequests.—The late M. Dupuytren, the most eminent

French surgeon of the present day, has not only bequeathed a sum of 8000*l.* (200,000 francs) for endowing a professorship of medico-surgical pathology in Paris, but has left 20,000*l.* (500,000 francs) for the establishment of an asylum for twelve aged medical practitioners.

University of Paris.—The present number of students registered in the faculty of medicine is 4500, and in that of jurisprudence upwards of 5000. The Polytechnic School has 302 pupils.

BELGIUM.

The 'Moniteur Belge' of the 2nd February contains four ordinances; one of which directs that a national museum shall be formed at Brussels, for the purpose of receiving the most distinguished productions of Belgian painters, sculptors, engravers, and architects; the second directs that a triennial exhibition of paintings, sculptures, engravings, architectural designs, and lithographical publications shall be held in the same city, from the 1st of September to the 1st of October—the first exhibition being fixed for the year 1836. The third ordinance establishes a board of commissioners, who are to advise with the minister of the home department on the subject of repairing such national monuments as are memorable on account of their antiquity, the recollections associated with them, or their importance as works of art, &c. And the fourth authorises the minister of the home department to employ native artists in executing statues of the most illustrious Belgians, and orders these statues to be placed in the Museum or other national edifices.

Adult Female School.—A school for adult females of the labouring class was opened in Brussels on the 1st of February last, when fifty pupils were admitted. None will be received but those who can read and write, nor will a greater number be admitted for the next two months, by the end of which time it is expected that, out of those fifty, a sufficient number of monitresses will be in readiness to assist. Females of all ages will hereafter be allowed to attend free of expense, provided they bring undeniable characters with them. They will be instructed in reading, writing, spelling, Christian morals, and such manual employments as are suitable to their sex and station in life. A *normal school*, set on foot by the benevolent individuals who have founded the adult female school,—was opened on the 1st of March, and is conducted without any expense to those who attend it. Its object is, by affording a more comprehensive range of instruction to such females as are desirous of becoming teachers in schools and private families than has been hitherto within their reach, to render unnecessary the assistance of males in the education of females. With this view, distinct branches of study are open to the attendance of the pupils. Those branches for which present provision has been made consist of history, geography, chronology, literature, grammar, logic, style, literary composition, and arithmetic, for each of which separate classes have been formed. It is intended likewise to form classes for foreign lan. guages and elegant accomplishments. A separate course will be established in which the science of education will be taught. The pupils are at liberty to attend the whole or any portion of the several courses, but none will be admitted who have not, to a certain extent, been educated.

HOLLAND.

Invention of Stereotype Printing.—Baron Westreenen van Tiellandt, who has already distinguished himself by several publications on the origin and early progress of the typographical art, has lately added to them a 'Rapport sur les Recherches relatives à l'Invention première et à l'usage le plus ancien de l'Imprimerie Stéréotype.' This work is the result of a commission. which the Dutch government gave him, to inquire into the earliest use of stereotype printing, with a view to ascertain whether Holland could fairly lay claim to the merit of the invention. The baron, in his present work, first mentions the attempts made by the celebrated Didot of Paris, when printing Callet's logarithmic tables, and shows that he cannot be considered the inventor of the stereotype art. He next proceeds to notice the previous discoveries of Carez. the printer, our countryman Tilloch, and more particularly Ged, the Edinburgh printer, whose duodecimo edition of Sallust in the year 1739 is quoted by Camus in his 'Histoire du Polytypage,' as one of the first essays made in this branch of typography. Whatever merit may attach to any of these attempts, it appears evident, from the careful investigation through which the baron has waded, that they were of a date long subsequent to the attempts made by a German clergyman, the Rev. John Müller of Leyden, who died in that town in the year 1710. This individual so fully matured his invention, as not only to incorporate every page of type into a solid mass by metal-casting at the back of it, but to take off casts from the face of the type itself; he was assisted by his son William, and as early as the year 1701, produced a small book of prayers, written in Dutch, by J. Havermans, which was stereotyped throughout. This was not the only essay he made ; for it has been now ascertained beyond all question, that Schaaf's 'New Testament and Lexicon' in the Syriac, a Dutch Bible both in folio and quarto, and an English folio Bible, were printed by him or his son, in stereotype, between the years 1708 and 1715. Baron Westreenen refers, in proof of this assertion, to several plates of these books which are still in existence ; they were collected by him in the course of his researches, and are now preserved in the Royal Library at the Hague, of which he is the keeper. He gives three specimens, actually printed from the plates in question, in his report. A fourth plate contains a fac-simile of the hand-writing of the celebrated scholar Prosper Marchand, who expressly assigns the priority of the invention to the reverend divine, and pointedly speaks of its peculiar applicability to the printing of Bibles, New Testaments, Psalters, &c. The baron has had the good sense to render this interesting publication more generally accessible by giving a French text parallel with the Dutch.

SWITZERLAND.

CANTON OF ZÜRICH.—*Seminary for educating Masters.*—This useful institution was opened with much solemnity on the 7th May, 1832; it is established in the town of Küssnacht, and calculated for the reception of between twenty-five and thirty pupils. The entire course of study extends over two years, and is conducted by a director and an under-master; but special teachers are called in for extra branches of study, which can only be pursued in extra hours. No pupil is admitted under the age of sixteen. The course comprises Christian doctrine and morals, biblical knowledge, and scripture history; arithmetic, geometry, the science of vocal harmony, national history, and such parts of natural history, geography, and agriculture as are generally useful. There is a second course, in which the pupils are instructed in the art of teaching, both theoretically and practically, and this is rendered still more effectual by placing them occasionally at the head of classes. The education given in this seminary is wholly gratuitous, and the expense is defrayed by the canton. The government buildings at Küssnacht have been appropriated to this purpose. In order that education may not stop at this point, *conferences* are directed to be held in every scholastic district, and all teachers and candidates for the situation of a teacher are required to assist at them. Four of these meetings are held in the course of the year; the subjects which engage their attention, are practical exercises in modes of tuition, the reading of papers on topics connected with education, whether original or derived from experience in other quarters, discussions on any new views or apparent results in the conduct of education, and the circulation of approved publications for advancing the science of tuition. A director presides at every conference; and the directors themselves assemble once a year, under the presidency of the director of the seminary at Küssnacht, in order to make the requisite arrangements for the quarterly conferences of the ensuing year.

We have before us the estimates of the ways and means of this canton for the year 1834, which are calculated at 1,333,380 Sw. francs, or about 88,900*l.*, as well as of the expenditure, which is calculated at 1,281,433 frs. or about 85,440*l.* Among the various items in these accounts we observe, under the head of 'Public Instruction,' the following appropriations:—to the *gymnasium* and *school of industry* 37,740 frs. (2500*l.*), the *university* (1575*l.*); salaries, fuel, and lights for the *cantonal seminaries,* 81,990 frs. (5470*l.*); for *educating masters,* 8560 frs. (570*l.*) For 167 schoolmasters with less than fifty pupils (80 frs. each), 262 with more than fifty pupils (100 frs. each), and ten assistants (40 frs. each),—in all 39,960 frs. (2665*l.*); and for the *higher classes* of

national schools 20,000 frs. (1335*l.*) These estimates are remarkable in several points of view. In the first place, the allowances to
the highest servants of the state are so small, that no individuals
can be tempted to take office but persons of property, who can
afford to make up the deficiencies in their yearly stipends by drawing upon their personal incomes. The burgomaster for instance,
though ex-officio president of the Diet for 1834, in which capacity
he received an extra allowance of 270*l.* (4000 frs.), did not altogether enjoy a larger income from the state than 375*l.* (5600 frs.);
a sum totally inadequate to meet the reasonable expences of his office.
The councillors of government too are not allowed more than 95*l.*
a year, which is not half as much as the expenditure which their
station requires from them. The whole net amount of the public
revenues does not exceed 1,302,780 francs, about 86,360*l.*, which,
as the number of inhabitants in the canton is at present about
225,000, would be but a fraction more than seven shillings and
eightpence per head. So considerable a portion, however, of these
revenues is derived from national domains, benefices, regalia, &c.
that scarcely more than one-third of them proceed from *taxes;* and
the actual sum paid in taxes, is thereby reduced to about two
shillings and five-pence per head. In fact, not only has Zürich no
public debt, but it possesses considerable funds lent out at interest.
We believe, too, there is no state in Europe which expends, like
this canton, *more* upon education, than upon its military establishments: to the former purpose it devotes 14*l.* out of every 100*l.* of
its expenditure, but to the latter only 10*l.*

BASLE-CHAMPAIGN.—The government of this canton have just
published the outlines of a new law for the regulation of the national schools; it proposes that every master should have a suitable and gratuitous dwelling, with firing free, a plot of ground, an
annual allowance of 250 Swiss francs (about 17*l.*), and a fee of
five francs (about 6*s.* 9*d.*), from each pupil. The masters will no
longer be permitted ' to indulge in the sports of the field.' Parochial ministers are to be bound to give every child of proper age
weekly instruction for six hours, in history and the German language; and a school is to be established in every parish. In
Liechstall (the capital of the canton), Waldenburg, Geiterkinden,
and Therwil, district-seminaries are to be opened, in which French,
history, geography, the mathematics, &c. are to be taught; as well
as Latin and Greek, where there are not less than three pupils who
desire it.—(*Zürich*, 21 *January*.)

Bern and Zürich Universities.—The latest accounts we possess
of these two infant institutions, represent them as in a thriving
state. The students at Bern have entered into a resolution to
inflict very severe penalties on duelling, a custom which has been
attended with the most mischievous consequences to many of the
German universities. Dr. Arnold, professor of anatomy at Heidelberg, one of the most eminent anatomists in Germany, has ac-

cepted the chair of anatomy at Bern; and M. Mittler, who lectured on history at Heidelberg, has been appointed professor of that science at Zürich.

LUCERN.—There are 165 primary schools in this canton, more than one half of which are open both in summer and winter; the secondary schools amount to sixteen. The town of Lucern, with a population of 6055 souls, possesses five primary schools for boys, and as many for girls; four schools for little children, and two secondary schools for both sexes. The number of pupils in all these establishments is upwards of 800. Secondary schools have been opened in the various districts of the canton, so as to supply, as was conceived, the wants of their communities; but the pupils are so greatly on the increase, that the government will soon be called upon to make an addition to the number of schools now in operation. In spite of the exertions made to improve the state of these schools and the means of the masters, there is no master at present in a situation to direct the education of more than 120 pupils.

ITALY.

THE TWO SICILIES.—A letter from Milan contains the following remarks:—'There is not at present a single parish or cure of souls in Lombardy, without a school; the number has now increased to 3746.' But our accounts from the two Sicilies show a far less satisfactory state of things. The business of national education in those quarters is wretchedly in arrear. There is many a district and parish there without a single school, and thirty populous towns at least have pressing occasion for additions to the solitary school, which is allowed them. The instruction of females is a point to which scarcely any attention is paid; the daughters of the nobility and of civil and military officers alone, are admitted into the two royal establishments in Naples; but the middle and lower classes of females are left to depend upon the limited stock of information which may be picked up in monasteries and convents. The low state of education may be inferred from the fact, that among the two thousand girls and young women, who attend the schools in the two Sicilies, there is not one in five whose acquirements reach beyond mere reading. You will rarely find a single peasant in the Abruzzi, who can spell or write his name; no wonder, therefore, that every attempt to ameliorate his condition has miscarried; and you will quite as rarely meet with a family in comfortable circumstances, or unencumbered by debts. An indolent unconcern for improvement seems to have laid hold of the entire body and mind of this uncivilized region. Ignorance is its universal characteristic; scarcely a book is to be seen in the whole country, for there are but two wretched dealers within its borders, and no pains whatever are taken to excite either a love of knowledge or a spirit of emulation. There is abundance of talent in the people themselves, and no quarter of the globe would sooner place itself on a level with the most enlightened nations in Europe, if it had the advantage of education.'

Genoa.—The number of students in this university, which is of so recent a date as the year 1812, has varied of late years between four and five hundred. It is conducted by a 'Curatorium' or senate, consisting of a president (the Cavaliere L. Provana di Collegno), and five members. There are four professors attached to the *theological* faculty, namely, for scholastics and dogmatics, divinity in general and its dogmas, the sacred scriptures, the Hebrew tongue, and moral theology. In the faculty of *jurisprudence* there are six professorships, namely, two for the pandects, and one each for the decretals, commercial law, civil law, and canon law. Nine chairs are attached to the faculty of *medicine*; namely, clinics and nosology, botany, natural history, materia medica and forensic medicine, pathology and physic, internal clinics and syphilitical diseases, surgery in general, midwifery, and the practice of surgery. The faculty of *philosophy* consists of seven professors, namely, of mechanics, chemistry, arithmetic and geometry, Latin elocution and Greek, the differential and integral calculus, logic and metaphysics, and Italian elocution. There are also seven 'Professori giubilati,' namely, for mathematics, canon law, clinics, technical chemistry, anatomy and physiology, divinity and dogmatics of the schools, and holy writ and Hebrew. The number of lecturers and supplementary professors is eight; namely, one in the theological faculty, one in that of jurisprudence; two in canon and civil law; three in surgery and medicine; and one in philosophy, for ancient philosophy and mathematics.

GERMANY.

Saxony.—Two years ago the masters of all the national schools in and about Dresden, in conjunction with the directors of the two seminaries, called the 'Freemason's Institute' and 'Blockmann's Institution for Education,' formed a pedagogic society ; the number of members has now increased to 109 regular and seven honorary, who hold their meetings in one of the larger school-rooms, where they discuss topics connected with their profession at stated times. The society held the second anniversary of its foundation on the 30th of January.

Baden.—*Heidelberg in olden times.*—Rupert the First elector-palatine, whom contemporary chronicles style 'a chivalrous prince,' and describe as 'magnanimous towards the helpless, a good neighbour, and of righteous bearing in the spirit of the age,' was the founder of this university. In his epistle to Charles the Fifth, king of France, he speaks of himself as being a simple layman, ignorant of any tongue besides that of his native country, but taught to appreciate the value and benefits of such an institution, by the example of Prague and his intercourse with the emperor Charles the Fourth, whom he had accompanied in several campaigns. He entrusted the entire organization of his new university to the celebrated Marsilius von Inghen, who had been professor of philosophy in Paris, where he had twice filled the office of rector. The seminary, which this scholar established here in the year 1346, and for which he obtained the pope's sanction thirty years afterwards, in all probability suggested the foundation of the university. Rupert having received the pope's approbation, directed the institution to be opened on the 18th of October, 1386; its foundation bears date, the 1st of the same month. In the first instance, there were but three professors employed: Marsilius von Inghen, as professor of the science then in the ascendant, 'scholastic philosophy,' read logic; Reginald, a Cistercian monk from the diocese of Liege, lectured on St. Paul's epistle to Titus; and Heilmann Wunenberg, of Worms, who had obtained the degree of master of the liberal arts at Prague, expounded one of the books of Aristotle's Natural History. The first lectures were delivered on the 19th of October. Scanty as such a beginning may at first sight appear, it was by no means so in substance and efficiency; for the scholars of those days frequently poured forth the whole store of their attainments upon a subject, professedly of narrow compass. On no other grounds can the attendance of upwards of five hundred students on the first year's courses at Heidelberg be in any way accounted for. Some weeks afterwards we find Ditmar von Swerthe lending his assistance by a course on the liberal arts; and before the year had expired, John of Noyt or Noet lecturing on canon law. Rupert having expressly directed, that Heidelberg should be modelled after the university of Paris, it was divided into four faculties: philosophy, theology, law, and physics; and until the year 1393, the rectors were chosen by the teacher attached to the faculty of philosophy, which included every branch of learning and science which was not connected with either theology, law, or physic. Besides the rector, the university had a chancellor, whose office and prerogative it was to confer academical dignities on such persons as were reported to him as worthy of promotion to them, after due examination. The head of the chapter of Worms, was ex-officio chancellor, and the first who held this station was Conrad of Geylnhausen. There were likewise a vice-chancellor, and four conservators, whose office it was to watch over and uphold the rights and liberties of the university. The professors and burgesses, who boarded students, were exempted from certain taxes, and, at Christmas in every year, the various lodgings in the town were examined and valued, and no one was permitted to receive a higher rent for them than what was then fixed.—(*Dr. Engelmann's Heidelberg in Ancient and Modern Times.*)

PRUSSIA.

BERLIN.—According to the official return, the number of matriculated students attending this university during the present term viz., from Michaelmas to Easter, 1835, is 1800; of whom 553 have entered for divinity, 571 for jurisprudence, 368 for medicine and surgery, and 308 for philosophical sciences. Besides these students, the courses are attended by 75 individuals from other universities, whose matriculation remains in suspense, and 554 non-matriculated individuals, such as pupils in physic, surgery, and pharmacy; others from the Institute of Frederic-William, and the Academies of Architecture, Woods and Forests, Mining, Horticulture, and Arts and Sciences, &c., all of whom are entitled to admission to the lectures. The lectures, therefore, are altogether attended by 2354 students, independently of the 75 whose matriculation has not hitherto been approved.

BRESLAU.—The institution, known by the name of the 'Franke Foundation,' comprises the following establishments:—1. A public school for boys and girls, consisting of eight classes, four of which form the boys' school, and as many the girls' school; 2. A female school (*Töchterschule*); 3. A civic school for boys of three classes: 4. Two gymnasia, namely, the 'Latin School,' consisting of six classes, and the Royal 'Pädagogium,' which also contains six classes, together with a pro-gymnasial class; and 5. A school of practical knowledge, or *Realschule*. The number of male and female pupils, who are educating in all these establishments during the present winter, is 2120; and 508 boys and 16 girls of this number are boarded and lodged, as well as educated upon the foundation. There are 132 masters and 12 mistresses employed in instructing and taking care of the children.

BAVARIA.

MUNICH.—20th November.—Though the interval allowed for matriculation has been extended beyond the fourteen days originally fixed, and such students as arrive after its expiration have been threatened with expulsion by the hands of the police, we have not more than 1300 inscribed on the books, instead of the 1800 or 1900, who entered the university on former occasions. A variety of circumstances have brought this unfortunate state of things about; the government have adopted measures to reduce the number of young men who are ambitious of a university education; and they have also issued rigid regulations with a view to put down their meetings in private houses, prevent their congregating (*zusammenkneipen*) in taverns, or treating young women to serenades; in fact, such recreations as these are no longer permitted without previous license from the police. Nor can any student give a comrade a night's lodging, unless he has intimated his intention beforehand to the constituted authorities; and every inhabitant of the town is required, under heavy penalties, to give notice to the police if he have the slightest reason to suspect, that arms are kept in any house in which a student resides, or that military exercises are going on in it. Another great drawback is caused by the vast number of students who are under arrest, as well as by there being a still greater number, who have been released with a caution not to show themselves in the lecture-rooms.

Munich Greek School.—A lyceum, designed for the education of Greek youth between the ages of nine and eighteen, has existed in Munich since the month of August, 1833. A printed address, dated on the 20th of that month, and drawn up by D. Parrhiniadis, the individual appointed by the present Greek government, has been circulated in Greece, powerfully enforcing upon the people at large the necessity of attending to the moral and intellectual improvement of their younger fellow-countrymen, and upbraiding them with the indifference which they have hitherto shown in this respect. The plan of studies to be pursued in the Lyceum at Munich, is varied so as to meet the wants of the pupils, whether they are intended for an ecclesiastical, a learned, a military, a commercial, or a mechanical profession. The several branches of instruction which this lyceum undertakes to teach are, ancient Greek, with constant reference to modern Greek, Latin, German, French, Italian, and English; religion, universal and special history, geography, arithmetic, and the higher branches of the mathematics, natural history, rhetoric, moral philosophy, drawing, writing, singing, dancing, gymnastics, and swimming. The pupils will also be taught, where it is their particular wish, to play on some musical instrument. The method of instruction is formed on the German model. Professor Thiersch has been appointed ephorus of this seminary by special desire of the Greek government. We have reason to believe, that it will remain at Munich for a few years only, and will then be transferred to the soil of Greece itself.

GRAND-DUCHY OF HESSE.—*Educational Reform.*—The *studien-plan*, or system of education lately promulgated, comprises seven languages, six branches of technical knowledge (*realien*), among which no mention whatever is made of natural history, and three branches of the fine arts. To the routine of education laid down for the gymnasia, which are to consist of eight classes, a youth is admissible at the age of ten years; but there is no class in which more than 30 hours' instruction per week are prescribed. After the eighth class has been mastered, a boy begins to learn *Latin* ten hours a week, and ultimately reaches the *prima* or first class, where the term is reduced to seven hours a week. *Greek* commences with the sixth class, at the rate of two hours a week, and the time is gradually increased to six hours, when a youth enters the first or finishing class. Instruction in the *native tongue* begins with the eighth class, at the rate of four hours per week, and ceases with two hours in the first. *French* is taught three hours a week in every class, and two are devoted to *Hebrew* in the two upper classes, commencing with the second. The *mathematics* are taught for two hours a week in the two lowest classes, for three in the fifth and sixth, and for four in the first, second, third, and fourth.

Natural philosophy occupies an hour per week ; *history* two hours in each class, and *geography* as many in the six lower classes ; but *ancient geography* is entirely omitted. Philosophy, logic, and experimental philosophy are studied by none but the first class. Writing is confined to the three lowest classes, and instruction in psalmody and singing to the four lowest, but private instruction is allowed to be given in the four highest. Drawing is taught in three sections ; and if it be desired the pupils may learn English and Italian. It is much to be feared, that under a system like this, whatever powers of mind the scholar may possess, they stand the fairest possible chance in the world of being dissipated by such a variety, so far at least as any depth or solidity of attainment is concerned.

GÖTTINGEN.—His Majesty has given the sum of 3000*l.* towards the erection of the new University buildings.

AUSTRIA.

National Schools.—Among the Austrian sovereigns none have paid greater attention to the intellectual improvement of the lower orders than Maria Theresa, Joseph the Second, and the present Emperor. In this important respect more has been done in the dominions of the crown of Austria than, until of late years, in any even of the western states of Europe. Of all its national schools those in the German provinces of that crown have been placed upon the most effective footing ; and there are some who ascribe their superiority to the stand which their directors have made against the introduction of what is termed the mutual instruction system—a system which ought not to be adopted, except where no better means of providing tuition are at hand. The national schools in Austria are of three kinds, primary schools, head schools, and schools of practical attainments (*trivial-schulen, haupt-schulen,* and *real-schulen*). The subjects taught in the primary schools are religion, morals, reading, writing, and arithmetic, with occasional instruction in such pursuits as are called for in common life ; such as practical mechanics, &c. These schools are open to every one, even to the children of the most humble individuals. Parents who are destitute of means, not only pay no fee for the admission of their children, but the latter are supplied with the requisite books gratuitously. In every place where a parochial register (*pfarr-buch*) is kept, a school of this description has been established under directions from the government ; many have likewise been opened in places which lie at a considerable distance from a parish church, or are situated under other peculiar circumstances. The *head schools* are designed for the benefit of those who are intended for employments connected with the arts or mechanics, and with retail trade, as well as for those who are preparing themselves for the grammar schools (*lateinische schulen*). The same course is here pursued as in the primary schools, but it is carried to a greater extent. There are several of these head schools in every province, one at least in every circle and every populous town. There are *model* and *normal* schools in the capital of each province, to which the head schools in minor spots are directed to assimilate their several methods and operations; and to these schools a fourth class is attached, in which the pupils are prepared for the real-schools or civic schools, or the education of those is completed who are not in circumstances to be able to attend any better class of seminaries. The additional instruction which they here receive consists of drawing, geometry, architecture, stereometry, mechanics, geography, and natural history; the whole of which are taught with special reference to the uses of common life. The fourth and last class of national schools is the real or civic school, which is designed for the use of boys whose destination is of a higher character, such as artists, merchants, brokers, stewards, accountants, &c. Here they are instructed in commercial operations, the laws of bills of exchange, the history of the arts, chemistry, design, foreign languages, &c. The superintendence over the conduct and moral government of the national schools, as well as the immediate direction of these schools, is intrusted to the clergy, as possessing in general higher attainments and a greater degree of influence than other individuals. The minister of the parish is the immediate superintendent of the parish school, and the deacon or vice-deacon of the district schools. These parties, whose duties are accurately laid down, are subordinate to the chief civil authorities of circles and to the Protestant consistories, who have concurrent jurisdiction over the schools; and they are themselves subordinate to the governments (*gubernia*) of each province, who, in all cases of emergency, take their directions from the board of education at Vienna. The children of non-conformists and Jews, in those places where they have no schools of their own, are admitted into the regular schools, care being taken to abstain from any interference with their religious instruction. Equal attention is paid to the education of the female portion of the community among the lower orders, and primary schools have been specially established for their benefit; but wherever the opening of such schools has not been practicable, the girls are instructed simultaneously with the boys in the ordinary parochial schools.—(*Blumenbach's General Survey of the Austrian Monarchy.*)

Protestant College at Debreczin in Hungary.—On my visit to Mr. Fay, the burgomaster of Debreczin, he afforded me an opportunity of examining his cabinet of coins, as well as several rare genealogical folios which the Protestant College will inherit upon his decease. They contain the genealogies of the most celebrated native reformers, from the earliest days of the Reformation. I observed one of Samuel Lowzahn's family, compiled by him in 1587; another of Gregory Mártonsalva and his son, from 1656 to 1721; a third by Francis P. Papai of the year 1710, in which Newton and Hutton have inscribed their names; a fourth was by Gregory Marotty, of the year 1731; a fifth by George Koeroesy, of the year 1726; and a sixth contained an original enumeration of the Hungarian youth who attended the University of Wittenberg between the years 1546 and 1608. The latter is rich in Esterhaszys, Palfys, Pechys, and Mariassys, sons of the most distinguished Hungarian nobility. The most remarkable institution in this enormous *village*, as some are fond of terming it, although it possesses above five thousand houses, and upwards of forty thousand inhabitants, is the spacious college which the Protestants of Hungary have established for the education of their sons. The youth are divided into students and scholars; the former are instructed in the higher branches of academical learning, whilst the scholars begin with the elements of knowledge, and gradually rise, as in our own grammar schools, to the study of the best Greek and Latin authors, or what are here called the ' Humaniora.' There are two descriptions of pupils in the college; the ' Publici,' who are of noble extraction, and not designed for the church; and the ' Togati,' young men who have slenderer means, and are intended for holy orders: they are subject to severer discipline than the others, and wear a uniform black dress. In the list of professors I observed one for the Eastern languages; and the modern ones also are not neglected. The college is a handsome structure; the library, which consists of thirty thousand volumes, occupies two large apartments; there is an old and splendid edition of Livy among the works, as well as several manuscripts of value, and an original epistle from Pope Ganganelli to Ambrosius Danzer. The ' Imperial Chapel,' (*Hof Kapelle* is the name given it), forms part of the college; it is neat, and of very substantial construction; it is capable of containing the whole 643 students and scholars who are at present educating here, and who are required to hear a sermon preached to them on Sundays. The majority of the inhabitants of Debreczin are of the Protestant faith; indeed there are few Hungarians in the eastern districts of the kingdom who do not profess Calvinism. Their number throughout Hungary amounts to nearly three millions, and I was informed by Professor Sárvary, that their clergy is not far short of fourteen hundred.—F***.

WALLACHIA.—Very great encouragement is at present given to the diffusion of knowledge in this remote quarter, and above twenty schools of a superior description have already been opened. At the close of October last they were attended by 3050 pupils, whose studies are directed by able professors, the greater part of whom have been educated in German Universities. There are 500 youth in the Central College of St. Sava alone.

RUSSIA.

SIBERIA.—The Mongolian and Buriatic school at Troizko-Ssawak, not far from Kiachta in the province of Irkutsk, contains 24 pensioned pupils and 7 boarders. The lower class is composed of 25, who are taught the Mongolian and Russian languages on the Lancasterian system; and the remaining 6 youths, who compose the upper class, are instructed in the same languages, with the addition of grammar and the elements of arithmetic. The elders of the Buriate nation in the neighbourhood of Troizko-Ssawak, have offered to build a wing to the school, at their own expense, for the purpose of lodging the pupils and increasing their numbers.

Magnetic and Meteorological Institutions.—The Russian government have directed a normal observatory for the instruction of a certain number of cadets in magnetic and meteorological observations, to be erected and attached to the corps of miners at St. Petersburgh; and their labours are to be connected with simultaneous observations which are to be conducted by the sons of employés at the mines themselves. A complete magnetic and meteorological observatory is also to be constructed at Ekatherinenburg, and the requisite instruments are forthwith to be provided for the observatories of the same description already built at Nertshinsk and Barnaul.

The Serf.—The bonded peasant is bound to pay undeviating obedience to his lord, to render due service to him, (which service the law has fixed at three days in the week for each married couple), and to pay the tribute which his lord imposes upon him. The public authorities are bound to lend their aid to the lord at all times. The bondsman is not, however, compellable to obey any orders contrary to law, which his master may require him to execute. He cannot marry without the consent of his master, nor can he be forced to marry against his own inclination. If there be any want of marriageable females on an estate, or the whole peasantry are allied by blood, and a neighbouring lord be possessed of such females, in such case the purchase of females may be effected; and in cases where neither the lord nor his peasants have sufficient pecuniary means wherewith to make this purchase, the buyer may agree with the seller to place an unmarriageable female at his disposal for every female he may deliver to him. Both the lord and his peasantry are responsible to the government for all public imposts, and the peasantry are personally liable for the poll-tax, for all burdens imposed on the land, and for the furnishing of recruits. The lord is bound to provide for the maintenance of his peasants, and cannot exact greater service from them than three days' labour per week. Grown-up children, so long as they are single, are not legally liable to do service; but this regulation is not in general much regarded. In case of need, the lord may compel his peasants to dwell under his own roof, or on his own farm, and employ the whole family in working for his support. The peasant cannot enter a complaint against his lord; nay, all his acts become null and void if the lord appear or plead in court; but he may denounce his lord for high treason and false returns of the numbers of his serfs. Though there may be no express law giving the lord a right of disposing of his peasants' property, the denial of a hearing before a public tribunal, and the ancient laws respecting slavery, are bars to any remedy which the peasant may seek. The head of every province is bound to prevent or punish the commission of any acts of tyranny, and may place the affairs of the lord in trust. It is not lawful for a peasant to change his place of residence; runaways must be delivered up to their masters; the lord has power to punish the peasant, but neither with starvation, maiming, nor death : he can make a recruit of him, send him to the house of correction, and compel him to settle on his estate wherever he thinks proper, if he be not fit for service. Compensation is due to the lord for every peasant slain by design or accident. The lord may emancipate his peasant and also sell him with or without any land ; but he cannot separate him from his family, nor dispose of him publicly to the highest bidder. Custom, however, has gradually modified many of these oppressive enactments ; and the harshest treatment to which the serf is exposed, takes place on the estates of small proprietors.—(*Treatise on the general Laws of the Russian State. St. Petersburg*, 1833.)

TURKEY.

The Constantinopolitans.—' The history of this city,' says Tenier, the French traveller, in a recent letter from the spot, ' is written in the physiognomy of its varied population. Arabia and Persia, the heart of Africa and the steppes of Tartary, have each of them supplied its contingent. Nation upon nation live side by side with the original owners of Byzantium, and yet never unite with them. Each have their separate homestead; each their distinct habits and prejudices. Constantinople is an abridgement of the whole East; an immense field of observation within a single precinct. Its population consists of four large classes, (from which I exclude the Europeans who dwell in Pera and Galata,) differing altogether in their religious tenets; they are composed of Greeks, Jews, Armenians, and Turks. The Turk are split into an infinite variety of nations, of whom the Ottoman empire itself is compounded; their characters are traceable to the ancient inhabitants by whom its provinces were peopled; here we have blacks, the issue of the Sennaar slave ; white or copper-coloured Arabs ; Trebizondese, Tartars, Persians, Turks, the children of Turk and slave ; Turks again, the offspring of Turkish male and female ; and then the soldiery, drawn from every province whether European or Asiatic. Looking at the custom prevalent among the Turks of contracting alliances with female slaves from various countries, it will be readily conceived that no race on the whole list of those out of which the population of Constantinople is compounded, is of more mixed a cast than the present rulers of the country ; among the Turks too, no blood is so mixed as that of the highest classes. In fact, the lords of the land, nearly the whole of whose mothers have been handsome Greek or Georgian slaves, exhibit a cast of countenance essentially differing from that of the lower orders of the people. The latter have always retained the features, which connect them with the Tartar race, such as the high cheek-bone, the temple slightly depressed, the arched brow raised towards the external angles, and the head elongated from front to back. The last of these traits is common to both classes, and is most easily detected, if you walk into a barber's shop in the morning, and take a glance at the Turks of all ranks in society, who bring their heads at once under the observer's eye and the barber's razor. The nose is short and rounded at the extremity, and the sides of the nostrils are somewhat thrown up. The more distinguished Turks are of Georgian blood, at times both on the father's and mother's side; for it is customary with the Moslems of rank to purchase children of that race, and, after adopting them, to raise them to the highest dignities in the state. This is the case with the majority of the Sultan's executive at the present moment; there are scarcely three of them who are of pure Turkish blood. The features which characterize the Turkish grandee, are what we account the type of the genuine Mussulman; for they include an aquiline nose, small but quick and oblong eyes, a round forehead, small mouth, a whitish rather than brownish complexion, and full ears, set however close to the temporal bone.'

Turkish School.—Extract of a letter from Bujukdere. ' I was walking with two friends along the main-street of one of the adjacent villages, when a confused murmur of voices drew my attention. I found that it proceeded from a mosque immediately at our elbow, and upon inquiring whether we might venture to go in, (for no stranger is allowed to enter a Turkish mosque without express permission,) I was answered in the affirmative. Following the direction from which the noise proceeded, we mounted a flight of steps, and, instead of finding ourselves launched into a place of worship, we discovered that we had made our way into a roomy apartment containing tables near the walls, at which a number of Turkish boys of all ages were posted with book in hand. It proved to be the village school; and scarcely a better one, as I afterwards learnt, is to be met with in Constantinople itself. In one corner of the apartment we observed the master reclining upon a decent carpet; he was an old mullah or ecclesiastic, with an enormous turban on his head, a long grey beard, yellow kaftan, and legs crossed in the true Turkish fashion. His left hand held a long pipe, which he was smoking; and his right lay quietly in his lap, except that it was now and then agitated by a fidgetty motion, as if something particular affected its owner. On his left we remarked a bag of tobacco, and in front of him a ponderous tome, probably the Koran; while an enormously long bamboo cane, which reached from the floor to the ceiling, stood against the wall on his right hand. He saluted us on our entrance with a nod of the head, but did not rise from his seat, or suffer his mouth to part for an instant from his pipe. The score and a half of urchins who were standing or kneeling, as their size required them, behind the tables, with carpets for their feet, were momentarily drawn off from their tasks by our appearance; but an involuntary glance at their master's brow, or perhaps some warning from the fingers of his right hand, which had not moved from his lap, set them all to work again. They appeared to be learning to read, and had certainly made considerable progress, as there was no spelling going on. All were reading rapidly, and as each of them was reading aloud, and none the same matter, I leave you to conceive the noise and confusion of tongues that filled the room. The bigger boys, or rather the wiser ones (for there were several little fellows among them), seemed to act as under-masters; for they were not reading, like the rest of their comrades, but were hearing and correcting them, and this not merely by word of mouth, but with the assistance of certain very unceremonious boxes on the ear. One diminutive urchin in particular, who was quick as lightning in correcting a *lapsus linguæ*, made no scruple of doubling his Lilliputian fists and directing them, might and main, at the face of a huge and seemingly incorrigible dunce, with whom he was playing the part of monitor; reckless, by the way, on what his blows fell, whether the giant's nose or his neighbour's. Throughout the whole scene, the pedagogue in the corner lay quietly smoking his pipe on his carpet as if he had not a limb to move. One of my companions who had a quantity of burnt almonds in his pocket, in a fit of mischief suddenly let them loose in the middle of the room. It was worth a day's purgatory to see the rout which ensued : monitors and scholars with one accord dropped their books out of their fingers and gave chase to the prey ; and the whole lot would have been devoured in a trice, had not the old mullah's fingers found their way nimbly to the bamboo-cane, and, without costing him the pains of uncrossing his legs, or even displacing his darling pipe, he belaboured the poor devils' backs with it in every direction ; for there was not a corner of the room which could escape its cruel length. All ran back to their posts as if Jack Ketch had been at their heels, and we ourselves took to our heels and made a rapid exit into the street. *Ab uno disce omnes :* you have here the model of a Turkish school before you."

EGYPT.

Extract from a letter to M. Jomard, written by Artin-effendi, a former pupil of M. Jomard's, and now a member of the Superior Council of Government in Cairo :—" His Highness the Pasha has entrusted M. Kœnig with the education of the young prince, Seyd-Beg, whom he is principally to instruct in the French language. It is doubtlessly intended that Seyd-Beg should hereafter command the Egyptian naval forces. His whole life is passed on board ship, and he is accompanied by about thirty pupils, who are pursuing a similar course of study to his own. All the young men educated in France have received appointments suited to their capacities. We have numbers of St. Simonians here, and several others are just arrived ; nor is there a school in the country which has not some of them for its teachers. A pupil of M. de Dombesle, whose ploughs are quite the vogue amongst us, has recently landed, and he has engaged, in conjunction with Olivier, a St. Simonian, to lay certain proposals with regard to agriculture before government. Previously to his arrival two millions of plants had been imported into Egypt.' The writer also mentions the establishment of two important schools in this country—a School of Civil Administration, and a Polytechnic School. ' The former,' he observes, ' is under the direction of his Excellency, Mouktar-bey, the President of the Council of Civil Administration, assisted by myself and S tephan. effendi, a contemporary pupil in France.' The school contains thirty students, who are taught Turkish, Arabic, Persian, French, the mathematics, and other subjects to qualify them as civilians. The Polytechnic School is to be established at Boulak: its object is to fit pupils for the special schools already in existence, and intended to be instituted in the Pasha's dominions. A long decree regulates the organization of this seminary in all its branches. Admission is only granted to those who are *bonâ fide* subjects of the Pasha, are not below the age of twelve, or above that of fifteen years, are able to read and write Arabic or Turkish, and have been vaccinated, or have had the small-pox. The intended number of pupils is two hundred; they are to be divided into four classes, each class representing one of the four years' courses of study of which the entire course is to consist. This course is to comprise at first the French, Arabic, Turkish, and Persian languages, drawing and linear perspective, the elements of arithmetic, geometry, descriptive geometry, algebra, analytical geometry, statics, hydrostatics, taking plans, natural philosophy, chemistry, and mineralogy, cosmography, history, and geography. A portion of the pupils will be qualified for giving early assistance to the teachers in their tasks, or opening courses of the same kind in other quarters. The functionaries employed are to be a commandant of the school and a director-general of studies, in the person of Elim-bey; the deputy-commandant appointed is Hekeken, an engineer, an Armenian by birth, who has been educated at the Pasha's expense in England; there are also to be four professors or sub-directors of studies, three of whom are sufficient for the present wants of the school, in which only a single class has yet been formed. In addition to these there are three masters for the three Eastern languages already mentioned, Turkish, Arabic, and Persian.

AFRICA.

CHILDREN's FRIEND SOCIETY.—' As a sort of controversy has arisen in England on the subject of juvenile emigration, and as the gentlemen who have devoted so much of their time to the relief of those destitute children have been roundly taxed in the public papers with the commission of very serious offences, such as transporting British subjects contrary to law, reviving the slave trade, cheating the public, jobbing in human misery, and so forth, we beg the reader's attention to a brief description of this new scheme of emigration. The Society for the Suppression of Juvenile Vagrancy, now called ' Children's Friend Society,' raised a fund by private subscription for the relief of children found in the streets of London entirely destitute of known relations, of lodging, clothing, and food. For the reception of these children they procured a house and grounds, where they were kept under proper discipline, education, and employment, in digging, gardening, &c.

Finding that only a very small number of children, compared with the extent of juvenile distress, could be relieved in this way, they proposed to their wards emigration to some of the British colonies, where they would be placed in the service of farmers and others, and trained in habits of order and industry. Where the relations of any of the children could be discovered, their consent was asked as well as that of the youths themselves. Where no relative could be found, the consent of the children to emigrate was considered sufficient. On their arrival in this colony, they are received by a committee of gentlemen, who see them safely housed and supplied with everything necessary for their health and comfort. Application is then made to the Supreme Court for authority to act as guardians, and to apprentice them under regular indentures to their employers till they come of age. The Supreme Court then appoints a barrister to examine each of the children separately, as to whether they left England of their own free will and choice, whether they have any relations or natural guardians in this colony, and whether they are willing to accept the committee as their guardians. These questions being answered to his satisfaction, he reports the same to the Supreme Court, and the authority prayed for is then, and not before, granted to the committee. This process has to be repeated in the case of every separate detachment of emigrants. These emigrants are children, minors who require guardians, and need to be instructed and taught some useful trade or calling: for these purposes they are apprenticed to respectable persons till they attain the years of majority. The committee at Cape Town are of opinion, that the services of the children up to the time of coming of age, were worth on an average 9*l.* or 10*l.*: this sum was charged, and it has been found nearly sufficient to meet the ordinary expenses of the emigration. For some who had eight or nine years to serve, a charge of from 12*l.* to 15*l.* has been made. For others who were eighteen or nineteen, the charge has been so low as from 2*l.* to 4*l.*, or 5*l.* For these, of course, the outlay was as great as for those whose services were worth 15*l.* The Society in London has, in several instances, received poor children from the parish workhouses; and the overseers, according to custom, paid to the Society the sum of 10*l.* for each, on being thus relieved of the burden of supporting them. Had all the children sent out been of this description, the Committee at Cape Town would probably have been authorized to apprentice them without exacting any premium from the masters; but out of about two hundred children, only five or six have been thus provided for by their parishes. It was, therefore, impossible for the Society to make any distinctions on this head; but they expect that in future, from the liberality of the public at home in making subscriptions and donations for this excellent object, and from occasionally receiving parish children with the above-mentioned allowance, they may be enabled to reduce the premium without endangering the stability and usefulness of the scheme itself. Such is the scheme of juvenile emigration, which has so strangely been misrepresented and misunderstood. As to the children themselves, generally speaking, their emigration has been like passing from death to life. They have the satisfaction of feeling they are no longer regarded as burdens on the benevolent and humane, or the niggard charity of the law, but as useful and respectable members of society, who have by their honest labour repaid their benefactors, and established a claim to independence of character.'—*From the South African Commercial Advertiser, published at Cape Town, November,* 1834.

BRITISH.

OxFORD.—The following summary of the members of this University is extracted from the University Calendar for the present year :—

	Members of Convocation.	Members on the Books.
University Coll.	109	218
Balliol	109	279
Merton	64	129
Exeter	125	307
Oriel	154	302
Queen's	172	343
New	64	147
Lincoln	72	131
All Souls	67	97
Magdalen	113	159
Brazennose	233	396
Corpus	86	129
Christ Church	479	986
Trinity	112	264
St. John's	119	220
Jesus	59	153
Wadham	84	228
Pembroke	101	192
Worcester	94	211
St. Mary Hall	24	43
Magdalen Hall	54	167
New Inn Hall	1	32
St. Alban Hall	10	35
St. Edmund Hall	46	83
	2551	5251

2 B

Matriculations . . . 369
Regents . . . 220
Determining Bachelors in Lent . 288

In January, 1884, there were 2519 members of convocation, and 5290 members on the books.

CAMBRIDGE, *Dec.* 31.—The Hulsean prize was this day adjudged to Mr. William N. Curtis, of Catherine Hall, for his dissertation on the following subject:—'How far the political circumstances of the Jewish nation were favourable to the introduction and diffusion of the Christian religion?'

The subject of the Seatonian prize poem for the present year is ' Ishmael.'

Jan. 10.—The following is the subject of the Hulsean prize dissertation for the present year.—' The resemblance between Moses and Christ is so very great and striking, that it is impossible to consider it fairly and carefully without seeing and acknowledging that he must be foretold where he is so well described.'

The representatives in parliament for this University give annually—

(1.) Two prizes of fifteen guineas each, for the encouragement of Latin prose composition, to be open to all bachelors of arts, without distinction of years, who are not of sufficient standing to take the degree of master of arts; and

(2.) Two other prizes of fifteen guineas each, to be open to all under-graduates who shall have resided not less than seven terms at the time when the exercises are to be sent in.

The subjects for the present year are—

(1.) For the bachelors,—' De fide historica rectè æstimanda.'

(2.) For the under-graduates,—' Utrum recte judicaverit Cicero iniquissimam pacem justissimo bello anteferendam esse?'

Jan. 23.—LIST OF HONOURS.—*Moderators.*—John Harrison Evans, M.A., St. John's College; Thomas Gaskin, M.A., Jesus College.

Examiners.—Edwin Stevenson, M.A., Corpus Christi College; Francis Martin, M.A., Trinity College.

Wranglers—Cotterill, Joh.; Goulburn, Trin.; Rawle, Trin.; Greatheed, Trin.; Dickinson, Trin.; Cross, Joh.; Ashby, Pemb.; Blackburn, Trin.; Scudamore, Joh.; Gibbs, Caius; Johnson, Caius; Ross de Bladensburg, Trin.; La Mottee, Trin.; Smith, Christ's; Abbott, Pemb.; Acland, Caius; Skelton, Christ's; White, Trin.; Girdlestone, Trin.; H. W. Smith, Joh.; De Saumarez, Caius; Gipps, Joh.; Lambert, Joh.; Leefe, Trin.; Howes, Trin.; Hall, Clare; Rigg, Christ's; Dunn, Trin.; Heisch, Trin.; Proctor, Cath.; Helps, Trin.; Merivale, Trin.; Cooper, Trin. *æq.*; Davis, Christ's, *æq.*; Allen, Trin.; Davies, Corpus; Budd, Pemb.

Senior Optimes.—Musgrave, Trin.; Gibbons, Joh., *æq.*; Grote, Trin., *æq.*; Wackerbarth, Corpus; Hilditch, Joh.; Rudd, Joh.; Nichols, Caius; Coape, Christ's; Watson, Trin.; Merriman, Caius; Garvey, Emm.; Jeremie, Trin.; James, Corpus; Lowe,

Trin. ; Drake, Joh. ; Burnett, Trin. ; Courtenay, Jesus ; Seager, Trin. ; Hoste, Caius ; Shortland, Pemb. ; Curtis, Joh., *æq.* ; Davidson, Clare, *æq.* ; James, Jesus ; Walker, Jesus ; Morris, Joh. ; Johnstone, Emm. ; Dixon, Sidney ; Tillard, Joh. ; Beadon, Joh. ; Hall, Christ's ; Bishop, Joh. ; Scott, Clare ; Jowett, Caius ; Pritchard, Joh. ; Ward, Pet. ; Eyre, Cath., *æq.* ; Forrest, Queen's, *æq.* ; Howes, Tr. H. ; Blunt, Caius ; Barber, Joh. ; Harris, Trin.

Junior Optimes.—White, Joh. ; Legrew, Joh. ; Berkley, Jesus, *æq.* ; Wilson, Clare, *æq.* ; Rogers, Joh., *æq.* ; Spiller, Cath., *æq.* ; A. Smith, Joh., *æq.* ; Thomas, Pet., *æq.* ; Waltham, Joh. ; Williams, Magd. ; Broadstreet, Emm., *æq.* ; Gilbert, Magd., *æq.* ; Scrivener, Trin. ; Richardson, Joh. ; Ramsey, Pemb. ; Etty, Joh., *æq.* ; Nightingale, Cath., *æq.* ; Schwabe, Caius ; Karslake, Magd ; Richards, Joh. ; Stocks, Trin. ; Laing, Joh., *æq.* ; Wilkinson, Clare, *æq.* ; Newlove, Clare ; Fergusson, Trin. ; Ellison, Trin. ; Clarke, Pemb., *æq.* ; Storer, Joh., *æq.*, Fox, Queen's ; Morgan, Trin., *æq.* ; Reid, Joh., *æq.* ; Williamson, Caius ; Manners Sutton, Trin. ; Harrison, Trin. ; Paton, Queen's, *æq.* ; Philips, Magd., *æq.* ; Meade, Caius ; Claydon, Trin. ; Hue, Trin.

Jan. 30.—The late Dr. Smith's prizes of 25*l.* each to the two best proficients in mathematics and natural philosophy among the commencing Bachelors of Arts, were this day adjudged to Henry Cotterill, of St. John's College, and Henry Goulburn, of Trinity College, the first and second wranglers.

The following are the subjects of examination in the last week of the Lent Term, 1836 :

1. The Acts of the Apostles.
2. Paley's Evidences of Christianity.
3. The Menexenus of Plato.
4. The Seventh and Eight Satires of Juvenal.

Feb. 13.—At a congregation held this day the following grace passed the Senate :

To rescind the regulation respecting the examination for the classical tripos, which directs that 'the examination shall continue four days, the hours of attendance on each day being from half-past nine in the morning till twelve, and from one till four in the afternoon:'

And to substitute the following :—' The examination (commencing as heretofore on the fourth Monday after the general admission *ad respondendum questioni*) shall continue five days ; the hours of attendance on each day being from nine in the morning till twelve ; and from one till half-past three in the afternoon.'

LONDON UNIVERSITY.—On the 25th of February, the annual Report was made to the proprietors. The total expenditure it appears exceeds the income, but this excess is stated to have been occasioned by items of a nature not of constant recurrence, such as the rent at the end of the term of the house in Gower-street lately occupied by the warden, and the expenses attending the application for the charter ; and that the ordinary income is more than equal to the ordinary expenditure. The number of students at present is, in the faculty of arts and law, 137, and in that of medicine, 371 ; the total number is 492, a few of the students attending both faculties. The pupils in the junior school amount to 303. The report also gives the following detail of the proceedings for the attainment of a charter, with the result :—

' In the year 1831, the Council first presented a petition for a charter of incorporation, the draft of which (as is usual) accompanied the petition. After receiving the approval of the law officers of the crown, and the royal signature in two instances, this draft was on the eve of obtaining the sanction of the great seal, its last stage towards completion, when the heads of the University of Cambridge, and afterwards those of Oxford, interposed, and demanded that a clause should be inserted, restraining this University from granting degrees.

' The Council declined to accept a charter encumbered with such a restriction ; and the matter remained in this state until the beginning of 1834, when, at the instance of the senate, the Council applied to the home-department for the determination of the Crown.

' The University of Oxford then petitioned the throne to be heard before his Majesty in Council against the grant, and similar petitions were presented from the University of Cambridge, the College of Surgeons, and the teachers in the hospital schools of London.

· ' The Council acknowledged with gratitude the petitions presented to his Majesty in favour of the charter by the City of London, and by the three denominations of dissenting ministers meeting in Red Cross Street.

' His Majesty referred all these petitions to a committee of the Privy Council, before whom they were argued in April last.

' The Privy Council came to no decision on the subject.'

The Report concludes by noticing the success attending the founding of the hospital, and its great use to the medical students. The College of Surgeons and the Society of Apothecaries have recognised it as a school of clinical instruction ; and the exertions of the professors, the attendance of the pupils, and the amount of the annual subscriptions, lead them to anticipate for it a permanent prosperity.

KING's COLLEGE, LONDON.—The Council have resolved upon conferring the academical distinction of ' Associates' on such of the regularly matriculated students as have gone through a three years' prescribed course of study in the Higher Department to the satisfaction of the several professors. The associates will be entitled to perpetual admission to the college library and museums, as well as to those courses of lectures, by diligent attendance upon which they have gained the distinction. Mr. Marsden, the well-known Oriental scholar, has munificently presented the college with a very valuable library of books connected with the study of philology, amounting to several thousand volumes. He had previously been a very liberal benefactor of the college by pecuniary donations. The Rev. R. Jones, Professor of Political Economy, has been appointed to the chair of the same science at the East India Company's College, at Hayleybury, in Hertfordshire ; the appointment had become vacant by the decease of the Rev. T. Malthus, but its duties will not interfere with Professor Jones' Spring Course of Lectures at King's College. M. von Dadelszen, a native of Holstein, who attended the college last year as a regular student, has been elected the first scholar on the Worsley Endowment, the object of which is to educate young men at the college as missionaries to British India. Another election on this foundation will shortly take place.

STAINES.—A society for the promotion of science and literature has been recently established at Staines, and has been extremely well supported. The subscription is 10s. per annum, and a museum and library are to be formed by degrees; the books, &c. to be consulted by the members, but not to be borrowed. The main object of the society is to 'encourage voluntary and gratuitous lectures upon scientific subjects, and essays upon general literature;' but 'all papers on subjects strictly professional, and on politics,' are to be excluded. Each member of the society is allowed to introduce his own family, and non-subscribers are admitted to each lecture on payment of one shilling. In an address delivered on the 1st of January, by the Rev. Robert Jones, vicar of Bedfont, one of the committee, he thus enforces the advantages of this mode of diffusing knowledge :—' Science, as applied to the arts, and illustrative of its experiments, must be very imperfectly understood without the aid of models, diagrams, and lectures. No mere treatise on chemistry, for instance, however clearly written, can possibly do justice to the discoveries revealed by modern research and experiment ;—we must not only read, or hear of, but actually behold its wonders, before we can arrive at any complete or practical insight. And though in the perusal of treatises on astronomy, we may, and do attain by study and in theory a fair proficiency in that noble and ennobling science ; yet with an orrery, and a living intelligent lecturer before us, we appear to see at once, and comprehend at a glance, the mysteries of the starry heavens, and the laws which rule them. The material and palpable delineation will strike and remain upon many memories, on which a dry treatise may have little interest and no hold. Dr. Jones also combats the objection raised upon the supposed necessity of having distinguished literary or scientific men as lecturers ; and contends that the aim of such societies is rather to call forth and encourage rising talent ; that the auditors seldom fail of being interested, even though the lecture is not of the highest order, when, as is often the case, they have a personal knowledge of the lecturer ; and mentions an instance of a course of lectures on German literature being announced at a similar society in Brighton, which were to be delivered by the clerk to a grocer in that town; and asserts that 'to compensate the injustice of Fortune, Nature is most impartial in her gifts; and, though it is in the power of few to obtain the advantages of academical education, it is in the power of most to reap the fruits of their own patient and persevering application. Whatever may be the aids that schools and colleges can afford, and I duly prize them, it is the after-study, the self-tuition, that stamps the man.'

PARISH SCHOOLS.—Some uncertainty having been felt, in several instances, as to the legality of applying the rates to the support of parish schools for the education of poor children, the following letter has been written by the Secretary to the Poor Law Commissioners :—" Sir,—I am directed by the Poor Law Commissioners for England and Wales to remark, that it appears, from the evidence in possession of the Board, that when the education of parish children has been carefully attended to, and where the master and mistress have been persons of intelligence and of good moral habits, those children have obtained situations, and got into industrious courses more readily, and have, in a much larger proportion of cases than where no such care has been bestowed, ceased to be burdensome to the parish, or the public at large. A careful additional expenditure for the promotion of a good education has always hitherto been proved to be the best course, with regard even to the mere pecuniary saving; and, on that account, a proper expenditure of the rates will therefore receive the sanction of the Commissioners."

THE CAMBERWELL COLLEGIATE OR PROPRIETORY SCHOOL, in connexion with King's College.—This School was opened in January, in the presence of the committee and upwards of 700 persons. An address was read by the Rev. J. A. Giles, the head-master, detailing the scholastic plan which it was intended to pursue.

HALIFAX.—There are twenty-three schools comprised in the Halifax Sunday School Union, which are attended by 4198 scholars, and 1064 teachers. The increase during the last twelve months has been two schools and 290 scholars.

BEVERLEY GRAMMAR SCHOOL.—This grammar school is of great antiquity, having existed many years prior to the Norman Conquest. It is supposed that it was originally a free-school for the natives of Beverley, who were probably instructed by the priests of the Collegiate Society of St. John. When or by whom it was founded is not known. Some of the first entries in the accounts of the Beverley corporation refer to sums of 10s. and 20s., paid to 'Alexander Metcalfe, for the use of his sonne Robert Metcalfe, at Cambridge.' Robert Metcalfe became afterwards a great benefactor to the School and to the borough. The items alluded to occur in the year 1605-6. It appears that in those early days the

School was maintained by the liberality of the corporation of Beverley, who were well-qualified to sustain such an institution, from the rich grants which had been made to them at various periods, especially by Elizabeth. An old school-room, which had stood a hundred years, was taken down in 1814, and a new school was built, in its present very desirable situation.

This School possesses two fellowships; one founded by " Master Robert Hallitreeholme, of Beverley, clerk;" its original endowment was 120*l.* sterling:—and another, founded by "Dame Jane Rokeby and her son, Robert Creyke," originally 10*l.* sterling. Both were founded in the 17th Henry VIII., both in St. John's College, Cambridge, and both were to be enjoyed by persons born in Beverley or some neighbouring town, having been educated in the Grammar School of Beverley.

Eleven scholarships have been founded in connexion with this School, which are described as follows :—

Date.	Amount bequeathed.	Intent.
1626 Mrs. Margaret Davey.	40*l.*	Maintenance of poor Scholars at the University.
—— Mrs. Margaret Ferrers.	2*l.* a year, and residue of certain rents.	A poor scholar at the University.
	£. *s.* d.	
1652 R. Metcalfe, D.D. . .	6 13 4 yearly.	One poor scholar ditto, till he take the degree of M.A.
—— R. Metcalfe, D.D. . .	6 13 4 do.	ditto ditto.
—— R. Metcalfe, D.D. . .	6 13 4 do.	ditto ditto.
1670 William Lacie, D.D. .	8 0 0	16*l.* annuity	ditto ditto,
—— William Lacie, D.D. .	8 0 0	ditto ditto.
1681 William Coates. . . .	6 0 0 100*l.* sterling.	ditto ditto.
1739 Lady Eliz. Hastings, .	28 0 0 yearly.	ditto. ditto.
1778 John Green, Bishop of Lincoln, ...	10 0 0	ditto ditto.
—— Robert Clerk, Fellow of St. John's College, Cambridge, ...	200*l.* sterling.	ditto ditto.

These scholarships are seldom claimed; and when no application is made for them, the money is distributed among poor persons, being settled inhabitants of the town or neighbourhood of Beverley A few observations may be made on some of these scholarships. The will of R. Metcalfe is very strongly expressed with reference to the appropriation of his bequest: and it states that "*no son of any of the aldermen, or of any other person of sufficient ability to maintain their children at the university, shall be capable of receiving benefit from the maintenance left by him.* The 10*l.* per annum, left by John Green, is suffered to accumulate (in conformity with his will,) when there is no applicant; and such accumulation is paid to the scholar next appointed to receive the exhibition. The scholarship founded by Robert Clerk is for a native of Beverley, first with respect to the kindred of the name of Clerk, and then of Johnston. The bequest of Lady Elizabeth Hastings is lost for the present to Beverley. No candidate having been sent from Beverley for four successive elections, the provost and fellows of Queen's College, Oxford, transferred the scholarship to Richmond School, in accordance with powers vested in them by the testator on the 5th of February, 1789 ; but this school also neglecting to send candidates for four successive elections, it is now displaced. To account for this apparent neglect, we must observe that while the conditions of the will are required, the exhibitions are not worth looking after.

A yearly benefaction of 10*l.*, left by Dr. Metcalfe, is the only permanent endowment, in the shape of salary for the master, which this school possesses. The master receives 70*l.* annually from the corporation, and a yearly gift of 20*l.* from the two representatives of the borough ; which, if not paid by them, is made up by the corporation: there is also a good dwelling-house for the master, at a merely nominal rent. The charge for teaching the classics and the mathematics to the free scholars is 40*s.* a year ; which sum the mayor has a right of lowering, in the case of the sons of the poorer freemen. A separate charge of 2 guineas a year is made if the pupils are instructed in the English grammar, writing, and arithmetic. The sons of non-freemen, who are day-scholars, pay 6 guineas a year for the classics, and 3*l.* for writing and arithmetic. The present master of the School is the Rev. L. S. Warren: the pupils now in the School are 10 freemen's sons, 10 other day boys, and 24 boarders. The school-room is very commodious ; and there is a fives-court erected by the late master, Mr. Richards, attached to a play-ground, which is two acres in extent. The library, which belongs to the School, contains 700 vols., many of which are valuable and scarce.

School for Chimney Sweepers.—An evening school, for educating the young chimney sweepers of this town, has lately been established in Warwick-street, under the patronage of our much respected vicar, the Rev. H. M. Wagner. A large proportion of those now in Brighton attend it regularly, and evince the greatest desire to obtain instruction. We have reason to believe that schools of the same description will soon be established in all the populous cities and towns in the kingdom. An evening school for adults has also been established ; which, under the zealous superintendence of the Rev. Mr. Langdon, is, we have reason to believe, doing much good.—*Brighton Gazette.*

LUTON.—Two new school-rooms, on the plan of the National School Society, have been commenced at Luton, Bedfordshire. The foundation was laid on Feb. 14, by the Marquis of Bute. Independent of the site for the buildings, which are to contain 300 children, his Lordship has presented 100*l.* in money, as well as the materials of the old school-room, worth about 50*l.* more. The remainder of the sum required will be made up by a government grant of 145*l.*, and by private subscriptions.

GLOUCESTER.—In accordance with a suggestion made to the committee of the National School Society, the Gloucester National School will for the future be considered a ' Central' or Model Institution; and will receive for training and instruction in the system those persons who cannot conveniently repair to the metropolis for that purpose.

WORCESTER.—Government has made a grant of 125*l.* towards the erection of a school-room for the Sunday and Day Schools connected with St. George's Chapel, in the tithing; and the National School Society have given 40*l.* for the like purpose.

MANSFIELD PAROCHIAL LIBRARY.—The Rev. Dr. Cursham, Vicar of Mansfield, is forming a library for the use of the poor of that parish. After a sermon, which he preached in aid of its funds, the sum of 13*l.* 8*s.* was collected.

HOLBECK YOUTH'S GUARDIAN SOCIETY.—A society has for some time existed in the manufacturing village of Holbeck, near Leeds, whose object is the dissemination of useful knowledge, and the protection of the morals of the youthful population of both sexes. It was commenced by a few persons, in an humble sphere of life, who were anxious to afford other attractions to the working classes than those to which they had been so long accustomed. These individuals met—they summoned public meetings of the inhabitants, by means of the bell-man, and afterwards issued a prospectus of their plan; the substance of which is the establishment of libraries, to which sixpence entrance money is contributed, and a halfpenny per week afterwards—the reading of lectures and papers on useful subjects—attendance at sabbath schools, both adult and adolescent—and more particularly the enforcement, both by parents and overlookers in mills, and all persons having authority over youth, of moral and religious discipline. By the liberality of several mill-owners, 25*l.* have been raised by the society; and a library of 600 volumes has been formed, to which 185 young men subscribe: 130 parents, heads of families, have signed their names, and thereby pledged themselves to act in co-operation with the society.

BRADFORD.—Upwards of 40*l.* have been subscribed at Bradford, for the purpose of furnishing the working-men of that town with standard works on political economy, and other useful branches of literature. The object of this subscription is to preserve the men from the demoralizing influence of the public-house, by providing them with rational means of recreation.

CHILLINGHAM, DURHAM.—The Bishop of Durham has forwarded to the Rev. L. Yarker, Vicar of Chillingham, the sum of 100*l.* towards the building of schools in that parish, for the education of the poor. The Right Hon. the Earl of Tankerville has also contributed the sum of 25*l.* to the same object, and has generously given a piece of ground and stone for the erection of a suitable building. In addition to these munificent gifts, the Rev. Vicar has received towards the same object the sum of 50*l.* from the executors of the late Bishop Barrington.—*Newcastle Journal.*

MANCHESTER.—At the annual meeting of the Manchester Mechanics' Institute, held on Thursday, Feb. 26th, a resolution was passed to the following effect:—"That the establishment of day-schools for boys and girls in connexion with this institution, upon the system of the Edinburgh Sessional School; the addition in the number of the evening classes, and the increased attendance upon them; the judicious enlargement of the library, and the great increase in the circulation of the books; are viewed by this meeting with the highest satisfaction: and that this meeting desires to express its sincere gratification at the prospect of future success which is afforded by the prosperity of the institution during the past year."

SCOTLAND.

General Assembly's Schools.—In an Address put forth by the General Assembly on the state of their schools, we see it stated that eighty-six schools are maintained by voluntary subscriptions. At these schools a suitable instruction has been given within the last few years to upwards of 20,000 of the young, and to not less than 4000 of the adult population of the Highlands and Islands. Some of the teachers derive no remuneration in money for their labours, but receive such provisions as the place affords. The average amount of the school-fees paid to each of the eighty-six teachers does not exceed 5*l.* per annum. It is further stated, that there are still 100,000 of the population who do not receive the slightest portion of elementary instruction; and in forty-four parishes it was lately discovered that there were 1320 families who did not possess among them a single copy of the scriptures.

Female Education.—On Thursday, Feb. 19, Dr. Cantor delivered an interesting lecture at Edinburgh on Female Education. He pointed out how unaccountably the education of the female sex has hitherto been neglected; showing, at the same time, how important their education is to the well-being of society. He then adverted to the neglected condition of the children of the poorer classes, and pleaded with much feeling for the establishment of infant schools, as a highly expedient means of infusing a spirit of morality and industry into the minds of the lower classes of females. Whilst he thus contended that the poorer classes should receive an education suitable to their station, he, on the other hand, was an advocate for throwing widely open to the higher classes of females the gates of knowledge; and alluded with much satisfaction to the Scottish Institution, in which nearly forty young ladies attended the mathematical class. Dr. Cantor concluded, by pointing out in forcible terms the utter insufficiency of the cultivation of the intellectual powers in females, unless the affection and desires of the heart be properly directed.

GLASGOW ASYLUM FOR THE BLIND.—A 'Statement of the Education, Employment, and internal Arrangements of this institution,' has reached us, together with the eighth annual report, which was read at a general meeting of its supporters, on the 19th January last. It appears that seventy-eight pupils have been admitted since the opening of the establishment in 1828, of whom twenty-four have left, six have died, and forty-eight are now remaining. Of these, twenty-three are men, twelve boys, seven women, and six girls. Boys under sixteen and girls under eighteen reside in the house; the adults of both sexes are employed as day-workers, and are paid wages at the same rate as other work-people would be paid, but a gratuity is given monthly as a reward for industry. It would appear from one of the items of revenue, that those who live in the house pay towards their own support, 71*l*. 11*s*. being stated as the 'amount of board from pupils;' but neither the scale of charge nor the number who reside in the house is given, though we infer, from a classification of labour in which boys and girls are distinguished from men and women, that the number may be eighteen. Indeed, the statistical details of the report are in several instances imperfect; they give, for instance, the amount of the sale of the manufactured articles for the years 1833 and 1834, but do not state the cost of the raw materials, which would have enabled us to ascertain the amount of their profitable labour. Instead of this we have an item, 'loss on manufacturing, 17*l*. 11*s*. 1*d*.' If the blind labourers are only paid like other workmen, we cannot understand this item. Leaving these points, however, as matters for local consideration, we are much pleased with the methods of instruction adopted, and the objects to which they are directed. An alphabet, formed of different kinds of knots, placed at different intervals, had been invented by two young men, both blind, in the Asylum at Edinburgh. This has been adopted with very great success, and parts of the New Testament have been prepared, (the string being wound round a horizontally revolving-frame,) which children of eight years of age can read with great facility; and other blind persons have corresponded in this way both with the seeing and the blind; it also forms a means of communication between the blind and the deaf and dumb, which has been exhibited at several of the annual meetings at Glasgow. Arithmetic is also taught by this contrivance, ' the ten numerals being represented by one characteristic pin, according as it is placed. It is simply a pentagon, with a projection at one end on an angle, and at the other end on a side. Being placed in a board, (pierced with pentagonal holes to fit the pin,) with a corner projection to the left hand upper cor-

ner of the hole, it represents 1; proceeding to the right hand upper
corner it is three; the next corner in succession (*i. e.* the right hand
side,) is 5; the next (or bottom) 7; and the last 9. In like manner
the side projection, by being turned to the sides of the hole progres-
sively, give 2, 4, 6, 8, 0. The size of the board used at the Asylum is 16 by 12 inches, and contains above 400 holes, kept about
a quarter of an inch separate.' Geography is taught by means of
a globe, very ingeniously constructed by Mr. Alston, the treasurer
of the institution, for the purpose. It is nine feet and a half in
circumference. The water is made smooth, and the other parts
are in relief; the earth is rendered rough by a coating of fine sand,
the rivers are denoted by smooth lines, the mountains by a range of
elevations, and towns by a small brass knob. The degrees are
appropriately distinguished, and all the other appendages are provided, 'only so modified as to enable the blind to solve geographical problems, and *feel* their way upon it, with as much precision
as those who have eyes, and can *see* their way upon globes of the
usual construction.' Very satisfactory proofs of the efficacy of
these methods have been given at the annual examinations, and
much pains appear to be taken in cultivating the minds of the
pupils, not only by these means, but by oral instruction.

SCONE, PERTHSHIRE.—The following extract from a late number of the 'Printing Machine' shows at what a very small
cost parish libraries may be established, and at how small an
expense a fund of entertainment and instruction may be provided
by all who are desirous of so doing. This plan seems to us better
calculated to do good than the establishment of gratuitous libraries. Here the contributor has a feeling of independence; he
has a voice in the selection of the books, and avoids the distaste
of having instruction thrust upon him, of being *schooled* as it
were; in fact, by following his own inclination, instructed and
modified by intercourse with his companions, he is far more likely
to acquire, practically, useful knowledge, whether in literature,
or science, than by any other course. "Towards the close of the
year just ended, 1834, it was thought by some persons who take
an interest in the parish of Scone, that with such a population
a library might be formed on a small and cheap scale, to which
every parishioner might be invited to become a subscriber.
Several years ago the same thing had been attempted in the dissenting congregation, but it had not succeeded, because, as is
alleged, the books were exclusively religious. It was determined
that in this case there should be no such limitation. The only objection to the formation of a library that anybody started, was the
facility with which books could be obtained from some of the libraries in Perth; but it was thought by the promoters of the parish
library, that greater interest would be taken by the people in a
collection of books exclusively belonging to themselves; and that
many might be brought to read, when they could obtain books
within the village, and in their working dress, who would not

make the preparation requisite for going to Perth, or take the trouble of seeking after books among strangers. The great difficulty is to get country people to make even the slightest exertion beyond that ordinary routine to which they have been as it were mechanically accustomed from their infancy. After calling several meetings of the inhabitants, the library has been set on foot; but it has not yet been joined, it is confidently believed, by one-third of those who will ultimately become members. The entry-money was fixed so low as 2*s.* for every individual, and 6*d.* per quarter. Books were bought as soon as the sum so collected amounted to 6*l.* In making purchases, the committee of subscribers experienced the benefit of the present cheap rate at which books can be bought. The library already possesses several volumes of ' Constable's Miscellany,' of Oliver and Boyd's ' Cabinet Library,' of the books published by the Society for the Diffusion of Knowledge, of the ' Family Library,' and of Bentley's ' Standard Novels.' The object in purchasing books is to select those which contain much in small compass, either by a process of condensation in respect of thought, or at least of letter-press. There have also been bought several of the new publications by the Book Society for promoting Religious Knowledge. But it is obvious that a sufficient number of books could not have been obtained at first from the very small funds. It was therefore proposed that any of the members who happened to have such books as they could spare, and as might be generally interesting, should give or lend them to the library. The result of this proposal has been most successful; upwards of 100 books, some consisting of several volumes—one, for instance, of sixteen, one of ten, several of four, three, or two, have been sent in, the names of which are all printed in the catalogue. There is, therefore, at a mere trifle of expense, provided ample reading for all the present subscribers; and as the pleasure of perusing entertaining and instructive books becomes more generally known and felt by experience, there can be no doubt that the funds will greatly increase. If the people could be persuaded to regard reading not as a task but as a luxury, it would certainly prevail much more generally than it does.''

WINCHESTER SCHOOL.—On making the best inquiry that we can, we are informed that Dr. Williams, upon his promotion to the office of head-master, made great changes with regard to fagging in commoners, but that the system still exists among the boys upon the foundation in its original form.

INDEX.

ABBOTT's Teacher, review of, 125—135; advantage of engaging pupils to instruct themselves, 126; importance of interesting them in their studies, 128; difficulties not to be disguised, 130; dialogue illustrative of Mr. Abbott's system of moral discipline, 132

Æschylus, Scholefield's Appendix to, review of, 110—117; remarks on Müller's, 118—122

Airy, Professor, Lalande medal adjudged to, 179

Algebra, Peacock's Treatise on, observations arising out of, and review of, 91—110; and 293—311; on extending the meaning of terms, 92; value of authority, 94; simplification of the mathematical sciences, 96; end proposed in teaching algebra, 97; relation of arithmetic to algebra, 98; use of algebra, 101; generalization, 102; meaning of algebraical signs, 103; extension of the meaning of terms, 294; supposed mistakes and absurdities, 296; review of Mr. Peacock's treatise, 297; degree in which the work is suitable for the elementary student, 298; and for the more advanced student, 300; science of suggestion, 302; Mr. Warren's Treatise, 303

Algiers, state of education in, 174

Allen, W., evidence of, with respect to educating the children of different religious denominations together, 220

Althans, H., evidence of, with respect to normal schools, 233

America, on the state of education in, 312—327; notice of the "American Annals of Education and Instruction," 312; education not under the superintendence of the general government, 313; manner in which education is provided for in the different States, 314; advantages of a uniform system under the superintendence of government, 317; present system of education in the different States, 318; want of education in some of the States, 322; effect of the interference of government in the common schools, 323; American associations for extending education, 324; objections to the interference of governments, 326

Argovia, elementary schools in, 159

Arithmetic, on teaching the elements of, 272—280; method of teaching numeration, 272; of teaching addition, 273; subtraction, 275; multiplication, 277; division, 279

Arnault, M., clause in the will of, addressed to the French Academy, 349

Athens, on the situation of Lycabettus near, 165

Aubin, Mr., his establishment for the poor at Norwood, 48

Austria, state of education in, 360

Basle-Champaign, substance of a new law to regulate national schools in, 354

Bath Education Society, observations on the principle of, 186; Bath Free Grammar School, account of, 183

Bavaria, admission into the High Schools of, 157

Belgium, Free University in, 150; ordinances for the establishment of a national museum and the encouragement of fine arts in, 351

Berlin, royal grant for improving the university buildings in, 157; number of students at the university of, 358

Bern, university of, appointment of medical professors in, 159; state of the Bern and Zürich Universities, 354

Beverley Grammar School, account of, 375

Bibliotheca Classica, by Dymock, notice concerning, 148

Birmingham Institution for the Deaf and Dumb, abstract of report of, 187

Bishop of London, observations by, on the principle of the Bath Education Society, 186; evidence of, with respect to educating the children of different religious denominations together, 214; evidence of, with respect to normal schools, 233

Bolton, in Lancashire, statement about the schools of, 72

Bradford, formation of a mechanics' library at, 378

Breslaw, "Franke Foundation" of, establishments comprised in, 358

Brighton, plan for educating the daughters of poor clergymen at, 186

British and Foreign School Society, debt of, 183

Brougham, Lord, evidence of, with respect to normal schools, 233; with respect to a national system of primary education, 238; with respect to compulsory education, 239

Brussels, adult female school at, 351

Bulwer, Mr., remarks by, on defects of character occasioned by the system pursued at our public schools, 89

Camberwell Collegiate or Proprietary School, 374

Cambridge Philosophical Society, meeting of, proceedings at, 179

Cambridge University intelligence, 177, 370

Canterbury Philosophical and Literary Institution, notice of, 187

Cape of Good Hope, account of emigrants sent out to, by the Children's Friend Society, 174, 367

Carlisle, Rev. J., evidence of, with respect to educating the children of different religious denominations together, 224

Children, Mr. Smith's garden-allotments to, 182

Children's Friend Society, account of the emigrants sent out to the Cape of Good Hope by, 174, 367

Chillingham, Durham, grants for the building of schools in the parish of, 378

Chimney-Sweepers, establishment of a school for, at Brighton, 376

Clark, Rev. G., evidence of, with respect to educating the children of different religious denominations together, 218

Constantinople, description of the inhabitants of, 364

Cotton, Rev. W., evidence of, with respect to educating the children of different religious denominations together, 216

Crossley, J. T., evidence of, with respect to educating the children of different religious denominations together, 233; with respect to normal schools, 233

Darmstadt, schools in, 151

De Beaumont and De Toqueville, substance of their Report on education in the State of New York, 56

Denmark, establishments for education in, 170; population of, 171

Devon and Exeter Savings' Banks, statements concerning, 63; large amount of deposits for children in, 64; larger proportionate amount of deposits in Devonshire than in any other part of England, 65

Dublin, Trinity College, examinations at, 189

Dunn, Henry, evidence of, with respect to educating the children of different religious denominations together, 223; with respect to normal schools, 229

Dupuytren, M., munificent bequests of, 350

Dymock's Bibliotheca Classica, notice concerning, 148

Edinburgh Sessional School, account of the, 11

Edinburgh, female university at, 188

Education, extracts from the Report of the Committee of the House of Commons on the state of, 213—243; evidence with respect to educating the children of different religious denominations together, 214; summary of the evidence, 225; evidence for and against infant schools, 227; evidence with respect to normal schools, 229; union of labour with study, 234; evidence of Professor Pillans with respect to singing and drawing, 236; evidence of Lord Brougham with respect to a national system of primary education, 238; his evidence on compulsory education, 239; general observations on the management of schools, 241

Egypt, progress of education in, 366

Elegantiæ Latinæ, critical notice of, 122—125

Etchilhampton, Wilts, school-room opened at, 180

Etymological Researches, by Dr. Pott, review of, 327—337; affinity of languages, 329; Sanscrit roots, 330; relations between the Greek and Latin, 332; Indo-Germanic languages, 333; etymology and import of proper names in ancient oriental history and geography, 334; Persian names beginning with Arta and Ario, 336

Female university at Edinburgh, notice of, 188; substance of Dr. Cantor's lecture on female education, 379

Females, project of a plan for the education of, 27—45; deficiency of the present system of female education, 28; advantages of a general system under the superintendence of government, 31; infant schools for poor females from two to six years of age, 33; elementary schools for poor females from six to twelve, 36; schools of industry for poor females above twelve, 38; importance of normal schools, 39; principles on which the normal schools should be conducted, 40

Flogging and fagging at public schools, observations on, 84—90; Montaigne's opinion of corporal punishment, 85 ; flogging of scholars censured by Quinctilian, 85; account of the fagging system at Winchester school, 86 ; defects of character occasioned by the fagging system, 88

France, abstract of the budget of the Minister of Public Instruction, 349

Freiberg, Switzerland, Jesuits' academy at, 158

French Academy, clause in the will of M. Arnault addressed to the, 349

Genoa, university of, professors and students in the, 356

Giessen, students in, 151

Gin-shops, corruption of children in, 180 ; table of number of persons visiting, 181

Glasgow University, Lord Stanley elected Lord Rector of, 189 ; account of the Glasgow Asylum for the Blind, 379

Gloucester National School to be a Central or Model Institution, 377

Göttingen, sum given towards the erection of the new university buildings at, 360

Greece, Thiersch's actual state of, review of, 135—148 ; establishment of national schools in, 165

Halifax Sunday School Union, 374

Hanover, constitution of, September, 1833, 153 ; money applied to purposes of religion and education in, 155 ; schools in, 156

Harrow School, observations on the rules and orders for the regulation of, 75—83 ; account of John Lyon's foundation, and observations on his statutes and regulations, 75 ; summary of proceedings in the Rolls' Court as to this school, 80 ; remarks on the decision of the court, 83

Hayleybury, East India College at, 374

Heidelberg in old times, 356

Hesse, Grand Duchy of, educational reform in, 359

Holbeck Youth's Guardian Society, notice of, 377

Holland, Dr., observations by, on provincial medical schools, 180

Hungary, protestant college at Debreczin in, 361

Huyghens, correspondence of, 151

Infant schools, evidence for and against, 227

Ireland, national education in, obser-

vations on, 193 to 213; commission appointed for the superintendence of, 193 ; returns presented to the House of Commons, 194 ; table of number of schools, scholars, &c. in each county of Ireland, 197 ; regulations of the commissioners with respect to religious instruction, 200 ; correspondence between the commissioners and the Synod of Ulster on that subject, 202 ; number of clergymen of different denominations who have applied for grants in aid of schools, 204 ; books prepared by the commissioners for the use of schools, 206 ; example of exercises, 209 ; treatise on arithmetic, 210 ; treatise on geometry, 211 ; elements of book-keeping, 212

Jena, university of, students at, 154

Jewish schools, notice respecting, 350

Johnson, Rev. W., evidence of, with respect to educating the children of different religious denominations together, 215; with respect to normal schools, 229

Julius, Rev. Henry, evidence of, with respect to educating the children of different religious denominations together, 222

King's College, London, intelligence relating to, 372

Latin and Greek exercises, observations on the writing of, 262—271 ; objections to the usual system of writing exercises, 263 ; plan proposed to be substituted, 265 ; example of the manner in which a teacher may make exercises, 269 ; comparative advantages of writing exercises and reading classical authors, 270

Law Students in France, 150

Llampeter, St. David's College at, notice concerning, 188

London University, abstract of the annual report of, 371

Lucern, canton of, number of schools in, 355

Lycabettus, on the situation of, 165

Lyon, John, rules and orders of, for the regulation of Harrow school, 75

Lyons, academy of, notice respecting, 348

Madrid, state of education, literature, and arts in, 161

Manchester Mechanics' Institute, resolution passed by the, 378

Mansfield, formation of a parochial library at, 377

Manwood, Roger, free-school of, at Sandwich, 256

Mechlin, University of, 151

Medical · Provincial Schools, observations on, by Dr. Holland, 180

Menars, present state of the schools at, 164

Montaigue's opinion of corporal punishment, 85

Moscow, institution in, for teaching the oriental languages, 167

Müller's Æschylus, remarks on, 118—122

Munich university, state of, and regulations at, 358 ; system of instruction at the Munich Greek school, 359

Naples, state of education in, 160

Nassau, institution for the education of teachers in, 154

Nauplia, state of literature in, 164

New York, state of, on the system of public instruction in the, 56—61 ; public school-funds created by the legislature, 56 ; local school-funds, 58 ; distribution of schools and number of scholars in the State, 59 ; working of the New York system, 60

New York, university of the city of, notice of, and list of professors in, 173

Normal schools, evidence with respect to, 229

Oxford University intelligence, 176, 369

Parish-poor children, on the education of, under the Poor-Law Amendment Act, 45—55 ; powers given to the commissioners, 45 ; elements of the pauper population, 46 ; corruption of workhouses, 46 ; Mr. Aubin's establishment for the poor at Norwood, 48 ; power given to the commissioners to establish workhouses and issue regulations for them, 49 ; this power might be applied to the establishment of schools, 50 ; how the education of the poor should be conducted, 51

Parker's Progressive Exercises in English Composition, review of, 338—342 ; Mr. Parker's answer to the charge of plagiarism, 338 ; charge against Mr. J. R. Priestley, 341

Paris, royal printing press at, 149 ; statistics of education in the public institutions of, 348 ; students in the University of, 351

Parish schools, application of poor-rates to the support of, 374

Pays de Vaud, schools in the, 159

Peacock's Treatise on Algebra, observations arising out of, and review of, 91 to 110, and 293 to 311

JAN.—APRIL, 1835.

Pillans, Professor, observations by, on the qualifications necessary in a schoolmaster, 18 ; evidence of, with respect to educating the children of different religious denominations together, 218 ; with respect to normal schools, 231 ; with respect to the union of labour with mental study, 234 ; with respect to singing and drawing, 236

Pott's Etymological Researches, review of, 327—337

Presbyteries in Scotland, remarks on the judicial powers of, 23

Proprietary Grammar Schools, observations on, 254—262 ; proprietary schools compared with others, 255 ; West Riding school, 256 ; free-school of Roger Manwood in Sandwich, 256 ; tenure of school property, 258 ; interference of proprietors, 258 ; regulations of West Riding school, 259 ; principles on which it is proposed to be conducted, 260 ; division of youths into two classes, 261

Prussia, examination previous to matriculation in the universities of, 156 ; Bible societies in, 157 ; population of, 157

Public schools, on the discipline of, 280—292 ; flogging a necessary part of school discipline, 282 ; treatment of older boys, 285 ; fagging indispensable in large schools, 286 ; false representation, with regard to Winchester school, 288 ; fagging not a degrading system, 290 ; difficulty of teaching Christianity in a large school, 291

Rouen, Society of Emulation at, 348

Russia, account of the university of Kiew in, 167 ; travelling scholars in, 168 ; account of the Kubatshine republic in, 169 ; magnetic and meteorological institutions in, 363 ; account of the serfs in, 363

Russian Conversations-Lexikon, 167

Salisbury Mechanics' Institute, notice of, 187

Sardinia, scholastic establishments in, 159

Savings' Banks, observations on, 62—66 ; statement of the Devon and Exeter Savings' Banks, 63

Savoy, state of education in, 159

Saxony, grammar schools in, 151 ; students' dress in, 152 ; book trade in, 152 ; grants for the promotion of education and science in, 153 ; gymnasia in, 155 ; pedagogic society in, 356

2 C

Scholefield's Appendix to Æschylus, review of, 110—117
Scone, Perthshire, establishment of parish libraries at, 380
Scotland, elementary education in, observations on, 1—26; establishment and regulation of parish schools, 2; former condition of the schoolmasters, 5; want of a sufficient number of parish schools, 8; measures recommended for increasing their number and efficiency, 10; account of the Edinburgh sessional school, 11; establishment of schools in imitation of it, 13; measures suggested for securing competent schoolmasters, 16; observations by Professor Pillans on the qualifications of schoolmasters, 18; schools for the education of teachers recommended, 19; qualifications and emoluments of the Scotch schoolmasters, 20; judicial powers of presbyteries, 23; promotion of education by the church of Scotland, 25
Scotland, General Assembly's Schools in, 378
Siberia, school at Troizko-Ssawak in, 362
Sicilies, the Two, state of education in, 355
Sidney Sussex College, mathematical exhibitioners in, 179
Silesia, seminaries in, 157.
Silkston, Yorkshire, free-school at, 188
Singing, observations on teaching, 243—253, natural capabilities to be first attended to, 244; purity of tone, 245; mode of practising the scale, 245; exercises for the voice, 247; execution, 248; adaptation of words to the music, 249; ornamental part, 250; style of singing, 252
Southwark Literary Society, notice of, 183
Spain, royal decree to regulate public instruction in, 162; royal order to establish Lancasterian schools in, 163
Staines, establishment of a society for the promotion of science and literature at, 373
Statistics of education in England, 66—74; government questions sent to all places in England and Wales, 66; observations on the questions, 69; statement about the schools of Bolton in Lancashire, 72
Stereotype printing, on the invention of, 352
Strasburg, school for the children of beggars at, 350

Teacher, Abbott's, review of, 125—135
Teachers in elementary schools in France, 149
Thiersch's Actual State of Greece, review of, 135—148; statement of the circumstances which led to his mission to Greece, 135; character of Capodistria, 137; view of the population of Greece, 139; general description of its surface, 142
Tübingen university, number of students at, 154
Turkey, state of education in, 172
Turkish school, description of a, 365

Universities of Belgium, Holland, Germany, Switzerland, Austria, Russia, Sweden and Norway, and Denmark, tabular statement of, 343—347

Wallachia, progress of education in, 362
Warren's "Treatise on the Geometrical Representation of the Square Roots of negative Quantities," observations on, 318
Westreenen van Tiellandt, Baron, researches of, on the invention of stereotype printing, 352
West Riding Proprietary School, Wakefield, Yorkshire, observations arising out of the report of, 254—262
Wigram, Rev. J. C., evidence of, with respect to educating the children of different religious denominations together, 215
Winchester school, account of the system of fagging at, 86; subsequent notice relating to that system, 190; another notice concerning, 381
Wood, Rev. J., evidence of, with respect to educating the children of different religious denominations together, 222
Woodbridge's American Annals of Education and Instruction, review of, 285—300
Worcester, grants for the erection of a school-room at, 377
Wright, W., evidence of, with respect to the union of labour with mental study, 235
Würtemberg, examination for admission into a university at, 153

Zürich, canton of, schools in, 159; seminary for educating masters in, 353; teachers in the university of, 159

Printed by W. Clowes, Duke-street, Lambeth.